UNDER EVERY LEAF

16-18 Queen Anne's Gate, home of British military intelligence between 1884 and 1901. Two Wyatt townhouses knocked together, they were deceptively commodious. At this period, some thirty to forty personnel were assigned there, the library was on the ground floor and the presses were in the filthy basement. In 1901 the ID moved to Winchester House, St James's Square. © London Metropolitan Archives

UNDER EVERY LEAF

WILLIAM BEAVER

Biteback Publishing

First published in Great Britain in 2012 by
Biteback Publishing Ltd
Westminster Tower
3 Albert Embankment
London
SE1 7SP
Copyright © William Beaver 2012

ISBN 978-1-84954-219-7

10 9 8 7 6 5 4 3 2 1

A CIP catalogue record for this book is available from the British Library.

Set in Adobe Caslon Pro
Cover design by Namkwan Cho

Printed and bound in Great Britain by
CPI Group (UK) Ltd, Croydon, CR0 4YY

To those who from their own experience and scholarship suspected that 'something must have been going on', including Sir Isaiah Berlin, OM of Wolfson College; Brigadier Sir Edgar Williams, CB, CBE, DSO of Rhodes House; Professor Ronald Robinson, CBE, DFC, Beit Professor of Commonwealth History and Dr Colin Newbury, University Lecturer in Commonwealth History. You were right.

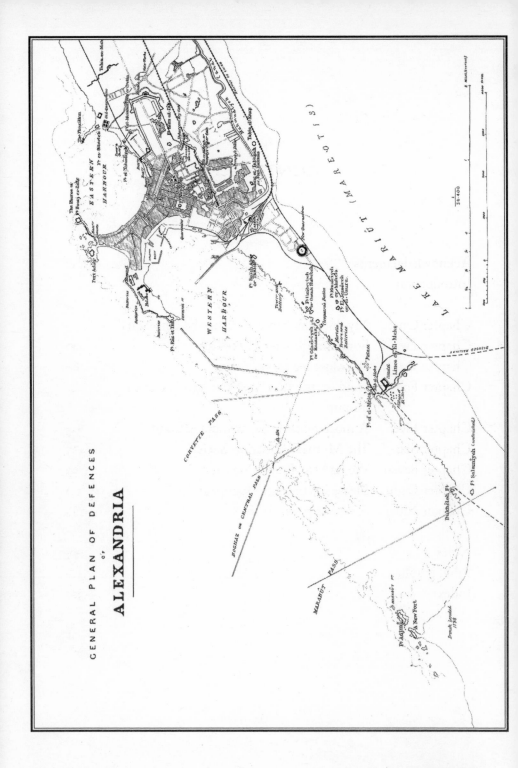

Dated July 1882, this simple tactical map for both military and naval forces was probably completed by May as part of the ID's preparation for the Egyptian expeditionary force. Although strategic and boundary maps made up the regular output of the ID mapping room, Alexandria is an early example of the up-to-date tactical maps regularly produced by the ID from the mid-1870s for deploying forces.
© National Archives

CONTENTS

Acknowledgements   ix
Introduction   1

Chapter One: My duty must in conscience be performed   9
Chapter Two: Something more is necessary   43
Chapter Three: We must see these islands   66
Chapter Four: Held up the Khedive? You have picked   101
                him up
Chapter Five: A most valuable department of state   133
Chapter Six: The Mutual Laudation Society   161
Chapter Seven: We had the French 'on toast'   197
Chapter Eight: Please lay in some champagne   232
Chapter Nine: A *vox clamantis in deserto*   268

Notes   294
Bibliography   316
Index   327

ACKNOWLEDGEMENTS

For originally suggesting the study of British intelligence in the scramble for Africa I am grateful to Dr Colin Newbury of Linacre College, Oxford. The subject grew in many different directions and the number of people to which I am indebted is correspondingly large, indeed, more than I can name. My debt to them all is real and deep. I am particularly grateful to those whom I have dedicated this work. Likewise the staff of the then Public Record Office (now National Archives), especially Mr M. D. Lea, Ms Veronica Graham-Green and the redoubtable ladies who patiently provided me with an endless stream of dusty tomes from their subterranean mine and rejoiced, no doubt with relief, when we eventually stumbled upon the right seam. In my gratitude I gladly include the helpful staffs of the National Army Museum, Royal Commonwealth Library, English Heritage, the London Metropolitan Archives, Rhodes House of the Bodleian Library, the Royal United Services Institution, and the British Museum.

Justly deserving of inadequate thanks, too, are Dr D. W. King, OBE, FLA and Mr C. A. Potts, ALA and the hard-pressed staff of the Ministry of Defence Library (Central and Army). Despite severe organisational pressures at the time, of which I was then only dimly aware, they welcomed me, lent me an office overlooking Horse Guards and gave me free rein of what was then a most remarkable collection.

Likewise, my thanks go to Ms L. E. Forbes, ALA and Ms Clarice Bates of the Oriental Library, University of Durham, who cheerfully gave me every possible assistance with the Sudan Archive as did the Duchess of Devonshire, Major T. S. Wragg, MBE, TD and Mr Peter Day with the Hartington Collection at Chatsworth House. In Oxford, Mr J. Wing and the staff of Christ Church Library opened the Salisbury Collection to me without let or hindrance and in an act of remarkable generosity Mr J. Browning of Maggs Bros withdrew a collection of diaries from sale until I could examine them.

So, too, the early historians of the Intelligence Corps of the British Army deserve my gratitude: Colonel Brian Parritt, MBE, Lieutenant Colonel W. W. Leary, BEM, Major Jock Haswell and Mr H. A. Hunter who greeted me as a colleague and guest on several occasions. Colonels J. E. South and E. E. Peel, RE and the staff of the Royal Engineer Library kindly admitted me to their mess and most important library as did Major R. G. StG Bartelot, RA and the Royal Artillery Museum.

Without the material assistance of the trustees of the Beit Foundation through the award of the Beit Senior Scholarship in the university, progress on this work would have been much affected. I am grateful to them and for the very real help from the Sudanese scholar Professor Richard Hill, General Sir James Marshall-Cornwall, CBE, DSO, Kenneth and Lynn Cunningham, David and Grizelda Vermont, Richard and Tam Frost, Sir Ronald Wingate, CB, CMG, CIE, OBE and the many descendants of the men I studied whom I plagued for papers or information about their forebears.

In bringing this work to publication I am grateful for the encouragement of Lord Hennessy of Nympsfield, FBA; and of Michael Smith, the acknowledged doyen of later British intelligence history, and Sean Magee of Biteback Publishing, who from the first has given the author the most wise and valued encouragement. He and the dynamic Biteback team have been a delight to work with. My long-suffering family I also mention with thanks and end with the standard yet heart-felt declaration that whilst praise belongs to the named and unnamed above, any opprobrium for the inevitable errors and omissions I reserve for myself alone.

William Beaver
Wolfson College, Oxford

INTRODUCTION

In the mid-nineteenth century, the world was ripe to be possessed by the powerful. Russia's steady subversion of Bulgar and Afghan alike, and her mysterious successes in the south, masked by distance and played over little-known lands, caused disquiet in London and blind worry in Calcutta. Later the threat would come from France, Germany, Portugal and even Italy, all passionate in their desire to expand into Africa. Behind every move was the threat of armed force against the most successful of colonial powers: Great Britain.

Yet Britain desired to live in a parallel universe of progress, freedom and peace. And, on the whole, this is the grand story of the second half of Victoria's reign. But it could only exist in the world it wanted to live in if it listened for, absorbed and used to advantage intelligence about potential foes and their tricks, knavish or otherwise. Britain could never win at shadow boxing and its magnificent navy was, when all was said and done, of little use away from the water's edge. In more subtle ways, however, Britain could combat that which she could detect and the result was that for well over half a century Britain was not involved in nor suffered from either a great European or a great Asian war. Britain played her cards well because she sat facing the mirror.

But who sat facing the mirror? Britain's diplomatic machinery was almost powerless to collect the right information, analyse it enough to turn it into intelligence or propose courses of action based on what it found in an increasingly complex world. To fill the vacuum, the governments of the day drew heavily on the experience and technical expertise of the little-known Intelligence Department (from 1888 the Intelligence Division) or 'ID' of the War Office. In short, the ID was useful to the politicians and great offices of state because it replaced conjecture with studied analysis.

Initially, ministers and their officials came to rely on the Division because it was convenient. If they did not agree, they could dismiss the ID's opinions with a polite 'Read and noted'. After all, it was but a separate, innocuous subunit which printed maps and dealt with strange places and even stranger people. From the beginning it was estranged from its notional overlords, the generals at Horse Guards, and on the surface carried no organisational clout. So, if they chose, the government could ignore the Division and its advice. But just the opposite happened and the young captains and majors with experience and expertise beyond their years wrote far-reaching memoranda which affected policy and the lives of millions. As the century drew to a close, an increasing number of Foreign, Colonial and Indian Office minutes ended with: 'Presume you have asked the ID?' And back would come the answer: 'Done.'

When the Division did propose courses of action, it did so with evidence not usually available to others. This gave it a cachet and weight. It did its best to be unbiased but by the 1890s the Intelligence Division was so convinced that it knew what was best for the Empire that when the government did not move as rapidly as the Division believed it should have done over the retention of the Sudan to Egypt and the capturing of the headwaters of the Nile, the Division took matters into its own hands and dragged the Empire behind it. This coincided with the Second South African (or Boer) War, which the ID had long predicted and planned for – warnings which the War Office ignored. This became public and by the dawn of the Edwardian era the value of intelligence was increasingly recognised, its insufficiency acknowledged. The great security organisations, both civil and military, which sprang into life then and subsequently all owed their origin to the ID.

THIS REMARKABLE ORGANISATION

These are remarkable claims for an organisation that is virtually unknown and only fleetingly shows up in histories of the period. So what was it? Who were the men who gave their lives to it?

The organisation for which so much is claimed was a particularly homegrown affair. From its inception during the Crimean War, the Department was a pariah to the rest of the Army, which did not understand it and actively discriminated against it. It resented the ID's 'semi-official' access to the Prime Minister and Cabinet, directly and through the great departments of state. It looked on the ID as a proto-general staff in an era when changes of that sort were not in fashion. Its officers were thought to get all the best positions on expeditions (which was generally true) and were self-serving cliques (which was also usually true). But above all, the ID injected a new technocratic intellect, planning and vision into the realm and service of diplomacy and operations which had not existed before.

The hundred or so officers who served in the ID before it was absorbed into the new General Staff in the early twentieth century were from the 'scientific' branches, i.e. the Royal Engineers and Royal Artillery for the most part, and were acknowledged to be the best technical brains in the Army. Unusually for that time, many had experienced higher education; about a dozen came from Oxford, Cambridge or Dublin and almost all came from the top of their classes at the fledgling Staff College. Again, almost all were practising linguists. Over the sixty years or so covered here, the average length of appointment at the ID was for five years. This was longer than normal and did not, as a rule, go down well with the losing regiment or corps, but it was necessary if the officer was to understand and get into the work, which was divided geographically. The age at time of appointment was around thirty to thirty-five years old.

If a snapshot, albeit a very detailed snapshot, of the ID *in medias res* is wanted, it exists in the report on the *modus operandi* of the ID by Captain (later Lieutenant General Sir) Edwin Henry Hayter Collen, RA written for the Intelligence Branch, Simla in 1878. In many ways it is regrettable that his *Report on the Intelligence Branch, Quarter Master General's Department* was not written a decade later, when the Division and its work were arguably at their peak. Yet through it all comes the inescapable conclusion that being in the ID was thrilling and a lot of very hard work by some extraordinary young officers paid off in the increased pre-eminence and security of the Empire. And this is how they will make their appearance in the pages that follow. For the most part these exceptional people will suddenly appear in the narrative with a report, an informed opinion or action which advances or influences the story and just as suddenly will quietly disappear from view, fading into the shadows, back to their vigil.

This is not to say that these men were meek or mild. For the most part they will break into history again when the much-needed organisational reforms they campaigned for finally come to pass. In fact the Intelligence Division of the last quarter of the nineteenth century produced three chiefs of the Imperial General Staff, two field marshals, six generals, eleven lieutenant generals, fifteen major generals, nine brigadiers and at least fourteen colonels. More than half became knights or peers in their own right. It could be argued that they were probably the first real meritocratic cadre in modern British government. Fewer than half ever married.

WHY WERE THEY SUCCESSFUL?

The success of the Intelligence Department/Division lay in its ability to generate trust, its unrelenting reliability, in its ability to gather information on every possible topic from demography to orthography, to collate and analyse it, then turn it into intelligence and strategy for, primarily, the Foreign Office, Cabinet and Queen (who had a considerable knowledge of foreign affairs and influence in their conduct). The ID was also speedy and clever: at one stage the Indian Army swore blind that the Russians were about to attack Afghanistan and India in large numbers, a 'Henny-Penny' stance it frequently took. But was it true? The ID quietly reassured the Prime Minister, Foreign and India Offices that it would not happen. Why not? They war-gamed it and it did not make sense, not least because an army marches on its stomach. The ID obtained and analysed the annual contract let by the Russian Intendance Branch for flour. There were no plans to have any new or expanded flour points advancing themselves down towards the south-east and the Hindu Kush. No flour points for bakeries, so no bakeries to bake bread to feed troops, so no troops, no invasion. Britain did not overreact.

WHY DON'T WE KNOW MORE ABOUT THE INTELLIGENCE DIVISION?

In the last two decades or so much has been written, and generally well written, about various aspects of Britain's intelligence effort in the hey-day of Empire, mostly concentrating on efforts in the field, e.g. the Great Game in Asia. Very much less has been written about what is behind that effort, i.e. the organisational heart of the intelligence machine, its role and its influence in imperial policy making. Part of the answer lies in the paucity of direct evidence. There is no depository of Intelligence Division papers for this era, per se, although some reports and memoranda of the most immense value remained in the Ministry of Defence Library (Central and Army) until the mid-1970s. Other examples of the Division's official work and the government's response (save those returned for burning) exist in the Foreign and to a lesser extent in the Colonial Office files in the National Archives. Much of this evidence has not been examined by historians interested in imperial defence and foreign policy simply because these papers are not where one would expect to find them.

As the Division was neither fish nor fowl, the clerks in Whitehall deposited the remaining evidence of the Division's influence in obscure files such as 'FO Diplomatic/Domestic Various', many of which were first opened since deposit in the research for this work. And there, after pages and pages of extra-territorial marriage licences (and a letter from an irate mother to the Prime Minister claiming that her son had run off to Russia with an acrobat called Gregory and what was he going to do about it?) one turns the page and finds a highly classified intelligence summary or plan of action, fully acknowledged by the Foreign Office, minister or Cabinet, which, when replaced into the decision-making process, was influential in forming British policy.

There are also clues to be found occasionally amongst the papers of politicians and officials. Finding explicit reference to the work of the Division within the collections of major politicians, like Lord Salisbury, is rare. But that does not mean it did not exist. It was the practice of Lords Salisbury, Hartington and Rosebery to conduct much of their most sensitive official business privately, a fact which annoyed their departments at the time and has irritated historians ever since. Hence much of the interaction which we know took place between the ID and its political masters will probably be forever lost to us in its detail.

But the ID was not completely hidden. During this period there were formal commissions and enquiries, and efforts to co-ordinate military, naval and imperial defence issues, e.g. in 1879 and 1885, in which intelligence matters were pointed to. But, as in the case of the 1885 Colonial Defence Committee, the proceedings were those of a committee of the Cabinet, and the tradition was not to take any record *at all*. When Sir George Clarke (later Lord Sydenham), secretary to the Committee, came to write about it, he noted his involvement and then turned away 'in discreet silence'.

There are also few answers from the practitioners themselves. They simply kept their secrets unto death. Almost all of the central figures destroyed their papers. The playwright Sir Terence Rattigan was adamant that Major General Lord Edward Gleichen left none and so were the families of Lieutenant General Sir James Wolfe Murray and Major General Sir Charles Wilson, amongst dozens of others.

One key collection, however, remains intact. This is the largely unexploited collection of correspondence from and to General Sir F. R. Wingate at Durham University. His son, the late Sir Ronald Wingate, was certain that his father planned to keep faith with his silent colleagues as almost all of this seminal correspondence was carefully ripped out of his letter books and put aside. It was death alone, he observed, that intervened between his father's intention and the fire.

The other exception is some of the correspondence and odd papers of Sir John Ardagh, director of the Division between 1896 and 1901.

After his death, his wife Susan, the Countess of Malmesbury, deposited a selection of his papers in the Public Record Office and, as will be shown, she did so to indicate the importance of the Division's work and to vindicate her husband from charges that he did not properly advise the government of the threat to Great Britain posed by the Boer nations in South Africa.

Finally, there are tantalising glimpses from corps histories of which the *Royal Engineer Journal* and *History of the Royal Engineers* stand out, not least because many of the authors had been in the Division themselves. Hints, too, occasionally appear in obscure autobiographies written decades after the events. But in the main they hollowly echo the memoirs of Lord Sydenham.

We must therefore look for evidence in the prescience behind policies propounded themselves, the measured actions taken. There is the proof of the influence of Britain's intelligencers. Whilst it may be hard for later generations to divine its depth and reach, there was no doubt in the minds of the players of that era that, on the whole, Britain knew what it was doing because it took the trouble to quietly, ever so quietly, find out what others were doing. As the Farsi expression had it: 'Anywhere in the world where a leaf moves, underneath you will find an Englishman.'

CHAPTER ONE

MY DUTY MUST IN
CONSCIENCE BE PERFORMED

It will always be to the credit of mid-Victorian Britain that its organising, technical and industrial energy was largely expended on peaceable progress and not on martial affairs. In 1854, when Britain was about to go to war with Russia over Turkish independence, the British Army was hardly more sophisticated than in Wellington's day. Whilst there had been some advances and changes for the better during that time, the notion of higher organisation was rudimentary compared with continental armies and what there was still consisted of officers dashing hither and thither on occasional training days with scrappy bits of orders. At the end of the century, the three-time Prime Minister Lord Salisbury told the House of Lords: 'The art of war has been studied on the continent of Europe with a thoroughness and self-devotion that no other science has commanded, and at the end of the day we find ourselves surrounded by five great military Powers, and yet on matters of vital importance we pursue a policy wholly different from those military powers.[1]

On the continent, the management of warfare was indeed receiving serious attention. By the mid-1850s the most dramatic changes in warfare since the invention of the firearm were well underway. Railways and the telegraph shortened lines of communications and lethal inventions, such as the breech loading rifle, the forerunners to the machine gun and dynamite entered the battlefield with devastating effect. Politically, warfare began to engage whole populations, as the American Civil War and the first steps to German unification proved. War became more destructive and with increasingly efficient

9

conscription and mobilisation, the ripples of distress it caused went wider and deeper than ever before.[2]

In this regard the British Army was out of step with the progressive spirit of the age. Unlike its Austro-Hungarian, French and German counterparts, Britain spent little or no time contending with the notion of how to manage increasingly complicated operations. Critical to this was the creation of specialised co-ordinating staff and functions, be it operations, logistics, medical or feeding. Most importantly, the British Army had no means of ensuring a favourable outcome of battle other than through sheer heroics and the square. It seems to have forgotten the lessons of the past when that key element of successful operations, viz intelligence work, played its crucial role in the shaping of modern Britain.

In consequence, the British were content to commit their small army to a campaign in the Crimea of which they knew little. They knew no more about Russian capability or intentions beyond that of conquest, and relied for battlefield success on the British Army's reputation for individual and collective pluck and gallantry rather than planning and organisation.[3]

If the British military establishment observed this changing world, it learned little from it. So, too, the politicians. The great Liberal politician of the day, Lord Palmerston (Premier 1855–58, 1859–65) put his faith – and the nation's money – into the south-eastern costal defence system of lonely forts, called 'Palmerston's follies' from the day the first stones were sunk. But the real threat was elsewhere. By 1853, Britain and its new allies, the continental powers, were on the brink of war with Russia over the independence of Turkey, 'the sick man of Europe'. For their part, the supreme ruler of the crumbling Ottoman Empire, the Sublime Porte, and his advisers were firmly of the mind that whatever happened the British would save them.

The 'whatever happened' was the sure advance of Russia, protected by a fog of diplomatic activity and anxiety over the ownership of the Holy Places in Palestine, an issue drummed up by the French for their own purposes. The British government was largely indifferent to the resolution of this problem, but was suspicious of the various conti-nental plots that lay behind it. Nevertheless, the spectre of Russian advances surpassed any mutual suspicion between the continental powers and France and Britain, especially, grew closer together.

In the months leading up to the Crimean War, there was more intrigue, more indecisiveness by the British and more bungling. There were also screeds of despatches and reports coming in from a number of sources, most of which were wholly unreliable, the government giving unmerited credence to excited despatches from the French Ambassador especially. In short, there was no filter, no analysis and no intelligence. The new telegraph that extended as far to the east as Belgrade transmitted more worthless information than good. But who could tell which was which? George Villiers, the fourth Earl of Clarendon, beginning the first of three terms as Foreign Secretary, fumed: 'These telegraphic despatches are the very devil. Formerly Cabinets used to deliberate on a fact and a proposition from foreign governments; now, we only have a fact.' His predecessor Lord John Russell agreed, lamenting 'the fatal facility of the electric telegraph'.[4] Despite further diplomatic activity, matters deteriorated and by March 1854 Britain and the allies had 'drifted' into war with Russia.

The British Army was not ready on any level. Comprising some 65,000 men at home, 40,000 in the colonies and 30,000 in India, it had not fought a major European engagement of any kind for more than four decades. Within Whitehall there was systemic fail-ure in governance, too, with the civilians at the War Office and the soldiers at Horse Guards wrestling with each other on major and minor matters. In the Army itself, the development of leadership was weak. The selection, education and promotion of officers were corrupt and chaotic. Commissions were purchased and the Royal Military College at Sandhurst was 'half empty, understaffed and paralysed through lack of funds'.[5]

Intelligence, be it operational or strategic, was a word to be used with caution. It was synonymous with 'advanced thinking' and, indeed, the core around which many feared or hoped an overseeing organisation would eventually come about at the highest level of the British Army, an organisation composed of the key high-ranking specialists who could train, maintain, move and support an army in the field, all working together in a combined operation. Within such an organisation the responsibility for objective, aim and thrust depended on intelligence, and in peaceable England there was one man who saw the folly of ignoring intelligence. He was Major Thomas Best Jervis, a Bombay sapper, recently returned to London on retirement.

Jervis had spent much of his career in India as a surveyor working for Major (later Colonel Sir George) Everest. His reputation was not especially high. 'Through great humility of disposition' it had taken him some seven and a half years to become a lieutenant and when Everest learned that Jervis had been selected *proxime accessit* to become his successor as the Surveyor of India in 1837, he was reputed to be so horrified that he reversed his decision to retire. In any event, it was Jervis who tendered his resignation and returned to England in late 1841 a disappointed man. No longer an East Indian or 'John Company' employee and 'freed from official trammels', he poured his considerable energies into any number of schemes both sensible and wild, scientific, religious and pastoral, here, there and everywhere, all for the improvement of mankind, not least the Association for the Discouragement of Duelling, dromedary postal services and the bringing of Christianity to Indian women. But in the midst of all this random energy and enthusiasm, 'cartography together with Christianity became the main elements in his life'.

According to his admiring son, Jervis's weathered appearance and large, balding head made him 'conspicuous in the largest assembly and [he] could not fail to command respect and veneration' but he was regarded in Kensington as he had been in Calcutta as an eccentric, intellectual gadfly. He may have caused mirth, but when it came to matters cartographic, Jervis knew what he was talking about. He was passionate about the benefits to be derived from strategic cartography. For years he urged a deaf government to establish a national depository of maps and statistics for British merchants and

shippers to consult. This depository, a treasure house of topographical and statistical information, would, in addition to its commercial
value, also serve the government as a repository of maps useful to any
British force deployed anywhere in the world. This was thinking on a
grand scale endorsed by the government's total lack of interest.

Integral in his thinking about maps was their value as a key contributor to intelligence. In Jervis's mind cartography and intelligence went
hand in hand. He had, at first, thought of intelligence collection and
analysis tactically, in the field. His idea had been to train mobile bands
of scouts who could read terrain and enemy dispositions accurately,
galloping back with the results of their reconnaissance to trained staff
officers who would collate the information gathered, analyse it and
turn it into battlefield intelligence for their generals. Enemy displace-
ments, intentions and the nature of the ground between the opposing
forces would be clear. Jervis, who knew his history, recognised the
contribution this innovation had made to operations at Jena in 1806
and knew it would be invaluable half a century later.

Yet even as war in the Crimea drew closer, Jervis had neither the
reputation nor the power to do more than draw attention to the
desirability of establishing such a cartographic depot with this remit.
Relentlessly he pressed his case to all who would listen until on the
eve of the Crimean War he was induced by his long-suffering wife
and son to take a holiday in Belgium.

In Brussels, Jervis proved as irrepressible as in England.
Investigating new map-making techniques, he stumbled on nothing
less than a copy of the Russians' latest secret staff map of the Crimea
– 'a document which no money could purchase' – and the equally
sensitive Austrian staff map of Turkey-in-Europe. How these gems
came to reach Brussels, Jervis never knew. Nor is it known if he ever
considered whether they were planted by one or other of the powers.
What is known is that they were authentic and up to date. Without
wasting any time, Jervis rushed them back to London to lay before
the Duke of Newcastle, then Secretary of State for War, and Lord
Raglan, the prospective commander of the British expedition.

Jervis was greeted with a studied coolness bordering on disdain. He found to his surprise they 'had not particularly considered the Crimea at all'. Raglan, it turned out, did have a copy of the Russian map, but he could not read the Cyrillic 'hieroglyphics', and so it lay uninterpreted. Jervis was unable to understand this cavalier carelessness. His faith in the value of accurate maps as critical to a commander's success on the modern military battlefield was so passionate it became his Achilles heel. He allowed Newcastle and Raglan to drive him into what he later described as 'a parsimonious proposition'. In short, he was to enter into an agreement by which, *at his own expense,* he would translate the staff maps into French and chromolithograph them across ten sheets. In turn the Crown would buy two copies. He was not allowed to petition Parliament for expenses nor sell the map on the open market.

Jervis agreed to the deal and sold much of his treasured library to raise the £850 he needed to accomplish the project. He thereupon produced the maps in a miserable coach-house and stables at 9 Adelphi Terrace, near the Strand in London.[6]

So when Raglan sailed eastward, he did have the new map in his possession and it should have served its purpose; yet when the finger of blame over the wretched performance of the British Expeditionary Force later turned towards him Raglan shrugged off all responsibility, complaining that Sevastopol had been 'completely unknown to him as it had been to Jason and his Argonauts'.[7]

But this was all in the future. When the first British troops arrived in the summer of 1854 it was clear that Jervis's map was the only one detailed and accurate enough to be of value to commanders. Printed by chromolithography in ten sheets in blue, black and brown, copies of it were like gold dust and much in demand. He was permitted to keep his presses turning and his reputation took a turn for the better.

From that hard-won base, he returned to his scheme to create a national map repository, now strictly for military purposes and, looking for a template, he lobbied Newcastle for permission to visit the French Depôt de la Guerre. This was eventually granted and he returned with 1,476 maps and prints, a gold snuffbox from Napoleon

III, and a further conviction that Britain should have a similar depot and have it now.

To this end he wrote yet another report for Newcastle in 1854 urging him to set one up. The war was not going well and, for the first time, William Howard Russell's despatches in *The Times* and the telling drawings by the new breed of war artists, Simpson and Crowe, in the illustrated papers exposed the government and the Army to the critical gaze of the British public. The once glorious British Army was accurately pictured as a sick, freezing, starving skeleton, sacrificed to arrogance and lack of planning. The British public was furious, the press and Parliament demanded action. Newcastle was finally forced to consider Jervis's proposal but the Aberdeen government, unable to cover its incompetence and negligence further, was forced to resign on 30 January 1855 when the independent radical, John Arthur Roebuck, gave notice of a motion to enquire into the conduct of the war.[8]

‡

The new government of Lord Palmerston came in on a wave of enthusiasm for military reform. In the vanguard was the new Secretary of State for War, Fox Maule, created Lord Panmure in 1852. A competent, loyal Liberal, he had entered the Commons in 1835 and served his first term as Secretary of State for War between 1846 and 1852. Panmure knew, of course, of the tension and lack of co-operation and co-ordination between the civilians in the War Office and the soldiers at Horse Guards, separated as they were physically and administratively: the civilians under the Secretary of State and the soldiers under the General Commanding-in-Chief (later Commander-in-Chief or C-in-C).[9]

As for the War Department, which until 1854 had also been responsible for colonial affairs, it suffered from 'a want of unity of arrangements'. It lacked a precise chain of command and had 'no separate office, no precedents and no experienced officials'. The administrators carried on in a fashion which Pepys would have recognised. At bottom they considered themselves responsible to the government and the soldiers looked upon themselves as responsible to the Sovereign. Two systems of professional status were at war and each blamed the other for reverses in the field. When, for example, the previous government was feeling the full force of blame for one disastrous operation after another, an angry Sidney Herbert, the able Secretary for War under Newcastle, told the House of Commons that 'the main responsibility lies with that collection of regiments which calls itself the British Army and not with the Government!'[10]

Official correspondence between Horse Guards and the War Department bristled with rancour. The politicians and the generals tended to regard each other almost as enemy powers. As they controlled the purse strings, the civilians eventually gained the ascendancy, but the stench of acrimony between the civilians and the soldiers lingered well into the twentieth century.

As Florence Nightingale learned in her campaign to improve the lot of the private soldier, Panmure was not generally considered a decisive minister despite the will of the nation to support military reform. Yet one of his first acts within a few days of coming into office was to put Jervis's plan into effect. The Topographical & Statistical Department (the T&S) suddenly came into being early in February 1855 with Jervis as its first director with the acting rank of first major then lieutenant colonel.

If the suddenness of this innovation startled the soldiers, what alarmed them even more was Panmure's announcement that the T&S was to be accountable to the civilians in the War Department rather than to them, the soldiers at Horse Guards. This could give the civilians, should they wish to use it, a potential source of information independent of the generals.[11]

The T&S embodied revolution, or so thought those hoping for its success or fearing its potential power. In Parliament the great radical Joseph Hume opined just before he died that the T&S would prove to be the 'first effectual step to the reform of our military organisation' and even Jervis allowed himself to hope that his department, if developed along French lines, would bring 'the whole military business of the country under the direction of a single head'.[12] In other words, the core of a general staff.

And so the T&S was, from the beginning, considered by Jervis at least to be the seed of a directing or general staff, the next great advance in military thinking. Even at that time, both France and Prussia were already evolving processes and procedures to co-ordinate and control the deployment of large armies. The Prussians proved the effectiveness of a *Großstab* or general staff so completely in the Prussian–Austrian War of 1866 and the Franco-Prussian War four years later that by the late 1870s most major European powers boasted a similar controlling organisation in one form or another.

However, owing to major organisational weaknesses and the lack of threat, Britain did not follow suit until some thirty years later. The value of such a staff divided opinion which, combined with organisational and political implications, became irrational at times. And the idea of a function dedicated to intelligence collection, analysis and dissemination was irrevocably identified with the notion of a general staff. This had its plus and minus points. On the plus side, intelligence work in Britain would, as will be shown, attract the finest thinkers in the Army, officers of exceptional ability who could hold their own with the two golden generations of British politicians who governed from the end of the Crimean War until the end of the Boer War. On the other hand those who would become involved with intelligence were held in a very real and deep opprobrium by their suspicious seniors.

But, again, all this was in the future. Back at Adelphi Terrace, Jervis was delighted with his appointment. He had a war to win and set out to make the T&S 'the most indispensable accession to the machinery of state'. He immediately recruited some twenty-six engravers, lithographers and assistants.

Alas, his scatterbrained approach continued to alienate as many as it attracted. He showered his seniors with so many schemes on so many subjects that he unwittingly consigned to the 'too difficult' pile his modern, innovative ideas on intelligence, not least the latest incarnation of his 'brigades of topographers' to map abroad in peacetime and serve as a 'secret intelligence corps in war'.

But he was no longer alone. The T&S became a notional home for the few military thinkers on active service such as Colonel J. H. Lefroy, father of the Victorian military education movement, some aspects of which Jervis anticipated. Lefroy allied himself with the new T&S. Together they introduced standardised projection, scales and nomenclature for field maps, delighting officers in the field and increasing the popularity of the T&S.[13]

The volume of work increased dramatically and the laborious engraving, the preparation of the stones, printing and despatching went on around the clock. By August 1856, the T&S had outgrown Adelphi Terrace and Jervis received permission to move to 4 New Street, Spring Gardens. There Jervis added to his number until the strength rose to some fifty-five skilled map makers. But it was not all straightforward. He told Panmure: 'I confess the results have overpassed my expectations when I revert to the number I have to prove and discharge for incompetency, insubordination and drunkenness.' One morning he found four aged ladies on his doorstep. They made it clear that they were there to colour in maps as 'a prescriptive right … the father of three of these having been charged by His Late Majesty George III, in the like capacity for very many years'. Their claim to employment was enhanced, he learned, as these women appeared to have 'rendered in early life the most essential services to His Grace the Duke of Wellington', whatever that meant.[14]

As the war progressed, Jervis, who had not been fully fit for years, worked at a frantic pace in spite of the unceasing inroads of pertinacious inflammation of the bowel until his health gave way, aggravated by a misprescription which was slowly poisoning him. Reduced to a skeleton, unable to eat, Jervis refused to leave his new department and was carried from floor to floor in a chair; the ever-optimistic, impractical gadfly countering all expressions of solicitude with 'My duty to the government must in conscience be performed; I will go down colours flying.' Finally on 3 April 1857 the 'scientific, Christian soldier, the philanthropic educationalist, the stanch [*sic*] friend of India and Indian Missions' died.

Few were surprised when Panmure promptly appointed a committee of enquiry into the running of the T&S under Assistant Secretary of State for War J. R. Godley. It found that whilst useful, 'the value of the work has not been proportionate to the cost, and that the work itself has not been judiciously selected... At this your Lordship will probably not be surprised.' The committee recommended substantial reductions and proposed combining the T&S with two Horse Guards functions: the Topographical Depôt (which had been left over from an earlier attempt at an intelligence department, the Duke of York's Depôt of Military Knowledge) and the Ordnance Survey.

But Panmure was not content to let the soldiers hold sway. Even though the Ordnance Survey had a budget thirteen times that of the two topographical offices combined, the T&S had become such a vital symbol of civilian control over Horse Guards that Panmure absorbed the Survey into the T&S, and decreed that the new T&S would 'remain an independent branch of the War Office'.

The civilians prepared for a backlash and when it came dismissed it with the airy comment that it would be against 'all precedent and practice' to hand the T&S over to Horse Guards, rejecting at the outset 'any reasoning by which it could be proved that the Commander-in-Chief ought to direct the surveys of the country, purchase books, maps and instruments, and carry on generally the functions which are now placed immediately under the Secretary of State'.

The Godley Committee stressed that in future, the Department should give more attention to Jervis's ideas about intelligence not only at field level but higher. Indeed, 'officers should in reporting on countries, study their practical strategy and resources' and for this purpose Panmure 'should be empowered to employ officers and men from any branch of the British or Indian armies, or from civil life'.[15]

Panmure was pleased with the main thrust of the report and approved it on 26 October 1857. He thereupon appointed the director of the Ordnance Survey from 1854 to 1875, Lieutenant Colonel (later Lieutenant General Sir Henry) James, to head the new office and implement the recommendations of the report.

Like Jervis, James was a technocrat. He was the first (by a hair's breadth) to develop photozincography, which instead of heavy stone used relatively durable, lighter and more flexible zinc. It was a revolutionary cost-efficient boon to the practical and precise reproduction of maps and James was knighted for it in 1860. Nevertheless, when he sought some remuneration for his invention James found (as had Jervis earlier) that the parsimonious government had no intention of honouring his request.[16]

James's focus was on map making so the T&S made little progress towards becoming an active intelligence organisation in the decade following, despite continued unrest in Europe, the Middle East and the American Civil War. James proved more interested in the Survey and the best that can be said of him and his long-serving deputy, Major (later Lieutenant General A. C.) Cooke, Royal Engineers, is that the T&S survived their leadership.

This, however, was no mean feat. In 1858, the Liberal government fell and reaction on the military front was quick to follow. Major General Jonathan Peel, the rather less able brother of Robert Peel and the Conservative's new war minister, could not stand up to Horse Guards. It tried to contract away from the T&S the printing of secret fortification plans and even that of the Armstrong gun. Strictures were imposed and James complained that 'even in the most trifling matters' he was compelled to refer to his seniors.[17]

When the ailing Sidney Herbert, Florence Nightingale's staunch ally, returned to office in 1859 he brought a brief respite, directing the T&S to collect 'the most perfect series of plans of all the great fortresses of Europe, and other parts of the world'. He also tried to find them more central accommodation as 'the Topl. Dept. has relations with all the great Government Offices', but before the move could take place, Herbert died from overwork and the reactionaries returned to keep the T&S in its place.

Thus on the eve of the American Civil War, the T&S was composed of James, Cooke and two other officers in the Topographical Section, a retired naval staff commander looking after the library, eighteen printers and draughtsmen and an administration section staffed by two Royal Engineer non-commissioned officers and a sapper who examined the colouring, issuing or selling of the finished product. Nevertheless, between 1857 and 1870, the T&S produced almost two thousand different maps from a total of 237,519 impressions. Active, too, were James and Cooke in advancing their scientific and military reputations, James with photozincography primarily whilst Cooke translated scientific papers, sat on the Council of the Royal United Services Institute (RUSI) and wrote seven books, most of which dealt with the military systems of other countries. Although this is what Jervis had planned for, in actuality, and given the climate of disdain, the T&S output was more than might have been expected.

The reactionaries at Horse Guards were thoroughly in control and to ensure it could not get up to any further mischief such as, presumably, studying the methods, strength and equipment of the continental armies, the T&S was ordered to take on four new projects which would sap most of the department's energy for the next decade: firstly, the seven years' labour of recording, drawing or photographing every piece of equipment a field army would take on active service; secondly to prepare colour illustrations of all the myriad dress regulations, a monumental task taking four years only to be scrapped on the eve of completion in 1867; thirdly, James, master of the process of photozincography, was ordered to reproduce the great historical manuscripts held by the state including the Domesday book; and, finally, the T&S was to survey and draw plans of all the barracks and forts in Britain and Ireland. Under the weight of these projects the establishment dwindled and there was rarely more than one officer present and often none at all, as James spent most of his time in Southampton.

Despite such straitened circumstances the T&S refused to die. Indeed, there were some advances. It worked closely with the Royal Geographical Society over technical instructions for the North American boundary survey and arranged for the loan of various instruments for John Hanning Speke's African expeditions to find the source of the Nile. The T&S even managed to retain a ray or two of its aura of reform. In 1864, it was accused of 'drawing up a Report upon what should be the organisation of the War Office'. James denied it but, tired of the endless sniping, he requested the establishment of a committee of enquiry to confirm or deny the value of the T&S. On that committee he proposed to put Colonel J. H. Lefroy as its head. As mentioned above, Lefroy was arguably the best known military reformer of the age. He had been a 'great influence over Lord Panmure' and was largely responsible for a staff college worthy of the name. Having served on the Godley Committee, he was on record as regretting that the T&S had not fulfilled the teaching role dreamed for it by Jervis.

James also called for the appointment of Captain Douglas Galton, one of the first modern military sanitary engineers and later an assistant under-secretary in the War Office, who was thoroughly identified with the medical reforms of Sidney Herbert and Miss Nightingale. James also proposed other leading scientists and engineers. Yet, the Secretary of State for War was Lord (later Marquess) Ripon, who, it was said kindly enough, was not master in his own house; so except for Galton, no other moderniser was picked.[18]

The enquiry was packed by Horse Guards. Pre-eminent was the Quartermaster General, Sir Richard Airey, who was no friend of Panmure's reforms as he headed the department from which the Topographical Department had been wrested. After a brief investigation, his committee found, no doubt with some justification, that there was 'a want of special supervision over the work done'. He thereupon recommended that he, as Quartermaster General, should approve all non-survey work. The resulting report was accepted, Ripon weakly reserving the right to use the T&S 'without reference to Horse Guards'. Large wagons drew up at Spring Gardens to take away most of the presses and Airey refused to consider rehousing the enfeebled department.[19]

Still the T&S somehow survived. Whilst James and Cooke displayed no particular insight into the collection of intelligence or statistics, they can be credited with laying one important foundation stone for the Intelligence Department's later success: gifted manpower. Starved of officers on their strength, James had the idea of luring to the T&S officers who had 'a special aptitude and talent for strategy, geography and statistical science' as secondees.

Panmure had the idea of a staff drawn from all arms, hence the early appointment of Captain Martin Petrie of the 14th Regiment, but the officers James knew would be most useful were mainly Royal Engineers who, like the gunners of the Royal Artillery, were considered a second order to any officer from a regiment of the line. Officers of infantry and cavalry regarded technical expertise as being rather too keen in the wrong way. The 'scientific soldiers', the sappers and gunners, were 'mad, married, or Methodist' and very few held senior appointments outside their area of expertise.

Excluded from such opportunities, the brightest gunners and sappers eagerly sought secondment to the T&S. Soon James realised that he could recruit the absolute best of Britain's younger military brains. As early as 1858 he selected his secondees only from those officers who had passed through the recently reorganised Staff College. He offered officers who did well there almost the only opportunity to practise at a national level their recently acquired staff officer skills. James's policy of only using trained staff officers influenced profoundly the reputation and development of the Staff College, benefiting the reputations of both the College and the T&S.[20]

A potential posting to the T&S was, therefore, attractive to ambitious young scientific officers, so much so that some took extra courses in mathematics which were deemed 'crucial to qualify for a coveted post in the Topographical Department', and almost immediately the leading scholars from the Staff College came to Spring Gardens. Captain Petrie, who had passed first into the first class of the new Staff College, took on the mammoth task of compiling the first large-scale *Organisation, Composition and Strength of the Army of Great Britain*. This ran to five editions and strengthened the link between the T&S and the Staff College, to which Petrie returned as a professor.

In 1864 his successor was the Rugby-educated Captain (later Colonel Sir Henry) Hozier, whose legal daughter married Winston Churchill. Hozier had passed first into and first out of his class at the Staff College. He openly advocated changes in the Army along the lines laid down by Panmure and was therefore regarded as a dangerous reformer, which he was. Largely on his own initiative he followed the victorious Prussian troops as they crushed Austria in the Seven Weeks' War as a correspondent for *The Times* and marvelled at the planning which decanted the entire Prussian Guard Corps onto the border with Austria within a week of their entraining.

Hozier's allegiance to *The Times*, whose correspondents had uncovered the negligence and ignorance of the Army's commanders in the Crimea, angered Horse Guards. J. T. Delane, *The Times*' crusading editor, warned Panmure that Hozier's investigation of modern efficient military systems would not be welcomed and he was right. Yet Hozier's talents could not be denied and he was selected to advise the government on the feasibility of the 1867 Abyssinian campaign. This he did so well that General Sir Robert Napier appointed him to accompany the expedition for 'topographical purposes' as his military secretary. On his return to the T&S Hozier wrote a history of the campaign and the image of the scholarly soldier engaged on intelligence work became the firm hallmark of the T&S and its successor for the rest of the century.[21]

‡

In the spring of 1869 Cooke left to command the Royal Engineers in Bermuda and James replaced him with Captain Charles William Wilson, RE. Wilson was to be a primary formative influence in the

Department's second generation and, as will be seen, a major, if unsung, influence in Britain's foreign and imperial policy in the forthcoming years. Wilson had been at school at St David's, Liverpool College and Cheltenham College and matriculated at the University of Bonn. He came in second in the open competition for commissions in 1855. He must have made a considerable impression at the Royal Engineer Establishment, Chatham, because only three years later in 1858 he was appointed to manage the entire logistical chain (interestingly called 'the interior economy') for the North American Boundary Commission and to be its secretary. Providing without fail the forage, feeding and surveying over hundreds of miles of wilderness, he soon made a name for himself and not long after his return he inveigled James to lend him to Miss Angela (later Baroness) Burdett-Coutts, she of the banking family and the wealthiest woman in England. She wanted Wilson to perform the first modern survey of Jerusalem for historical and sanitary reasons.

Wilson enjoyed every minute of this new assignment. Besides the painstaking survey, he turned his hand to archaeology and became a noted amateur in the fledgling science. Indeed, Wilson's Arch in the Temple in Jerusalem was named after him. Between 1865 and 1869, he surveyed most of Palestine and the Sinai for the Palestine Exploration Fund and when James called him to fill the post of executive officer of the T&S, Wilson was already an active fellow of the Royal Geographical Society and a council member of the Royal United Services Institution.[22]

Wilson entered the cold and dingy house at Spring Gardens and found everything wanting, not least 'authentic information'. With Hozier away most of the time, Wilson must have wondered what he had got himself into and how could he, single-handedly, arrest the decline of the T&S? But a new dawn was at hand. Wilson returned to London just as the first Gladstone administration was finding its feet and the party of Panmure and Sidney Herbert was about to play again a significant role in the development of British intelligence.

Gladstone's new Secretary for War was hardly less remarkable than

Panmure. He was Edward (later Viscount) Cardwell of Winchester, a double first at Balliol and an energetic Peelite lawyer who was responsible for a number of maritime reforms and the abolition of transportation. In 1868 Gladstone asked him to become Secretary of State for War, following Ripon, a post he held until 1874. Once in office he resolved to complete Panmure's assertion of the control of the government and Parliament over Horse Guards. He thereupon cut drastically the number of British troops in the colonies, saving £1 million on the vote. He then turned to domestic military expenditure and his eye fell on the Ordnance Survey, which was mainly engaged in civil mapping although notionally under the T&S. He considered transferring it to the Department of Works.

James opposed this saying that if the T&S was not all it should be, it was because 'nothing had been done to remedy the disadvantages of the scattered arrangement of the offices'. On 14 January 1870 he told the Treasury that without the aid of the Survey, the T&S could not publish the maps and plans that he claimed were required by the War, Foreign and Colonial offices. In making his case he no doubt feared that in the transfer he might lose the military element of the Survey, viz twenty officers and four companies of Engineers, not to mention his own command. But Cardwell and the Chancellor of the Exchequer, Robert Lowe, had their way and transferred the Survey away from the military and James with it. Lowe tersely noted: 'I believe it has never been looked after by the War Office and the question is between some direction and none.'[23]

Thus within a few months of his arrival Charles Wilson found himself director of a dilapidated office, the odd press and a few clerks who were all that survived of Panmure's first reform. On 30 April 1870, the eve of his formal appointment, Wilson set out to distance himself from what had gone on before. He wrote to the War Office about the deplorable state of the T&S and especially its lack of information from all quarters. Whereas James had been content to see the T&S primarily as a map maker and secondly as a repository of lessons learned from previous campaigns, Wilson saw a department which should be an active collector of current military information from all around the globe.

If this was a bridge too far at that moment, Wilson must have been cheered by the arrival of a like-minded colleague: a young captain of artillery who had passed out first from the Staff College in 1869, Captain Evelyn Baring, later Lord Cromer, the virtual ruler of Egypt between 1883 and 1907 who had a mind so incisive it 'frightened people'.[24]

Baring and Wilson were contemporaries. Whilst Wilson had been sighting the North American boundary, Baring had observed the US Civil War at first hand. Horrified by the results of poor leadership and lack of organisation, Baring returned to the Staff College and disregarding the potential damage to his career, pointed to the wasteful effect of bad military management. Before long he became a recognised advocate of higher Army schooling. He railed against the purchase of commissions, fulminated against officers who saw no gain in further military education and told Lord Dufferin's Royal Commission on Military Education so. A tireless writer, he published the first *Staff College Essays* to 'show some of the officers of the Army that at all events *some* useful work is done at the Staff College'.[25]

Now at Spring Gardens, Baring concentrated his purposeful energy towards helping Wilson and Hozier develop the neglected interests of the T&S. And if to emphasise Wilson's concern about the paucity of current information on foreign armies, Prussia marched on France in mid-July 1870. The reaction of the British government was alarm and astonishment especially as within weeks 'what was unmistakably the most efficient army in the world' was before Paris. War fever gripped London. Cardwell told the Queen that England should have 20,000 men ready for action in forty-eight hours. On 20 July the Queen replied that if that was his intention, 'no effort should be spared at this moment to place every department on its most perfect footing'. The initial panic passed, but the awe inspired by the advance remained. Possibly inspired by Wilson, Cardwell told Lord Granville, the Secretary of State for Foreign Affairs, that it was 'most important to us to have accurate and complete intelligence of the causes which have led to the wonderful success of the Prussian troops'.[26]

Luckily for Wilson, Hozier and Baring, no one seems to have asked them for information in the early days of the war. This was just as well, because the latest issues of the French and German military newspapers in Spring Gardens were over a month out of date as Horse Guards, a quarter of a mile away, insisted on taking delivery of all the T&S's post. Wilson complained that on one occasion 108 back copies of an important foreign journal were delivered in one lump. To his disgust, Wilson said that on the outbreak of the war there was not one 'trustworthy account of any foreign army, and I am almost ashamed to say that had any complications arisen with France ... we should have had to translate a German work on the French army as giving a better account of it than we could prepare ourselves.'[27]

The Foreign Office, now aroused, turned to the British military attachés to explain the lack of forewarning and how it had come to be that the French, long acclaimed as the military masters of the post-Napoleonic world, had been reduced to cutting bombproofs in the Bois de Boulogne. Horse Guards reacted as if stung. The idea of any military attaché being brought to account by a civilian department was completely unheard of. The Commander-in-Chief, the Duke of Cambridge, proudest of all reactionaries, said that Colonel Walker, sometime attaché to the Kaiser's army, was 'admirably fitted for the post', but Granville found his reports were 'wretched' and the FO was reduced to 'a septuagenarian general sending information [from Paris] by balloon'. Cardwell agreed as to Walker's inadequacy and sent Hozier to the front. When the Duke was told of Hozier's appointment, he replied tersely: 'You could not have done better.'

Hozier, of course, thrived on his new task. His reports were popular with the Cabinet and the Queen, containing, as they increasingly did, readable, sophisticated analyses of what might happen next, based on solid fact and supportable premise. After reading one on Prussian attitudes towards Britain, Granville marvelled: 'How well Hozier writes. I have heard all that he says.'

Meanwhile in the backwater of Spring Gardens, Wilson and Baring rushed to produce maps and studies of the campaign whilst not losing sight of their larger goal. They again requested an urgent reorganisation of the T&S with its first objective to:

> collect in peacetime such information relating to foreign armies that, on the outbreak of war with any one country, we should be able at once to send to press, and publish for the use of officers of our army, a pamphlet containing the fullest and most recent details concerning the hostile army.[28]

Cardwell agreed and responded by appointing his Under-Secretary of War, the Earl of Northbrook (Captain Baring's second cousin), to head yet another enquiry on 'the best means of turning the Topographical Department to the greatest account'.

Northbrook, too, was remarkable He was a principled, high-minded and intellectual aristocrat, who had been in constant public service since coming down from Oxford. Shy in the extreme, he had been briefly an under-secretary at the War Office and his appointment to the War Office was Cardwell's one stipulation before taking office. His young wife and a son having recently died, Northbrook converted his grief into working every waking hour. He formed a committee to look into the T&S with the aged Airey as its head, but he clearly meant it to be dominated by the enquiry's secretary, Charles William Wilson.

During the four months the committee sat, Wilson, Baring and Northbrook unveiled for it the reality of the military world around them. They concluded that intelligence, then wrapped up in the almost mystical cloak of a *Großdienststab*, was the key to Prussia's success. They compared their small office with the large staff of Prussia and, for that matter, of France and widened their horizons to compare the difference between it and the effectiveness of the Russian and Turkish armies, all in an attempt to demonstrate that they, too, could produce intelligence.

When it was completed, Cardwell was impressed and Wilson did not hesitate to suggest to Northbrook that the time had come for there to be a functional role for intelligence in the British Army. Northbrook sent it on to Cardwell saying: 'I think you will consider it well and ably drawn up. I agree with a great deal of it...' They then sent Wilson to see the siege of Metz as a 'tourist' and in his resulting *Notes on a Visit to Metz and Strasbourg* he again emphasised that battlefield success depended on good intelligence. The case was complete.[29]

On 24 January 1871, the Northbrook Committee's report was formally laid before Cardwell. It condemned the bureaucracy of Horse Guards, which had prevented the T&S from collecting information scattered amongst various official sources, and it went some way towards recommending the restoration of the T&S as a separate office under the Secretary for War.

It was thorough. The T&S should be able to receive its own mail and establish a confidential registry. It should be allowed to spend some £600 p.a. on books and maps and it should retain its own printing presses. The T&S should be in the position of encouraging officers travelling abroad to 'make or obtain plans of and notes on foreign fortresses' and the permanent establishment should be increased by three officers who were to travel themselves. As for relations with others, the T&S was to liaise with the Royal Navy and military attachés all over the world should be encouraged to contribute information regularly to Spring Gardens. The Committee hoped that future attachés would be drawn from officers who had served in the T&S as they would 'know the class of information required, and take an interest in supplying it to a Department in which they had spent some years'.

In conclusion, the Northbrook Committee saw the mission of the T&S as collecting:

all possible information relating to the statistics, equipment and organisation of foreign armies; the resources, railways, available means of transport &c., of Great Britain and Ireland, the colonies (exclusive of India) and foreign countries; and to prepare any information relating to foreign countries which might be required for the heads of Departments in the War Office.

Cardwell immediately approved the report.[30]

At the time, it cannot have been lost on any observer of the military scene that the Northbrook Report was a considerable step forward in British military organisation. Yet putting the accepted recommendations into practice was no small undertaking. The first thing Wilson and his colleagues did was to reform the office. So that they could preserve information about foreign armies 'in such a form that it can be readily consulted, and made available for any purpose for which it is required', they broke the T&S into three sections, each covering a third of the world.

Using their language skills, Hozier, Baring and their attached colleagues now began perusing the newspapers daily and increasing the number of military periodicals from the places under their purview, pasting articles of note into large scrapbooks. More permanent references were kept in the expanding library along with reports from 'travellers' and attachés, which now, for the first time, came directly from the Foreign Office instead of via the War Office.

Soon Wilson was using the power of his own presses to publish extended orders of battle for various countries in a new *Armed Strength* series. These eventually became so thick and detailed that they far exceeded Wilson's hope of providing 'such information as every staff officer should possess upon taking the field'.

‡

So as the T&S's modest reorganisation was taking place, what did the world facing Wilson and his colleagues look like? As noted previously, the story of Europe in the nineteenth century is the story of growing militarism in Russia, France, Germany, Italy,

Austro-Hungary, in fact in most places except Spain, Switzerland, Norway and, especially, Britain. In the aftermath of the Franco-Prussian War, as the Prussians withdrew, France lost no time in recreating and modernising her legions and their command with one view alone: to avenge the loss of Alsace-Lorraine. The new Germany, for its part, anticipated an eventual revanche by strengthening the *Landwehr* or Reserves by instituting a form of national military service which in Bismarck's eyes had the added benefit of acting as a *Bindungsglied* or binding force to make a reality of the dream of a truly united Germany. Russia also smarted over the Crimean War and despite a peace faction in the heart of government, its ascendant military coxed and boxed southwards into Central Asia, causing concern in London and Calcutta.

Part and parcel of this militarism, along with more destructive weaponry and refined tactical and logistical reform, was the acknowledgement that covert intelligence activities were an indispensable part of every nation's armoury. This meant employing spies about whom honourable soldiers were ambivalent, as Hozier found when analysing the Seven Weeks' War:

> Spies have a dangerous task, and not an honourable one, consequently, except in very rare and extreme cases, officers will not accept the invidious duty. Money is the great means of obtaining good spies; needy adventurers and unscrupulous men will, if well paid, do the work and run … the risk of certain death.

The whole idea of spies and spying thrilled public imagination. Spying became at one and the same time an explanation, an excuse and a prime contributor to each nation's paranoia. Everyone in France suddenly remembered German 'tourists' taking long walks along railway lines in the late 1860s. And when, in 1875, the French War Minister General de Cissey had an affair with the Baroness de Kaula, it was obvious to the man on the street that she must be transmitting secrets back to Berlin. In the new Germany charges of spying became a convenient weapon against Social Democrats and other liberals as they would be for the French anti-Semites who persecuted and prosecuted Captain Dreyfus a few years later.[31]

But spies do not exist without an organisation behind them and, in the latter half of the nineteenth century, the continental powers spared no expense in establishing modern intelligence systems within their police and general staffs. In his first sweeping survey of the military forces on the continent, Wilson found that both Austria and France had not been slow to learn from their enemies. By 1873 the Austrians had forsaken their traditional 'heroics of the most futile sort' and boasted a new organisation of sixty-eight officers, a paymaster and ten clerks engaged primarily in military intelligence. The French, too, had Prussianised their intelligence and general staff 'as far as French national habits admit of' and by 1874 had fifty-three officers and nineteen clerks engaged in intelligence work.

The original Prussian system, which they all took as their model, was expanded for the new Germany and in 1874 carried a peacetime strength of 101 trained officers, nineteen clerks and direct operational command of a number of 'survey' teams.[32]

Thus directed, Cardwell and Northbrook saw the merits of investigating the idea of a general staff further. They turned to the T&S. Cardwell told Gladstone: 'Hozier will be the best man I know to consult on Prussian arrangements, and I intend doing so.' This made the work of the T&S even more suspect to the soldiers at Horse Guards, who saw in it the embryo general staff they so feared.

Yet is this not overegging the pudding? Prince George, the second Duke of Cambridge, who had a brief and wholly lacklustre record in the Crimea, had become Commanding-in-Chief in 1868 at the age of thirty-seven. The son of Adolphus, the prized seventh son of George III, he held that position until 1895. The original young fogey, it was rumoured that he would wax with apoplexy if the two words 'general' and 'staff' were used in the same sentence. He considered such an organisation would erode his personal authority and made his views widely known, not least to the Queen. In fact, she only approved the

Northbrook Committee's report after assuring herself that the Duke of Cambridge's functions would be 'in no way impaired'.

Whether it was the Queen's attitude or the Duke's, it only strengthened the resolve of the Liberal government to hasten further reform. The Earl of Kimberley, then Gladstone's Colonial Secretary, thought that the Duke's conduct was a 'miserable shilly shally' and Cardwell even hinted at dismissing him. Marshalling 'an uneasy coalition of politicians, civil servants and military reformers' Cardwell and Northbrook pressed on and Horse Guards were jostled as never before. When in the midst of this the Adjutant General learned that the Duke intended to take the waters in Germany (which he did for several months every year), he pleaded with him not to go. 'I am quite unequal to combat the ideas of five civilians inspired by Ld. Northbrook which is an "out-and-outer" backed by Mr Knox who has not a military idea in his conformation.' From the purchase of commissions to regimental titles, from the establishment of linked battalions to length of service, the conservatives of Horse Guards were being swept from the field. Soon Horse Guards was officially made subordinate to the War Office.[33]

One unwritten consequence of the Northbrook reform of the T&S was arguably a move towards that embryonic general staff which the reformers believed should come into existence. In any event, the reforms only increased the animosity to the T&S and its work. Officers in the T&S complained privately and increasingly publicly about the prevailing attitude of Horse Guards to the T&S and, indeed, to the act of collecting information, covert or overt. 'I may perhaps be allowed to repeat', Wilson wrote, 'that there is nothing new or un-English in the idea of studying ... such statistics as must be known in order to make sound plans for the eventualities of war.'[34]

Whilst on paper the gains made by the T&S were staggering, the reality was that the ability of the T&S, as then constituted to do much of anything at all (besides the *Armed Strength* series), was limited. What could Wilson, a captain, do faced with the reactionary might of Horse Guards already nibbling into the Northbrook recommendations? Hence, when Cardwell asked Wilson for the next step in expanding the effectiveness of the T&S, Wilson made a 'self-denying' request that an officer of 'high rank and position should be placed at the head of the department'; in effect a proto-Chief of Staff without executive duties. And as Britain was 'the only country in Europe which did not possess a scheme of national defence', Wilson urged an expansion of the existing sections of the T&S to include offices capable of dealing with home and colonial defence, mobilisation issues, railways and telegraphs.

Again, the Duke maintained his opposition to a Chief of Staff, considering that the 'duties of such an officer belonged to himself...' but Cardwell was having none of it. He needed to find a general who understood what the government wanted and yet was able to work with the Duke.

He existed. He was Major General (later Lieutenant General Sir Patrick) MacDougall, who had spent ten years organising the Canadian militia and had been the first commandant of the Staff College. His third book, *The Army and its Reserves*, won him the chairmanship of Cardwell's enquiry into the reserves where his considerable ability and hard work earned for him the approbation of the government. At the same time it was known that he was 'respected and listened to by the Duke'. He fitted exactly Northbrook's definition of what the head of the T&S should be, namely one 'specially selected for his knowledge of military history and strategy', attentive to the smallest details and prepared to work 'silently in the shadows'. He would make an excellent Chief of Staff, backed up by the T&S.[35]

On 24 February 1873, Cardwell was addressing the House of Commons on the Army estimates when, in mid-speech, he suddenly announced the creation of a new department of the War Office to handle what:

is called, I believe, logisticks; but it means, not any interference with generalship but the careful preparation of those measures which may enable generals to act best according to the exigencies of the case, and so as to prevent those mistakes which at the outset of any operations are so fatal and difficult to retrieve.

The new department would be created:

without any additional expense by attaching to His Royal Highness the Field Marshal Commanding-in-Chief a general officer who shall not be overwhelmed by daily executive duties but whose function it shall be to be responsible to the Commander in Chief and to the Executive Government for the proper conduct of what may constitute a real Intelligence Department...

MacDougall was the man and the existing T&S 'consisting of scientific officers, under that most excellent officer, Captain Wilson' would form the heart of the new department. On 23 May 1873 Wilson was promoted to major and the next day the new Intelligence Department was in being.[36]

It is clear that the government meant that 'practical and prophetic theorist' MacDougall, now a Deputy Adjutant General, to be a Chief of Staff in all but name. As for the new department and its work, Colburn's *United Service Magazine* described it as 'promising to be very lively'.

This is exactly what it set out to be. If the T&S had learned two lessons from the Franco-Prussian War they were that Britain needed to modernise and it needed to be able to mobilise. To assist him he brought in Captain (later Major General Charles) Brackenbury, whose brother would become the director of the organisation some years later. Charles Brackenbury had already provoked the Duke's wrath as he had 'criticised rather sharply the support of the HRH of sometime honoured absurdities', not least the parlous state of the Volunteer movement. This he did having, like Hozier, watched the Austrian Army collapse in the Seven Weeks' War of 1866. Again like Hozier, he wrote on military affairs (he was 'The Military Critic' at *The Times*) and enjoyed a substantial reputation in Europe. Constantly under the dark and threatening clouds of Horse Guards, he reached the comparative cover of the Intelligence Department only under the protection of Cardwell and his editor, Delane of *The Times*. Referring to Brackenbury, Delane hardly needed to remind Cardwell that 'at the Horse Guards there is a great desire to snub all scientific officers and to cling to the dear old system... We can't afford to have *all* the brains knocked out of the service.'[37]

Another early arrival was Captain (later Colonel) Robert Home, RE, the man who would catapult to extraordinary heights the role of intelligence in British policy making during the next decade and whose influence would last long after his untimely death from typhoid fever in 1879 at the age of only forty-one. Home was one of the first to pass into the new Staff College and then saw service in Canada between 1864 and 1867 on the defence of the frontier against the Fenians. He came to the T&S in 1871 to support the ramped-up effort during the Franco-Prussian War and was one of the first appointments to the new Department in 1873. After the shambolic autumn manoeuvres of 1872 an authoritative book of tactics for officers was much in want. Home, a prolific writer (on reform, usually anonymously), prepared *The Précis of Modern Tactics*, which, when published, stood for more than thirty years as 'universally considered the best tactical work in the English language',[38] and was translated into many foreign languages.

With talent like this in the Department, work on a realistic scheme for mobilisation began in earnest. It was an established preconception (which lasted until the Entente Cordiale in 1904) that France headed the list of threatening powers to Great Britain and Ireland. Defence and mobilisation plans had heretofore been focused on the Royal Navy and Palmerston forts. In 1858, General J. F. Burgoyne wrote that if the French landed they would be opposed by 'a collected field army'.[39] What he failed to do, however, was explain of what this force would be composed, where it would come from, how it was to be gathered, deployed, fed, watered and resupplied. This required planning, staff work, pre-positioning of stores and a hundred problems solved. Yet Britain lacked the capability to plan and mount even the most rudimentary defence of its shores, plain and simple. As for the Volunteers, the refusal of Horse Guards to take their contribution seriously drove literally thousands of well-intentioned but now disillusioned men to resign.

MacDougall, Wilson and colleagues thereupon set out on a programme to put this right. They rode the coast of south-eastern England, looking for likely landing places whilst Home worked up plans to counter an invasion. He estimated that based on France's capability, it would take at least eight army corps to repulse an invasion. As Britain did not have even one corps, Home had the order of battle for all eight corps published annually in the *Army List* without the name of a single officer or unit under them. He did this to 'keep our deficiencies in a prominent position, with a view to their being rectified'.

Soon the Department was immersed in a welter of detailed planning issues:

- The best arrangement for the defence of the capital, or any other important strategical positions if threatened with attack.
- The topography and resources of Great Britain and Ireland by sub-districts embracing:
- acreage, grass, and arable resources in grain, cattle, horses, carts, wagons, mills, bakeries, and billeting capacity of towns and villages.
- resources of the various lines of railway in respect of rolling stock, its nature and quantity, extent and capacity of platforms at all important stations, and amount of shunting accommodation, the fullest details in short of the available means of transporting troops by rail…

Strategically, Home's plan was clear: find and fix the enemy. It was unlikely the French would land within range of coastal batteries, but wherever they did come ashore they would be met by one or more of the eight planned corps, imaginatively composed in tiers according to depth of experience and quality of training, viz Regulars, then the reserves of Militia and Yeomanry. To their rear, the Volunteers would defend a ring of forts around London. Once the nature and direction of the invasion was identified, uncommitted corps would form the counter-attack and, possibly, counter-invasion. As a background to this military activity, Home had a hunch that the British government would have, at best, some six weeks warning of an impending invasion. He also had a hunch that the government would be wholly incapable of responding to the predictable civilian reaction of unbridled panic.

The detailed planning and those blanks in the *Army List* caused considerable mirth within the officer corps. Like civil resilience of a later age, mobilisation and defence were regarded as hot air or '*windbeutelei*' leading only to a 'desultory and technical discussion'.[40]

This was not the reaction MacDougall and Home wanted. What they wanted was 'to tie our bundle of military sticks into a wieldable fasces', but what they got was an uncooked marble cake of ridicule, ignorance, lack of support for a larger Army and an ill-equipped reserve force with only a notional role. Faced with this reality, Home concluded that *passive* defence and mobilisation would be a long, slow business. In short, Britain could not withstand a properly mounted invasion. Britain's weakness at home therefore needed to be overcome. The solution, they opined, was to compensate for Britain's lack of preparedness by gathering intelligence abroad.

The action of this country under certain contingencies must embrace offensive as well as defensive action, and this all the more on account of certain treaty obligations. It then became apparent that there were certain facts connected with foreign countries that should be ascertained.

This became the Intelligence Department's *raison d'être* and guiding principle for concerted collection activity from then on.

Using the rationale that 'mobilisation required preparation and preparation was impossible without information', Home asked Lord

Stanley at the War Office for authorisation to spend about £4,000 a year on overseas collection. Home's proposal, to say the least, was one of 'extreme delicacy' and so Stanley visited the Department with W. H. Smith, the Chancellor of the Exchequer, in tow. Smith, the model for Gilbert's 'Ruler of the Queen's Navee', had a reputation for being safe and sound. He 'examined the work that was being done, and what was proposed to be done, and he not only expressed his approval of the proposals, but his astonishment at it never having been before worked out'. Smith immediately offered to increase the secret grant if it was wanted.[41]

Cardwell, too, made good. He visited Spring Gardens and upon finding 'services intolerably crowded here', moved the ID to Adair House in St James's Square. The number of officers was increased to thirty-seven and considerable new work was begun. The *Armed Strength* series was moving apace and mobilisation plans were on a new footing.[42]

But there were still major deficiencies. As with the Franco-Prussian War, the Department could provide very little information to support Colonel Garnet (later Field Marshal Viscount) Wolseley's punitive expedition to Ashanti in 1873. When Charles Brackenbury's brother Henry called on Wilson for maps and information on West Africa, he came away almost empty handed. Belatedly the Department set to work and before the November reinforcements left (commanded by another future director, Sir Archibald Alison), the ID was able to provide better maps and even a Hausa vocabulary book.

Long-term strategic intelligence work vying with providing tactical intelligence for immediate operations became a two-edged sword for the Department. Whilst its officers proved it could support tactical operations relatively rapidly, its identification with Wolseley, 'an out and out reformer' who had vocally and practically supported all the Cardwell reforms, and the bright young officers he selected for his staff, called 'the Ashanti Ring' (like the Milner Kindergarten in South Africa thirty years later), gave Horse Guards fresh grounds for regarding the intelligencers with disdain. After all, there was immense jealousy from soldiers not selected for the expedition towards Wolseley and his Ring of 'heaven-born' reforming officers.

And no wonder, for it included the brightest and the best, most of whom served or would serve in intelligence functions in London, Cairo or Simla in the coming era. The interlocking membership of the Intelligence Department, Wolseley and the officers of the Ring did nothing to improve the Department's relations with Horse Guards.[43]

But despite the promising start, dark clouds soon gathered. Gladstone's government fell in 1874 and Cardwell was replaced by Gathorne Gathorne-Hardy, a man more susceptible than Cardwell to the influence of the generals at Horse Guards. Although he supported the ID to a degree, the new Secretary was unhappy at the War Office and only spent a few hours a day there, lamenting in his diary 'what I would give for a very safe and good military adviser. HRH won't do.' Yet the reformers believed 'Mr Hardy seeks for no opinion except those given to him by the Duke. We can expect no healthy reform of any sort.'[44]

That proved to be the case. In July 1874, the ID was peremptorily subjugated to the Quartermaster General's Office, which was itself being pushed into oblivion by the increasingly powerful Adjutant General's Office. Three of the Department's officers were removed to other duties and the collection of foreign statistics was stopped. MacDougall was told in no uncertain terms that:

> Any change in the working of the branch was to be laid before the Adjutant-General, who would receive instructions from His Royal Highness. The Adjutant-General was to be informed by the Quarter Master-General of all new information collected, in order that it might be laid before His Royal Highness.[45]

Wilson protested and MacDougall was apparently able to assuage the Duke, so that on 16 April 1875 the foreign sections were reinstated. But on paper at least, the Department was now under the thumb of Horse Guards. Wilson's posting was over in March 1876, when he went to command the Ordnance Survey in Ireland, and MacDougall left in May 1878 to command the forces in Canada. It seemed like the end.

But once again, the Department would not die. Another reformer and leading member of the Ashanti Ring, Major General Sir Archibald Alison, came from the Staff College to be MacDougall's replacement as the new head of the Department. He took the bit between his teeth and ensured that, even though starved, the ID would not be ignored. Having grown from Jervis's cartographical enthusiasm, by the mid-1870s its scientific, logistical and reforming spirit was giving heart to new generations of bright soldiers, ambitious for Britain's safety in a changing world. As will be seen in central Asia, their time was at hand.

CHAPTER TWO

SOMETHING MORE IS NECESSARY

When Gladstone's government resigned office in 1874, it left behind the remarkable legacy of a reformed Army. The transformation was little short of a miracle and together with a larger Royal Navy gave both Liberal and Conservative governments more than two decades of worldwide power and prestige.

Although Sidney Herbert paved the way for major military reforms, their actual implementation was brought about after his death by two men: Edward (later Viscount) Cardwell, Secretary of State from 1868–74, ably supported by Lord Northbrook, his Under-Secretary for War and a future Viceroy of India. Their catalogue of achievements remains breathtaking. They increased the size of the Army by twenty-five battalions and increased the reserve forces available for overseas service from some 3,000 to almost 36,000. They made being a soldier tolerable. They abolished flogging in peacetime and reduced the number of years of enlistment from twenty-one to an initial period of service based on six years in the Regulars and six in the Reserve. They brought back troops who had been kicking their heels in self-governing (and often pestilential) colonies and gave each infantry regiment a home base from which it would recruit and retrain for active service, making family life possible. They also abolished the purchase of commissions. Most remarkably, they achieved all this without an increase in Army expenditure. In fact, they reduced it.

Another seminal change was to make the Commander-in-Chief, in the person of the Duke of Cambridge, accountable to the government of the day. The Queen agreed to this most reluctantly, having been strongly advised not to by the idle and irascible Duke, who fought tooth and nail against it (and any other change). But, as was pointed out to her, it was the government who paid the bills and concomitant with that was accountability to Parliament. The Duke remained in post until 1895, resolute in his opposition to new thinking, and, as shown in the previous chapter, he decried the concept of a general staff, marginalising its proto-manifestation, the Intelligence Department, at every opportunity.

Another of Cardwell's changes, as noted in the last chapter, was to put intelligence on a sounder footing than ever before with a clear set of responsibilities which brought the ID into an acknowledged – and closer – relationship with the government.

But it was a relationship which demanded constant maintenance by the officers of the Department and key to their burgeoning relationship with the government was the consistent quality and usefulness of their product. Ministers and senior officials at the Foreign, India and Colonial offices did not normally entertain high opinions of the abilities and advice of generals in particular or military men as a whole. Without a military organisation that formally allotted or fixed responsibility for supporting government policy or providing advice, hordes of military men thought it their duty to opine on such matters. Experience showed, however, that their opinions often complicated matters. Thus the enthusiasms of soldiers were only valued in the clinch. At other times they were regarded as monochromatic, dangerous and lacking in political vision. On that both Conservatives and Liberals agreed. The Marquess of Salisbury, when Disraeli's Foreign Secretary, cautioned Lord Lytton, then Viceroy of India:

> You listen too much to the soldiers. You should never trust experts.
> If you believe the doctors, nothing is wholesome: if you believe the
> theologians, nothing is innocent: if you believe the soldiers, nothing is
> safe. They all require to have their strong wine diluted by a very large
> admixture of common sense.[46]

Ministers needed impartial and informed military knowledge which could be integrated into the processes of statecraft. This the new invigorated ID sought to provide.

In 1874 when the new Prime Minister, Benjamin Disraeli, swept into office he appointed Robert Gascoyne-Cecil, the third Marquess of Salisbury, to the India Office. In time Salisbury would become one of the most remarkable Prime Ministers Britain ever produced and first India, then the Foreign Office, were to be his training grounds. When appointed, his abilities had already been widely recognised. In the early 1870s the young 'fêted champion' of the Tories came to show as much enthusiasm for the new technology of intelligence as he did for chemistry, electricity and the telephone.

In office, his problems were many, not least keeping the government of India itself on an increasingly strong imperial lead. His other main problem was Russia's real and imagined expansion southwards. Simultaneously the long, sharp claws of the bear were eroding Ottoman control in the Balkans and western Asia as well as toying with Afghanistan and the approaches to India. This gradual encroachment had been going on for decades, but by the early 1870s the pace quickened. For London, the question was whether or not the Ottomans could withstand Russia in the west and, in the east, to what degree was India's north-west frontier, indeed all of India, menaced? If the Russians expanded to the Black Sea and beyond could they interdict communications between India and London? If Russia suborned the khanates of central Asia and Afghanistan, could they set aflame a revolt in India itself?

Everything was an unsatisfactory muddle. Diplomatically, Britain had to contend with the new *Dreikaiserbund* of Austria-Hungary, Germany and Russia, that loose triumvirate under Bismarck's sway, which staggered under Russian-encouraged Bulgarian unrest, the vicious Ottoman response and Russian support for a Serbian state of sorts, all of which caused considerable alarm in Vienna, Berlin and London.

It could not last. Separately and together each of the interested states danced an increasingly complicated quadrille of diplomacy and counter-diplomacy with the Ottomans and Russia until the *Dreikaiserbund* broke up in 1878 as Austria-Hungary, Germany and the new nation of Italy could no longer accommodate St Petersburg's intentions. But what were St Petersburg's intentions? It sent out conflicting signals to each of the major powers, reflecting the confusion within. The Czar's expansionist ministers for war were responsible for central Asia, whilst de Giers, the moderate Foreign Minister, was kept in the dark. Indeed, London was learning that what Russia said to the west was often quite different from the actions she took in the south and the east. For example, Russia promised the powers it would not seize Kiva on the Afghanistan border but the nearest Russian army unit took it anyway. There would be a flurry of diplomatic activity then all would go quiet until the next time. As Salisbury lamented: 'I cannot understand why the Russian Government does not insist on being obeyed ...They get all the inconveniences and few of the advantages of an aggressive policy.'[47]

Russia's perpetual interest in Afghanistan was not always easy to fathom. The Russian generals looked on it as a political *tabula rasa* but one which should naturally fall to their God-given place in the sun. Afghanistan was populated but sparsely by tribes who moved to the plains in winter and back to the hills and mountains during the summer. Raiding was a way of life – and death. Afghanistan's misfortune was to lie between the Russian and Indian empires. Watching the bear move ever nearer, the government of India had long wanted to establish a 'scientific frontier'. They also wanted to create a buffer state between India and Russian expansionists as early as the 1830s, a full decade before Britain annexed the Punjab.

But the bear was treading on unstable ground. Afghanistan's age-old tribal disputes laid it open to outside intrigue. The British had tried to set up a friendly regime in Afghanistan once before, in 1838, but it swiftly led to four years of conflict and humiliating defeat for the British. It did not suit the Afghans to be hemmed in. Later, the British press were convinced that the Russians were behind the refusal by the nominal Amir or ruler of Afghanistan, Sher Ali, to allow a British mission to examine the north-west boundary, thereby thwarting British designs to define the border accurately. And they were probably right. Successive generations of mishandling and interference by the Indian government had done little to draw the Amir towards the British. In any event, with her conquest or subjugation of Tashkent (1865), Bokhara (1866) and Samarkand (1868), Russia carried on advancing gradually towards Merv, which, with Herat, became an *idée fixe* in the minds of the Indian military as the key to unlocking India's defences.

Persia, too, was ripe for Russian intervention. For a century the Persians had a love–hate relationship with the British that deteriorated further during the 1870s before and during Russia's war against Turkey. In 1874, W. Taylour Thompson, the British envoy in Tehran, urged London to inject British aid and Indian officer cadres acting as consuls along the Persian border to the north. But nothing happened as Salisbury, the India Council in London and the Viceroy of India (Lord Northbrook from February 1872) could not agree on a common approach or who would pay. So Lord Derby, the Foreign Secretary, did nothing and the muddle drifted on.[48]

This taught Salisbury a valuable lesson. After the mutiny in 1857, India's government, headquartered in Calcutta and Simla when the weather turned, found its policies and actions increasingly second-guessed by London. Inevitably the hazy delimitation between imperial and Indian spheres of influence and differing points of view hampered any co-ordinated response. Despite the advance of the telegraph, or perhaps because of it, differences in policy and outlook between London and the government in India become more pronounced. Initially this was regarded as simply bothersome, but with increasing demands on the British Exchequer and the rapid growth of Britain's global responsibilities, Salisbury and Disraeli became convinced that it was high time for Indian government thinking to be brought into line with emerging imperial policy.

This would take time and in the meantime there was little Salisbury could do but watch Russian power and influence spread.

Yet even that was difficult as information from the contested areas was patchy and often highly inaccurate. This is not to say that the Indian government was inactive. On the contrary, ever since the days of the East India Company, there was first a Political, then a Political & Secret Department which fielded agents or consuls throughout neighbouring principalities and states. It is to this department which Salisbury was no doubt referring as 'your Intelligence Department' in the period before the Intelligence Branch, Simla (IBS) was formed. In any event, they were there to keep the flag flying, promote what commercial possibilities were available and report back on the political situation. Often they were high-ranking Indians who, as in the case of the envoy to Afghanistan, had been in Kabul for thirty years and, it was widely believed, had gone so native as to be useless.

Coming at the collection of information from a different angle, Thomas Best Jervis had been very conscious of the unsatisfactory state of information about the potentially contested ground, viz the nature of the great swathes of unmapped approaches to India as battlefields. He came up with the concept of a Corps of Guides, but his ideas fell on stony ground in the East India Company military of the 1830s and 1840s. Similarly an intelligence function was created in the Northwest Provinces during the mutiny, but subsequently disbanded. So by the 1860s, what political or military intelligence there was on Afghanistan and the border came back to London via the Punjab government. This resulted in:

> delay, lukewarm interest, weakening of responsibility, first in the Punjab, and then in the Supreme Government, with consequent diplomatic debility, and all the concomitant results on border management, of which only those can judge who occasionally meet the Border Officers, and talk with them in familiar confidence. It is almost incredible, but it is true, that according to this extraordinary system Candahar news, which is very often most important as regards the dynasty in possession of Cabul, reaches the Government of India through the Commissioner of Sinde and the Government of Bombay.[49]

As it was, the Quartermaster General of India had the responsibility to 'collect and record military information' but other duties 'tended somewhat to obscure this'. Whether independently of Jervis or at his behest is not clear, but as early as 1849, small units of Guides appeared within the order-of-battle formations stationed in Bengal, Bombay and Madras. The *Punjab Administrative Report 1849–50* clearly set out that they were to be 'guides and spies who would be of the utmost assistance to the Quarter-Master General's Department as intelligencers'. Nevertheless they were little more than scouts and mounted infantry. As late as 1878 an Indian staff officer noted 'only one solitary instance on record of a Guide sketching and mapping on the frontier'.[50]

Back in London, the India Office was deeply sceptical of information from India itself. It reckoned that such news about Afghanistan, the border, the tribes and the Russians which was selected for onward transmission to London was 'derived from the tales of native merchants and travellers, whose stories, magnified in the bazaars of the different cities through which they pass, reach India and Persia in a most distorted state, and give rise to rumours utterly devoid of foundation'. When one set of the 'Cabul Diaries' arrived in bulk in the India Office, an official wrote on the bundle: 'These are copies of the latest Cabul Diaries: Implicit reliance cannot be placed upon them.'[51]

On another occasion the British agent at Ley announced the arrival of an 1868 Russian mission to Kashgar a full year after news of it had first been sent to London by the Ambassador in St Petersburg.[52] Sir Richard Temple, the highly influential financial member of the Council in India, was not bothered in the least. He claimed that there was 'as much information as could be fairly expected' and if London wanted more or different intelligence external to what India was providing, it should pay for it.

Cardwell found this wholly unsatisfactory and had urged Salisbury's predecessor as Secretary of State for India, the Duke of Argyll, to provide funding for an officer in the Intelligence Department who would be responsible 'for all questions relating to the defence of India'. Argyll refused on the grounds of lack of money. Rebuffed, Cardwell wrote back: 'I will discontinue the Asiatic portion of the labour in our Intelligence Department relying for that knowledge being furnished to the Cabinet, whenever it is wanted by the India Office. I should, however, like it to be on record that such is the arrangement.'[53]

Yet despite Cardwell's claimed withdrawal of ID support, the Department could hardly ignore India. As early as the late 1860s the T&S began a semi-official or 'Blue Book' series entitled *Russian Advances in Asia*. Wilson revised it in 1873 and Salisbury found it when he came into office. It was unique.[54]

Drawing on reputable foreign material and despatches from a wide range of sources, *Russian Advances* described the Russian's *modus operandi* of expansion from the planting of military outposts, then political intrigue and faction favouring and finally absorption. It went on to sift through the scanty evidence of feints and advances, testing the viability of each by applying the new science of *Kriegspielen* or war games on paper, a skill at which Evelyn Baring was particularly adept. This was important because the war gaming allowed the ID to analyse the types and sizes of units rumoured to be involved and apply to each 'the amount of time it would take a military force of known composition to travel over a given distance of known terrain and weather patterns and arrive at a selected point in a battle-ready state'.[55] If the analysis indicated that the right units were not in the right place at the right time, the rumour remained a rumour.

In the 1873 volume, Wilson concluded that the Russians were gradually canalising their efforts on a push towards Merv and then on to Herat. Salisbury agreed and was hungry for more information from India. Yet Northbrook had little to offer. When he and his private secretary, Captain Evelyn Baring, fresh from the ID, first arrived in India, they did their best to foster military reform and save expenditure only to find little enthusiasm at home and none in India itself. They did manage, however, to propel forward the creation of the Intelligence Branch, Simla (IBS) in October 1874. The IBS consisted of two officers under the Quartermaster General, Major General Frederick (later Field Marshal Earl) Roberts. Along with his Commander-in-Chief, Lord Napier of Magdala, Roberts was a leading advocate of the 'Forward School', holding that India would only be safe if it deployed forces beyond the Indian frontier along probable invasion routes. Thus the IBS was set the task of identifying these routes leading to India from central Asia and the Bengal Presidency.

To accomplish this required exploration and mapping. 'What we want are *routes*,' Roberts told one officer keen to begin a mapping mission. 'Any number of them will be most valuable; and you will assist the Department greatly if you will send me every route you can get hold of. I have got sanction for two additional officers to be attached to our office for six months, to collate information; and I intend to set them to work at *routes beyond our border*, so as to have a Central Asia Route-book.'[56]

Mapping missions were not a new concept, but they were problematic; thrilling and dangerous, they caught the popular imagination. And once in the British press St Petersburg knew of them as well. Given the terrain, tribes and presence of Russians on the same quest, wherever the Indian missions went they threw up great dust clouds of suspicion. The antics of these missions, such as the MacGregor–Napier missions of 1874-75, convinced the Russians, the Afghans, the Persians and every tribe facing Russian encroachment that Britain was extending her formal influence westwards. And with some reason. Major (later General Sir Charles) Metcalf MacGregor and Captain (later Lieutenant Colonel) George Napier rode towards Persia as if all of India's prestige and power rode with them. As the twin son of the Commander-in-Chief and heir presumptive, Napier was more than a little conscious of his dignity. MacGregor's wish was simple. He wanted a Victoria Cross.

Soon M. deBerger, the Russian minister in Persia, was complaining that MacGregor and Napier were doing much more than determining something of the ill-defined Russo-Persian border for the Foreign Office. To judge by their actions, he concluded they were aiming to assert an Indian presence along the River Atrek. Thompson, the British envoy to Persia, was equally alarmed. He was worried that Napier's presence in the Khorassan–Atrek border region in north-east Persia would give false encouragement to the nomadic Tekke-Turcomans, the 'most Turk of the Turks', who roamed widely throughout central Asia at least as far as east as Xinjiang and whose relations with the Russians were quixotic and ambivalent to say the least.

Back in London, the ID agreed. On purely practical, physical and political grounds it could see no advantage in this method of proceeding. The locale was totally inaccessible to an Indian expedition to thwart the Russians without the active co-operation of Turkey or the friendly neutrality of Persia. But on the mission went and when details of Napier's salary leaked out in Tehran, the Persians were quite convinced that he outranked Thompson, the London-appointed envoy, and that the mission had the explicit backing of the British government. Nothing loath, Napier thought to ride to Merv. When he did not, his decision was greeted by the Foreign Office 'with something akin to relief'. MacGregor, the officer to whom Roberts had written with so much verve, was also off the lead conducting himself in a way which was just as disturbing to the Foreign Office, exercising as it did the Anglophobic Grand Duke Michael and his expansionist circle in St Petersburg to fever pitch.[57] These rides were, in the minds of the Foreign Office, the India Office and the Intelligence Department, worse than useless. Information could be collected without causing all this disquiet.

'It struck me that your Intelligence Department is inadequate,' Salisbury wrote to the Viceroy, Northbrook, in May 1874 and in July he returned to the theme: 'We ought to be thoroughly informed on all matters strategical, geographical, political.' Again in December he gave vent to his irritation at the lack of reliable information. 'You must think me very tiresome in reiterating the same observation: but all I hear of their mode of proceeding convinces me that strategic knowledge of the probable lines of march and sufficient means of obtaining intelligence from various parts of Afghanistan are necessary to your security; and that arrangements to obtain them ought to occupy your earliest attention.'[58]

Northbrook was in the middle. Here was the man who, with Cardwell, had put intelligence on a sound footing and was now receiving yet another wigging from Salisbury:

> Her Majesty's advisers cannot but be struck with the comparative scantiness of the information which it is in your Excellency's power to supply. For knowledge of what passes in Afghanistan and upon its frontiers they are compelled to rely mainly upon the indirect intelligence which reaches them through the Foreign Office.[59]

Northbrook was deeply unhappy but Salisbury kept up the pressure. He urged, and then ordered, Northbrook to appoint native agents at Herat and Kandahar and a British agent at Kabul to gather information as 'it is not to be expected that a Native Agent would be either able or willing to collect for your government...'. Northbrook baulked. He was afraid that such an agent would become a source of as much antagonism as the rides, irreparably damaging what Lord Mayo, the fourth Viceroy, had called 'that moral influence which is inseparable from the true interests of the strongest Power in Asia'.[60] He also disliked being, in effect, demoted to a mere ambassador under Salisbury's imperial thumb.

It was a tragedy as both men had India's best interest at heart, as demonstrated by their co-operation over the handling of the famine in northern Bengal and Bihar. Yet Northbrook had, according to Argyll, 'a somewhat ungenial manner, amounting almost to a dryness and hardness in the impression it conveys'[61] and whilst he made some attempts to satisfy Salisbury, not least by pressing Derby at the India Office to appoint a military attaché in Teheran, his reluctance to collect the intelligence Salisbury wanted meant that relations between the two men, hitherto always courteous, finally broke when Sir Henry Rawlinson, a member of the India Council and recent envoy to

Persia, published a Russophobic book, *England and Russia in the East.* In it were facts and figures Northbrook suspected were obtained from the home ID with Salisbury's connivance. Northbrook's resignation soon followed. Disraeli, now Lord Beaconsfield (from 1876), told the Queen that Northbrook refused to spend secret service money '*on moral grounds*'.[62] That was not the whole story; he also failed to build an intelligence system to Salisbury's liking.

Northbrook's successor, the first Earl of Lytton, was of a different stripe. A popular poet born into a family of romantics, he was the first Viceroy generally considered to be a party man. Lytton was convinced that Britain had mishandled its relations with Sher Ali and that even modest support would win him over. After all, he reckoned, Sher Ali's brothers held the principal cities of Kabul and Kandahar and were serious contenders for the Amir's weak throne. As for Sher Ali becoming 'a tool in the hands of Russia, I will never allow him to become. Such a tool, it would be my duty to break before it could be used.'

Deeply misreading Salisbury's intentions, Lytton launched a 'spirited foreign policy' in which more missions figured. There was no shortage of men to answer his call. Captain (later Lieutenant Colonel F. W.) Butler wrote to Roberts that:

> My idea of going to Central Asia and mapping out a part of the world, hitherto almost blank in our charts, was instigated by the doings of Stanley and Colonel Gordon in Central Africa. The thought was no sooner formed than the mode of fulfilling it was begun. I got the latest WO maps from Major Wilson, RE, who was head of the Topographical Department at the War Office; and on my telling him that I intended going to the Atrek and then on to Merv, he smiled, saying that it had been tried before; that without the slightest doubt if I persevered, I would have my head cut off; but that, if by any chance I came out of it with a whole skin, I deserved to be canonised.[63]

Based on Butler's reports, Lytton wanted to arm the Tekke-Turcomans to stop the Russians taking Merv. Lytton thoroughly agreed with his military advisers that 'according to modern notions of military science, India could only be safely defended against an enemy advancing from the west by the British occupation of the whole mountain mass of Afghanistan, that is, by securing the western passes leading into the valley of the Oxus, as well as those debouching on India'. Lytton demanded to know from London at what point the Russians would not be allowed to pass without a fight.

All this put Salisbury on the spot. Intelligence gathering was one thing, swaggering throughout central Asia was another. He had always believed that the central Asia question had to be settled on the spot, a resolve which was to prove prescient the more Russia prodded the Ottomans and Persians. As he had earlier remarked to Northbrook: 'All diplomatic remonstrances and threats must have a background of force. What I desire is that background must be Asiatic.'[64]

The wider effects of the missions in the politics of Europe were of little or no concern to the Indians. When General Roberts was reminded by an official that intelligence work outside India might be subject to formal permission from London, Roberts wrote that he could not 'refrain from remarking that to make an Intelligence Department really valuable, it is most desirable explorers should have access to the countries adjoining India ... in order that, on the outbreak of hostilities, the defence of our frontier, or the conduct of an offensive war, may be arranged with every possibility of success.'[65] More missions were despatched and the rumour mill ground fine.

Meanwhile, Lytton and Roberts hoped to strengthen the expertise of the fledgling IBS ('...something more is necessary...') by sending an exceptionally able officer to study the methodology of the ID. He was Captain (later Lieutenant General Sir Edwin) Collen, who authored an encyclopaedic 145-page report on the organisation and *modus operandi* of the ID. Salisbury approved this move, no doubt hoping some of the ID's calm professionalism might rub off on those responsible for Roberts's intelligence.[66]

But time was slipping by and Lytton was daily warning London that the 'rich plains of India might prove a too alluring bait to the occupiers of the barren and profitless mountains of Afghanistan'. Unfortunately for London, the Russians kept stirring the fire, threatening to march on other expeditions. More reconnaissances, more feints. The Great Game was being played on a grand scale. The Foreign Office and the ID could see nothing but trouble ahead.

All this bellicosity was being stoked with a great stick in the British press as well and from every quarter the government was besieged with opinion and advice, most of which was costly and thoroughly impractical. What was needed was a fresh, dispassionate perspective on the overall situation, an assessment which would carry weight. This task fell on Captain Evelyn Baring, who it will be remembered was one of the first officers to strengthen the weakened T&S and Northbrook's private secretary in India. Returning to the Department after Northbrook's fall he composed a 72-page *Memorandum on the Central Asia Question*. Using factual analysis and war game modelling, he concluded that the proponents of the Forward School were guilty of seeing a danger where none existed.[67]

Baring tested the issues dispassionately and came to support the ID's long-held view that a Russian attack on India would be so difficult as to be unlikely. He called into question the strategic value of Merv, considering it 'enormously exaggerated', and reasoned that as Russia was then overstretched by her involvement in Turkey, her remaining army, 'however colossal it may appear on paper, is in reality less formidable than is generally supposed'. In fact, he went on, an invasion of India was well-nigh impossible. 'I am, however, well aware that it is not so much invasion that is feared as that the near approach of the Russians would be damaging to our prestige...' Like Salisbury, Baring was loath to exacerbate Afghanistan's instability by planting consuls or agents. He knew that the best news regarding these regions would reach London through Russia.

Nevertheless matters on the ground were moving ever faster. On 13 June 1878, the day the Congress of Berlin opened to confront Russian pressure on Turkey, the Russians sent a mission to Afghanistan which soon succeeded in establishing paramount influence over its ruler,

Sher Ali. Reports of this soon reached London, but so used were they to constant rumours of this kind, both the ID and the India Office were caught out when it proved to be true. Lytton proposed counter-missions under Sir Neville Chamberlain and Major Louis Cavagnari with plans to place British residents at Kabul and Herat.

News of this new Indian mission was greeted by Sher Ali and his Russian advisers with a refusal to entertain it. Lytton was unable to accept the loss of prestige and unleashed the Indian Army in a large punitive expedition led by Roberts in November 1878. As the Indian battalions moved westward in three columns, Afghanistan's independence and stability, ostensibly what the Raj had wanted to preserve in the face of Russian aggrandisement, was trampled underfoot.

Now placed in the position of supporting the expedition, the ID placed all its information on routes at Roberts's disposal and recommended that he should head for Kabul, as it was, in their opinion, the key to India and 'without its possession, invasion of our territory cannot be undertaken'.

Throughout the winter and spring the Indian Army headed for Kabul and Kandahar, and shook the Afghans in a series of short, sharp engagements whilst the London ID prepared arguments in favour of an advance of India's scientific frontier to include the command of the Pishin Valley. The ID settled on Pishin because it did not share the common opinion about the importance of Merv. Of more immediate importance, however, was their reasoning that if the Russians successfully invested Herat they would not be easy to dislodge, so India should keep outposts at Kushi in the Pishin Valley and at Quetta in order to keep an eye on routes from Kabul and Kandahar. Quetta was not in Afghanistan and if Roberts took Kushi 'and the point beyond the Khyber with the command of the valleys leading to these two places we would not be under the necessity of claiming any other portions of the Ameer's territory. Without these, however, our military frontier could never be considered secure.' This proposal, moderate by comparison with what the Indian military wanted, became the basis of the post-campaign strategy of 1880–81.[68]

Obliged to support the campaigns with maps and proposed plans, the Intelligence Department's Russian watchers also kept a close eye on its reverberations. Concern focused not so much on a counter-vailing Russian advance into Afghanistan, which the ID knew was unlikely, but they were mindful that rather more energy was being expended on further advances into Persia and the possible final subjugation of the Tekke-Turcomans. This concern was matched by those ID officers assigned to monitor Russia's progress in Turkey. Their joint conclusion was that Russia was definitely on the move south and that the only weapon Britain could bring into play, as it did not have the power to counteract a Russian advance on one let alone two fronts, was more accurate intelligence to support its diplomacy.

As usual, the ID found that information from India was ill digested and flavoured with opinion. The officers of the IBS had all deserted their offices for the field and material was reaching London which did nothing to alleviate anxiety. Looking at the latest reports from the Napier expedition, the ID found huge discrepancies in his maps and reports. His memorandum of May 1879, *Report on the Late Movement of the Russian Force in the Trans-Caspian District, etc.*, was so alarmist that Salisbury refused to distribute it, telling his officials that it was 'so partisan as to be of little value'.[69]

In monitoring and analysing Russian moves, the ID moved centre stage. Yet, as so often happened before, the bureaucracy of Horse Guards stifled the speedy collection of information. As a very minor office, the ID had to request information from the Foreign Office through the War Office and this resulted in delay and a much higher profile with the wrong people than the officers at Spring Gardens would have wished. When the new director of the ID between 1878 and 1882, Major General Sir Archibald Alison, who had just relin-quished his post as commandant of the Staff College, realised this was the case, he appealed directly to Salisbury for immediate and regular access to all the FO's eastern sources, not least the valued reports from the consul in Tiflis. Salisbury responded affirmatively and from the spring of 1879 the Foreign Office sent confidential prints and despatches directly to the ID, noting that 'the current despatches can in future be sent to the War Office [i.e. the ID] in regular course'.[70]

With more sources at its disposal, the ID now began regularly contributing reports to the Foreign Office detailing its close and careful monitoring of Russia's activities. The Foreign Office welcomed these reports, printed many of them for use internally and for embassies abroad and asked for more.

As always, the ID's increasingly profitable relationship with the Foreign Office depended on its analytical skill based on the accuracy of the information from which it created its intelligence assessments. With peripheral sources, i.e. reports from embassies etc., now reaching Spring Gardens regularly, the next step was to increase the quality and quantity of information gathered locally. This led to the proposal to the Foreign Office to increase its flow of reliable information from the field by the establishment of a number of 'listening stations' thrown out like a piquet fence in front of India. Promoting this scheme, Alison, the ID's new head, reminded the Foreign Office that 'the situation in Asia at the present time is obscure and involved. Early and reliable information with regard to Russian or other military movements near the Northern Border of Persia therefore appears to be most important, and this information can only be satisfactorily obtained on the spot.'

The ID had been working this project up since at least July 1878 and advanced it during and after the Congress of Berlin. It was designed to be a logical extension of the ID's sister scheme of listening posts manned by British officers in eastern Turkey which was then being set up. The Department's proposal was to link Britain-in-Turkey with Britain-in-Central Asia by the establishment of outposts at Girishk and Bamian, the outposts before Kandahar and Kabul respectively, with possibly a cantonment at Washir, upon which to hang the whole intelligence screen 'strong in her security from surprise, and with the means at her disposal to take the initiative in two directions when necessary. England might then afford for the present to look on calmly awaiting the further development of events affecting the safety of her Asiatic possessions.'

With so much else on their plate, the government did little to advance the ID's plan and in March 1880, Alison suggested that as a stop-gap, an officer be accredited to the Persian court with authority to travel. Lord Tenterden, the Permanent Head of the Foreign Office, minuted: 'If anyone is to be appointed for this … he ought to be a very judicious person and carefully selected.' But the Conservative government soon fell and when Thompson in Tehran answered that anyone like Napier prancing around northern Persia would only excite the Russians and do the British no good, Lord Granville, the new Liberal Foreign Secretary, let the matter drop.[71]

‡

In the field, January and February 1879 saw the Indian field force supreme. Sher Ali fled into Turkestan hoping to go to St Petersburg to plead his cause, but he was dissuaded in doing so and died at Mazar-i-Sharif in late February. His son, Yakub Khan, became the Amir and the British forced him to sign the Treaty of Gandamak, which ceded the areas of Kurram, the Khyber, Sibi, Chaman near Kandahar and Pishin to India. It also hoped to put the direction of Afghanistan's foreign policy in Indian hands by the stationing of a British resident at Kabul. This treaty had been largely engineered by Major Pierre Louis Napoleon Cavagnari, Deputy Commissioner at Peshawar, who was rewarded by Lytton with the appointment as Resident. The appointment of Cavagnari, now Sir Louis, was even more disturbing to the Afghans than the missions. Yakub Khan was looked upon as a tool of the British and many of his followers were ready to turn against him.

On 3 September 1879, some of Yakub Khan's regiments mutinied over pay and in the uproar Cavagnari and his mission were murdered. The Indian armies took to the field again. Yakub Khan swore he was not involved and not surprisingly fled into exile in India as Roberts,

'Bahadur Bobs', led his troops the other way. For its part, the ID spent the campaign concentrating on terrain and route analyses as before.

And again, the Afghan chieftains mounted an exacting campaign but the Indian Army pushed onto Kandahar and took Kabul in October. Yakub Khan abdicated. Sporadic fighting lasted for another month ending with Roberts's victory over Yakub Khan's rival Ayub Khan. Hopes were placed on Sher Ali's nephew, Abdur Rahman, taking the throne and Lytton, having learned his lesson, no longer insisted on a British mission.

India was now responsible for a weak vassal state. Roberts despaired at finding a reliable ruler and along with many Conservatives back home pressed for the 'disintegration' of Afghanistan, dealing instead with powerful warlords. If Abdur Rahman were to take over, perhaps he could meld his country-in-name-only into a viable security buffer? Yet as with others in his position before and since, Abdur Rahman was an enigma. Having spent some years in Russia when Sher Ali was Amir, he was nevertheless encouraged by the British to take over Kabul and consider himself Amir. In exchange, he would be able to rely on the Indian Army if needed to put down 'foreign aggression'. He agreed.

It was important to get the situation resolved rapidly. Beaconsfield's government was being severely criticised in the press over its policy towards Afghanistan. However, before a conclusion, satisfactory or otherwise, manifested itself, the general election of May 1880 put Mr Gladstone into power. Lord Lytton resigned to be succeeded by the Marquess of Ripon. The new Secretary of State for India was the Marquess of Hartington, later Duke of Devonshire. Standing over six foot four, monosyllabic and almost a caricature of the aristocratic politician, Hartington knew quite a lot about modern soldiering. He had been a militia officer in the 1850s and in 1863–66 he was Under-Secretary for War, succeeding to the secretaryship in 1866, during the closing months of the Russell administration. He visited the American Civil War and watched the Prussians return triumphant to Berlin after successfully defeating the Austrians in seven weeks. The effect of both experiences was not lost on him. Although Postmaster General in Gladstone's first administration, he fervently supported his Cabinet colleague, Cardwell. As will be shown, it is not difficult to see Hartington as Salisbury's alter ego in his use of intelligence and appreciation of the work of the ID.

When it came to matters *Indiana*, Hartington was alarmed at Lytton's bellicosity and had long wanted him recalled. There was continued confusion over the degree to which Rahman should be 'brought on' and Hartington disapproved completely of dividing up Afghanistan into a series of separate provinces. He doubted if Kandahar, nearest to the Russians, could remain an independent province without British assistance and, unlike Lytton, favoured the inclusion of Herat in the Amir's dominions. [72]

It was a discussion held in public as well. By the spring of 1880, retired generals, old Indian hands and serving soldiers all sent their ideas in to the new government or the newspapers. Senior Liberals seemed to encourage this whilst despising the authors. Gladstone told the Queen: 'Military men charge their so-called professional opinions with political element, and thus give authority to very worthless doctrine.' Hartington told Sir Henry Ponsonby, Queen Victoria's private secretary and former soldier, that:

> I am sure that Ripon will give all due consideration to military opinions as such, but before we can judge how much weigh shd. be attached to them, we must know on what reasons they are formed, & whether they are not really as much political as military opinions, wh. soldiers are as apt to form as other people, with no better materials for coming to a right conclusion.[73]

In this debate, the ID maintained its consistent stand for the establishment of the listening posts and for eventual withdrawal. The Intelligence Department's Executive Officer, Major C. J. (later General Sir Cecil) East, wrote a paper in August 1880 which made the same point as all its predecessors during the previous four years.

In his *Memorandum on our Future Policy in Afghanistan* he pointed out that Russia was too weak and committed elsewhere to undertake any operations against Afghanistan 'at present'. Russia had her hands full with the Tekke-Turcomans and in undertaking various plots against the Ottoman Empire and Persia. East reiterated the Department's long-held belief that India's real (and cost-efficient) security lay in the close monitoring of Russian troop movements. It was critical, therefore, to build and maintain an intelligence screen through the posting of good consuls at Asterabad and Meshed, who could watch over Herat, north-west Afghanistan and the southern trans-Caspia. He added:

> If we were kept accurately informed of the state of affairs in those regions the Government would be at once able to dispel the discreditable state of alarm into which this country is periodically thrown by rumours of Russian expeditions against Herat or Northern Afghanistan. If knowledge is power, ignorance is weakness, and this weakness we constantly show by the undignified fear displayed at every report of the threat of Russian movements. It is frequently said, and occasionally truly so, that our military disasters are attributable to the defective information obtained by our Generals. It is probably safe to say that in the conduct of foreign affairs the same cause is at work, and that when we are outwitted by foreign powers, it is owing to our being deficient in the necessary information.[74]

East could not understand the Forward School's *idée fixe* on holding Kandahar and tying down troops needlessly.[75] It would be much better, he argued, to create a fortified cantonment at Kushi in the Pishin Valley, an idea the ID had mooted before. This would not violate the new Anglo-Afghani Treaty of Gandamak and 'by occupying Kushi, or the upper Kurram Valley, we are in a position to enter Kabul, either as a friend or enemy, whenever we may wish to do so, and from Pishin we can advance in a few days on Kandahar whenever the necessity arises'.[76]

Soon after East's memorandum was written, Northbrook, then First Lord of the Admiralty, urged Hartington to recommend a slow retirement. Hartington knew the new Viceroy, Ripon, would have his whole council against him if he suggested an unconditional withdrawal and told Gladstone that the retention of Pishin, as suggested by East, might be a good middle ground. Withdraw from Kandahar, perhaps withdraw from Quetta or even Pishin. But with Pishin the Indians would retain control of Kurram and the Khyber without the disadvantages of occupying Kandahar. Hartington asked Gladstone for a decision as soon as possible. He feared the increasing influence of the Indian military authorities upon Ripon, who would 'not understand my anxiety about the military opinions'. To give him his due, Ripon agreed with Hartington that it might allay some of the criticism of the government if Pishin were held, but Northbrook argued that it had the same drawbacks as the retention of Kandahar.

All this talk of withdrawal angered the Queen, who believed that the retention of Kandahar and the delimitation of the border would go no little way in preventing 'a repetition of those murderous and expensive wars'. Yet the argument was over. Slowly and clumsily, the government's mind was being made up and withdrawal became policy in early November 1880. Communicating the decision to Calcutta, Hartington stressed the point that had been made over and over again by the ID that the Russians were not going to invade:

> Her Majesty's Government are unable to admit that the mere fact of the existence of Russian military positions some one hundred miles nearer the North West Frontier of India constitutes in itself any cause for anxiety, or for apprehending the possibility of an invasion of India from that quarter.[77]

London at last found her voice and from that moment on, India was no longer able to go it alone. Its affairs were now being regarded, in the metropolis at least, as only one part of an increasingly confident Empire where, as will be seen, all was interrelated. So, whilst Pishin was retained until late spring 1881 as a warning and an insurance policy, withdrawal was the order of the day, a result insisted upon by London and in which the Intelligence Department had played a large part.

CHAPTER THREE

WE MUST SEE THESE ISLANDS

Russia's dance with the Afghans and the Tekke-Turcomans was just one part of a concerted push all along her southern borders which had been going on for decades. Despite protestations to the contrary from the Czar and his ministers, Russia's soldiers felt the humiliation of the Crimean War keenly. If there were weak rulers in the east who could be suborned or subjugated, so be it. If pan-Slavism in the west was a potential instrument by which Russia could reach the Mediterranean, that, too, was to be desired. In response, all the west had at its disposal to bottle up this expansion was the Ottoman Empire and its ill-governed provinces. It being their desire to weaken the Ottomans at every turn, the Russians found Constantinople their greatest ally.

The major western powers were vocal in their support for the Ottomans, but in reality it was only Great Britain which was, at that stage, prepared to bolster the Sublime Porte against the Czar. Ever since Palmerston's day, Britain had been the Porte's primary champion. Now that the pressure was on in Asia and the Caucasus as well, Britain slowly realised that the link between Britain-in-the-East and Britain-in-the-West had to be forged and once in place could not be broken.

As the 'Eastern Question' in all its bewildering complexity oozed to the forefront of world politics, Britain found herself drawn into that dance she had hoped to sit out. Not yet seeing the need to bolster the Turk, the British public held the Turkish administration in low esteem. The first nationalistic rumblings of the Balkan provinces caught the imagination of Victorian liberals who railed at what was widely perceived as Turkish cruelty to subject peoples, especially

Christians. Beaconsfield's government came under fierce pressure to 'do something'.

The problem, as ever, was lack of reliable intelligence as to what was really going on. As in Asia, there was a dearth of reliable information from which to make intelligence. Although there were British consuls in some major cities, e.g. Cairo, their responsibilities as to the collection of information was ill defined and received little emphasis.

Even in Constantinople, the mechanics of collection were virtually non-existent. As M. E.(later Sir Mountstuart) Grant Duff, then Under-Secretary for India, wrote about the Turkophile Ambassador to the Porte, Sir Henry Elliot: he 'remained without anything like adequate means of information, there was no one in the Foreign Office to collate that information and to put it in such form that when need arose it could be used by the Secretary of State.'[78]

For his part, Elliot was ill, did not have a military attaché and dismissed or held back the increasing flow of alarming reports from his consuls and other sources. It was all too difficult. Then in June 1876 the Turks viciously suppressed the Bulgarian insurrection. Beaconsfield, without accurate information, misled the House as to the situation on the ground. He vowed it would not happen again. Angrily, he wrote to the Foreign Secretary, Lord Derby: 'I must again complain of the management of your office. It is impossible to represent the FO in the House of Commons in these critical times without sufficient information.'

Elliot, faced with his Prime Minister's intense irritation and a rapidly deteriorating political and military environment, finally asked for an attaché. The War Office agreed, but W. H. Smith at the Treasury thought, as one of his officials put it, that attachés were usually more 'ornamental rather than useful'. Finally a Horse Guards appointee was posted to the Embassy only to arrive on Christmas Eve 1876, a month before the outbreak of the Russo-Turkish War. Whatever expectations there were of him, his appointment was not a success.[79]

Throughout 1876 the FO and the Embassy were almost daily shown up as being unable to meet the collection task. Information sent in to the Indian Office was not always shared with the Foreign Office and vice versa. It was in this befuddled state that the Intelligence Department found its niche.

The gap the ID increasingly filled was as simple as it was sophisticated. By the mid-1870s, it was possible to see a *modus operandi* evolving at Spring Gardens, a real advance in the processes of collection, analysis and dissemination of intelligence which was, for Britain, unique. And it was the constant drive to improve which was the predominant theme of the next thirty years. First of course was the Department's insistence upon the consistent collection of 'news', which is to say information, up-to-date reliable information, not just from pinch points, but from all around the world, hence the constant press for knowledgeable consuls. The Department could never understand why politicians did not grasp this point and it is why the ID kept on hammering away at it. Until the Intelligence Department existed it was news of varying veracity and immediacy (the 'facts' cited by the Earl of Clarendon in Chapter One) from and upon which ministers made or delayed their decisions. This may have been tolerated in a slower past, but it was intolerable in an age of more rapid communications.

Secondly, what was missing was a careful analysis of these facts to turn them into full-blown intelligence. This is the second gap the Intelligence Department filled. From the mid-1870s, therefore, the ID's reputation within the highest level of government grew because the analysis and comment on the presenting issues was undertaken by some of the most intelligent, selfless men of the age.

The third missing was dissemination of their product. And that, as the officers of the Department often noted, was the most problematic. As it had its own press, it could rapidly generate the reports and comments which could be easily read and circulated as appropriate. This was, however, not without some internal cost and apprehension as all too often material emanating from the ID led to opprobrium and personal reputational risk of a high order from Horse Guards.

By late 1876, the Department was not only providing the government with enough accurate intelligence to allow Beaconsfield and Salisbury (his Foreign Secretary after the resignation of Derby and the Colonial Secretary, Lord Carnarvon) to manage the Eastern Question, it was preparing Britain for a much greater imperial role.

‡

The Intelligence Department had paid some attention to Turkish affairs from its inception, but only because it was there. Turkey had not won a single war in the past century, yet its real and notional suzerainty was vast. In November 1870, when Wilson, Baring, Hozier, Brackenbury and Home eagerly sought to prove the worth of the T&S, one of the first intelligence summaries Baring produced was on Turkey. Yet by 1875 the Ottoman Section (E) ran far behind the Russian Section (D) in number and accuracy of sources. Wilson lamented that the most recent holding in the Department's library he found on his arrival was an 1856 *Sketch of a March in Asia Minor and Syria*.

As the Russians stoked the first flames of nationalist struggles in Bosnia and Herzegovina, Wilson transferred more of his scant resources into the Ottoman Section (E) and by October 1875 had enough information to produce three papers which left the government in no doubt that the Ottoman forces were in a lamentable state and that Russian advances in the Balkans were gathering pace. The Foreign Office was at first somewhat exercised at receiving these unexpected contributions but, as the situation grew worse, admitted their usefulness and had them printed, albeit almost a full year after receiving them.[80]

Meanwhile Section (E) received a new head. He was Captain (later Major General Sir John) Ardagh. A 36-year-old sapper, a graduate of Trinity, Dublin with honours in mathematics and a prize in Hebrew, Ardagh was destined for Holy Orders, but against his family's wishes he opted for a career as a military engineer. His reserved persona and delicate build hid a remarkable capacity for work and a photographic memory and he passed in first into and first out of the Royal Military

Academy, Woolwich. After an eventful early career, which included saving his Canada-bound vessel and holding the important position of secretary to Admiral Sir Frederick Grey's 1868 Fortification Committee, Ardagh astounded his seniors by applying for Staff College in 1870. The Deputy Adjutant General, Royal Engineers wrote: 'I am rather surprised at his application. It is in his power to compete in the *final* examination of a class so as to obtain his certificate without wasting two years.' Be that as it may, Ardagh passed in second and setting his cap for the Intelligence Department, joined on 1 April 1875.[81]

Ardagh was immediately stimulated by the tasks at hand and took over in July 1876 when the Section's three papers were before the government. The Foreign Office, now desperate for news, with the added delay of appointing an attaché to Elliot in Constantinople, immediately sent Ardagh to the Turco-Serbian frontier where he joined the Turkish forces at Nisch. Ardagh arrived in Turkey after a summer of escalating violence, the death of the Porte and the murder of his ministers of war and foreign affairs. The new Porte or Sultan, Abdul Hamid, was 'reckoned to be one of the worst tyrants in Turkish history'.

With Russia as its patron, Serbia declared war on Turkey and all the apples began to spill out of the cart. Russia made further moves on Bulgaria and Beaconsfield was certain that Austria would move to overshadow Bosnia with considerable force.

By September the major powers proposed a conference, but as ever, it was the Turks themselves who posed the biggest problem as they had made it clear that they were the aggrieved party and would not countenance any form of mediation. Faced with this blancmange, Beaconsfield considered playing another card to find a solution, viz Britain's armed might. This led him to rely less and less on the Russophile Lord Derby at the Foreign Office and more and more on Gathorne Gathorne-Hardy (later the first Earl Cranbrook), his Secretary of State for War from 1874 to 1878 and Secretary of State for India between 1878 and 1880. On 30 September Beaconsfield told Gathorne-Hardy that it was time for Britain to take a stand. He thought that this active intervention might take the form of the occupation of Constantinople as 'a material guarantee'. He wrote to Gathorne-Hardy: 'On the water side all is easy, but how about the land side? You must have in your archives at the War Office large materials on this matter, probably all sufficient. What are the fortifications there? What force required to hold them and others might be erected?'[82]

As the answers existed only in part in the ID, the Foreign Office sent a message to Elliot in late September ordering Ardagh to report on Constantinople's defences. This he did with astounding efficiency, providing sketch surveys of almost 150 square miles in fifteen days.

Whilst Ardagh was at work in the field, the Department made a new contribution in the form of a twenty-page *Memorandum on the Probable Course of Action which would be adopted by the Russians in the Event of their attempting to occupy Bulgaria and march on Constantinople.* Authored by Baring, it complemented his paper on India, which argued that a Russian assault on India was, at present, out of the question.

In *Probable Course,* Baring contended that England could support Turkey without the inconvenience of landing troops if the Royal Navy controlled the Black Sea and defended the Bosphorus and Dardanelles. These strokes alone would complicate a Russian advance, giving the weak Turkish Army just enough time to organise defences at just the right locations – the last line of which Ardagh was already sketching. It was vital, he argued, for the Intelligence Department to have more information about the possible area of operation: 'Timely forethought in this respect may be the means of averting defeat, or of paving the way to victory.' He added:

It would perhaps be sufficient to send out Engineer officers to lay out and prepare lines for defence of the Bosphorous and Dardanelles, and to obtain information as to the roads, transport, supplies, &c., in the immediate neighbourhood of Constantinople.[83]

Baring's report was well received. The FO sent it to the embassies in St Petersburg and Constantinople and continued to ask for extra copies in the months ahead. But action was needed and so after meeting with officers from the ID, Gathorne-Hardy went to Beaconsfield on 24 October 1876 urging the continuation of the defensive survey and to 'look forward to guarding it in case of need'.[84]

Thus the Foreign Office's minute on Baring's memorandum 'Further information required' was answered with 'Done. 25 October.' The Intelligence Department had entered the machinery of decision making. The ID's *entrée* was based solely upon its ability to supply 'significant information' and interpret it in ways which made sense. Gathorne-Hardy and Beaconsfield welcomed Baring's report. It brought all the known 'facts' together, analysed them and produced intelligence. No one else was doing it.

Whether ministers were alive to the evolving process of producing creditable intelligence or simply found the result valuable, they still hankered after the latest unprocessed information. 'News, want of "news"', was felt most keenly. In November 1876, Gathorne-Hardy confided in his diary his distress at the lack of current news from Turkey. He wrote to Salisbury, still at the India Office, that he feared Derby was not telling his colleagues everything he had heard. 'I hope Derby will not "let us burst in ignorance", but at least furnish us with knowledge enough to enable us to form and justify opinions.' Salisbury was well aware of the problem as his contretemps with Northbrook showed and it is highly probable that Gathorne-Hardy and he resolved to keep each other up to the mark. It certainly embarrassed Gathorne-Hardy to appear before Beaconsfield without being at least as well informed as the Prime Minister. 'No news yet from Salisbury', he wrote in his diary, 'so that I am not behind...' Beaconsfield, of course, pressed for more news and all too often for his own comfort Gathorne-Hardy would have to reply: 'I go on obtaining what I can of interest from different sources, and intend to lay what I collect before you when ready.'[85]

Baring had called for Engineer officers to gather more information on the spot in the event of any exigency and on 27 October 1876, two days after Gathorne-Hardy had approached Beaconsfield with the request, Lieutenant Colonel Robert Home, RE of the Department boarded a train for Marseilles with a captain and two lieutenants of Engineers. The captain, (later Major General Sir) Thomas Fraser, later wrote: 'We were all in the state of mind that men are in, when at last it seems their chance had come.'[86]

Set against the backdrop of an administration dividing against itself over the handling of the Eastern Question, the despatch of this secret party was undoubtedly the only non-diplomatic choice open to the government. The FO gave Home every facility, HM Treasury wrote him a financial *carte blanche* and Gathorne-Hardy waited anxiously for their reports.

But the Army was the Army. As soon as Horse Guards learned of the mission it rushed to assert its control over it. Home was ordered to report through the Duke to Gathorne-Hardy, yet would be under the local command of Elliot at the Embassy. As he was ostensibly concerned with fortifications, his line of command was not to the head of the Intelligence Department, the reforming Major General Sir Patrick MacDougall, who had been closely involved in liaising with the Foreign and War offices, but to the Duke's safest pair of hands, the aged Inspector General of Fortifications, General Sir John Lintorn Simmons. Fraser was the IGF's man on the mission.

Simmons's orders to Home, which Gathorne-Hardy approved on the date of his departure, were not drafted at Horse Guards but at the FO with information supplied by the ID. Home was to prepare plans for the defence of Constantinople, the peninsula between the Black and Marmora seas (the Buyuk-Tchekmedje-Derkos line), the Gallipoli peninsula, controlling the sea defence of the Dardanelles, and, of course, the Bosphorus. He was also to report upon the force necessary for occupation of both sides, the best landing places, availability of water, hutting, 'in fact on all matters required to be known by the authorities in England in the event of a British force being sent to hold that position'.[87]

This was a mammoth task, but the party consisted of men who were its equal. There was Fraser and Lieutenant (later Lieutenant General Sir Herbert) Chermside, who had, like Ardagh, witnessed the latest sophisticated civil defences used in the Franco-Prussian War. The leader of the party, Home, was the author of the 1865–66 Canadian Defence Plan against a possible Fenian incursion from the USA. All trained under a Staff College curriculum which placed a premium on doing just what they were setting out to do.

Compared with the absence of planning before the Crimean War, this was a major leap forward in preparation. Inevitably word of Home's mission leaked out and he arrived in Constantinople on 11 November preceded by wild rumours. Ardagh rode down to meet them and presented his surveys. Home told Simmons: 'I am amazed at what he has done.'

Back in London, the War Office refused to tell the Admiralty where Home's party was or what they were doing. On the spot, Home ignored these bureaucratic niceties and immediately involved the stationnaire's commander, Captain E. C. Anstruther, who provided every assistance he could. Time was against them. There was no let-up in violence in the east and winter was settling in. In steadily deteriorating weather, the intelligencers each set out to do as much as they could as rapidly as possible within a month. Fraser rode or walked over 500 miles in twenty-three days and the others almost equalled him. Cold and rain came unrelentingly. Home's waterproof froze and as it cracked whipped around in the wind and cut him deeply across his face. He and Ardagh both caught fever. Home especially felt it and his 'sensitive and overworked' brain denied him sleep in whatever barn he was occupying for the night.[88]

At the end of the month, they rendezvoused in Constantinople to compare and compile. Thanks to Anstruther's help in getting the results back to London, the Department's presses were soon turning out the first sketches and maps for incorporation in the 300-page intelligence estimate *Reports and Memoranda relative to the Defence of*

Constantinople and other Positions in Turkey, and also routes in Romelia.
This was intelligence worthy of the name.

A commentary survives from those frantic days. It was penned by Captain Edwin Collen, the Indian Intelligence Branch observer sent to study the ID's methodology. He watched *The Defence of Constantinople* come together. Citing it in his own report on the workings of the Department, he said that Home's report was done 'under circumstances of the greatest physical difficulty, under great pressure, and involving the deepest responsibility. The reports and reconnaissance are examples of the application of trained military knowledge and power of observation. These labours received the strongest recognition from the highest authorities.' Speed, too, was paramount. Printed and bound, *Defence* was on the desk of the Foreign and War offices forty-five days from inception.[89]

It was not before time. Events were moving rapidly in Constantinople. Salisbury arrived in Constantinople as Beaconsfield's representative and frequently Home was called to ride in and consult with him and Elliot. In such heady company, Home was determined not to fall into the trap of having his opinions dismissed. He wrote to Simmons: 'The peculiar position in which I am placed, and the very peculiar people with whom I am in contact, render me rather chary of committing myself to strong opinion of any kind.'[90]

Whilst his colleagues were still in the field, Home made his initial report on 15 November, just six days after Beaconsfield had assured the world that Britain's military resources were 'inexhaustible'. Be that as it may, Home prepared for war. He estimated that it would take at least 65,000 British and Indian troops to hold the straits. This force would have to be backed by 120 defensive guns of various calibre and a secure telegraph line through Malta and Crete. Three days later he provided a second chapter which included building a railway from Hadem Keue to Baghchetsh as a primary logistics route. He estimated it would take six weeks for the construction of fortifications east of the city.

As the team sketched and planned, Home prepared contracts,

located observation posts, plotted the course of redoubts, and positioned hutting and steam pumps for water supply. He sent Ardagh and Anstruther to select landing places. When Admiral Sir James Drummond, Commander-in-Chief, Mediterranean, arrived in Constantinople, he and Home rode over the ground and confirmed each site. As for ship-to-shore supply, Home told Simmons that he would adopt local customs and enlist local supply, using lighters to construct wharfs, doing everything in 'the true spirit of military engineering'. By 25 November, Home was able to signal that he had plans in place to support 35,000 troops.

Home successfully pressed for more help to do the detailed staff work. Five officers came out, as distinguished a batch as their freezing predecessors: the Department's authority on mining galleries, Lieutenant W. H. Anstey; Lieutenant (later Major Leonard) Darwin, son of the great naturalist and later Member of Parliament; Captain (later Lieutenant General Sir Henry) Trotter; Lieutenant W. A. H. Hare, (who passed in first just ahead of Ardagh at Staff College); and Captain (later Major General Sir Hugh) McCalmont.

Not included in this list of the capable was the Duke's son, Captain G. W. A. Fitz-George, who was sent travelling through Turkey and the Balkans at this time. Wolseley wrote in disgust: 'That most useless of fellows Fitz-George has been shoved by his father into the Intelligence Department although he has not been through Staff College or shown himself in any way fitted for staff work...'[91]

Now with more Royal Engineers on the ground, Elliot authorised the railway survey between Hadem Keue station on the Adrianopolis line to Jaserin. Home planned to build five to six miles of railway that winter as soon as he could get the materials to the site. Home told Simmons: 'The advantage of having the rails and sleepers on the spot is very great, especially at a moment when a very large amount of vessels must be taken up for the transport of stores, horses and men.'

Home's energetic activities in preparing for a British expeditionary force outpaced diplomatic efforts to get Russia and Turkey to the conference table. Unlike *Defence*, the Foreign Office realised it was only getting Home's reports from the War Office as a courtesy. Perhaps it was just as well. The cautious permanent secretary at the Foreign Office, Lord Tenterden, suggested to his chief, Lord Derby, that the officers should be brought away before questions were raised in Parliament. Derby agreed but he reckoned without the Prime Minister. Beaconsfield was fully ready to consider sending a force to make and man Home's defences. He told Salisbury as much on 27 November.

It had the potential for becoming a very big enterprise indeed. On 6 December, even Gathorne-Hardy was becoming nervous and wrote to Beaconsfield:

The engineers in Turkey want more help... The demands for men and material for the suggested works to defend Constantinople grow. More guns of heavier calibre – 50 per cent more men – a railway for stores – telegraph lines and telegraph wires to make 'entanglements' in front of the forts. It is rather embarrassing for me, as I can only defer considera-tion, not having it in my power to decide such questions now.[92]

'The "Intelligence Department" must change its name,' Beaconsfield wrote crossly to his secretary. 'It is the department of Ignorance.'[93] The proposals would embroil the British into 'a very big business in which the present state of affairs hardly justifies us in embarking'. Now that he knew the real cost of an armed intervention, that is to say the reality of the undertaking as opposed to the wish for it, he wired Salisbury that an armed intervention by Britain was no longer a viable option.

Thus another tack would be necessary and Derby and Salisbury again pushed forward their plan of 4 November for an all-power conference designed to force the Sublime Porte into accepting reforms. The thinking was that if this were set in train, Russia would be robbed of her *casus belli*.

What then exercised Salisbury was the extent to which any reforms could be enforced unsupported by military force. How could he convince the Porte that Britain would abandon Turkey unless he began instituting reforms, when everyone knew Home, Ardagh and colleagues had been actively looking for places where British troops could land in large numbers?

One answer Ardagh came up with was the 'appointment of foreign commissioners, Judges, or officials [who] would I apprehend excite no opposition among the people, but rather the reverse for the Turk often suffers just as much as the Christian from maladministration of justice, and official corruption'. Thus it was that the idea of commissioners was at the core of Britain's proposals. This carried weight with the powers but not, hardly surprisingly, with Turkey. The conference broke up without resolve on 20 January 1877.

Home was not surprised. He had never been confident of the conference's success and on the day the conference opened suggested that if it did not go well, Britain would need strategical compensation to balance the continual Russian gains. As he told Simmons on 16 January: 'It is possible that war may be staved off for a little time, but come it must. Let us be ready to collar our share and hold it.' And Home knew exactly what compensation looked like. The month before he had suggested to Gathorne-Hardy and Beaconsfield that what Britain needed was 'a *pied à terre* to cover the Northern End of the Suez Canal, a naval station for men of war, a coaling station for vessels en route to India, a halfway house and *point d'appui* between Malta and Aden.'[94]

As the conference plodded its way into the sand, Home continued in his role as one of Salisbury's most trusted advisers, being 'much consulted' and 'occupied in giving his lordship information on military matters well within his cognisance'. Presuming the conference would fold, Home weighed up the options. If it collapsed and war against the Turk came, then Britain would have to hold Gallipoli. Yet no one knew better than he that nothing on the mainland could be held without enormous risk. He thereupon told Simmons: 'I want to get charts of Rhodes and Cyprus sent out as we must see these islands.'[95]

As soon as the conference petered out, Salisbury ordered Home and his officers to comb the Levant for the right *pied à terre*. He told Home to deploy his intelligencers, telling London that 'Colonel Home will furnish reports on these Islands – he will also visit Egypt if he considers it requisite.' Home sent Ardagh to Egypt and he and Lieutenants Chermside and Cockburn headed for the islands.

Then, as had happened so often, the bureaucracy of Horse Guards crashed the party. Logically, the government was waiting for Salisbury to return to London before deciding what to do with the intelligence officers, but they reckoned without the irascible Inspector General of Fortifications. When Simmons heard of these reconnaissances, he exploded and ordered all the officers home immediately. Being directly under Simmons, out of touch with Salisbury and not yet enjoying the extended protection of the Foreign Office, the travellers had to comply. A detailed examination of Cyprus was not made until later.

It is highly likely that as Inspector General of Fortifications, Simmons felt increasingly eclipsed by the Intelligence Department's attention to defence of the United Kingdom and abroad, issues for which he believed himself responsible, and issued the recall. Indeed as far as Simmons himself was concerned his outburst was not some sudden tempest. Simmons's irritation with the ID had been building for years. In 1870, he was the only senior officer to criticise Baring's seminal report on Turkey and he did the same with its successor. He poured ink over Home's reports from Constantinople littering them with petty criticisms. And he sought to rein in the intelligencers by appointing, at long last, a military attaché who would ostensibly co-ordinate all British military activity in the Ottoman Empire. This officer, a Colonel Lennox, arrived in Constantinople on Christmas Eve 1876 and Home reported immediately to him. Two days later, on Boxing Day, the new attaché complained to Simmons that he had not received the latest Intelligence Department report from Home and burst out: 'As you may remember HRH desired that we should work in harmony, and I have remembered that direction very often.'[96]

To make such an extraordinary observation after only two days in post gives a very clear hint that Lennox knew upon which side his bread was buttered.

Simmons also fretted about the intelligencers' reconnoitring. He warned Home not to examine the Asian side of the Dardanelles as that would be to exceed instructions. He was convinced that Home would talk the government into taking both sides of the Dardanelles then to fortify and man them at great cost. Warming to his theme, he thought the idea of securing an island base 'upon the scale of Malta' would be such a huge move it might even lead to conscription! 'The magnitude of the question cannot therefore be exaggerated,' he wrote when shown the FO minute detailing Salisbury's authorisation of Home's reconnaissances, 'and I venture to submit, that the material guarantee, secured by the occupation of the Dardanelles in the manner contemplated, is one, which should only be entertained after the most serious consideration.'[97]

At this distance it is difficult to say whether Home's privileged position as Salisbury's principal military adviser was the chief cause of Simmons's precipitous resignation in the very week the Constantinople Conference collapsed, but it was no doubt a contributing factor. The Duke asked Simmons to withdraw it as a personal favour and he even may have allowed him to recall the intelligencers in mollification.

For the government, Simmons's behaviour was deeply unacceptable. Gathorne-Hardy returned his letter of resignation without comment, irritated with the 'grudging way' in which Simmons took it back. He wrote in his diary: 'He has shown such a temper as makes it unlikely that he will not be under its domination again.' In the months which followed Simmons's abortive resignation, his comments and reports received less and less attention until soon they were routinely filed by the FO unread. The opposition, too, knew with whom it was dealing. When in 1881, Simmons was proposed for the post of Adjutant General, Hugh Childers, then Secretary of State for War, asked Lord Hartington what he thought. The Secretary of State for India replied: 'I could not recommend him.' In his experience, he added, Simmons 'urged proposals which we consider very retrograde and is very impractical. He would be a very proper officer to send to Gibraltar...'[98]

On the other hand, when Home arrived back in London, he was promoted to Brevet Colonel.

‡

With British irresolution to the fore, the Russians felt it safe to declare war on the Ottoman Empire, which they did on 24 April 1877. Although the Russian Army's organisation was primitive, its training woeful, Russia was in a remarkably strong position politically. Its suborning of the Khan of the Crimea was going well as was disruption of Ottoman provinces to the east. The British Foreign Secretary and Lady Derby were openly pro-Russian and any secret from the FO was known in St Petersburg within days.

With minimal effort, Russia's efforts in Afghanistan produced paranoia amongst the soldiers in India. The domino theory reigned supreme. It would only be a matter of time before Russia would be the lord of Persia, indeed the entire Levant, and the prize of access to the eastern Mediterranean and the Suez Canal would be theirs. In reaction, Beaconsfield rattled his sabre, but he and Salisbury knew that to back it up with any chance of swift success would doubtless necessitate the largest deployment of British troops in the Empire's history.

The despatch of a force of such size to back up the Porte would be 'a big business'. Indeed it would. Whereas in the early 1870s there had been some seventy battalions at home and abroad, by the late 1870s there were fifty-nine in Great Britain and Ireland and eighty-two abroad. A parliamentary committee in 1876 had pointed out how weak the Army really was. Britain's supply of reserves was hardly 'inexhaustible' and public opinion was, as Granville said, 'pronouncing itself thoroughly in favor [sic] of neutrality'.[99] The Cabinet itself became more and more divided on what to do and every talk of military action brought Derby and Carnarvon closer to resignation.

Beaconsfield knew the cost of action, but would not waver. Salisbury told Home that whilst he would not fight for the Turk, he would fight for Turkey and not for the Bosphorus but for the Dardanelles and the Persian Gulf.[100]

The ID wholly expected this and before they had been forced home, two of Home's young officers, Chermside and Hare, had surveyed as much of the Russian's probable invasion route as they could. If Adrianople were cut off from the sea, the Dardanelles would be threatened. Back in Spring Gardens, Anstey finished his detailed report vaunting Russia's chances which he sent to Gathorne Gathorne-Hardy on 9 April.

On 17 April, Beaconsfield called on Gathorne-Hardy to consider what steps should be taken to prevent the Russians occupying the Dardanelles. After that meeting 'full of the future and our course', Gathorne-Hardy confided to his diary that he was certain that the Prime Minister had the occupation of Gallipoli in mind. 'Gallipoli is his object and no doubt that Col. Home who has been with him has suggested that course.'[101]

He was right. Beaconsfield fully intended to establish the British in the Dardanelles, 'engaging to retire from the occupation when a treaty of Peace was concluded, which would secure the requisite balance of Power'. He told the Queen that Gathorne-Hardy and his military advisers had 'worked out the measures in detail', which they had. The Cabinet sat on 21 April and Lord Carnarvon, the timid Colonial Secretary, opened the batting by suggesting that the least risky course of action was to send the fleet to the Bosphorus. That evening, Beaconsfield wrote to the Queen:

Upon this, Mr Secretary Hardy read a report, from one of our military authorities in which it was stated, that all accounts, and secret military documents, stated, that, when the Russians had arrived at Adrianople, it was their intention to occupy the Dardanelles before they advanced on Constantinople. This declaration which startled the Cabinet, led them at once to consider the plan of Ld

Beaconsfield without the inconvenience of his personally bringing it forward.[102]

The Turks were not battle ready and the Russians initially made rapid progress. General Gouko's cavalry seized the Shipka Pass on 14 July and pressed hard on the Brijuk–Tchechmedjie line. The Cabinet met and again the ID was asked for advice. As the one fixed tenet of British policy towards the east for the past half-decade was to keep the Dardanelles out of Russian hands, they decided, in desperation, to destroy the batteries on the European side of the Dardanelles. Thus it fell to Captain Fraser of the IGF to do and so he immediately set off on the night train to Paris with 50 pounds of guncotton in his portmanteau:

> Leaving from Victoria Station, I got into an empty carriage; but at the last moment an old lady was handed in by a footman and a maid; I had a box of detonators in my hand, and on starting she found her footstool had been forgotten, and begged me to let her have my small box instead. I knew that if anything happened it would make no difference to either of us where the box was in the carriage; so I let her have it, and a great comfort it was to her in the bliss of ignorance.

Yet before he could arrive, Osman Pasha rallied the Turks and twice defeated the Russians at Plevna on 29–30 July. And when Suliman marshalled for a counter-attack on Shipka, the new ambassador, Sir Henry Layard, took heart that the tide was changing and postponed Fraser's mission. The Cabinet was considerably relieved and the minutes indicate that whilst Fraser's mission was in play they were as much if not more concerned about his safety wandering around the Bosphorus with his case of guncotton than in the task itself.[103]

Looked at from London, the Russo-Turkish War of 1877–78 was a confusing seesaw with fortune changing hands so often and the news so perplexing, that it was hard for the government to keep up or to tell who was on top. It was crucial therefore to have exact and accurate military intelligence so as not to over- or underreact.

The ID bombarded the consuls with questions, but always through the Foreign and War offices. Consul Ricketts at Batoum was, for example, very adept at gathering useful material, but he was unusual. Most consuls were ill educated as to what or how to report military matters. Even the military attaché to the Court of the Czar, Colonel Wellesley, son of the Duke of Wellington, felt he needed to ask the FO what he should collect. He had nurtured sources in the Asiatic Department of the Russian War Office but needed to canalise his collection. 'I am sure that you will understand my position,' he wrote to Tenterden at the Foreign Office. 'The more papers I buy the greater the expense, and the more irons I have in the fire, the greater the risk.'[104] But little matter, because from February 1877 until the Russians attacked in April, Wellesley reported back that he did 'not apprehend any present intention on the part of Russia of embarking in war with Turkey'.

What poor Wellesley did not know until he read it in the newspaper *Russki Mir* in May was that he had been duped all along. It took him another month to get permission to visit the front but with one incident after another, he finally resigned his post in August 1879.[105]

The attaché Lennox, Home's antagonist at Constantinople and, like Wellesley, a ducal appointment, also proved ill fitted for his post. By October his relations with the Ambassador had deteriorated to such a degree that when he tried to go over the Ambassador's head over some long-forgotten issue, Layard was outraged and Simmons was ordered to rebuke him. His recall was only a matter of time and it came in December. He returned to London to be interviewed by Gathorne-Hardy, who came away from the encounter singularly unimpressed with his judgement or foresight.[106] Horse Guards then visited another headache on the long-suffering Secretary when war broke out. High-ranking attachés were needed, it was claimed, and two generals were sent out only to shower Gathorne-Hardy with profuse and conflicting advice. What Gathorne-Hardy wanted, what Salisbury and Beaconsfield needed, was proper intelligence.

‡

In spite of collection problems large and small, there now emerged a spirit of co-operation on intelligence matters between the Admiralty and the War and Foreign offices. Fraser noted that all three departments were in close touch through the Intelligence Department 'and all information was passed round to the three departments. We subordinates, of course, got the permission of our respective chiefs to show everything.'

The ID was producing more concrete intelligence than the Inspector General of Fortifications and both Simmons and the Foreign Office knew it. The winter of 1877–78 was particularly bitter and questions naturally arose about its effect on the 'New Order' Turkish Army. Fraser received the order to produce such information for Beaconsfield, but it was Home who collected and reported it via Foreign Office channels. Since then the FO requested, as a matter of course, to receive extra copies of all ID reports.[107]

The ID was not slow in making itself indispensable to the FO. It set up a map in the FO itself of the area of operations and provided the FO with a weekly update of operations. MacDougall transferred officers from quieter sections of the ID to strengthen the Ottoman Section, which then had an authorised strength of four officers and one other rank. With this extra help, the Section produced voluminous accounts of strengths and operational matters which increasingly became more professional and complete. The FO appreciated this effort and reciprocated by authorising ID officers to travel to Algiers, Tunis, Russia, Scutari, Altoona, Monastir, Thessaly, Athens and Crete for the purpose of 'obtaining information in regard to Military Matters'.

The reputation of the Department was swelling by leaps and bounds. It was at this time that Gathorne-Hardy approved the Department's request to create a separate mapping and library section under Captain G. Grover, the pioneer military balloonist. Grover set to work using the first-hand knowledge of the recently returned officers and this was reflected in the quality of the Department's map making. Commenting on one such (Shipka Pass and Plevna),

Gathorne-Hardy remarked that the Queen 'has been so taken with Captain Ardagh's map, that she has not returned it to me. Everyone who saw it thought it admirable, as I need not say I did myself.'[108]

But the Turkish hey-day was over as soon as it had begun. As the year turned, the Russians gained more victories and Gathorne-Hardy described the Turkish armies as falling back in an 'utter crash'. Public opinion was sharply divided and whilst armchair generals and many in Parliament were all for sending an expeditionary force, liberal opinion was exactly the opposite. Then the Sultan asked if he might take exile in Britain if Russia won, a request which deeply dismayed the Cabinet. It dithered over every proposal to bring Russia to heel and there was no succour from the other powers. Diplomatically and militarily, Britain was alone and Gathorne-Hardy moaned: 'We have done too much or too little.'[109]

In mid-January, the Russians gave assurances that no matter what happened they would not seize Gallipoli, but the Cabinet no longer trusted such assurances. Simmons convened a meeting on 16 January, to which no ID officer was invited. He asked Fraser if there was still time to occupy the Dardanelles. Fraser thought that there was just time enough. Fraser was ordered to ready his portmanteau of gun-cotton for the second time but in the event, all the government was prepared to do was to send in a strong fleet, which weighed anchor for the Dardanelles on 23 January.

With a fleet sitting in Beskka Bay, the British hoped it would have its desired effect on the advancing Russian forces. It did for a moment and an armistice (Adrianople) was arranged, but the Russians, so close to their goal, soon resumed their advance towards Constantinople. Beaconsfield could only respond by announcing plans for an expeditionary force and for a week in early February the War Office prepared for war. There were grave deficiencies in artillery and transport and Gathorne-Hardy could only lament: 'Too late – too late! Rings in my ears.'

If Constantinople fell, that was one thing. If the Dardanelles went, then there would be, as Gathorne-Hardy noted, 'a still more inconvenient advance to the coast of Asia Minor which would threaten the Suez Canal, and the Euphrates Valley, and so intercept our communications with India.' The Dardanelles must not be allowed into Russian hands. In this atmosphere Derby at the Foreign Office and Carnarvon at the Colonial Office resigned. Derby was coaxed back but only for a few months.

On 3 March 1878, the Russians engineered the Turks into signing the Treaty of San Stefano, which created an outsized and 'independent' Bulgaria. The treaty was concluded without recourse to Britain, France, Germany or Austria-Hungary. On 20 March, Gathorne-Hardy managed to get Home through the maze of Horse Guards bureaucracy to see Salisbury with as much secrecy as he could manage. Salisbury wrote to Home: 'Gathorne-Hardy said you were to report yourself to the Adjutant General as having gone to consult me about affairs in my department which all Asia is. Do not otherwise say anything about this.' On the twenty-eighth the Queen authorised Beaconsfield to mobilise the First Class Reserves, testing for the first time part of Home's mobilisation plans.[110] This was too much for Derby and when at the same Cabinet another Intelligence Department plan was tabled to take control of Cyprus, he again resigned, this time for good. Salisbury became Foreign Secretary.

It is more than probable that when the new Foreign Secretary met the deputy head of the Intelligence Department, Home reiterated the caution with which Britain had to act in responding to the Treaty of San Stefano. Neither man had any faith in it, a caution born of weakness. As the blanks in his mobilisation charts so dramatically proved, Britain possessed relatively few trained reserves and the Volunteer movement, as a serious, deployable force, was just getting underway. The government would thereupon have to turn to India for muscle. Indian troops could be sent to Malta for possible deployment to the Dardanelles, but it could be no more than a bluff. Home warned Salisbury that the Indian Army could not take to the field quickly. And there were other pressures on the Indians. Before he resigned, Carnarvon had considered asking for Indian troops to help stabilise affairs in Zululand, but above all, a few Russians roaming around Afghanistan and the Northwest Frontier were capable of tying down the entire Indian Army.

When the request did come through from London to Calcutta for help, it was for 7,000 men, a request that the government of India acceded to most reluctantly. After all, they possessed an obscure semi-official journal published in Tashkent reporting that General Kauffman was moving a whole field army down to Tashkent and would need every man they had. The Intelligence Department answered coldly:

> What is the nature of the blow to be struck? Is it a movement in force against India, or a demonstration in order to stir up the border tribes on our frontier, with the object of giving employment to our Indian forces, and thereby preventing any further detachments being sent to Turkey? Undoubtedly the latter.[111]

Indian troops were despatched to Malta in late April only to be packed back home by August.

With Salisbury at the FO, there was a sudden increase in the Department's already hectic programme. Collection, as ever, was crucial. Home began teaching Layard, the new Ambassador to the Porte, the finer points of recruiting and running a network of agents. By letter, he taught the Ambassador how to recruit and despatch operatives, ensure their veracity and process the results. It was crude but it worked. For example, for a given mission Home suggested sending out six agents, all unknown to each other, and then to check their answers against each other.[112]

Tradecraft being what it was, the ID itself began handling some resources. Some were external, some from within. Amongst numerous assignments large and small, typical was Captain Fife watching Russian troop movements near the Dardanelles and the redoubtable Major East, head of the French Section (A), who went quietly to Paris to obtain 'if possible some Confidential information from the

French War Office which had been prepared in the time of the 3rd Napoleon'. All this 'in view of possible complications with Russia'. This was very high-risk behaviour and when the contact was late for their meeting, East grew suspicious, aborted and cut out.[113]

But much more was needed. On the day Derby resigned from the Cabinet and the Reserves were called out, Salisbury authorised Home to send officers to Syria and Cyprus. Home, himself, was later seen in Beirut. The ID requested help from the FO in securing up-to-date plans for Alexandria, Cairo, Port Said, Ismailia and Suez. Explaining his reasoning to Layard, Salisbury pointed out that if the Russians kept up their rate of advance, Kars would fall, exposing Syria and Mesopotamia to Russian incursion, further weakening a visibly shrinking Turkey. In fact it was 'a question of existence'. The Russians had to be stopped and Layard was therefore authorised to offer the Porte help in defending Turkish dominions in Asia. Salisbury hoped the pledge would encourage and stabilise the Porte in order that reforms could be advanced and 'may enable the Turks to set up a system of administration which shall be recognised as superior to anything that Russia has to offer'. In exchange for all this Layard was to ask the Porte for Cyprus.

The idea of Cyprus under British control had at least one root in Disraeli's novel *Tancred* but its more immediate origin was in Home's *pied à terre* memorandum of 1876. Salisbury, having ordered the reconnaissances of January 1877, had Cyprus much in mind and the question came up in the famous Cabinet of 28 March, a week after Salisbury and Home were known to have conferred together. Home wrote another memorandum, noted above, and Simmons believed that 'it was upon this paper that the Convention, then secret, had been agreed upon with Turkey for ceding Cyprus to Great Britain'. The Cabinet agreed to investigate the possibility and Derby was sure enough that the decision to seize Cyprus had been taken there and then that he resigned.

In this memorandum, Home focused on Cyprus as being the least troublesome of all the alternatives. It would provide a base from which to protect and pressure Turkey, it could become a commercial depot and it would:

> allow the experiment of what good government will do being fairly tried. The political effect produced by observing the rapid development of a country under English rule – the peace and prosperity that would reign in it and the satisfaction of the inhabitants at the change from Turkish to British government – would be incalculable and would do more to maintain English prestige than half a dozen campaigns.[114]

Having arranged to take Cyprus, Salisbury and the ID turned their attention to stopping the Russians once and for all.

The fragile Armistice of Adrianople gave Beaconsfield and Salisbury the opportunity to wage peace and make it stick. Thus the idea came about for a grand conference of the powers in early June 1878, a congress, no less, in Berlin with all the major interested parties including Russia and Turkey, each wearing its heart on its sleeve.

Beaconsfield, well into his seventies, led the British delegation. Often ill, he summoned up all his reserves and was the lion of the congress. As Bismarck noted: *Der alte Jude, das ist der Mann.* He delivered his opening remarks in English, laying down a marker that Britain would be intransigent on Turkey's behalf. Despite continuing leaks from the Foreign Office which signalled to everyone British intentions, matters on the whole went Britain's way. But the devil, as always, was in the detail and much of the detail was in demarcating borders.

Salisbury turned again to the ID. The first technical appointee to the British delegation was Ardagh. He had new ID maps and a wealth of knowledge at his disposal. Predictably, however, his appointment set off an explosion at Horse Guards and Simmons demanded that he, Simmons, be made a delegate, too, which he was some five days after Ardagh.

Nothing loath, Ardagh built fraternal bonds with the rising stars from the Foreign Office, who found his knowledge and ability prodigious. He was key in combating Russian chicanery over numerous technical, military and cartographic issues and felt it very keenly: Serbia, Montenegro, Novi Bazar, all required minute attention and when the shape of the two Bulgarias (Bulgaria and Eastern Roumelia) was finally decided, Ardagh alone of all the delegates took careful tracings of the new boundaries. From start to finish Ardagh found the congress 'a most anxious one, from the great interests and serious responsibility connected with it'. Beaconsfield agreed, describing the congress as a 'curious history of plots and intrigues' all of which had to be battled with firmness.[115]

The treaty was signed on 13 July. The British mission returned to London in triumph, so much so that Gladstone would later record that it was undoubtedly Disraeli's finest moment. The Prime Minister and his Foreign Secretary received the Garter and Ardagh was made a civil, rather than military, Companion of the Bath for services to the Foreign Office. It was an honour unheard of for a serving officer and even the modest, shy Ardagh admitted it was 'all the more agreeable' for that. Salisbury wrote to express his congratulations and thanks:

> for the assistance which has been so frequently and so ably rendered to the Foreign Office on many occasions during the recent Congress, and the preceding diplomatic negotiations, by the Intelligence Department of the War Office.[116]

And Home, too, wrote to Salisbury congratulating him on the outcome. 'I cannot help telling you how infinitely better than I ever dared to hope, the whole matter has turned out. That it has done so, I know just enough to feel sure, is due and entirely due to your Lordship.' To which Salisbury replied:

> I am very much obliged to you for the expressions contained in your letter. Cyprus was the acquisition on which your mind was originally bent – & now that we can judge the matter as an accomplished fact I am heartily glad that your advice prevailed – & that we did not touch

either Crete or Alexandretta. I am glad to think that – at all events during my remaining term of office – our official intercourse is likely to continue – for 'intelligence' is a commodity we are very likely to require in the affairs of the East. If I do not err the next act will open in Persia – are your pigeon holes full of Persian facts?[117]

‡

The Treaty of Berlin brought a collective sigh of relief to Europe. Indeed, the western signatories had recreated Turkey-in-Europe, for a while at least, and in Asia Russia was still separated from India by vast distances of desert wastes and high mountains. The one outlet for Russian expansion was between the two: from the Armenian plateau to Persia; hence Salisbury's offer to the Sultan to assist him in defending Turkey-in-Asia and his remark to Home about the 'next act' in Persia. Without anticipating events, Salisbury's observation proved correct. At the time it was already happening as the Russian expansionists and Pan-Slavs were pointing to the unfavourable outcome of the Treaty of Berlin as far as they were concerned and blamed the moderates from St Petersburg. After 13 July 1878 the Russian expansionists were very much in the driving seat and this did not bode well for Turkey or for Persia.

The Intelligence Department was aware of the hole in the dyke. In his Cyprus memorandum, Home showed Salisbury that the island 'shall give us potentially the keys to Asia Minor' and reasoned that as long as the Dardanelles and the Bosphorus were 'maintained in status quo', Britain's concerns were in Asiatic Turkey and eastwards. Thus Home's reckoning that Cyprus would be 'a secure base for checking any hostile advance from the Caucasus or the headwaters of the Tigris and Euphrates or either the Persian Gulf or Suez Canal'. In a revealing letter Salisbury told Lord Northcote, Leader of the House:

As to the strategic question, of course I speak with bated breath. But my apprehension is that Cyprus is to be looked upon as a polite expression for Alexandretta, [undecipherable], and that its value consists in this – that it gives us a second line of attack in case of Russia advancing Southward. Of course the Black Sea will retain all its advantages; but being ex hypothesi allies of Turkey, the Bosphorous will be our base for such operations. Alexandretta will be our base for raising, arming, officering and supplying the Asiatic populations whom we may hope to bring up against Russia from the south and south-west.

We should attempt the same operation from Poti and Trebizond on the North and Northwest of her armies. That is my idea of the strategy of the matter conceived after many conversations with Colonel Home.[118]

To put this into effect was another 'big business' and would require the resources of the ID at the very time when the War Office, having woken up to the ID's potential as a general staff, was relying on it for various movement, loading and other staff functions in relation to the outbreak of war in Natal Colony, South Africa. From London, Grover in the Library & Mapping Section wrote to Ardagh:

Everybody here has fled away, and it is a sad wilderness. Wavell, Frank Russell, James, and East are all at the Cape and I, to my sorrow, am in Adair House – longing to inscribe on its walls 'Ichabod!' [Four of the six sections were being worked by attached officers, thus] I have consequently had a very great deal on my shoulders, as you may imagine – and I cannot flatter myself that the result is at all satisfactory. The good old Intelligence Department is almost defunct – and it has lost its pristine 'offensive' usefulness. A passively useful institution is out of place.

For its services in the Eastern Question, the ID had levied no claim on the FO. The training and rise in prestige was worth every penny. Grover did, however, ask Ardagh to secure a £10 gratuity for Mr Kelly, the chief printer. 'He has done a lot of work very promptly for them during the last two years. We have not charged the FO with any cost at all.'[119]

Grover was right. The ID had displaced to the front lines. Those ID officers so recently concerned with the Russo-Turkish War were now delimiting the Bulgarian, Serbian and Romanian boundaries to check the Russians. Home was appointed chief British commissioner for the Bulgarian delimitation and he swept in Ardagh, Chermside and two other officers from the Ottoman Section. Charles Wilson, still revered in the Department, rushed over from the Irish Ordnance Survey to head the Serbian Boundary Commission along with Ross of Bladensburg. Brevet Colonel A. H. Wavell, head of Section B (British Colonies, etc.), returned from Africa to oversee the Roumelian portion. Captains Sale, Hare and Gill joined them soon after.

Each of the commissions had two tasks. The official one was to create accurate borders. This loomed large in Victorian thinking. The British commissioners were to give Turkey 'every possible advantage' in laying out a good military frontier so that, if threatened in the future, she would not have to throw outposts over her border, itself a provocation. They took care not to separate villages from their traditional water and fuel supplies and insisted on a bridge being built to unite the two Romanian shores as well as gaining topographical advantages all along the Balkan frontier of Eastern Roumelia. As later events would prove, their work was on the whole exceptionally sound.

Like the 1876 reconnaissances around Constantinople, the surveys were conducted under appalling physical conditions punctuated by the threat of 'inspired brigands'. Their careful survey work brought them into constant conflict with their Russian counterparts who practised the same energetic deception in the field as they had in Berlin. On 4 December all the commissioners met and Ardagh noted disdainfully that the other plans:

such as they are, were ready. Colonel Bogolinbow at once put his finger on the point most favourable to him. The croquis general which I have compiled shows that the line to frontier proposed by the Commission gives Roumania about two hundred square kilometres more than they thought. Bogolinbow claimed a reconsideration of the vote. The

Commission made a Jonah of one – repudiated the accuracy of the croquis, which I did up to a certain point, stating that the villages were certainly not more than a kilometre out of their true position, and that in the main there could be no doubt that the sketch survey [by the British] was far more accurate than the Austrian map. Bogolinbow then proposed that in consideration of the above mentioned discoveries the Commission should reconsider its decision. Home thereupon [moved] an amendment (at my suggestion). The amendment was carried and consequently Bogolinbow's motion lost.

On another occasion, Ardagh realised that the Russians would benefit from an inaccurate sketch survey between Tchain Kouron and Ai Gedik. Without losing a moment, he gathered what officers he could and galloped off to survey thirty miles in one day at 1:30,000. Presented at the same time as the Russians introduced their map, the finished character of the British map carried the day. The Russians were incensed.

Still with that sense of urgency, Ardagh, now a substantive major, rushed his maps back to Adair House for the Department's stone grainers, lithographers and pressmen. The result was of such a high quality that they quickly became the all-power maps. But the Russians were not finished. They insisted on a meeting at ambassadorial level with the intent of overthrowing the commissioners' work, especially the Romanian boundary which they had worked so hard to dismantle. Home got wind of this and warned Layard, who wrote: 'Colonel Home has done the Roumanians good service by giving them the boundary they require. I hint that Her Majesty's Government will not be a party to having the question reopened.'[120]

Delineating borders was the commissioners' first task. The commissioners' second mission was to collect intelligence. Home decreed that nothing about the Russians or the topography was to be missed. Both Home and Salisbury saw 'the next act' in the Fertile Crescent and Home, who better than any man knew how weak the British Army was, determined that if war did come, an arriving British force would need to be masters of the terrain on arrival. Salisbury agreed and pressed the Treasury for a special one-off payment of £4,000 for the systematic reconnoitring of Asia Minor 'under a central authority in England [i.e. the ID], where the whole work might be centralised and the information focused'. The Treasury, however, thought the work might be done in some other, cheaper way and the plan was shelved, a harbinger of a Liberal policy to come.

As indicated above, Home and two intelligence captains worked daily with Layard to improve the Ambassador's collection capability. All were passionate advocates of a string of military consuls stretching up and to the east to link with a similar string played out from India. And all had to collect to an exacting standard.

Then Home again received orders from Salisbury to examine Cyprus. Unfortunately, the Robert Home who went to Cyprus late in 1878 was a different man than he had been when he first suggested its acquisition two years before. Almost seven years of constant, unremitting labour 'as the real head' of the ID took its toll. Home, the first meritocrat of the Cardwell School who advanced 'without influence and without money', brought the Intelligence Department into the corridors of power and ensured it stayed there. His friends were worried when he was assigned as chief British boundary commissioner as 'he had already overtaxed his powers, and that rest, rather than fresh and worrying work, was what he most needed. But to him the call of duty was sufficient...' Whilst on the Turkish frontier, Home contracted typhoid fever and returned, via Cyprus, to die in his forty-second year in January 1879.

Beaconsfield was said to have wept and *The Times* had to explain their obituary of an unknown man: 'It can very rarely happen that a man should have been so little before the nation and should yet have performed for it such signal services as Colonel Home.' His colleagues at the Department raised £100 for a window in his memory at Rochester Cathedral. A wife, four sons and two daughters succeeded him. The Admiralty, not Horse Guards, made the handsome offer of a cadetship for one of his sons.

He was not forgotten for a long time. His name occasionally surfaces in Foreign Office minutes during the next twenty years where whatever statement was attributed to him assumed Gospel-like proportions. And even at the remove of thirty-one years, his near contemporary Lieutenant General Sir William Butler wrote in anger at the financial neglect suffered by such early staff officers, for he believed that it was that which really killed him.

At the moment when Colonel Hume [*sic*] was finding brains and knowledge ... for ministers and statesmen ... he frequently sat late into the night at home working a sewing machine to keep his children in clothes! What a lot of splendid human steel I have seen cast on the scrap heap in my time, in the fullness of strength and usefulness, through the selfish stupidity of a system which never seemed to know the worth of any human material it had to deal with.[121]

‡

It will be recalled that Ardagh had reported two years before that foreign commissioners would be welcome in Bulgaria and could maintain themselves without force of arms. Thus Derby had approved the posting of military vice consuls to Serbia and Bosnia under the agent at Belgrade. Both were linguists attached to the Intelligence Department. Another intelligencer, Captain (later Lieutenant General Sir Henry) Trotter, became consul at Erzeroum. A singularly reserved and secretive geographer, in fact a perfect model for a Great Gamesman, he made extensive low-profile journies throughout Armenia, Diarbekir and the neighbouring Kurdish provinces. It was upon his recommendations that a British Consul General was appointed in Sivas with the intention that he would supervise a number of vice-consuls who would protect the minorities as best they could. Layard supported the scheme, Salisbury accepted it and after the Congress made plans for the establishment of consuls throughout Anatolia and Kurdistan.

As with the boundary commissioners, the consuls had two missions. One was to supervise the implementation of Article LXI of the Treaty of Berlin, which placed on the Porte responsibility for such 'improvements and reforms' as would satisfy all the powers including the Russians. Their second mission was to maintain an alert presence in Asia Minor and link up with the intelligence screen which the Indians were starting to build. In this way Salisbury could protect India without the expense of occupying Persia, Mesopotamia or even Afghanistan. Writing to Sir Richard Temple, then Governor of Bombay and active in sending the Indian force to Malta, Salisbury spelled out very clearly his vision:

> There is an intermediate course between military occupation and simple laissez-faire. It is a process of which there are already some examples: but for which there is at present no expression. I will call it the pacific invasion of England. It has been largely practised in Egypt, with excellent effect: it is going on, more slowly, in China and in Japan. The principle of it is that whenever you bring the English into contact with inferior races, they will rule, whatever the ostensible ground of their presence. As merchants, as railway makers, as engineers, as travellers, later on as employers like Gordon, or McKillop, or as Ministers like Rivers Wilson, they assert the English domination, not by any political privilege or military power, but by right of the strongest mind. The taking of Cyprus, and the acquisition of a right to reform Asia Minor and Mesopotamia, will I hope give opportunity for this pacific invasion. If it is to be effective, it will furnish the best of bulwarks against Russian advance. Cannot something of the same kind be done in Afghanistan? Once obtain the unrestricted right of access and in a few years you will govern without ever drawing a sword.[122]

In the west, Salisbury wasted little time. The man chosen to build the screen was none other than the creator of the modern ID, Charles Wilson, who was appointed Consul General for Anatolia on 14 April 1879. The vice consuls under him were Trotter, J. D. H. Stewart (who would serve with Gordon), Chermside, Kitchener, William Everett (who would be the deputy director of the Department in the 1890s) and two other officers, a gunner and sapper, straight from Adair House.

Wilson was discouraged by the quality of Turkish official he found. He regarded them as inferior to those he had known fifteen years before when he surveyed Palestine. Nevertheless, he was convinced that radical reform was 'absolutely necessary, if a permanent settlement of the country is to be affected, and if all pretext for a further extension of the Russian frontier is to be removed'. Initially the consuls corrected many wrongs just by their presence and by threatening recalcitrant officials with exposure in British *Blue Books*. As Salisbury acknowledged: 'The Sultan and his Pashas flinch when their misdeeds are held up to the whole of Europe – as may be seen by their eagerness to exculpate themselves.' But before long the power of these threats waned when the local officials realised that the consuls were not harbingers of 'a large number of competent and honest European officials...'

Trotter felt that Salisbury was 'perhaps over sanguine in expecting great results from the work of myself and others who have less knowledge of the country and its language than I have...' But Salisbury was pleased and encouraging, reminding Trotter that 'the diplomacy therefore of the consuls is really all to which at present these wretchedly ill-governed populations have to look'.[123]

The story of the consuls bringing fair play and justice to far-flung places is one of selflessness, zeal and despair. It is also one of danger. Not only did 'inspired brigands' abound, but Everett was the victim of an assassination attempt which left his hand maimed. Nevertheless, the consuls set up what would become the Stafford House Fund for Relief, quelled insurrections, badgered Layard for more money and more good men, English or Turkish. Above all, they never lost heart. Everett wrote to Layard: 'I feel like an exhausted battery. If you can give another turn to the generator I can go on again...' But reality was dawning on Salisbury about the likelihood of reform.

In 1879 he acknowledged that 'our responsibility for Turkey is at an end'.[124]

In the spring of 1880, the Liberals returned to power and, missing the real point of the consular apparatus, or perhaps grasping it all too clearly, sought to dismantle it. Wilson and Trotter went to London where they campaigned for its extension. Try as they might, they could not induce the new government to see the global picture. The most active threat to Britain's eastern Empire was the continuing instability of Egypt, a financial and political insecurity, a legacy of the collapsing Ottoman hegemony and an increasing threat to the neutrality of the canal and communications with India.[125]

In shoring up the Khedive of Egypt, Britain could not count on disinterested support from France. Britain in Egypt was alone her own saving grace. Months before the Foreign Office and government realised it, the balance of British security in Asia had shifted westwards to Egypt. Fortunately, British intelligence was already there.

CHAPTER FOUR

HELD UP THE KHEDIVE?
YOU HAVE PICKED HIM UP

In the fullest sense of the word the Suez Canal was wonderful. Trade between west and east was simplified, safer and cheaper. Commercial possibilities became realities and the world's shipping was drawn to the canal as if it were a whirlpool, British shipping most of all. In 1874, in only its fifth year of operation, the managing director of the Pacific & Orient Steamship Company estimated that Britain's annual tonnage through the canal ran to £16 million 'and probably much more'. The eleven member nations of the canal's Tonnage Admeasurement Commission acknowledged that predominance when in the same year it asked Britain, the twelfth partner, to contribute 72 per cent of the cost of dredging the Mediterranean mouth.

There was another side to this wonder and Lord Derby at the Foreign Office looked at the canal from a strategic rather than commercial angle, citing the military advantages of 'direct sea communication with India' above the more obvious business argument when asking W. H. Smith at the Treasury for the 72 per cent.

This was the rub. The land around the canal was under the control of the French Suez Canal Company. The adjoining territory belonged to Egypt, an Ottoman province as open to pernicious influences as Bulgaria or Anatolia. In Egypt, however, it was not the Russians but the French and French bankers who were openly pressing the whole debt-ridden Egyptian administration into ruin. To the British, the other 'protecting power', it was clear; the French had designs on establishing their suzerainty over the whole country. By 1875, informed observers in London saw the French playing a similar game in Cairo as the Russians were playing in Constantinople.

A s noted previously, British support for the Sublime Porte was a Palmerstonian legacy, the importance of which was diminishing in 1875–76 at the very moment when the Eastern Question lit up and it looked as if Britain's protective stance would be put to the test. The canal was the diminutioner, a point recognised by Smith who responded to the request from the Tonnage Commission by warning Beaconsfield that its members might well 'go on spending our money for us until we quarrelled with them. If it were possible for England to purchase the Canal outright it would in my judgement be a safer financial and political option than that which is now suggested.'[126] Smith's canny idea was well received by the Prime Minister and when the opportunity presented itself in 1875, Disraeli swayed a largely sceptical Cabinet into purchasing 44 per cent of the ordinary shares.

As Parliament was not sitting, the money would have to be raised through a loan. So in the story polished by many tellings, Disraeli's secretary, Montagu Corry (later Baron Rowton), recalls how he waited outside the Cabinet meeting until Disraeli appeared at the door and hissed: 'Yes!' Corry hastened to Baron Rothschild and asked him for £4 million. 'When?' 'Tomorrow.' 'What is your security?' 'The British Government.' 'You shall have it.' And have it the government did.

Britain was now, in the eyes of the world, truly Great. The purchase of these shares gave it a major defence responsibility. No longer was India mentioned without mention of the canal, but the location of the canal was a problem. Egypt, as much as, if not more than, any other Ottoman province, was a liability with France in this case making her presence increasingly felt.

With French naval and colonial activity all along the shores of North Africa, France saw herself as the leading partner in the Anglo-French dual control over a country rapidly heading for the abyss. The Khedive Tawfiq of Egypt, notionally under the suzerainty of the Porte, but really under the sway of French bankers, and the parlous financial state of the Egyptian government enforced a reduction of the Army. Parts of it mutinied and fuelled a nationalist movement under the charismatic and highly able Egyptian Army officer, Urâbî Pasha. Riots followed. The Khedive sought to turn this to his own advantage and was summarily deported. Appeals to the Turks by Lord Granville bore no fruit and unrest grew. The youthful French Premier, M. Gambetta, made no secret of his desire for a joint military occupation with the French in command. But he was forced out of office in January 1882 and his successor, M. de Freycinet, obsessed with what he perceived to be a continuing threat from Germany, abrogated Gambetta's diplomatic upper hand over *affaires égyptiennes*. This left Britain, the once reluctant partner, now the senior partner, and in reality the sole partner. This change in French policy was dramatically played out when the French fleet sailed away from Alexandria as the British fleet and troops moved in to quell riots and prevent the threatened massacre of the Coptic Christians.

The result was the British occupation of Egypt in 1882, the suppression of the nationalist movement, the restoration of the Khedive as notional ruler and the establishment of a relatively sound civil and military infrastructure. Egypt thereupon became the northern pole in Britain's eventual mastery of Africa. In this the Intelligence Department played a leading role.

In 1875, as concern was growing about Turkey itself, the Intelligence Department's Charles Brackenbury became secretary to a joint Admiralty–War Office committee charged with co-ordinating the deployment of British troops overseas. It, too, was concerned about Egypt and declared that in prelude to any deployment almost anywhere, a British expedition would have to be despatched from Berehaven in Bantry Bay 'for the purpose of holding possession of the Suez Canal'.[127]

Although the ID's primary task was to provide information on possible areas of operations, knowledge of Egypt was scant. Charles Wilson and his chief, Patrick MacDougall, found no report more recent than 1856. More up-to-date information was needed rapidly for two reasons. First, memories were fresh of how little the Department knew about the west coast of Africa when the Ashanti Expedition brewed up. Second was the potential collapse of Turkey. Home, Ardagh and their colleagues would soon be bound for Constantinople and Egypt would surely appear in any equation they might need to cast.

Thus in December of 1875 travelling 'for the benefit of his health', MacDougall arrived in Cairo. His presence was soon known and aroused the suspicion of the chief of the Egyptian General Staff, none other than the ex-Confederate States of America officer General Charles P. Stone. Stone worried that MacDougall's visit was a prelude to annexation, but he co-operated and even obtained an audience with the Khedive for MacDougall. The Khedive gave MacDougall permission to conduct a military reconnaissance of the canal 'based on my belief in the probability that, at some future time, English troops might be called upon to fight side by side with His Highness' army'.

With a Khedival escort at his heels, MacDougall toured the canal and on his return wrote and printed one of the first papers under the ID's imprimatur solely for the Cabinet and the Foreign Office.

In it, MacDougall surmised that England could defend the canal *and Egypt* against a Russian force holding command of the Mediterranean if an Army corps, comprising troops from both Britain and India, were to meet and take possession of Port Said and other key points. He posited that an overland invasion through Palestine was not impossible either and set his officers to 'organise by anticipation' alternative ways to transport troops from Alexandria to Suez. In all his calculations the main point was a given: 'The object of England at all times will be the protection of the Canal from injury or interruption.'[128] In the ID's mind this was axiomatic. It soon found general acceptance and remained so until 1956.

As with Turkey, the Department's attempt to collect intelligence in Egypt faced opposition from various quarters in London. It must be remembered that Egypt was still in Disraeli and Salisbury's mind's eye a potential gift from the Porte in exchange for holding back the Russian bear. But others either did not know that or did not see it.

As previously noted, when in February 1877 Salisbury and Home instructed Ardagh to return home via Egypt, Simmons insisted on Ardagh's immediate recall, scoffing to Gathorne-Hardy that 'as to Egypt, I can scarcely conceive that all necessary information is not in the possession of Her Majesty's Government...'[129] Fortunately, Simmons's influence was on the wane and by August 1877 his objections to collecting information no longer mattered.

Simmons was the least of the ID's problems over Egypt. The situation merited an intelligencer on the spot. To that end the Department began a war on the bureaucracy which lasted on and off until they got their way in 1882. Their first move was to press the Foreign Office for a vast welter of information the ID knew it did not possess. The ID wanted details of Egyptian defences, the manufacture of war stores, how many 'camels, horses, mules and asses could be bought at a fortnight's notice – where and at what price?' It was especially curious about the number of men trained in torpedo work including 'who is charged with the administration of this branch and what are his antecedents and character?' On and on went their requests.

The Foreign Office did not, unsurprisingly, have any of this information and that same month two of the Department's officers, Captains East and Clarke, both highly capable veterans of the ID's early work in Turkey, left for Egypt to begin to find the answers.[130]

By April of the next year, 1878, the collection of 'the latest and best plans' was still underway, but with a slightly changed emphasis. By then Home had fixed on Cyprus as Britain's eastern *pied à terre*. As Salisbury noted, it was 'the polite expression for Alexandretta' and altogether much less trouble.

Meanwhile the ID was labouring to set up the consular screen between Turkey-in-Asia and India. But what was Roumelia to Britain when compared to Egypt? In Gladstone's eyes they were both trouble, and that opinion mattered as the Liberals came back into power in April 1880. The Grand Old Man had an abiding dislike of the Turks and during the Russo-Turkish war had been the author of two angry pamphlets against Turkey's abuse of subject peoples.

He also considered the idea of a consular screen provocative and as for the canal, he passionately disagreed with England's purchase and 'retained thenceforward an unconquerable distrust of the route-to-India argument'.[131]

Simply put, Gladstone's heart was in solving the Irish problem and any other overseas issue was a distraction. As Salisbury observed about Gladstone some years before:

> His mind, with all its power, has this strange peculiarity that his reason will not work vigorously on any question in which he does not take a hearty interest; and he can take a hearty interest in one question at a time. On any question, therefore, which crosses the subject of his heart … his perceptions are blunted and his reason will not work true.[132]

Yet no matter how much Gladstone wished the canal to disappear, its spectre daily grew. By 1881 the French Navy was firmly established in Tunis and Northbrook, now in charge of the Admiralty, had to consider the implications of that. His conclusion, possibly informed by Gladstone's opinion, was that in the event of war with France, Britain should block up the canal!

As for the Intelligence Department, it was convinced that the French were actively promoting instability. The Egyptian Army, now very much at the heart of the nationalist movement, was deeply disaffected and in open revolt. Charles Wilson, the Consul General in Anatolia and the pivot point in Salisbury's consular piquet line, was convinced that the French were fanning the revolutionary flame. Indeed, he concluded that overall France, not Russia, was the biggest threat to the emerging British Empire. And the Empire's most insecure point was the canal.

But all that was idle speculation until the Khedive suddenly cut his army drastically to save money and the large number of dispossessed officers saw external meddling as the root of Egypt's trouble. The Egyptian Army's revolt was put down without bloodshed but worse was to come. Wilson came to Gladstone's London hard upon the heels of a further revolt by Egyptian officers. He urged the extension of consular posts not only in Turkey-in-Asia but nearer to the canal. It was not a view likely to find favour. Again, the Department ran into caution and intransigence. At the Foreign Office, the wary Tenterden immediately divined that Wilson was planning 'to extend Lord Salisbury's system of military consulships from Asia Minor to Syria and Arabia'. This would introduce Britain into the world of the southern Levant and from there to the rim of the Suez Canal.

To Tenterden, Wilson's scheme of extending consuls was 'wildly impractical and would not stand examination'. He minuted 'I cannot think that such a policy is judicious or would be really politically useful. The system of pitting English consuls against French consuls is incompatible with the present manner in which our Consular Service is conducted.' To be successful it must be backed by bribes and 'the unscrupulous use of the political authorities'. The real way to counteract French influence, Tenterden added, 'is by straight forward diplomacy at Constantinople, Paris and not by Consular bickerings in which an English consul is invariably worsted'.

FO opposition to consular piquet schemes of any stripe was hardening, even though the alternative, missions such as those conducted by Napier, McGregor and Burnaby, were even more disruptive. Throughout 1881 the Foreign Office had professed scepticism of the plan to extend the line further down towards the canal. This suited Gladstone and, just before the invasion of Egypt, the War Office wrote to the Foreign Office that with the exception of Major Henry Trotter, now the attaché in Constantinople, there were no longer any places for British military officers in Ottoman western Asia.

But the ID did not give up. Major General Sir Archibald Alison, MacDougall's replacement as head of the Department, agreed with Wilson. Had nothing been learned in Constantinople? How could Britain deal effectively with the French or the Khedive from a standpoint of ignorance? Events were moving rapidly in Egypt, there was real unrest and now blood was being shed. Accurate, up-to-date intelligence was needed, but the government was not in a mood to listen and no new consuls were appointed.

The ID kept up as much pressure as it could muster. Just after the second uprising on 9 September 1881, the Department formally petitioned the Foreign Office through the War Office to allow an officer to examine the canal afresh. Lord Granville, the Foreign Secretary, turned it down saying normal Foreign Office channels would no doubt serve. The ball in their court, the ID batted it back with a highly complex questionnaire about railways and harbour facilities. The FO had no means of answering the questions put and, probably to their irritation, ended up asking a retired Indian officer, Major General Sir Frederick Goldsmid, to provide the facts. When nothing had been received by November, Alison again applied to send an observer to the canal. Granville again told him to wait. Events, however, grew no better for the waiting and the Cabinet stumbled under the increasing weight of Disraeli's legacy.

In December Granville at the Foreign Office, Northbrook at the Admiralty and Childers at the War Office met to consider the deteriorating situation. Alison and Captain (later Vice-Admiral Sir Edward) Rice of the Admiralty were invited to join their discussion. Alison was not happy. Like his predecessors discussing Turkey, Alison had little fuel for their deliberations. The FO had just informed him that there was virtually no news. This, and the 'poor' and 'indiscreet' nature of Goldsmid's report on the canal when it finally came, caused Alison to press once more for an experienced intelligence officer to be sent to Egypt. But it was all to no avail.[133]

Frustrated, the Department resorted to other means. This time Major (later Major General Sir Alexander) Tulloch, RE provided the answer. Tulloch was in the ID mould through and through. He had introduced himself to the ID in 1875 when he submitted papers to MacDougall on the Carlist Wars and Belgian and Egyptian defences. This enterprising placement-by-essay was possibly unique but it worked and in 1876 he was attached to the Department, preparing home defence schemes. After his period at the ID or quite possibly because of it, he found himself in Portsmouth where he was to supervise the embarkation of troops bound for the First South African War. As he himself admitted, he was exceedingly bored and seeing the need to recoup, requested six weeks leave to go snipe shooting ... in Egypt. Sir Garnet Wolseley, the Quartermaster General (1880–82), quickly approved Tulloch's request without referring it any further and sent him straight to the ID for instructions. When Tulloch announced his sporting plans to Alison, the head of the ID exclaimed: 'Thank goodness you are going! We wanted to send out two officers some time ago, but it was forbidden.' Tulloch was briefed and left for Egypt in January 1882 with shooting snipe low on his list of priorities.[34]

Tulloch had a difficult task. Single-handedly he had to analyse the nature of the threat and potential operations from three different viewpoints: those of an Anglo-French force, Britain supporting Turkish forces or, as was increasingly likely, Britain going it alone. He also had to lay the groundwork for sabotage and the recruitment of operatives.

Tulloch found that because of the amateurish spying of another 'English tourist' (probably Goldsmid) he was often under surveillance. Nevertheless he photographed the locks at Ismailia and made friends with the few Britons in Egyptian service. At Zagazig he arranged for the British telegraph superintendent to look out for likely interpreters and the most reliable contracting firms 'in the event of an occupation of the country'. He also toured the Cairo-Ismailia-Suez Railway and 'arranged with the [English] manager of that line that, in the event of an intervention being imminent he should contrive to have a huge amount of rolling stock and engines at Zagazig for some plausible reason, and, at the last moment, he was to send them down the line where an accident was to be contrived which would prevent their being brought back'.

His enquiries led him to believe that disaffected Egyptian officers were busy perfecting waterproof dynamite and submarine explosives, devices which they would not hesitate to use to block the canal in the case of an armed intervention. In that event the Urâbîsts might well become reckless and to get a chance of success would obstruct the canal by sinking all the ships they could and by calling out the Bedouins who would swarm on the canal banks... Consequently it is very necessary to consider what force naval and military should be ready in the Mediterranean to prevent the Egyptians interfering with our eastern shipping trade, on the supposition that the Turks might go to Cairo and that we should confine ourselves to keeping the canal open.

A French company was trading in the requisite waterproof explosives and Tulloch believed the Egyptians were about to obtain enough of them to put the *bouche de canal* out of action should they wish. So when the French salesman returned to France, Tulloch waited until he was aboard his ship then telegraphed the man's description far and wide as fitting that of one of the Phoenix Park murderers for whom there was a sizeable reward. The dynamite merchant never returned to Egypt.[135]

Back at the ID, Alison kept up the pressure on the government to legitimise the collection effort. Finally, in February 1882, Granville and the Consul General, Edward (later Sir Edward) Malet, in Cairo agreed to Alison's request for an officer to visit Egypt 'with the object of obtaining and forwarding at once to this country such information as is necessary to enable detailed arrangements for an exped[ition] to be matured in this country on a perfectly sound and reliable basis'. Tulloch, now legitimate, finished his collecting and planning and began writing his report in the spring of 1882.

By this time, Gladstone simply walked out of the picture. He was both unwilling and unable to come to grips with the concern over Egypt and the diplomatic to-ing and fro-ing between London, Constantinople and Paris. Two days before the British and French sent a stiff note to the Khedive deploring the deteriorating situation and threatening action, Gladstone called upon Childers to lower the Army's budget. He apparently knew nothing of Tulloch's mission and two months after it was officially condoned, casually asked Granville if there was any source of information on Egypt besides that found in the newspapers or diplomatic telegrams.

More importantly, Gladstone failed to understand the growing French Anglophobia or to comprehend the worsening situation sufficiently to assist Granville in turning it to Britain's advantage. He lived in hope that the Powers would take a united stand and was disappointed in the French refusal to subscribe to Granville's call for the Porte to restore order in Egypt using the Turkish Army. Gambetta's memory was being twisted into something approaching xenophobia and the mood of the French Chamber was such that there was no longer any hope for French participation in any concerted international action. The surprise at this attitude was purely Gladstone's. France's designs on Tunis, its intrigue in the monitored Turkish provinces, its havering over Egypt and a mood of general colonial aggrandisement seeped from every telegram, every memorandum and every report arriving at the Foreign Office.[136]

On 11–12 June 1882, inspired riots occurred in Alexandria. Both France and Britain considered the canal to be directly threatened and despatched fleets to Alexandria. On 15 June, Gladstone forbade the unilateral despatch of British troops to accompany the Navy. Then on 16 June, Tulloch's report, which had been confidentially printed and held ready since May, was officially sent by the ID to the Foreign Office and the Cabinet. Cast into the pond at this point, even the cautious Tenterden urged the preparation of an expedition and the alerting of Indian troops. Hartington, Northbrook, Childers (the splinter Cabinet of moderate Liberals who were taking measure of the situation) and the service chiefs used the report to bring enough pressure on Gladstone so that on 21 June he reluctantly agreed to allow two battalions to prepare for embarkation. The Suez Canal directors were told to take 'every precaution' against sabotage and Tulloch and Sir Cooper Key, First Lord of the Admiralty, were formally asked for their advice on the best way to protect the canal if the nationalists made their move.[137]

At last the ID contingency plans drawn up by MacDougall in 1875 were in play. Tulloch left for Alexandria immediately and on 29 June the two battalions left England under the command, somewhat surprisingly perhaps, of Alison. Back in London, Gladstone vainly hoped the Khedive would somehow give the Powers assurances that the canal would remain open and a week later he complained to Granville that it was impossible, for him at any rate, to understand what was going on.[138]

Matters were indeed moving rapidly. During the first week of July, the splinter Cabinet continued to hold Egyptian affairs in their hands, even though each step 'seemed to be dictated by circumstances rather than will'. Childers at the War Office had constituted a Confidential Mobilisation Committee on 29 June, including MacDougall, which met almost daily during the crisis. It became the key decision-making body. Its first action was to wire for Ardagh, who, having returned from the Turco-Greek Boundary Commission, was teaching at the School of Military Engineering (later the Royal School of Military Engineering, Chatham). Given no notice and charged with the gravest secrecy, Ardagh left to join Tulloch on 6 July. Presuming he would be watched, he chose Belgium as his cover destination.

The day before Ardagh left, Gladstone professed his opposition to landing a force to guard the canal. The next day, however, Childers authorised more British troops to go east to Gibraltar and arranged for a company of sappers from the Rock to meet Alison's two infantry battalions in Malta. The game was afoot.[139]

Upon arriving in Egypt, Tulloch immediately obtained Goldsmid's services and together they operated a civil-action-cum-intelligence department off the decks of HMS *Invincible*. They set up an Arabic press and published proclamations. Tulloch also put his plans for an agent network into operation, a service which proved so effective that Urâbî later complained that the English major knew more about the coastal fortresses than he did.

And the expedition set sail with more intelligence on the proposed area of operations than any British force in history. A week before it left, the Department published a 461-page *Handbook on Egypt* complete with politics, customs, details of the canal, even the number of bakers in provincial towns and their daily turnover. Closely following it were coloured maps of lower Egypt. But the ID's main contribution, then and in the months following, was the provision of intelligence officers. Ardagh to Alexandria, Tulloch to the canal, Gill into the desert to the Bedouin tribes and Alison as commander of the expedition.[140]

‡

The French and British fleets were gathered off Alexandria when on 11 July the British admiral's rusty French (he thought a Nationalists' signal using the French '*demander*' meant 'demand') was said to have inspired him to begin shelling Alexandria. Oddly, as it worked out, the French set sail leaving the British to it. Alison, who had been impatiently waiting at Lymasol, embarked his troops on his own authority (Childers had told him to wait) and headed straight for the canal. When he neared Port Said, Admiral Hoskins rushed out to inform him that the Nationalists had fired Alexandria on 12 July. Alison thereupon veered away from the canal towards Alexandria, landing to restore order on 17 July. There he met Tulloch, who was able to give him a complete order of battle on all Urâbî's forces and their locations.

Ardagh now also reached Alexandria and as he had done in Constantinople began a close examination of the city's defences and water supply. Gill and Professor Palmer, a Cambridge don who had offered his services, headed for the desert to suborn the Bedouins and ensure the telegraph wires were not cut. Unfortunately for them, they were betrayed and murdered.

The French were astonished by Britain's unilateral, rapid and well-planned action. They made overtures of co-operation by asking to see Tulloch's 16 June report which led to the despatch of troops, but this was refused. Egypt was now a British show and a British show alone.[141]

Armed with Tulloch's report, Admiral Sir William Hewett occupied the canal on 2 August and on 14 August Granville gave him orders to keep it clear by force if necessary. Thanks to Tulloch, the Navy had no trouble occupying Ismailia and the Ismailia–Suez railway and the canal was indeed safe. Whether de Lesseps, the builder and manager of the canal, had simultaneously done a deal with Urâbî to keep the canal open is a moot point. What is certain is that the British on the spot, securely holding the canal, now began to consolidate their hold over the rest of Egypt and its administration. This was not what Mr Gladstone had intended.

However, Urâbî and his forces were still on the loose. Troops were en route from Britain and in mid-August Sir Garnet Wolseley arrived to take overall command. As he had in the Ashanti Ring, he brought with him bright, young intelligence officers of proven ability, notably Kitchener, Fraser and Maurice. Alison, junior in rank to Wolseley, took the first brigade in the Second Division. Colonel (later General Sir Redvers) Buller arrived to head the field intelligence effort, which 'exceedingly disgusted' Tulloch, who at that late stage was robbed of his chance to see his efforts through. But it all came to a head on 13 September when, as Tulloch had predicted, the Nationalists took their stand against the British at Tel-el-Kebir and were resoundingly defeated. Egyptian history was entering a new era.

So how did matters stand? Since 1875, the ID and the ID alone had supplied the military intelligence, analysis and prompting upon which the British had taken Cyprus as a *place d'armes*, extended the line of military consuls in the Levant and made sure of Egypt. All within six years. Commenting on the victory, Salisbury told Northcote that any congratulations should go to Northbrook at the Admiralty and Childers at the War Office 'for the successes have been purely departmental'.[142]

Gladstone's contribution to Britain's unilateral action in Egypt was to sweep up after it and square it with the other Powers. He wanted to place the Egyptian military, police, financial and local institutions on as sound a footing as could be in as short a space of time as possible and then hold a conference on Egypt's future (like the Congress of Berlin). After this the British would withdraw. The very people who would be tending to the infrastructure, however, were Intelligence Department officers who appear yet again, this time to steer Egypt, indeed the whole Empire, into a course the Grand Old Man never envisaged.

The Liberal government had overseen the dispersal of the Egyptian Army, upon which the Khedive's authority rested, and restored him to his throne by dint of their infidel army. Granville could only say that it was the policy of the government to uphold the Khedive. To this Salisbury replied:

> You have not held up the Khedive, you have picked up the Khedive. Nothing could be more widely opposed than those two processes in their results. Unless we are prepared … [to] leave Egypt to an anarchy which is inconsistent with all our professions and fatal to our interests, he must be sustained by that which is the only thing left upright in that land – namely the power of Great Britain.[143]

Enter then again the concept of consuls and a new contributor to the debate, viz Philip (later first Baron) Currie, who had been a précis writer to both lords Clarendon and Salisbury and as the Assistant Permanent Under-Secretary of State was, in effect, the senior civil servant in the Eastern Department of the FO. He worked closely with Salisbury and Home during the gestation of the Eastern Question and the acquisition of Cyprus. He cautiously depreciated Gladstone's stand against consuls and thought it 'a pity that their knowledge of eastern languages and habits should not be utilised'. Granville, his interest now awakened, asked Currie what he had in mind. Currie immediately wrote a memorandum suggesting the despatch of Wilson (now Lieutenant Colonel Sir Charles) and two or three of the other ex-consuls to Egypt:

> Chermside, Stewart, Clayton and Everett are all first rate men and have been employed for the last two or three years in collecting information in Turkey and communicating with Officials. Their services

would I think be of great value, either as members of an Intelligence Department under the direction of Sir C. Wilson (who was formerly employed in the Intelligence branch of the War Office) or to be attached to the British military and Naval Commanding Officers for the purpose of procuring intelligence and communicating with the natives. In the event of a Turkish force cooperating with us in Egypt, Sir C. Wilson would be specially fitted for the post of Commissioner with Vice Consuls acting as deputy Commissioners.

Even Tenterden agreed. 'Sir C. Wilson would make an admirable Commissioner and it would be a mistake not to avail ourselves of the services of men specially trained and used to dealing with Turks and Orientals. It will be a difficult job and we shall want all the ability available.'

Childers, too, thought Wilson would make an excellent commissioner, suggesting to Granville: 'Could you not attach Sir C. Wilson and some of the V.C.s to Malet or whoever is to be our Political Representative in Egypt, and let them be available for us as matters advance?' This gave the proposal the head of steam it needed and it went to Lord Dufferin, then Ambassador to the Porte, who agreed. The deal was done. The FO assigned Wilson, Stewart and Chermside directly to Malet in Cairo and continued to pay their salaries.[144]

Although two of the vice consuls, Stewart and Chermside, had never been formally posted to the ID they had, as Currie noted, acquired their intelligence training serving under Wilson. Chermside was a tall, striking Etonian who had passed first into Woolwich. Like many intelligence officers, he had a taste for adventure and won a reputation for reliability on Leigh Smith's Arctic expedition. He went to Turkey with the other intelligence/engineer officers in 1876 and stayed to work with Wilson on the Turkish Boundary Commission and as consul in Anatolia. After a year on the frontier in Kurdistan, he spent the next decade as military attaché in Constantinople. He was an accomplished linguist, who had a photographic memory – a trait he shared with Ardagh - and was as fluent in court Turkish as he was in street Arabic.

Chermside's peer, Stewart (later briefly Major General Sir Herbert), also knew Arabic. A Wykehamist, graduate of the Staff College and a member of the Inner Temple, he had served under the late Major General George Pomeroy Colley at Majuba in the First South African War in 1881. With the invasion of Egypt, Stewart joined the cavalry and was responsible for the swift taking of Cairo and its citadel. He was an XIth Hussar and cut such a figure that even the highly critical Kitchener considered him the finest soldier he had ever met. Together with Baring, who was brought in to be effectively Chancellor of the Egyptian Exchequer, these three extraordinary officers were to exercise in Egypt that reforming influence which Salisbury had hoped that they might have exercised in Asia Minor.

Wilson was delighted with his new assignment, not only professionally but as a first-rate amateur archaeologist. A few days after the battle at Tel-el-Kebir, Wilson landed and went directly to the *Mouseion* to prevent looting and then secured the Museum of Antiquities at Boulac. But that was the icing on the cake. The real work to be done, if peace and stability were to be the order of the day, was the rapid rebuilding of infrastructure and good governance. Looking at all the presenting problems in detail, Wilson addressed himself to healing one of Egypt's largest running sores: its prisons. A wide range of legal and prison reforms put into effect rapidly and publicly was the result. With Alison's help he secured a fair trial for Urâbî and served as a general referee on the court, all of which astounded the Egyptians.[145]

With such reform underway, Wilson was ready to address the future of the disgruntled and largely disbanded Egyptian Army. By late September 1882 he laid plans before the Cabinet to reinstate it, creating a new Egyptian Army of 10,000 with an ethnically mixed officer corps, a gendarmerie and military schools. In order to make it work, Wilson stressed the need for a cadre of English officers from the active list to serve as advisers.

Again, this did not coincide with Gladstone's objective of leaving Egypt as fast as he could. In his wake Granville, too, questioned this part of Wilson's plan, but Alison, General Officer Commanding

British troops in Egypt, considered it an immediate operational matter and approved Wilson's scheme on 22 February 1883, without, apparently, further recourse to the government.[146] By March when General Sir Evelyn Wood arrived to assume the mantle of Sirdar or General Officer Commanding the Egyptian force, Chermside, now all of thirty-two years old, was already in place with an elite infantry battalion; Fraser had insinuated himself into the post of Adjutant and Quartermaster General; Kitchener (who was much brought on by Wilson) became second-in-command of a cavalry regiment and Charles Watson, another Royal Engineer, Arabic scholar and later Wilson's biographer, became Surveyor General, from which position he made it his business to keep 'a general eye' over the Minister for War.

Needless to say, the rest of the British Army in Egypt and at home looked upon the new advisers as a new Ashanti Ring, 'favoured' whilst smugly predicting that the Egyptians would never make soldiers, even less dependable officers. As early as July 1882 Tulloch and Watson had to disagree publicly with this view, but the patronising attitude towards the Egyptians and their British officers by many in the British military party in Cairo, unfortunately led by Wolseley, was only dispelled by successes in the field in the late 1880s and 1890s. They also regarded those officers who had thrown their lot in with the 'Gyps' as *outré*. All too many British officers found all this language and customs business, coupled with running around the desert with ragtag Egyptians, simply unnecessary. Moreover there was the imperishable stigma of being involved with intelligence, another murky sideline. This disapproval did not die for many years and flavoured many subsequent events.

Meanwhile, Wilson and his colleagues got on with rebuilding the Egyptian Army not only to bolster the Khedive, but to address the growing political problems to the south in the Sudan. After years of uneven rule over the vast regions south of Wadi Halfa, the Egyptians were largely pushed aside by an alternative, indigenous government, the charismatic leader of which maintained he was the Prophet, elect of God to rule. This was Mohammed Ahmed, the Mahdi, who was said to lead an army of several tribes numbering 10,000 by some, by others 100,000. In any event, Wilson was convinced that the Mahdi and his followers, labelled Dervishes in a generic lump by the British, were a major threat to Egypt's stability and that Cairo was largely to blame for the Mahdi's ascendency and popularity with the people. If the term Dervish was meant as an appellation for all Mahdists, then it was repaid in kind by the Mahdi who labelled every Egyptian and Briton as 'Turks' and loathed them all.

The Sudan was alive and Wilson told Malet at the Embassy that the weak, disordered and expensive state of the Sudan had been brought about by 'the useless conquests ... strained relations with the Abyssinians and the manner in which trade had been forced along an unnatural route down the Nile, instead of allowing it to follow the road to its natural outlet at Souakin'.

The Mahdist movement capitalised on this misrule and Wilson predicted that a greater portion of the Sudanese people would willingly join the Prophet if he secured a capital, namely Khartoum. As for the Mahdi himself, he had already announced his intention of leading his people to Mecca, directly through corrupt, impure and infidel-ridden Egypt, Egypt without a serviceable army to defend it.

Thus in September and October 1882, Wilson wrote two memoranda for London in which he forcefully outlined his plans to secure the Sudan to Egypt, eliminate the Mahdi and make the province pay. From the first, Wilson made the case for binding the Sudan to Egypt, no doubt because of the revenues it could produce for the insolvent and unstable Egyptian government and partly because of the very real threat to Egypt and the canal itself.

He reckoned that if the Khedive's government were to withdraw its southernmost garrisons and fix a line at Khartoum (then defended by demoralised units of the Egyptian Army under the command of an English officer, William Hicks, who carried the Egyptian rank of pasha or general), allow the reopening of the Suakin–Berber trade route, make peace with the Abyssinians over land disputes and create a free port at Messoweh for Sudanese and Abyssinians alike, then much would be put right. Alongside would stand a new Egyptian Army, peppered with British officers, and an eager Royal Navy interdicting slavery from the Red Sea. If these plans were effected, Egypt's southern problem would be solved at a stroke.

Key to this was crushing the Mahdi before he consolidated his power base. Wilson plainly told Malet and Granville that:

Khartoum may fall soon, and consequence may be so serious as to necessitate despatch of a large force from England. The relief of Khartoum must be effected from Souakin. English officers should be sent at once to Khartoum to organize defences and report on the real state of affairs. [An] Indian contingent should be stopped at Aden, with a view to its eventually operating from Khartoum; 5,000 infantry with due proportion of cavalry and artillery, might be sufficient. Points to meet False Prophet would be at Korobut and Assuan, if he advances this way. Reappointment of [Major General Charles] Gordon Pasha or another Englishman is recommended. Direction of military operations against the False Prophet should be placed in the hands of General commanding Her Majesty's troops in Egypt, as the only available troops are British, and British officers must be largely employed.

Wilson wanted more intelligence:

I think that, considering the present excitable state of the Muslem population of Turkey, Syria, and Egypt, and the general uneasy feeling with reference to the events which are to occur in 1300AH, and the appearance of the Mahdi in that year, it would be advisable to send two English officers to the Soudan to report on the state of the country and the steps which will be necessary to ensure its pacification.

Alison, Malet and the War Office seconded the proposal and Granville reluctantly agreed. Thus on 28 October 1882, Wilson's subordinate, Stewart, was allowed to embark on his 'quasi-military' mission, the

British government taking no responsibility. Gordon's appointment, for which Wilson argued long and loud, required a longer campaign to bring about.[147]

It was the spectre of an invasion into Egypt proper by the Mahdists as set out in Wilson's memoranda that led those on the ground to reject the Liberals' avowed policy of leaving Egypt within a year. Indeed the British advisers were going about the business of evacuating Egypt by entrenching. Although the Cabinet was at sixes and sevens about Egypt, even it realised that a lasting withdrawal could only be secured if the necessary reforms were undertaken. To this end the government called the Marquess of Dufferin and Ava from Constantinople to Cairo. Dufferin brought with him an immense reputation as a career diplomat. Early on in his career in Syria, he prevented the French from making the Lebanon a client state. He had then gone on to be Under-Secretary of State for War in the mid-1860s and Governor General of Canada between 1872 and 1878. He was the British Ambassador to Russia from 1879–81 before becoming Ambassador in Constantinople in 1881.

As soon as he arrived, Dufferin took Wilson as his chief adviser. Dufferin worked well with Wilson and the other intelligence officers, indeed it had been he who had recommended them. Malet was due to be promoted to Brussels and Dufferin proposed Wilson (who was but a few days away from a brevet colonelcy) to fill the post of 'Colonial Governor' over Egypt, provided Baring was not to be put forward. From that position Wilson was to 'exercise surveillance' over the Khedive and Egypt.

Meanwhile, the French, still angry at Britain's *coup de main*, made exercising notional 'dual control' over the Khedive's affairs almost impossible and in December Dufferin offered up Wilson to stand in as financial adviser to the Khedive. Sir Auckland Colvin, then English Controller of Egyptian Finance, Northbrook and Granville supported him, although Colvin wrote that he found Wilson 'so quiet & silent that he hardly filled the eye'. Wilson accepted on 13 July 1883 but withdrew, probably with no little relief, when the Egyptians requested a trained and proven financier.[148]

Dufferin soon learned that Wilson and Malet had absolutely no intention of turning their backs on the Sudan and he came to agree with them. Together they reasoned that a Sudan loyal to Egypt would also patrol the Red Sea shore. A Sudan loyal to Egypt would help control or even abolish the slave trade. A Sudan loyal to Egypt would produce much-needed revenues to help free the Khedive from his French creditors.

Wilson thought the first step must be the introduction of good government at Khartoum, much as he had wanted to do in Anatolia. By serving the tribes of the Sudan, parleying with the Abyssinians and understanding both, Wilson hoped to begin binding the Sudan to Egypt with prosperity for all. That was why he and the other intelligence officers were sensitive to the Sudanese wish to trade through Suakin and why he was insistent on defeating the Mahdists, who not only rivalled the Egyptians in governance of a sort, but were daily becoming an increasingly creditable military threat to Egypt itself.

Although Hartington at the War Office and Northbrook at the Admiralty agreed with him, Gladstone and Granville, intent on evacuating Egypt as rapidly as possible, refused to permit the serious military blow in the Sudan which Wilson insisted would be needed to set his reforms in motion.

The problem was that the government in London was living in a parallel universe. When the Egyptian government off its own bat ordered Hicks Pasha to take 6,000 of his troops and retake Kordofan in the south in November 1883, Granville forbade Malet to convey to the Egyptians the danger he and his colleagues felt the proposed expedition would be under. Living under the legal fiction that the Egyptian government was independent, Granville refused to allow Malet to offer any advice or support: 'Her Majesty's Government could assume no responsibility for the conduct of affairs in the Soudan.'

‡

Hicks and his force were slaughtered almost to a man. The victorious Mahdists continued their advance and within days Khartoum, 'with its now miserably attenuated' garrison, was in danger. That was not all. In the eastern Sudan, one of the Mahdi's lieutenants, Uthmān abū Bakr Diqna (Osman Digna), was besieging the forts of Sinkat and Tokar near the Red Sea coast. The Egyptians having no real army to send to their relief and British troops confined to barracks by order of the government in London, it was left to a small corps of gendarms under Baker Pasha to relieve the forts. It too was destroyed in its first engagement with the Mahdists, losing almost three quarters of its strength.

When news reached London, the public was confused and cross. Votes of censure were moved in both Houses on 12 February. As Lord Salisbury's daughter, Lady Gwendolen Cecil, put it: 'Popular feeling was now rising in England, and under its pressure and assisted by who knows what subterranean processes of Cabinet controversy [i.e. the splinter group], the ministerial obsession of irresponsibility was abandoned.' During the next few weeks the government advanced by swift stages from pure detachment to advice, from advice to insistence, from insistence to action. The Khedive was told to renounce his responsibility over the Sudan and it was to be evacuated.

Gladstone's special envoy, Dufferin, was deeply disappointed. He wrote to Ardagh, the Commanding Royal Engineer in Egypt and chief of British forces intelligence:

> It pains me to think that Khartoum and the command of a thousand miles of uninterrupted river navigation is to be relinquished. I had always hoped that under our guiding hand the Egyptian administration in the Soudan might prove a civilising influence. Now I conclude that [the] whole of those districts will lapse into a Nigritian Pandemonium.[149]

This was the way it was shaping up yet no matter how much Gladstone wanted to show a clean pair of heels, from then on the fortunes of the Sudan, Egypt and Britain were thoroughly entwined. Early in January 1884, Wilson's 1883 memorandum on the Sudan was tabled at Cabinet. That was the memorandum in which Wilson argued that the best course was to secure Suakin, keep the Suakin–Berber road open and post a strong Egyptian force at Aswan. There was just enough time, he argued, to organise the local tribes against the Mahdist advance but that depended on a strong British presence from Suakin to Khartoum. Without that presence, Khartoum would surely fall to the Mahdi. Once peace was restored, a notable and powerful local chieftain like al-Zubair Pasha Rahma Mansūr might be approached to become a regional governor.

Wilson then went on to propose that the assistance of the Abyssinians be purchased to wage a final push on the Mahdists in exchange for concessions of Sudanese border lands. He then rounded off his ideas with the insistence that a British officer be sent forward for intelligence purposes and possibly to organise the resistance at Khartoum. He concluded:

If the Mahdi is allowed to remain supreme in the Soudan the effect on the finances of Egypt, already in a bad way, will be disastrous. The constant fear of his advance down the Nile, and of an outbreak of religious fanaticism caused by his emissaries will keep the whole country in a state of unrest; paralyse all attempts to introduce reforms; prevent the investment of capital; and necessitate the retention of a British force in Egypt for an unknown period...[150]

Gladstone read Wilson's memorandum and told Granville that whilst he had been 'most struck' by it, he was nevertheless still suspicious of military advice and forbade the very British effort which Wilson's scheme required. Thus the Cabinet aligned with Wilson's hopeful futurology without sanctioning the means for him to achieve it.[151]

The opposition came to learn of all this and on 16 February 1884 carried a motion of censure on the Gladstone government's conduct of the whole affair. In pressing their point they demanded that the government produce Wilson's 'preliminary enquiry'. As Wilson had argued that increased involvement in the short run was the only way out of Egypt in the long run, it was hardly surprising that the Cabinet refused to produce his memorandum.[152]

Turning to Wilson's other recommendations, the Cabinet ordered the taking of Suakin, but only just in time. General Graham with a small British force landed there in the face of mounting Mahdist pressure after Sinkat and Tokar, two outposts of Suakin, had fallen to Osman Digna. Graham then countered with successes at el Teb and Tamai in February and March 1884 and looked forward to Berber. Ardagh was there and planned to secure Graham's advance with buffer upon buffer of tribal alliances along the way to keep the road open. Hartington assisted by despatching Chermside to Graham's force 'as an officer accustomed to dealing with Arabs, to carry on negotiations with Sheikhs'. From the other end, Wilson proposed sending six Arabic-speaking officers with 'experience in dealing with natives' directly to Berber where they were to set up an intelligence screen to monitor the situation there and in Khartoum. It was in this capacity that Kitchener, the future Sirdar, and Captain (later General Sir Leslie) Rundle were ordered to Berber.

Acting on that portion of Wilson's report which suggested Gordon's deployment, a Cabinet committee of Hartington, Northbrook, Granville and Sir Charles Dilke authorised Gordon to go to Khartoum even though Granville, and others no doubt, suspected him of being 'a little cracked'. Wilson's deputy, Stewart, was to go with him. Wilson himself would have stood in Gordon's shoes had not Granville wanted him for what Sir Julian Pauncefote, the Foreign Office's legal expert, called his 'special knowledge'.[153]

‡

The rest of this story is a tragedy authored by dithering in London and in the Sudan, by hugely difficult terrain and an able enemy. And, above all, the whole episode need never have happened. As it was, it seared itself into the mind of the British nation as an avoidable failure. As Watson Pasha, Wilson's biographer, put it: 'Unfortunately the British Government failed to realise the intimate connection between Egypt and the Soudan, and disclaimed any responsibility for the latter.' Gordon had been sent to Khartum to withdraw the remaining Egyptian troops and soon found himself besieged. As noted above, Colonel Sir Henry Stewart and Wilson set out to tell Gordon that a British force was coming to relieve him. On the way, marked by sharp engagements with the Mahdists and constant sniping and harassment, Stewart was fatally wounded and Wilson took over. For easily understandable (and blameable) reasons he did not arrive in time and to quote Wilson's biographer again it was just as well. 'Imagine what Gordon would have felt had Wilson met him in the midst of the starving people and given him the message: "I am not sent to help you and cannot stop with you, but there will probably be a British force to relieve you in about six weeks."'

The operation began well enough. Then, when Sir H. Stewart's column was only a fortnight away from Berber, Gladstone, like some huge vulture, suddenly vetoed the expedition. He blamed the poor climate and high risk.[154] Outflanked at every turn by members of his Cabinet, his special envoy, his diplomats and the soldiers, he rued the landing at Suakin as much as he regretted the appointment of Gordon. Kitchener and Rundle were suddenly recalled and the partially constructed consular piquet line disappeared. Stewart, as disgusted as Gordon by Gladstone's shilly-shallying, realised the game was up and wrote to Baring: 'I shall therefore follow the fortunes of General Gordon.'[155]

The Mahdi then upped the stakes by cutting the telegraph between Shendy and Berber. Then news reached Cairo that the Bahr el Ghazal and Berber had fallen. Regular communications with Khartoum were also soon lost, so that by May 1884 the remaining Egyptian garrisons in the Sudan were wholly at the Mahdi's mercy. Fortunately for them, British forces had not been forced to leave Suakin and from there Chermside (since October 1883 Governor of the Red Sea Littoral) negotiated with the Abyssinians to secure an escape route for the isolated garrisons. As matters stood, Wilson's Suakin–Berber strategy had been sabotaged and Wolseley and Wilson now tried to make the best of a botched job by agreeing to station the Egyptian garrison at Wadi Halfa where it could defend Egypt and 'give much moral support' to Gordon. The ID in London then suggested keeping the main body of troops at Aswan to cover 'all the Nile Valley that is *worth holding*', retaining Wadi Halfa and Korosko as frontier posts. On 4 April 1884, Hartington agreed using almost the identical phrases as the ID used in its reasoning.[156]

Yet the harvest of half-measures was not over. Gordon refused to withdraw. Hartington asked Wolseley for an operations plan to pluck Gordon off of his branch 'occupying little time and leaving no trace behind it'. Wolseley thereupon planned a four-to-six-week push up the Nile on his best Red River model, commanded by himself. Gladstone was so pleased that he suddenly became deeply involved in this project, bizarrely involving himself in the minutiae of staff work whilst generally criticising the ID for not knowing enough about the Sudan. For example, the Grand Old Man fretted over the changing water level of the Nile and thought that an English businessman would be better at measuring it than either a naval or military engineer. On 23 April, he dashed off a note to Northbrook: 'I have little doubt that you have not let drop the question of the Nile at high flood, which was opened yesterday at the Cabinet & wh. our "intelligence" department seems to be woefully behindhand.'[157]

As will be discussed in a later chapter, Wolseley was immensely strong willed. Virtually no other senior officer agreed with him in choosing the river route. Even the Duke of Cambridge sided with Wilson and other officers with Sudanese experience. Ardagh, who had measured the Nile in February, concluded that any expedition up-river would be a tricky business at best, requiring portages of 140 miles in one place and 241 in another. Hartington told Gladstone that Wilson believed that 'Wolseley had underrated the difficulties and delay of the Nile route, and [Wilson] thinks that the Suakin-Berber route, which has always been used by the Egyptians, should be used, at all events, in parts'.[158]

Over half the Cabinet agreed with Hartington and Wilson. Northbrook now was the one to become cautious. He was alive to the 'grave political difficulties' which would occur if something as permanent as a railway, for example, were pressed to Berber. Although he knew from Chermside that the opening of the route would have a settling effect on the large and important tribes in the eastern Sudan, he also knew that the intelligence officers on the spot wished to exercise 'some kind of authority' over the Sudan. He was therefore just as leery of the Suakin–Berber plan as he was of Wolseley's scheme.

Despite the Cabinet's misgivings, Hartington received authority in June to 'make some preparations for putting the port of Suakin into a condition to receive the heavy stores required either for a railway or an expedition'. The ID prepared mobilisation plans and provided five members for the small Mobilisation Committee under Alison, but it was not until 8 August 1884, after constant prompting by Hartington, that a vote of credit was passed. Twenty days later, Gladstone approved Wolseley as commander. He certainly did not want the soldiers to build a railway to Berber and complained to Childers that 'any contraction he cd. effect of War Office ideas wd. be a good [thing]'.[59]

Now that an operation was sanctioned, Wilson, who in the meantime had been exiled to the Ordnance Survey in Dublin, hurried back to Egypt to serve as Wolseley's chief of intelligence. With characteristic energy he produced orders of battle, blood-feud lists and long rosters of tribal allegiances; he also made proposals to gain the co-operation of those sheikhs who had not yet joined the Mahdi.

Meanwhile, whilst Wolseley was preparing the expedition, Chermside and the other intelligence officers continued to develop their network of informal influence in the eastern Sudan and with the Abyssinians. Chermside could point to his success in signing a treaty with the Abyssinians to evacuate the Egyptian garrisons; but his resources were limited and although he constantly laboured to gain the confidence of the lesser tribes around Suakin and Agig, the British government never allowed him to reap the reward of such friendships. By December 1884, the tribes having received little help from the British faded away to Osman Digna. An Englishman who was a long-term resident of Suakin angrily wrote:

In these circumstances it is to be regretted that HM Government should, by permitting the employment of their own officers in active service, in a manifestly hopeless cause, have given an indirect encouragement to a course which it is clear they expected would have a calamitous termination, or they would not have taken every occasion to disclaim any responsibility.[160]

On 30 December 1884 Wolseley split his forces and Sir H. Stewart crossed the Bayuda Desert towards el Matemma whilst the River Column laboured up the Nile. As Chief of Intelligence, Wilson moved out with Stewart's Desert Column, which, as noted above, suffered most of the way through unrelenting sniper fire and small feints. When Stewart was fatally wounded, the command devolved upon Wilson, who dragged his battered troops across the desert to the Nile where they met the equally brave Egyptian sailors who had kept Gordon's steamers free. Lord Charles Beresford, Wilson's naval brigade commander (who later became crucial in the establishment of the Naval Intelligence Division), made the boats as ready as he could for a reconnaissance up to Khartoum. They arrived two days too late and Mahdist flags flew everywhere over the conquered city.

From January 1885 all Chermside could do was try to save the remaining Egyptian garrisons. Wolseley, beside himself at having failed to rescue Gordon, objected to Chermside raising an irregular force to save Kassala. Chermside told Baring on 6 January 1886 that 'things could not be much worse'. The Liberals denied Chermside the wherewithal to save the Egyptians and Kassala fell in dreadful carnage later in the year. But when it became clear that Gordon was dead, the public outcry in Britain forced the government to give way to Hartington, who now offered Wolseley 12,000 troops and the services of Alison, the former director of the ID, to smash the Mahdi once and for all.[161]

Mentally, Wolseley was in a bad way after losing Gordon. On 10 February, Gladstone warned Hartington that Wolseley, downcast, might cause trouble. He did. The very next day, after almost a year of opposition, Wolseley surprisingly changed his mind and agreed that a Suakin–Berber railway was needed. Hartington immediately sent him fifty miles of track and rolling stock to Suakin only to have Wolseley change his mind again. Hartington was 'much embarrassed' by this *volte face* and on 12 March forbade Wolseley to make any pronouncement about the future of the Sudan, nor to style himself Governor General as he wished to do.[162] The government and Wolseley were wholly fed up with each other. Hartington was disgusted with Wolseley[163] and Wolseley was disgusted with the government. As he angrily wrote in his diary:

> I hope if this [the war with Russia, which as noted in a previous chapter was simply another scare] is forced upon us now, the people in their anger may lynch the coward Harcourt, hang the plucky Gladstone & throw Dilke and Chamberlain into the rain. As for men of the Northbrook calibre, merely tar, feather, and kick them with the contempt they deserve.[164]

Meanwhile, Wolseley and some of the British press tried to lay the blame for Gordon's death at Wilson's door. Wolseley wrote to Hartington: 'I gather from the tenor of your telegrams about Sir C. Wilson that you are surprised I do not praise him. I could not bring myself to do so. From the moment that Stewart was wounded everything went wrong…'[165] When Northbrook described Wilson as a political officer, Wolseley waxed apoplectic, telling Hartington that 'he has been, and is, the head of the Intelligence department, and absolutely nothing more. He collects information for me and keeps the threads in his head of all the complicated connections between tribes but he has no more to do with the policy adopted towards them than I have to do with Lord Northbrook's policy and the Navy.'[166]

Leaving Wolseley to fume, Hartington and Northbrook by-passed him and asked Wilson and Kitchener what Great Britain should next do with the Sudan. Wilson's resulting memorandum could have been written as easily in 1882 as in 1885. He believed that 'control of the Sudan is necessary to Egypt. If abandoned now, it will have to be reconquered in ten years.' In saying this Wilson was not only consistent but prescient. All along he and the other intelligence officers had advocated the retention of the Sudan by smashing the Mahdi and erecting an intelligence screen from Suakin to Berber and up to Khartoum. Again, he advocated the value of weaving local alliances at Suakin and now at Dongola, too, so similar to those which Salisbury and Home had designed for western Asia.

Wilson contended that without these steps in place a withdrawal from Egypt would be impossible. Gordon, Stewart and thousands of men died as Gladstone vacillated. But in his new memorandum Wilson stuck to his conviction that the retention of Dongola with a showpiece local army to defend it was key. Without that informal paramountcy in Dongola, it would be impossible to come to a settlement with the Mahdists from a position of strength. Baring agreed.[167]

But Gladstone had heard it all before and with a finger-hold on office, ordered the total evacuation of the Sudan on 13 June 1885. The Conservatives on assuming office ten days later did nothing to reverse the decision. In December they tidied up the line and agreed to defend Egypt's frontier, holding onto what had been built of the Wadi Halfa railway. In early 1886 the ID recommended that the remaining British troops be withdrawn to Wadi Halfa and when this was accomplished the politicians put Egypt out of their minds.

As for Wilson, he returned to command the Ordnance Survey in June 1885, first in Ireland then as Director General for the whole Survey, a post he held until 1894. And Alison, who had done so much for the Staff College, the Intelligence Department and Egypt, was also cast aside by Wolseley. He returned to Aldershot, was briefly Adjutant General in 1888 and quietly ended his career as a major general on the Council of India.

After this withdrawal of the bulk of British and Egyptian troops, *affaires égyptiennes* receded from the public gaze as well. Barely five months after Gordon's death, the Mahdi himself died, leaving his command to Khalifa Abdulla, a patient and canny disciple who was prepared to bide his time. And so Egypt seemed to slip into a hot, interminable afternoon. Whatever uncertain, and possibly dangerous, night lay far off, no one was concerned about the future, except, as it happened, the Intelligence Department of the War Office.

CHAPTER FIVE

A MOST VALUABLE
DEPARTMENT OF STATE

When Sir Archibald Alison left the Intelligence Department to lead Gladstone into Egypt, affairs in the east were quieting down (albeit briefly). This coincided with a remarkable continuity in Britain's management of foreign affairs. Lord Salisbury became his own Foreign Secretary for seven months between 1885 and 1886, then between January 1887 and August 1892, and again between 1895 and 1900. Meanwhile, the Liberals were anything but united. The Irish Question gnawed at Gladstone and notional leadership of the Liberals, on international matters at least, passed to Lord Hartington. Irritated by the dithering which beset Liberal governments in the early 1880s, Hartington, Granville, and other of the able 'Liberal Imperialists or Liberal Unionists' were drawn into a coalition with the Conservatives on foreign and Irish affairs. Salisbury was even prepared to serve under Hartington but Hartington repeatedly turned down the offer of premiership.

Hartington and Salisbury. It is perhaps surprising that the two scions from two of the oldest houses in England hardly knew each other, but it was so. As Lord Salisbury's daughter recalled, her father 'knew Lord Hartington to speak to, and that was all'. What they did have in common, however, besides agreeing on the Irish Question, was a reasonable knowledge of naval and military issues. During Lord Salisbury's second administration (1886–92), Lord Randolph Churchill, Salisbury's Chancellor of the Exchequer, determined to make major cuts in naval and military expenditure despite the fact that the combined estimates from W. H. Smith and Lord George

Hamilton for the Navy were lower than in 1885. Salisbury would not back the cuts Churchill demanded and Churchill resigned. This allowed the brilliant Liberal financier, George Goschen (he was always very much *Mister* Goschen until he became Viscount Goschen in 1900), to take over as Chancellor with W. H. Smith becoming First Lord of the Treasury. Salisbury again took responsibility for foreign affairs, except for a brief period when it was held by the increasingly ill Lord Iddesleigh, who collapsed and died in front of Salisbury the day after he was dropped from the government.

The co-operation between Hartington and Salisbury matured into a remarkable and agreeable partnership, Salisbury's verve and energy matching Hartington's steadfastness and caution. 'Far better not' was the latter's predictable watchword. Although already familiar with naval and military matters per se, Salisbury was not overly interested in them, leaving the bulk of this work to Hartington. There was considerable public and private unrest following the failure to rescue Gordon and by 1888 it built up to such a head that a long overdue Royal Commission was set up to enquire into the civil and professional administration of the Naval and Military departments and the relation of those departments to each other and the Treasury. It was led by Hartington. As far as the Army was concerned, it failed to usher in a great general staff for which the reformers hoped. On the naval side its management, too, was unreformed but as an effective fighting force it fared better as the Commission led to the Naval Defence Act of 1889, which brought about a quantum leap in the size and power of the Royal Navy. No longer was it the maxim that the combined British fleets should be a third more in size and might than her nearest rival. From 1890 the maxim was that the Royal Navy must be twice that of any other country in the world. This meant that Britain entered the 1890s with orders for a staggering ten new battleships, thirty-eight new cruisers, eighteen torpedo boats and four gunboats – £20 million between 1889 and 1893.

Another area where Salisbury and Hartington had shared experience was in their relations with the Intelligence Department. Both men were used to the ID performing its walk-on part, but in an increasingly complex world frequently as a key player. And the ID needed a larger dressing room, too. Thus in 1885 the Department moved from crowded Adair House to the slightly larger premises at 16–18 Queen Anne's Gate, two eighteenth-century Wyatt town houses. It appeared as it was, 'a secluded and shuttered house which had all the ambiance of the fictional hideout of an Intelligence service'. Still removed from Horse Guards and 'all the more appreciated by us for that reason', the printing establishment went into the basement and the library over it. A constable patrolled the vicinity at night and the Department spent annually some £5 for 'inspection of Fire appliances and instruction of staff in their use' by one of Captain Shaw's officers. Although Queen Anne's Gate was not all they would have wished, it was not as bad as the quarters for the Admiralty's new intelligence function, which were directly under a room used as a dustbin.[168]

Alison's time as head of the Intelligence Department having come to an end whilst he was in Egypt, the Duke of Cambridge replaced him with the former commanding officer of the King's Own Scottish Borderers, Colonel Aylmer Cameron, VC. Cameron was not able to sustain the Department's influence at home, partly because of his comparatively low rank, partly from the Liberals' distrust of soldiers and, no doubt, partly from the ID's stand on retaining Pishin instead of retiring rapidly back to India. Neither did Granville, the Liberals' Foreign Secretary, use the ID as Salisbury had done; initially he looked upon the ID as map makers and jobbing printers.

Despite the flurry of activity in Afghanistan, Persia and the whole of the Ottoman Empire in the early 1880s, surprisingly little military information reached or left the Foreign Office in the period which followed. There was traffic, but what news did arrive was rarely forwarded to the War Office and there is no evidence that much was passed onto the intelligencers as a matter of course. Yet the quietude between 1882 and 1886 was more apparent than real. On one hand, ID officers were learning, indeed inventing, the craft of field intelligence in active operations in Egypt (even more than in the more traditional setting of the First South African War in 1880–81). On the other, the Department was amassing facts about an undefined future, as though storing provisions before an uncertain winter.

In January 1886 the Department received a new director, Brigadier General (later Lieutenant General Sir Henry) Brackenbury, CB. It is quite certain that his appointment had little, if anything, to do with the Duke's approbation or lack of it. In any event, Brackenbury's genius was to tap the ID's factual energy and exploit it. Within five short years he introduced realistic strategic planning into the government's thinking, at the same time raising the ID to the status of an influential and virtually autonomous department of state.

From the existing accounts, Henry Brackenbury was a solitary, restless youth from a solid, middle-class family. He 'attended' Eton for a time as he did a number of other schools. In the early 1850s his disgruntled family sent him to Canada as an articled clerk. This did not suit and the tall, broad young man soon came back, no doubt influenced by his older brother, Charles, to join the Army, passing out from 'the Shop' at Woolwich just in time to experience the horrors of the Crimea. He then returned to the tedium of garrison duties in Britain and, like his brother Charles, began writing on military theory and supporting Cardwell's reforms. In 1868, when he was only thirty-one, he was appointed to the Chair of Military History at Woolwich and remained there until the outbreak of the Franco-Prussian War in 1870 when he inveigled his way to the front as a superintendent of the British National Society for Aid to the Sick and Wounded, which would later become the British Red Cross.

Like Hozier in the Austrian War and Wilson in the Franco-Prussian War, he was one of the few British soldiers to see at first hand large-scale modern warfare. His pen soon gave vent to his reflections on what he had experienced and his reputation as a military authority grew. His break came when Wolseley appointed him to be his military secretary in 1873 for the Ashanti Expedition and as Wolseley's diaries for both the Ashanti and the Zulu campaigns show, 'Brack's solid administrative prowess' was an important component in the fashioning of Wolseley's reputation, a reputation for efficiency and effectiveness which made the catchphrase 'All Sir Garnet' a household expression.

Because of, or perhaps in spite of, being a charter member of 'the Ring' of handpicked young officers, Brackenbury's stock rose rapidly. Like other ID officers, Baring, Ardagh and later James Grierson, Brackenbury served a spell as secretary to the Viceroy of India, Lord Lytton. When Lytton resigned, Brackenbury went to Paris as the military attaché. But he was not there for long as Sir William Harcourt, then the Home Secretary, called for him to be Under-Secretary for Police and Crime in Dublin, soon after the Phoenix Park murders in 1882 when Hartington's brother was killed.

Whilst at Dublin Castle, Brackenbury learned much about secret service work and had a free hand in operations backed by a substantial budget. But every day the papers carried more and more news about Egypt and when Wolseley wrangled his way to go out, vice Alison, Brackenbury considered himself part of his baggage.

In asking to go, Brackenbury crossed Gladstone himself. The Grand Old Man was furious. Egypt was of passing importance in comparison with the resolution of the Irish problem and he was thoroughly displeased by Brackenbury's wish to return to active service. He thereupon referred to the post-murders phase as 'the breakdown of Brackenbury'. He opined that soldiers did not make good policemen and punished him for turning his back on Ireland by placing him on half-pay and forbidding him to go to Egypt. What Brackenbury thought of this can only be guessed, but he bided his time and when Wolseley returned to the Nile in 1884 to try and rescue Gordon, Brackenbury went with him as Deputy Commander of the River Column, which he took over upon the death of General Earle.[169]

Although the attempt failed it was, essentially, a political failure and Brack's reputation was unsullied. Given the ID's activities in Turkey, Cyprus, India and Egypt and its relations with the Foreign Office in particular, it is improbable that the selection of Cameron's replacement was any longer wholly the preserve of Horse Guards. In any event, in January 1886, Brackenbury returned to take over the ID from Cameron as DQMG Intelligence (from 1887 Director Military Intelligence). The Duke cannot have been pleased with his appointment. He fulminated that Brackenbury was 'a dangerous man' and said so in public. The Duke also poisoned the Queen's mind against Brackenbury so successfully that no government was able to secure a knighthood for Brackenbury until 1894, six years after he had reached the rank of lieutenant general. It was W. H. Smith, Secretary for War, who had known the Department during the Eastern Question, who insisted on Brackenbury's appointment that a major general should again head the ID and paved the way for Brackenbury's promotion.[170]

Brackenbury found his niche in Queen Anne's Gate. Intelligence work fascinated him and he had a remarkable aptitude for it. He had come across it early when his older brother had been in the Department and he affirmed its value at first hand when he witnessed the efficiency of the Prussian General Staff in 1870. He gained further insights as the attaché in Paris and there are strong indications that he learned some practical intelligence tradecraft from American Pinkerton detectives whilst hunting secret societies in Ireland. He then schooled himself in combat intelligence in Egypt so that by 1885 he was convinced that intelligence held the key to productive staff work, leading to winning conflicts great and small.

Just before taking over, he wrote a letter to Captain (later Lieutenant General Sir Henry) Colvile, chief of the Egyptian Frontier Force intelligence, congratulating him on receiving the Companionship of the Order of the Bath. 'No one knows better than I how well you earned it. Don't think of giving up intelligence work at present. It is the highest class of work and whenever we have at Head Quarters in London a proper department of the Chief of Staff it will take its proper place.'[171]

Brackenbury returned from Egypt with bigger plans than simply running a useful intelligence function. With Wolseley as Adjutant General and Redvers Buller as Quartermaster General, the three moved to reawaken the Cardwell age. Each of these able officers saw on the Nile, as they had in no less than a dozen previous campaigns, that there were systemic failures at the top. They felt the want of a proper general staff very keenly. In this they were not alone. In this drive for efficiency, the military education movement, the Volunteer movement, technological advances and real or perceived threats from continental powers all pointed in the same direction. The debate was not conducted behind closed doors either. In an age in which progress was pervading almost every walk of life, military reform interested the public. Wolseley, and to a lesser extent Buller and Brackenbury, were in the public eye.[172]

Each of these able officers was strongly ambitious. Even as he returned from Egypt, Wolseley angled for a peerage so he could speak his mind in the House of Lords as a serving officer. Citing Lord Napier as a precedent probably did not help his case and he had to wait until his later elevation to the peerage, yet the fact was that each of the three was in competition for the highest posts, meaning they were united only by the loosest bonds of patriotism and professional concern. This played into the hands of the counter-reformers at Horse Guards, who pointed to the naked ambition of the reformers cloaked in a Trojan horse of reformation.

The reformation and counter-reformation raised a great deal of dust. Much of it was conducted in the public gaze and neither political party was in the least bit comfortable with the unseemly row which ate up a surprising amount of column inches in an age when speeches were often recorded verbatim. The reformers for their part became more vocal, with Wolseley's outspoken criticisms of the military establishment to the fore. Within government and its immediate circle, Horse Guards held the upper hand despite the dash of the reformers. They served to alienate not only the soldiers at Horse Guards, but also the civilians in the War Office and the government of the day as well. Minutes, notes and letters from those who had to deal with these matters all betray a deep irritation with the whole issue and the reformers in particular. No minister of either party trusted the opinions of soldiers who talked to newspapers about expenditure and policy, since modernisation was likely to prove costly and usually politically embarrassing. Guy Fleetwood Wilson, private secretary to four War Ministers, summed it up when he wrote: 'Fortunately no two soldiers ever agree, so the wretched tax-payer is able to live.'[173]

Within the troika, Wolseley now regarded Brack, his protégé, as a threat. He knew that Brackenbury was 'not one of the cleverest but *the* cleverest man in the British Army'. When it became clear that he could not rescue Gordon in time, Wolseley was seen to sink into a blue funk and never regained the enthusiasm necessary for field command. As the criticisms mounted, he transferred the blame to others, not least Wilson and Brackenbury. In his diary he complained that Brackenbury had a:

quarrelsome overbearing temperament. He favours those in power and bullies his subordinates without any regard for their feelings. Indeed I have looked upon him as 'quite a gentleman'. Neither has he the tact of the educated & experienced gentleman. He thinks he is the ablest of diplomats an amusing assumption according to the views of those who know him best. But, he is very able and will serve you with real interest and great ability as long as he thinks that doing so will be to his advantage. He has Greek blood in him and consequently does not know what real loyalty to any man – except to himself can possibly mean or why it should be cultivated in man.

On the subject of selfishness, Wolseley again wrote:

I have long been witness to a great deal of it in one man, namely Brackenbury, who is a worshipper of his own vile body more than most men I have known in the world… He is a man of great talent and will do well in any capacity; his selfishness which he hides under an assumed affectionate manner, & by well chosen sentiments expressed in a melodious tone, make enemies for him, and will prevent him from ever rising to any great position.[174]

Knowing this, what place would Brackenbury have in Wolseley's scheme of things? As the bonds between the reformers loosened, it became clearer that in the Adjutant General's train, Brackenbury would be shunted off as Wolseley's 'Chief of Spies'. But if the ID had a momentum of its own, Brackenbury, as its head, could perhaps re-enter the main line ahead of Wolseley as the first chief of an imperial general staff.[175]

Throughout this period Brackenbury kept his own counsel. He made few, if any, recorded speeches, yet he was in charge of the Department, which would be the obvious power base for a continental-style general staff and, of itself, a vehicle to further reform. Perhaps it would not be wholly inaccurate to view the energy behind the general drive and significant advances by the Department from 1886 in the light of what were probably Brackenbury's ultimate ambitions for it, laudable or selfish as they may be.

Wolseley no doubt thought they were was selfish. From 1888 onwards, he attempted to reclaim some of the privileges that as Adjutant General he had so freely dispensed when the troika began their campaign of reform in early 1886. But by the time Wolseley and the counter-reformers at Horse Guards combined to crush Brackenbury's embryonic general staff, the Intelligence Department was no longer dependent upon military approbation.

‡

So what did Brackenbury find when he entered 16–18 Queen Anne's Gate? He quickly discovered it not only had semi-official entrées to the great departments of state, he found it possessed the ultimate engine of dissemination: its own printing presses.

Brackenbury, as every extant file shows, immediately infused a purposeful energy into the Department, the like of which had not been seen since Wilson's time. Within a few weeks of his arrival, old methods were thrown over and mobilisation, staff planning and imperial defence took on a wider aspect. He revelled in the information the Department had been quietly gathering and he appreciated the abilities of the men he found. Men like Ardagh, who would become his deputy, and his Asian specialist, Captain (later Lieutenant General Sir James) Wolfe Murray, later Chief of the Imperial General Staff, and at least a dozen more were men of singular ability who were capable of producing revolutionary contingency plans of the broadest scope and undoubted quality.

Brackenbury thereupon set out to market the fruits of their labours apart and above the unsolicited, politically biased and babbling memoranda of other 'military authorities'. 'To my mind,' he wrote, 'if an ID is to be really useful, it must not only prepare and print papers but of its own initiative send them to those who have to decide questions at issue.'

As an officer who had 'in unusual measure the gift of expressing himself appositely, clearly, and concisely on paper', Brackenbury knew that he also had in abundance what everyone wanted to buy: information and creditable analysis which added up to intelligence. It was the crystal ball everyone sought. Brackenbury also knew whom he wished to cultivate. As he wrote to Ardagh, when he took over in 1896:

> I hope the ID will never cease to be not only the eyes & ears of the Army, but a most valuable Department to the State generally ... I am quite certain that your power of obtaining military information depends directly upon your friendly relations with other Departments of the State – Foreign, Colonial, & Indian Offices – and those friendly relations depend upon the help you give them.

To begin with, the ID's renewed enthusiasm rather annoyed the Foreign Office: 'This laudable thirst after knowledge is somewhat embarrassing at times,' fumed one official. Another scribbled: 'They are most inconvenient people. Cannot they wait until this crisis is over?' Yet inconveniences were not a problem. At this period, the Foreign Office had a procedure for dealing with outside or awkward memoranda: it took them in and after a considerable time they reappeared again, printed in bound volumes. Thus whilst these various contributions were officially on the record, in reality they were stale and the events about which they were concerned had been eclipsed by more recent happenings, diminishing whatever value, if any, they possessed – often to the embarrassment of their authors.

Brackenbury's idea was therefore to provide the government with the ID's reports and maps already printed. This allowed the recipients, usually at this stage the Foreign and Colonial offices, the opportunity to distribute the ID's contribution rapidly and wider, picking up the disseminating department's approbation as they passed. Brackenbury would send the ID's contribution over, attaching to the top one ID's informal internal 'yellow slip' prepared by the section responsible, giving credit to its young authors and revealing the steps in their thinking. In his formal correspondence to the Foreign Office, Brackenbury very occasionally toned down a recommendation or idea, but he always sent the original along to seal his point and give credit where it was due. 'At first there was some little jealousy,' the new director admitted, 'but when they grew to see how useful we could be, and how much trouble we saved them, it all ceased.'[176]

Back at Queen Anne's Gate, Brackenbury tackled his internal organisation first. Ardagh, now a full colonel, was brought in as his second-in-command as Deputy Assistant Adjutant General. He became directly responsible for mobilisation and home defence. Alongside his section (Central) were six other sections each with two officers and a military clerk. (A) handled France, Belgium, Italy, Spain, Portugal, Mexico, and Central and South America. (B) did British possessions and protectorates, southern Africa, Polynesia and Cyprus. (C) monitored Germany, the Netherlands, Scandinavia, Switzerland and the United States. (D) took on Russia, India, Afghanistan, Burma, China, Japan, Siam, Persia and central Asia. (E) was responsible for Egypt, the Ottoman Empire, other parts of Africa not covered by (B), the Balkans and the Austro-Hungarian Empire. (F) was the engine room composed of the library, map rooms, seven draftsmen, three printers and two storekeepers. Altogether the ID comprised some forty officers, other ranks and civilians.

Each section assembled information collected from several sources: the Foreign Office, Admiralty DNI, Colonial Office, the world's press, as well as from more shadowy fissures. On the desks of each section the material gathered would be sorted, analysed and co-ordinated, the results being stored or sent back to the several sources without the administrative inconvenience of cumbersome acknowledgements, registration books, or each office having to conduct long, ponderous and potentially revealing correspondence on what was still raw intelligence material. It informed. It worked. It was valued.

From 1886 there was a renewed emphasis on processing skills, that combination of melding fact, expertise, professional experience and imagination which made the ID's product so different, so well informed and reliable. No longer were officers 'groping after a system' in 'cutting passages out of British and foreign newspapers and having them pasted by clerks into vast tomes of the scrapbook order'. By 1887 the 28-year-old author, prize winner and linguist Captain (later Major General Sir Charles) Callwell described how material was processed to become useful intelligence:

- Collection of information by means of special reports, newspapers, periodicals, volumes reaching the daily growing War Office library, which was under charge of the department, and enquiries addressed to individuals known to, or likely to, possess knowledge;
- Methodical registration of the information for further use; and
- Collation into reports. The first and second headings were in reality the most important, although the third took up most of one's time, and the second ... required the greatest care of all.

The officers were teased by their fellow officers outside the Department with the taunt that they spent their time looking at risqué French periodicals when in reality they were searching an increasing number of foreign journals and gazettes for 'facts, always facts'. By the close of 1886 the Department library held some 38,000 volumes, increasing at 1,500 volumes annually, all at a working cost of £440. The librarian, Quartermaster W. H. Cromie, who will play a much more dramatic part later in this narrative, had but one assistant. This compared with the FO's library, which had twice the ID's volumes, a staff of ten and an annual budget of £4,121. The Colonial Office had 12,000 volumes and a staff of three against a budget of £728. The Lords' library had but 30,000 volumes and the Commons 40,000 most of which were records of its own proceedings, viz Hansard or its predecessors.[77]

What made the ID library different was not only its up-to-date and specialist nature, but the rapidity with which information could be extracted from the ever-expanding holding. How? In 1878 it adopted the Dewey Decimal System only a few months after it had been promulgated and took it several places past even that envisaged by Dewey himself.

The library grew and grew until in 1891 an official at HM Treasury told a surprised secretary of the British Museum, Sir E. Maunde Thompson, that Britain possessed what was 'believed to be the best military library in the world'. Thompson, needless to say, did not credit that claim at all. But after meeting Cromie he became a great supporter and was passionately interested in the Department's attempts to catalogue information not immediately revealed by a publication's title or chapter headings.

To augment printed information, the Department again began training consuls and attachés throughout the world. Soon it was allocating them specific collection tasks. It also encouraged the garrisons in Gibraltar and Malta to establish their own intelligence functions and to report back information gleaned from the multi-levelled monitoring of *affaires africaines*.

Recalling Caldwell's 'individuals known to, or likely to possess knowledge', the ID also carried on a discreet correspondence with those who made up Kipling's 'Lost Legions'. British subjects working all over the world, such as the British railway manager in Egypt already mentioned, railwaymen in Canada employing large numbers of Irishmen, a riverboat captain plying the Congo in the employ of the King of the Belgians, not to forget the head of Persian telegraphs or a wine merchant in St Petersburg, all were encouraged to write from time to time to 16–18 Queen Anne's Gate. The ID had no budget to speak of for running sustained covert networks and, on the whole, they did not need the inconvenience of financial oversight as these trusty nondescripts had faith in Britain's mission and would help if they could. They were the true empire builders.

Another area where pioneering efforts led to signal advances was in confidentiality. Establishing a culture of workable secrecy and procedures to preserve it took time but it was successful in two ways. Firstly by codifying the prevailing practice that anyone assigned to the Department was not to speak or write for the public without written permission. This was a particular bugbear for Salisbury, who deeply resented seeing comments and opinions in the press by any officer whom he had consulted on affairs of state.[178] Secondly, it involved coping with the burgeoning amount of material which contained sensitive information and needed active management. On the continent security was a mania, but not in Britain. Once it was recognised that even amongst this sensitive material, not all of it was of the same importance, a standardised classification system could be created. This Colonel (later Major General J. C.) Dalton, the head of Section (F) and later president of the Royal Geographical Society, did. It was he who set up the categories of 'top secret', 'secret' and 'confidential' which have since become the world's basic security classification system.

In August 1886, the ID obtained approval to assign a grade of security classification for *all* War Office despatches before they went to their destination. It is highly probable that this astonishing, overarching and onerous task was intended by Wolseley and Brackenbury as part of their reformation, especially as the ID was suddenly made responsible for the distribution of classified documents throughout the whole Empire.[179]

But as the ID grew away from the War Office and Wolseley became ever more paranoid about Brackenbury, the AG's office changed its mind and from January 1888 refused to send to the ID any official circulars 'unless that branch is directly interested and an opinion is required'. For the next few years security issues were batted back and forth between the AG's Department and the ID. In 1889, Brackenbury proposed making the ID the depository of all secret documents not in use. Surprisingly the Duke agreed. Then in 1890 the key to the Z cipher went missing in Sierra Leone and in 1893 the estate of Sir Robert Morier sold the classified papers in his possession, including ID memoranda, on the open market! By 1894 the bulk of work grew to such a proportion that the ID gladly handed most of it to Adjutant General's department (AG 7) whilst retaining some responsibility for exceptionally sensitive documents.

At the same time as this bureaucratic skirmishing was going on, Brackenbury prepared for the biggest campaign of all: the claim to running a separate registry. As he later explained to the Marquess of Lansdowne, then Viceroy of India and a future Secretary of State for War (1895–1900) and at the Foreign Office (1900–1905), the ID had learned:

> by practical experience that the other departments of State while willing to send their most secret documents to, and to consult upon secret affairs an officer at the head of a Secret Department, were unwilling to confide their secrets to the War Office where their papers passed through as general registry, and where the system of military hierarchy and the heavy pressure of business were the cause of great delay.[180]

He opened the battle within a month of his arrival. When Mr Perry, the Consul General in Odessa, was thought to have overestimated a Russian troop count by 8,000 men, Brackenbury wrote to the Foreign Office: 'Can Mr Perry be kindly asked to look into this without my having to move S.S. War, to move S.S. Foreign Affairs, etc.?' He made the same request of the Colonial Office, asking them to supply Section B with information semi-officially 'not only for South Africa but any part of the world'.[181]

And almost by accident everything he wanted fell into his lap. On 9 February 1886, the ID had written to the Colonial Office about disturbances in Sierra Leone and the letter, as usual, went through War Office channels. It somehow crossed the desk of the long-time Under Secretary for War, Sir Ralph Thompson, who tersely wrote back to Brackenbury: 'In all such matters I have no desire whatever to be the channel of communications between you and other departments – in fact I should decidedly object to it.'

It was the ID's golden opportunity and Brackenbury seized it. By May 1886, the Department was corresponding directly with the Foreign and Colonial offices weekly, often more frequently. By June 1886, the Earl of Rosebery, future Prime Minister and then Secretary of State at the Foreign Office, observed that it would be of 'great advantage and assistance' if the ID would send their memoranda to the FO as a matter of course. The Colonial Office, too, began to use the ID, although the hey-day of CO–ID co-operation did not come until the early 1890s when the Colonial Office had almost completely lost control of its obligations and opportunities in West Africa.

The War Office was not blind to what was going on. 'This is surely an innovation,' wrote one official. It was. As Ardagh later recalled: 'At first there was a certain amount of resentment by the military side of the War Office. Whilst it lasted the requisite communications and studies were made by private and conf. intercourse of individuals.' Indeed, the AG's office stepped in to forbid the ID corresponding directly with the Foreign Office yet the advantages to the FO and CO were so obvious that the AG and the War Office were overruled. In an Order in Council of February 1888, the practice was regularised and the Department was permitted to correspond directly with other departments 'semi-officially'.[182] Thus the former hierarchical formalities of communications between the ID and the great offices of state became more simple, personal and direct. Brackenbury had won.

As with the civilian departments, so it was with the Royal Navy. The ID had provided the Admiralty with intelligence for a number of years and had been involved both in setting up the Naval Intelligence

Department (NID) in 1886–87 and its forerunner, the Committee on Foreign Intelligence. The father of naval intelligence, Lord Charles Beresford, enjoyed close ties with officers of the Department including Wilson, Ardagh and Captain (later Colonel Milo George) Talbot of Malahide. Beresford, too, looked for efficiencies and proposed to the Sea Lords that in creating the NID it should be both an intelligence agency and a war staff. It met with unanimous opposition.

Nothing loath, Beresford went straight to Salisbury where he found immediate backing. Captain W. H. Hall, the first director of the NID, was in close touch with the ID as were his successors. Together the ID and NID briefed the ID's 'travellers' who thereupon took on Admiralty tasking as well as military. And, most importantly, the ID co-ordinated its strategical thinking with the NID. Each took account of the other's problems and ID memoranda, on the whole, echoed the NID position and vice versa. Relations between the two agencies were so good that when in 1896 the War Office distorted an ID memorandum on a question of submarine cables, the NID went to considerable lengths to reassert the ID's view.[183]

Yet all was not well, not least with Brackenbury's own colleagues. There had been an air of impermanence about serving in the ID and calls to active service had almost emptied it in 1879 and 1882. As Jervis, James and Panmure had intended, many officers were still attached for short periods of time. This allowed the ID to have the temporary services of the best staff college graduates from each class. For all the opprobrium from Horse Guards, it was a prized assignment and helped to spread an appreciation of the uses of intelligence throughout the Army. Yet it was deeply unpopular with the regular establishment. It smacked of 'rings' and was highly inconvenient to the attached officer's parent unit. His place had to be held open and what was more, it was the losing unit which paid, not the ID.

In 1886 more than half of the fourteen or so officers in the Department were liable to be recalled to their regiments at a moment's notice. In that year of 'profound peace', three officers were suddenly removed at one time. The Royal Artillery so disliked the attached system that it successfully petitioned the Duke to be exempted from it. Brackenbury was also frustrated and told the Treasury: 'Some of the best officers in other regiments have declined to take service in the Branch either because they were unwilling to throw additional regimental work on their brother officers, or because they knew how strongly their doing so would be resented in their regiment.' All this at a time when the Department was working hard to prove its worth.

The short-lived Liberal government of January to July 1886 was not going to do anything to help. Henry Campbell-Bannerman at the War Office refused to 'add to the already great number of seconded officers' when almost in the same breath he asked for a substantial study comparing British and German army estimates. Exasperated, Brackenbury wrote back: 'Give me time and it shall be done,' adding that Brevet Major F. B. Innes had been taken away and Wolseley refused to give him back; that the head of the German Section (C), Lieutenant Colonel C. W. Bowdler Bell, was 'sick, laid up with over-work, and I don't know when he will come back'. Added to that, 'five of my best and most highly trained officers have been taken away for Regimental duty since 1st instant. Is there any other office where such wicked waste of fine steel to cut brushwood would be tolerated?'

Brackenbury thought that the boil would be, at least partly, lanced if he could second several of the attached officers to the Department at an average annual salary of £450. Negotiations went on for a whole year but finally the War Office put the idea to the Treasury, which baulked, arguing that the new Naval Intelligence Department would reduce the ID's workload. This led to a predictable row over the boundaries of Treasury control. Explaining to the Treasury offi-cials why a seconded officer was preferable to an attached officer, Brackenbury cited the need for each to spend a much longer time in the ID than for a normal attachment. He told them that 'an officer is of little use when first appointed. It is only after months of study of the subjects with which his section deals that he commences to be really efficient; and the present system of constantly changing the men results in waste of public money, as it involves inefficiency in a large proportion of the officers which receive the same payment as if they were efficient'. The Treasury finally saw his point and on 12 October 1887 seven staff captains, one for each section, were put upon the strength and those staff captains whom he had selected to head sections as DAAGs could look forward to six or seven years' service *in toto*, something no other Army staff office could do.[184] This, too, was a major advance.

‡

As Wolfe Murray and his colleagues had pointed out to W. H. Smith on the eve of Brackenbury's appointment, Britain was not thinking hard enough about the military and naval implications of a growing Empire. The first issue to resolve, the ID reckoned, was mobilisation, to be sure, but also that of creating an effective imperial fire brigade. Indeed, the War Office was 'so dominated by ideas of home defence and the security of India that it neglected to provide a mobile army for service abroad'. When Brack took up his post the ID pointed out that for an annual budget of £21,500,000 Germany could mobilise *eighteen* complete army corps. For an annual budget of £18,000,000 Britain could not mobilise even one.

Faced with changing governments, in April, September and October 1886 the ID doggedly carried on enumerating the deficiencies in detail, particularly 'the want of any systematic arrangements necessary to put a force into the field'. Finally, in September 1886 the War Office established a committee to look into the ID's warnings and by November W. H. Smith asked Brackenbury and Sir Ralph Thompson (the under-secretary who refused to be the ID's postman) to report to him on the ways and means whereby a small field force would be mobilised rapidly and despatched across the seas wherever it was needed.

The issues of an imperial fire brigade and home mobilisation were wholly intertwined. Thompson and Brackenbury had already found that there was little if any co-ordination and almost no agreement on mobilisation between the various departments and agencies which should have been involved. The War Office was content to rely on the slow construction of coastal forts, an inadequately supported militia and Robert Home's mobilisation plans, even though the measures to render them effective had never been put into place nor had they been updated since the early 1880s and were now seriously obsolete.

At an equally high level, the Admiralty resented the expenditure on coastal defences and the raising of volunteer battalions as an aspersion on its ability to prevent an invading force from landing. In short, the Navy believed that the Army's money would be better spent on the Navy. For almost the next two decades whenever these matters occurred to them, the admirals and the generals would bicker about the threat and argue about the relative merits of the composition of the second line of defence, i.e. increased land forces or coastal defences, which was only a valid consideration if the Royal Navy was unable to hold the English Channel, which, until a naval scare in 1893, they were convinced they could easily do.

Below decks, so to speak, the ID and the NID took a cold, hard look at potential enemies and, not surprisingly, the French fitted the frame. The ID believed that unless there were strong secondary defences, France could secretly mobilise and invade Britain with between 100,000 and 150,000 men *if* she controlled the Channel for three weeks. The NID agreed and took upon itself the responsibility of ensuring that the Admiralty would have at least ten days' warning were a mobilisation to occur, time enough to bring the Royal Navy into the Channel.

But concerns further afield also worried the ID and NID. Britain's burgeoning imperial responsibility because of her increased involvement in Africa and the nature of a conceivable intervention meant that the Army should look to raise a mobilisation force of two army corps which would be, as Admiral 'Jacky' Fisher saw it, a large projectile to be fired by the Navy. Brackenbury put the ID forward to do the planning and organisational staff work necessary to bring this into reality. Yet whilst he might identify what was needed to create this force, there was not the political will to bring it into existence. Money, as ever, was the key. As recently as 1885 India had shocked the government by being unwilling – or supposedly unable – to pay for their regularly scheduled draft of 10,000 replacements. Senior politicians of both parties and HM Treasury thereupon realised that except for some global cataclysm, India was a reluctant and unreliable partner in the imperial dance and certainly had no intention of leaving Aden, Mauritius or the Cape permanently on her dance card.[185]

In these circumstances, Thompson and Brackenbury reported to Smith on 7 December 1886 that the mobilisation of two corps was impracticable: 'We can never hope to reach the same perfection of mobilisation as those foreign nations whose very existence depends on their being first in the field...' But if the general level of preparedness of the British Army was raised, then the mobilisation of one corps might be possible. In January 1887 he told the Cabinet: 'Unless our Rulers will take a business-like view of the situation, we shall suffer heavily in our first war with any great European Power, and have to buy peace at a price compared with which any expenditure upon armaments now would weigh but as a feather in the balance.' This found favour and the Duke was pushed to set up the inevitable mobilisation committee. It consisted of Brackenbury as chairman, two officers from the AG's office and Captain (later Lieutenant General Sir Percy) Lake, of the Central (Mobilisation and Home Defence) Section as secretary.

A veteran of the Afghan Wars, the Suakin expedition and an honour graduate of the Staff College, Lake was well suited to draw the many strings together. However, the subcommittee was established in late December 1886 just as Lord Randolph Churchill resigned as Chancellor of the Exchequer and funding for mobilisation plans went firmly on the back burner. Nevertheless, Brackenbury did not lose sight of the need for a prepared field army and Ardagh, his new deputy, was the man to work with Lake and others to deliver it, if anyone could. He had long experience with planning of this nature. He had served on the 1859 Royal Commission on National Defence, the 1868 Committee on Fortifications and the 1870 Committee on Coastal Defences. Apprenticed to Home he also served on the Standing Defence and Fortifications committees. He came back to the ID as soon as Brackenbury could persuade the Treasury to fund him and immediately picked up the threads. 'I feel that although we have, in our mobilisation scheme, laid the foundation of a great national work,' Brack told his new deputy, 'we have only laid the foundation, and that the whole superstructure has yet to be built.'[186]

Ardagh found a decided 'want of correlation' between military departments. The Engineers considered defence to be their responsibility whilst the IGF was to build the forts without knowing exactly where or whether or not there would be men to man an unknown number of guns which had not been contracted for. Ardagh and his section (Lake, a colonel and two captains) methodically set about putting all this right. From macro to micro they looked at home defence, colonial garrisons, war scenarios, the state of Ireland, the degree of emergency at any time, the location and dislocation of units, the selection of points of concentration and the provision and storage of equipment, ammunition and vehicles at each.

There were ports to consider, maintaining the registry of reserve horses, farriers who could cold-shoe, right up to the mechanics of calling up individual reservists and moving them all to the right location to be fed, paid and dressed. 'All had to be devised,' Ardagh insisted, 'so as to work with rapidity.'

Binding up all the myriad detail in his secret reports, *The Defence of England* and *The Defence of London*, Ardagh reckoned that in 1888 the effectives of regular and auxiliary forces in Britain and the colonies was 554,135 men, some 163,865 men short of what it had been considered necessary to keep under arms in 1804 during the Napoleonic War. Whereas Home, in his mobilisation planning, had counted on six weeks' warning, Ardagh expected little or none. Home had planned to concentrate a repelling force where the invaders would land and hoped to ring London with forts. Ardagh, with the threat increased and his warning time reduced to nothing, called for four corps of Regulars to deploy to Sussex, Essex, Kent and Dublin, the three in England to be 'distributed by brigades or Departments at certain railway junctions between London and the coast, in such a manner as to give the maximum degree of mobility by railway, and admit of a concentration with great rapidity upon a variety of positions selected with a view to meet different contingencies'.

Then, between the Regulars and London, would be the whole of the Volunteers (minus garrison troops), comprising three more corps complete with artillery. In front of it all was to be a screen of three huge formations of regular cavalry and a Yeomanry cavalry brigade.

Reporting in November 1887 it supposed that Britain could mobilise *one* corps, including Reserves, alongside an oversized infantry brigade, i.e. an imperial fire brigade, and a brigade of cavalry. Brackenbury thought the whole scheme was the absolute minimum, but told the Cabinet that if brought about it would 'place our Regular Forces in a condition sufficient to meet whatever emergency may arise'.

Recognising the Navy's massive new shipbuilding programme, Edward Stanhope, then War Minister, was unprepared to consider any extra expense for the Army and delayed consideration of the foundation scheme until three months after the 1888 Budget had been passed.

Nevertheless, Stanhope and the Duke bought the concept. Turning it into reality was another story. But even in its early stages it provided some focus. By 1890, Stanhope was able to tell the Commons that he believed most of Britain's ports to be adequately defended. Three corps of 110,000 Regulars and militia had been told off and plans for the concentration of equipment was advancing apace. The second line of defence was also organised upon points of concentration consisting of eighteen infantry brigades with artillery support.

As far as Stanhope went, as long as it was on paper, it was alright. But he would not condone troops training *in situ* and as for the calling up of Brackenbury's fire brigade, the minister stated on 1 June 1888 that 'it would be distinctly understood that the probability of the employment of an army corps in the field in any European war is sufficiently improbable to make it the primary duty of the military authorities to organise efficiently for the defence of this country'. Captain (later Field Marshal Sir William) Robertson, an intelligencer under Ardagh in the 1890s, pointed to this 'improbable possibility' as the brake retarding any commonly accepted and comprehensive design for imperial defence during the next decade.

Knowing what we do of Wolseley's temper and jealousy, it is not to be wondered at that just when Brackenbury and Ardagh were finding favour for their defence schemes with the Duke and Stanhope, he suddenly transferred the Mobilisation branch to his office. But in so doing, all he took unto himself was the responsibility for fleshing out Ardagh's finished plans and the onus of pestering the politicians for money. Ardagh himself soon left for India to serve as private secretary to the new Viceroy, Lord Lansdowne. For intelligence and definitions of actual threat, Wolseley still had to turn to Brack, which, as will be seen, he was loath to do.

Brackenbury was not content to rest on his gains. In a series of cautious and considered memoranda for the Queen and Cabinet, he sought to raise the question of defence estimates above party conflict. At this remove it appears that it was part and parcel of his stealthy quest to gain total independence from the Adjutant General's office and to make the ID a general staff in all but name. He told Lord Randolph Churchill's Select Committee on Army and Navy Estimates that waste and inefficiency would be reduced if the ID were developed into a 'thinking department':

> I cannot help but feel that to the want of any such great central think-ing department, under a much greater man than myself, in our War Office, to which all the different plans and different estimates of the various Departments are now working upon parallel lines in the War Office without ever meeting should be submitted, is due to that want of economy and efficiency which to a certain extent exists in our Army.[187]

It worked. According to his own account, Brackenbury's testimony 'induced the Government to organise the department in a satisfactory manner and from that time it obtained new life and vigour'. Although Mobilisation stayed with AG 7, the ID became a separate Division of the War Office in the reorganisation of February 1888, reporting directly to the Commander-in-Chief with Brackenbury now styled as Director of Military Intelligence (DMI). Its new terms of reference were encyclopaedic:

> The DMI is charged with collecting and distributing information relative to the military geography, resources, and armed forces of foreign countries, and of the British Colonies and possessions; and with the compilation of maps for military purposes; he is authorised to correspond semi-officially with other departments of state ... for preparation and maintenance of information relative to the defence of the Empire, other than the United Kingdom.

In June Salisbury made it clear in a Cabinet memorandum that the resources of the Foreign Office were available for the collection of information if the ID needed assistance.

Brackenbury passed off his victory with the droll comment that the 'grounds for change was the recognition of the fact that the Adjutant General of the Army had not time to devote to the close study of intelligence questions...' In reality the success was wholly Brackenbury's. He took advantage of the Department's growing reputation with senior politicians at a time when doubts were increasing as to the capability of Wolseley to lead or reform. That the Duke was a busted flush went without saying.

When the vicissitudes of the War Office reached the stage of public notoriety, a Royal Commission was established to enquire into 'the Civil and Professional administration of the Naval and Military departments and the relation of those departments to each other and the Treasury'. Set up by Salisbury and chaired by Hartington, it included W. H. Smith as First Lord of the Treasury, Stanhope for War, Lord George Hamilton for the Admiralty, Randolph Churchill, the radical Liberal Henry Campbell-Bannerman and Brackenbury.[188]

When the Commission finished its work, it, too, had come to favour a 'central thinking department' which would report directly to a Chief of the General Staff, who would in turn be responsible to the Secretary of State for War for all aspects of imperial and home defence. The rest of the report was so critical of existing arrangements that Campbell-Bannerman urged Hartington to tone it down lest every minister involved would have to resign.

As there would be no general staff for another generation, what went wrong with this green shoot? It was Campbell-Bannerman to begin with. 'I confess to having regarded this commission from the first as a farce, and I feel pretty sure that it will produce nothing but smoke...' He disliked the idea of a new 'Pope at the War Office ... and therefore I am against him'. But he was particularly anxious about an expanded central thinking department. He could see it dragging Britain into a great continental war: 'There might indeed be a temptation to create such a field for itself; and I am thus afraid that while there would be no use for the proposed office, there might be in it some dangers to our best interests.'

Campbell-Bannerman refused to sign and he knew where to place the blame: 'The general scheme is Randolph's inspired by Brackenbury and others. Hartington seems bitten with it.' He was no doubt right. The first DMI of the twentieth century, General (later Field Marshal Baron W. G.) Nicholson, told the famous Army reformer and academic, Spencer Wilkinson, that 'it was perfectly notorious that the report of the Commission was drafted by General Brackenbury to suit his own ends, and that most of the members ... knew little and cared less about the subject.'

Another spanner was thrown by Wolseley, who wasted no time in telling the Queen, through Sir Henry Ponsonby, her secretary, that: 'We surely want a doctor I admit, but Brackenbury and Co. have sent us an executioner.'

When in 1895 Wolseley knew that he was to replace the Duke as Commander-in-Chief, he admitted to his new DMI, John Charles Ardagh, that:

I always felt that the main influence at work upon that Commission was that of dear Brackenbury. He knew well that there was no possible chance that he would ever be made Commander in Chief. He consequently devised a scheme under which he would be able to pull the strings and exercise all the power and influence now belonging to the position he coveted. The creation of a Chief of the Staff as proposed by the Commission was Brackenbury's Chef oeuvre. But he made his civilian colleagues believe that their? [*sic*] Chief of Staff was nothing more than an English von Moltke ... I remember how I laughed when I first read the Commission's report & said to myself, 'well done Brack'. But I confess I never dreamed that any Government would attempt to act upon it.

Gladstone listened to Campbell-Bannerman rather than Hartington. Nothing was changed. The Liberal politicians' fear that the soldiers would push Britain into a great European war was at the root of it. When in 1904 the government of that day was investigating the root of the disasters of the South African War, its damning report held that 'if the recommendations of the majority of the Hartington Commission had not been ignored, the country would have been saved the loss of many thousands of lives and of many millions of pounds subsequently sacrificed in the war'.

Yet, surprisingly, the fate of the Commission was not shared by the prototype of the central thinking department; instead it vaunted it. Men like Salisbury and Hartington regarded good intelligence as vital for successful diplomacy and security, indeed, as a substitute for adequate security, whilst men like Campbell-Bannerman looked upon the ID as the existing organisation which rendered a potentially dangerous general staff unnecessary. Campbell-Bannerman seemed to believe that himself when he wrote:

All that is in fact required for our purposes can be amply obtained by an adequately equipped Intelligence Branch, which, under the direction of the Adjutant General, would collect all necessary information, and place it at the disposal, not of one officer or Department alone, but of all the Military Heads whose duty it would be to advise the Minister.[189]

The ID turned its back on the War Office. It was not through institutional reform that the Department would be able to prove its worth or growing influence, but rather through the new, closer connections it was fostering with the great civil departments of state.

CHAPTER SIX

THE MUTUAL LAUDATION SOCIETY

'One of the most difficult problems involved in the study of the foreign policy of a statesman', mused the twentieth-century historian Dame Lillian Penson, 'is that of determining in what form the issues of the day presented themselves to him.' The theme of this chapter is to examine the turbulent state of affairs in central Asia during the last quarter of the nineteenth century with Penson's observation in mind.

Britain's responsibilities abroad were large and growing and for the top of the governmental pyramid to keep it all in balance, without the under-pinning of a huge policy machine, was plate spinning on a large order. Yet on the whole Great Britain did it and did it without becoming involved in either a great European or Asian war. Much of this was arguably due to that most remarkable of all Prime Ministers, Lord Salisbury. In a way which later generations would find hard to fathom, he was perfectly content to enlist the aid of prominent moderate Liberals, such as Mr Goschen and, above all, the Marquess of Hartington, to work with him in keeping foreign affairs on a relatively even, responsive and responsible keel.

Three aspects of this approach made it all possible. First, of course, was Salisbury's decision to retain for himself the office of Foreign Secretary for most of the century from 1885 (i.e. the seven months Cabinet of 1885–86, from the beginning of 1887 until August 1892 and then returning again in June 1895 through November 1900).

Second was that, on the whole, the government of the day was obeyed even when the people on the spot wholeheartedly disagreed with it. And the third, of arguably equal weight, was prescience. Penson wrote of the difficulty of determining 'in what form the issues of the day presented themselves'. Salisbury, Hartington and increasingly the Colonial and Indian offices came to rely more and more on one voice, that of their intelligencers, for facts and what to do with them.

The growing cacophony which the telegraph brought simply heightened the scope for mischief and misunderstanding. It would be nice, albeit boring, to assert that the lessons in the handling of intelligence which so marked the Home–Wilson years were by the mid-1880s adopted practice at least in the Foreign Office. Yet, truth to tell, the collection of information, the transformation into intelligence and its timely dissemination was still haphazard and remained so for the rest of the century and, indeed, beyond. Departmental jealousy, private letters, resistance to technological advances (the Queen insisted on reading despatches in manuscript until the late 1890s) and a wholesale want of process bedevilled the efficient infusion of intelligence into the workings of government and its relations abroad. When Sir Eyre Crowe wrote a memorandum in 1907 on relations between Britain, France and Germany, he noted: 'For the whole of Lord Salisbury's two administrations [*sic*] our official records are sadly incomplete, all the most important business having been transacted under the cover of "private" correspondence.'[190] That such inefficiency, mischief and misunderstanding were outpaced by prescience was down to the mutual regard and trust between the highest level of government and its intelligencers.

Early in 1882, after the Second Afghan War (1878–80) and the British government's decision to withdraw from Afghanistan, Russian expansionists redoubled their efforts, imperiously playing their peace-loving foreign minister, M. de Giers, for a fool, or at least so thought Granville at the Foreign Office and so, too, the first Earl of Kimberley, the highly experienced and respected Secretary of State for India. The British made some attempts to hem in the Russians by urging them to delimit the Persian and Afghan borders, but the battered Afghans regained their self-respect in petulance and the Shah shrugged off any real compliance despite ample inducements from the Indian Exchequer.

The Russians also spurned the exercise and the Liberals were forced to quietly drop negotiations on 29 April 1882.

None of this came as a surprise to the Russian Section of the Intelligence Department. Two years before, Major F. C. H. Clarke wrote a memorandum for the Foreign and India offices in which he foretold that Britain would be unable to stop the Russians before they took Merv. He hoped that the shock of this eventuality would give the British the resolve to press the border issue to a negotiated climax. Indeed, when Merv passed under the Czar's sway in February 1884, talks resumed as Clarke had hoped. Yet the danger of a collision between the Afghans, Russians and Persians in the area south of Merv was very real. This region, the Penjdeh, bordered by the Oxus to the north-east, is a desolate land of plains and dark mountains. It is the land of Sohrab and Rustum and the gateway to Herat, the ancient door to India. Preceded by a screen of Turcoman cavalry, the Russians in Transcaspia were slowly but surely filling the vacuum left by the Shah of Persia and the Amir of Afghanistan. The government of India, alarmed and alarmist as always, encouraged the Afghan border fiefdoms to resist and Indian military aid brought initial successes in 1884. But by the end of the year those tribes were very much on the defensive, their light resistance no match for the ponderous progress of the whole Russian colonial move-ment, its subversion of local tribes, its injection of forces, its railheads and its settlers beguiled by the mirage of prosperity on the back of fields of grain or at least a better life than that found on the steppes.

As Clarke had predicted, Britain's only hope of containing the Russians around Merv was by diplomacy. Britain's strength now lay with the increasingly sophisticated sciences of cartography and geog-raphy; nineteenth-century science brought to serve nineteenth-century diplomacy. To Clarke and the other scientific officers of the Intelligence Department, accurate, indisputable mapping of contentious areas was *prima facie* the essential framework for peaceful co-existence. Borders tidied things up. Such frontiers brought with them European implica-tions of national sovereignty and, most importantly, the consequences of transgression. The view of London's Intelligence Department as to whether India itself was best served by a firmly defined tripwire or a nebulous stretch of frontier changed from time to time with the nature of the external threat or the state of development of a creditable military response; but of one thing they were agreed throughout: the Penjdeh had to be mapped and apportioned to Afghanistan's advantage or there would be no holding the Russians.

Their reasoning was clear. If Russia held the Zulficar Pass leading out of the Penjdeh and the wedge into existing Afghan territory between the Murgab and Hari Rud rivers, she could build railways which could easily bring her down to invest the fortress city of Herat and then India would be hers in due course. When the Russian expansionists' long-term plans came into the ID's hands in 1886, this prediction was found to be accurate.

Many of the natural landmarks and villages in the Penjdeh were ill defined if not notional. This vagueness had plagued the Foreign and India offices since the first abortive attempt at negotiations. The ID, still sceptical of the ultimate value of missions, nevertheless spent much of the 1880s gleaning every scrap of information it could find from any source on the topography of central Asia. The Ambassador at St Petersburg, his attaché and all British consuls throughout the Russian Empire sent as many maps as they could collect to the ID.[191] For its part, the Indian government sponsored Indian intelligence and survey officers on long reconnaissances of the Indian border areas at some considerable risk to those involved. Not surprisingly, the Russians, too, had an aggressive cartographical service in Asia and the ID spent no little time attempting to obtain the information they were gathering although much of it was wildly inaccurate.

As their results reached London, the Department correlated and added them to the master stones and the sweating jobbers in the basement of Queen Anne's Gate pulled them off. How many copies after working for so many hours on the stone? Often no more than a dozen, perhaps a score, other times several hundred. The ID was delighted to fill the gaps and more than once pushed an unappreciative War Office to thank the travellers officially.

By the early 1880s, whilst the ID was forging a new reputation in Egypt, the Foreign and India offices were taking the Department's technical services for granted. Indeed, one important piece of the mapping puzzle, which arrived just days before the Russians occupied Merv, was lost for eight days in transmission between the Foreign Office and the War Office before frantic officers from the ID could find it. In 1883, Major W. R. R. Fox of the Mapping Section (F) told a senior Foreign Office clerk:

> I should like you, privately, to know what the production of these maps had entailed upon us owing to the very short notice you gave. Two draftsmen have been working since Tuesday morning through each night up to 4 o'clock in the morning. They were taken off other pressing work which has been in hand for so long a time that great technical risk is run in further allaying its transfer to stone. I hope the map and tracing are what are required.

Indeed, some in the FO continued to believe that Stanford & Co. were the government's primary map makers. Finally the ID was forced to point out its special contribution to secret map making through its presses and those of the Ordnance Survey. Certainly Currie at the Foreign Office, for one, knew and valued the ID's expertise in this area and willingly supported the ID's application to expand its lithographic section in 1884. Yet the War Office financial authorities gave it only half-hearted support, an old story, and the ID continued to wring miracles in the ill-lit, damp cellars of Adair House and later at Queen Anne's Gate.[192]

‡

As presaged by Clarke two years before, the Russians took Merv in February 1884. Nevertheless consternation swept Simla and London, and the British and Indian press worked themselves up to a fever pitch. The Liberal government's reaction was typical and feeble. What could it do unless it knew Russia's intentions for certain? It could do little but protest to M. de Giers for all the good that would do. Then in April a diplomatic pouch from St Petersburg arrived at the ID containing amongst a number of maps one unmarked, nondescript map of the whole area. It was nothing to cause comment except to the keen-eyed observers in the Department who saw enough clues to convince them that it was not only an official Russian map but in fact it was nothing less than the long-sought-after proof of Russian intentions in Asia. Thomas Best Jervis would have been very pleased.

What was interesting is that the old policy of vagueness between Afghanistan and Russia was replaced by a projected border which was, unsurprisingly, entirely to Russia's advantage. The Sarakhs and Penjdeh would be completely enclosed. As for the Russo-Persian border, which the British had for some time insisted included to Persia's advantage the northern watershed of the Atrek, that was left blank, but advances here, too, were obviously intended. This was a map beyond price and the Department believed it was the work of the expansionists under General Kuropatkin.

Granville was immediately informed. He alerted the Cabinet and it was decided to confront de Giers with it. Thus armed, the Ambassador called on de Giers and reported back that the Russian Foreign Minister was genuinely surprised at the scope of the expansionists' plans.[193] The British thereupon immediately proposed a joint boundary commission and the Russians, caught flatfooted, could only agree. As for Britain, it was very much in their interest to put a well-briefed boundary commission on the disputed ground before the Afghans suffered any further reverses. The Persians, too, were pressed to concur and on 12 July 1884, Kimberley appointed Major General Sir Peter Lumsden of the Indian Army as the British commissioner.

Using ID maps, Lumsden's new deputy, Colonel (later Colonel Sir Joseph) West Ridgeway, formed a delegation and brought them overland from India. This cartographic mission was composed in the main of officers who were or had been in the Intelligence Branch, Simla (IBS). Twenty-five Britons with a 465-man Indian escort soon

LEFT A daguerreotype of Thomas Best Jervis c. 1855. His many earnest enthusiasms made him an object of ridicule and mirth both in India and England, but he was above all tenacious and lived to design, create and lead Britain's first modern intelligence organisation.

© Private Collection

BELOW Then a Colonel, Henry James is the officer on the right. He greatly prized commanding the four companies of Royal Engineers, here outside the purpose-built photographic building for the Ordnance Survey in Southampton.

© Southampton Archives

Fox Maule, Lord Panmure and 11th Earl Dalhousie. Taking up the office of Secretary of State for War in the middle of the Crimean War, he faced a deluge of neglect and incompetence. One of his first acts was to create the Topographical & Statistical Department.
© National Portrait Gallery

Edward Cardwell was a highly respected and assiduous Member of Parliament. His great military reforms included a complete restructuring of the Army. He also brought Horse Guards under the control of the War Office and reinvigorated the T&S, making it for the first time a real intelligence organisation.
© National Portrait Gallery

Major General Patrick MacDougall, the first Commandant of the Staff College (1858–61),was Cardwell's selection as head of the new Intelligence Department. Encouraging Wilson, Baring, Hozier et al., it was during his tenure that the ID began to flourish.
© National Army Museum

Lord Hartington, later the
8th Duke of Devonshire, was
Salisbury's Liberal alter ego
in foreign affairs. Having lost
a wife, a son and a brother, he
was an indefatigable worker and,
unlike Gladstone, was able to deal
with many issues simultaneously.
He valued the ID's assistance
in contending with Britain's
growing overseas responsibilities.
© National Portrait Gallery

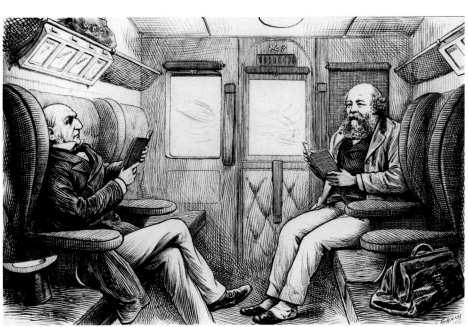

Gladstone and Salisbury in a rare Furniss cartoon. Two of Britain's greatest prime ministers,
they had very little in common save for high principles and quick minds. © National Portrait Gallery

Head of the T&S at an early age and key to its transformation into a functioning Intelligence Department, Charles Wilson's reputation was nevertheless irreparably, but unfairly, sullied by the failed attempt to rescue Gordon in the Sudan.
© National Army Museum

Henry Brackenbury as a Brigadier General. Wolseley called him 'the cleverest man in the British Army'. He was an ambitious and talented organiser and reformer, widely respected by politicians and the Foreign Office. As Director and then Military Member on the Viceroy's Council, he reformed both the home and Indian intelligence organisations.
© National Army Museum

Robert Home was an officer of prodigious ability and energy, and built some 279 bridges as chief of engineers in the Ashanti War of 1873–4. He died in 1879 whilst serving as Commissioner for the delimitation of the boundaries of Bulgaria. His memory is celebrated in the stained-glass Good Centurion window in Rochester Cathedral.

© National Army Museum

A characteristically severe photograph of John Charles Ardagh taken c. 1859. Opposite his picture the album's compiler wrote:

Now Englishmen pronounce this name
Or else we'll go no farther.
It's hard as any in the book
Oh no! I'm sure 'tis H-ardagh-r!

© National Army Museum

Albert Edward, Count Gleichen served in the ID 1886–8 and 1894–9 and on the General Staff 1907–11. Gleichen excelled as both a field and strategic intelligence officer in the Middle East, Africa and London.

© National Army Museum

James Grierson produced penetrating analyses on the armed strength of Japan, Germany and Russia. He was instrumental in setting up the intelligence branch Simla and was responsible for reports which the home ID found alarmist. He later became Director of Military Operations (1904–06) in the new General Staff.

© National Army Museum

Gifted but tragic, Henry Colvile was 'one of the best intelligence officers in the army'. He was selected to lead the push into Uganda before a posting to South Africa, where a combination of illness and bureaucratic machinations saw him relieved of his command by Lord Roberts.

© National Army Museum

F. R. Wingate founded the highly successful Egyptian Intelligence Division. His sympathy for the people of the Sudan earned him a lasting reputation there as well as in London. He gathered the best intelligencers around him, insisting on language skills, and supported his dissemination efforts through good publicity.

© National Army Museum

The snide pen portrait accompanying the Spy cartoon of James Wolfe Murray said he was an administrator, not a soldier, 'who had enough brains to know Russian and not make mistakes'. In reality he was a careful intelligencer whose analyses were highly valued. Chief of the Imperial General Staff at the start of the Great War, he died in Russia in 1919.
© National Army Museum

W. H. Cromie on the eve of taking his LLB (Gray's Inn). The ID fought hard to advance him but was often rebuffed by the War Office or HM Treasury. His ambitions for himself and his career ended amidst suspicions of collusion with the French.
© National Army Museum

found themselves very much alone in the middle of bitterly cold terrain, stalked over by vaporous bands of highly mobile and lethal Turcomans and Afghans of uncertain allegiance or discipline. The commission arrived on station and waited and waited until spring when the Russian commission finally arrived, convincing Lumsden and the Indian authorities that behind the Russian commission the local commander was hurriedly moving south-east and consolidating his territorial gains.

Whilst they waited, Lumsden, West Ridgeway and the IBS officers spent the winter reconnoitring, mapping and sending the results to the ID as often as they could. Determined to define the northern boundary of Afghanistan with or without the Russians, Lumsden began independent conversations with the Afghan warlords. Gladstone found him an 'extremely bad narrator' and he and the Cabinet were confused as to what Lumsden was saying or, more importantly, offering for allegiance. A request for an immediate shipment of 8,000 Snider rifles for the defence of Herat did nothing to increase the FO's confidence in Lumsden. More than once he was chastised by both the Foreign and Indian offices, viz: 'Your telegram No. 10 of March 20 which is couched in a very unusual tone shows that you do not understand the situation of the Government, which is firmly to support the Ameer but to endeavour to settle the difference with Russia by negotiation.'[194]

During the long, difficult winter, Lumsden fell out with West Ridgeway. And then there was the problem of the press. 'You would hardly believe it,' wrote one officer to Currie at the Foreign Office, 'but a third of the Indian party seem to have received permission from the Indian Govt. to correspond with Indian and other papers. Ridgeway heads them as the representative of *The Times* and I was told a day or two ago that the clerk in charge of the office and the confidential archives is likewise the representative of some paper.'

As time went on tempers frayed even further and this flavoured Lumsden's official exchanges with the FO. It reached the point where Granville himself had to point out to Lumsden that 'the tone of many of Sir Peter's communications to this office was such as in an official experience of considerable length he never remembered as between an officer in employment and his official chief'. In January, Lumsden infuriated Gladstone by threatening to resign. Whitehall only tolerated all this because it was well aware of all the strains and dangers faced by the commission.[195]

Back in London, it was a difficult time as well. De Giers was a broken reed and promises came and went. If the Russians were not going to send a commission, should Britain take a stand, defend Herat, draw an arbitrary border and declare its crossing a *casus belli*? Casting around for the troops to accomplish this, what British reinforcements existed were already tied down on the Gordon relief expedition in the Sudan, whilst within India a full-scale Russian scare was building with much talk of pitting Sepoy against Cossack. A 'vast polemic literature' sprang up in an increasingly belligerent press both in Britain and in Russia.

It was difficult for Granville to know what to do because he did not know what was going on. The FO was receiving most of its information on the developing crisis through its consulate in Tehran and via the Indian government, which is to say it reached London as ever: garbled, thick, dated and unreadable. It received the damning 'X' and was filed away unread, as for example, the Indian government's *Gossip in Kandahar about Boundary Commission*, Sept–Oct 1884. It arrived on 5 January 1885. 'These are very old...' ran the comment on Mitchell's *Russian Abstract*. 'Already received from St P...' In February 1885, the 19 December 1884 *Peshawar Diary* arrived and was promptly filed away unread. This was common. These reports were so cluttered with obscure place names and tribes that they could not be properly digested. The clerks could only minute to Granville on the Kabul newsletters: 'Not much of interest in them. See one or two passages...' And on 8 September 1884: 'Nothing of much interest.'

In addition to problems of credibility, processing and simply addressing the mission, further delays occurred because the government of India often printed her lengthy reports before sending them on. The FO was loath to circulate such material beyond those most immediately involved. When *Rumours of Military Movements: Government of Kandahar* arrived, it was duly initialled by Currie and Granville but when one of Currie's officials suggested giving part of it wider circulation, Currie minuted: 'Not necessary, I think' and Granville concurred.[196]

This mass of indigestible information from the field meant that the FO relied more and more on the India Office and the Intelligence Department to separate the wheat from the chaff. For the ID the problem was with its Indian counterpart. The IBS was not running straight. It was clearly salting its reports with alarmist rumour which took on the mantle of truth. Not only that but Francis (later Viscount) Bertie at the Foreign Office suspected 'a wider want of arrangements' at the India Office itself. The poor, raw or partially processed information from India and the boundary commission was steadily eroding the reputation of the entire Indian establishment with the Foreign Office during these months of increasing tension.

Predictably, when the Indian Army's *Defence of India: a strategical study* was leaked to the press and St Petersburg, it was Russia's turn to point to the sentence: 'There can never be a real settlement of the Russo-Turkish question *til Russia is driven out of the Caucasus and Turkestan.*' Is this British policy? they asked. It was certainly gospel truth to the anti-Liberal press both in Britain and in India. The ID despaired. It was 'one great cause of difficulty in coming to an amicable solution of the dispute between the two countries'. What made matters worse for the ID was that the notional author was India's third most senior general, the Quartermaster General, responsible for the IBS, Charles Metcalf MacGregor, he of the trouble-making Napier–MacGregor mission in 1875.

Cameron immediately wired MacGregor for six copies which the Indian QMG, no doubt aware of the storm it was causing, sent with the disclaimer: 'I do not give them to you in your official capacity as head of the Intelligence Branch, War Office.' When they arrived, Cameron and Major L. A. Gregson, head of Section (B) (British

Colonies), demolished the arguments one by one in a succinct report to the War and Foreign offices discrediting the whole enterprise.

Cameron wrote that for every sound modern military reason the idea of an Indian invasion of Transcaspia was nothing short of ridiculous:

> It will be seen that we are recommended to operate on a general front of 600 miles from our frontier, along routes completely separated by wide tracts of impassable, rugged, mountainous country, and probably in most cases without telegraphic communications. For reasons already given each of these seven [Indian] Departments would require over 30,000 camels, or their equivalent in other beasts of burden.

What saddened the ID was the lack of balance at the IBS, which Gregson sighed 'was a mere branch of the author's office and would therefore probably repeat the opinion of its chief…' In fact, the book was written in large part at the IBS by 'a junior officer of imagination', Captain (later Lieutenant General Sir James) Grierson. In any event, the FO and the ID now had to deal with the fall-out: 'Prior to the appearance of the book all was quiet, there was no sign of any immediate disturbance; may it not, therefore, be fairly argued that our present difficulties with Russia are due in a great measure to the "Defence of India"?' Granville agreed. The report was publicly disowned. MacGregor was forced to issue disclaimers, Grierson was made to apologise and in 1886 he found himself packed off for a spot of re-education at Queen Anne's Gate.[197]

‡

By March 1885 the reality of Russia's actions was filling the intentional lines of her 'unofficial' map. When in March the expansionists let it be known that their frontier would run south of the Zulficar Pass and south of Penjdeh, an IBS officer assigned to the boundary commission wrote: 'They have nothing further to gain by an advance to Herat itself.' The Russian boundary commissioners still had not arrived and with the Indian boundary commission stuck out in no man's land, the Cabinet was forced to consider taking a stand against any further encroachment, not least defending Herat.[198]

In all this to-ing and fro-ing it was often hard then, as it is now, to see what would have tipped two countries over the edge into a vast Asian war without, in the eyes of the imperial government at least, any concrete reason. Yet there it was. The irresolution of the Liberal regime had arguably led to the fiasco in Egypt and the Sudan. Central Asia seemed to be going the same way. In late February, the Russian Ambassador to the Court of St James's wired to de Giers that if a Conservative government had been in power there would have been war.

Thus on 12 March, a message from Ridgeway arrived with the news that the Russians were arming 'their Turcomans' with breech-loaders and pleaded for permission to begin the wholesale defence of Herat along with a request for thousands of rifles to arm those Afghans who were allying themselves to the British. The possibility of this escalation in Asia gave the Cabinet all it needed to leave the Sudan, which it decided upon the same day, and the next day Ridgeway reported that the Russians were preparing to sweep over the Penjdeh.[199]

Russia's determination, Russia's forcefulness, Russia's bluster and the Indian Army's crying wolf led to three more months of bewilderment and vacillation. At its root was the question: was the Russian movement in the Penjdeh a continuation of its controlled expansion or was it the beginning of the long-awaited attack on India itself? Was it another feint or the end game? Should the troops being pulled out of the Sudan be deployed immediately to Afghanistan? How long would it take? No Liberal minister or officer of state was competent to assess the complex strategic question which now faced the imperial government without more facts.

Then, at this crucial juncture, the head of the ID's Russian Section, Captain (later Lieutenant General Sir James) Wolfe Murray, lanced the boil. The day after the decision to leave the Sudan he sent to the

FO one of the first 'special secret studies' from the ID, viz an intelligence estimate drawing all the strings together and the forerunner
of the type of report which Brackenbury would later use to maintain
and extend the Department's influence and reputation from 1886.[200]

If ever a report arrived in the nick of time, it was *Russian
Communications with the East*, coming as it did from a Russian specialist who had the necessary background to make sense of the welter of
indecipherable eastern information and more than enough skill and
experience to draw germane conclusions from it all. Certainly no other
person or agency was doing such analytical work, nor is there any
evidence of anyone within the FO or India Office attempting it.[201]

Like the pen-pictures drawn by Wilson and Ardagh, the author of
Russian Communications with the East, James Wolfe Murray, was said
to be spare, silent, shy and very bright. His nickname was 'Sheep'.
Educated at Harrow and Woolwich, like other scientific officers he
pressed to go to Staff College as early as he could and passed out first,
whereupon he was immediately posted to the ID in August 1884. In
Russian Communications with the East Wolfe Murray argued that if
Russia seriously meant to go to war, lines of communication ought
to begin appearing from deep within Russia down into Transcaspia
towards Penjdeh, the intended front. If she found it politically expe-
dient not to rile Turkey or further stir the Bulgarian pot (which was
spilling over already) then she would avoid the Black Sea, forging
ahead through Tzaritzin-Astrakhan to Krasnovodsk on the eastern
shore of the Caspian. The Volga was the avenue and, as it would not
be free of ice until April, 'if it be her intention to engage in a struggle
on the north-western frontier of Afghanistan … every day's delay at
the present moment is of value to her'.

Where was the evidence that lines of communications were being
laid? The ID enquired of the redoubtable Mr Peacock, consul responsible for Transcaucasia: 'Can you furnish designations or numbers
of Russian regiments reputed to have left Tiflis and details as to
composition and movements. Does "three more regiments" signify
regiments or battalions?' Other consuls and sources were alerted and

by the time Wolfe Murray's paper reached the FO, the ID reckoned that there was no evidence that there was even a reconnaissance-in-force moving towards Penjdeh much less an invading army. Nothing was heard. There were no lines, no preparations for war. The government's measured reaction (which is to say it did nothing) points to the reasonable presumption that the ID's analysis was pivotal.

Then, on 18 March, the ID followed up Wolfe Murray's paper with a comprehensive troop strength report based on 'a careful collation of all the information hitherto received' which placed the number of Russian troops in Transcaspia no more than 15,000–20,000 and revised the number of field artillery pieces downwards from seventy to twenty. These troops were clustered into three groups centred on Merv, Ashkhabad and the Sarakhs without any swift means of coming together. The consul at Tehran was pressed to find out how far the Russian railhead was from the Sarakhs. It was many miles away. Therefore when the Russians engineered and won a border skirmish with the Afghans on 30 March the government again did not overreact, as it knew from the intelligence supplied to it by the ID that, whilst the situation was volatile, there was no possibility that it was a signal for the large-scale invasion which the Indian authorities had feared. If, as later happened, it was claimed that this crisis was the primary reason for the withdrawal of British troops from the Sudan, it would be more accurate to say that it was a convenient excuse.[202]

Having looked at Russian capabilities, Major J. S. Rothwell, an acknowledged Russian expert who had just come to the ID from a professorship at the Staff College, performed the same analysis upon British and Indian forces. Delivered on 10 April 1885, *England's Means of Offence against Russia* pointed out that Britain's military might *vis-à-vis* Russia was 'far less favourable' than it had been on the eve of the Crimean War. A 50,000-man Russian force attacking Herat would successfully tie down the whole Indian Army, leaving the Royal Navy and, at the most, the rest of the British Army (36,000 troops in Britain and Ireland) to strike back. Using import and export figures, Rothwell showed that blockading the Baltic against Russian shipping would be useless. Attacking Cronstadt or other ports would be costly and absurd, and a lightning strike on St Petersburg would be worse folly. Indeed the peacetime strength of troops around the Czar's capital was only 6,000 short of Britain's worldwide maximum offensive force and within a fortnight the Russians could mobilise and arm three times that amount.[203]

If the Liberals needed any incentive to find a peaceful solution in the face of ignorant jingoism, the ID gave it to them. But, of course, the Department was not operating in a private world with the Foreign and India offices. With MacGregor's book came the whole supportive might of Horse Guards proposing grandiose operational plans against the Russians which, at that most inconvenient moment, the Department had to find time to refute convincingly. One such scheme, probably drawn up by a senior general with experience in riverine operations, sought to land a British force of 30,000 at Batum, join a Turkish force of 60,000 men, then together take the Batum–Baku railway, put transportable gunboats on the Caspian 'with a view to becoming complete masters of that sea' and from there strangle the Russian lines of communications, lines which the ID had shown were dormant at best.

As was standard practice by now, Wolfe Murray analysed the proposal. If he had found it to be feasible, he would no doubt have found favour at Horse Guards, but he could not. Asking the question as to what would make it work, he began by saying that Turkey's co-operation would be absolutely essential. As Muslims they could turn the tribes of the Caucasus mountains into allies. Their aid would make the Black Sea a British lake, tying down large numbers of Russian soldiers, creating thereby a two-front war which would complicate Russian logistics to such an extent that Afghanistan would rapidly become a secondary theatre.

Taking into account Russia's ready reserve and her powers of mobilisation, the situation would then improve for Britain – if the Austro-German coalition could be induced to actively join! Knowing of course that neither scenario was even remotely possible, Wolfe

Murray encircled his castles in the air with detailed planning, using *Kriegspiel* to play out the permutations. He even wrote a deception annexe to the main operational plan, based on a worldwide input of fake telegrams which, he was sure, the Russians would tap.

But try as he would, he concluded that if the Turks could not be swayed, then the difficulties facing the arriving British force could 'certainly be reckoned as enormous...' Indeed, he went on: 'Everything depends upon rapidity and secrecy of movement, and that therefore it would be almost useless to undertake the operations without having a force most fully equipped for an immediate advance upon landing.' Britain had no such force and did not even have enough equipment to support one army corps within Great Britain.[204]

Submitting this damp squib of all damp squibs, Wolfe Murray must have wondered at the worth of his career. But, like many other intelligencers, but like many other intelligencers of his generation, his time would come in the new century.

More and more wearisomely grand schemes continued to come in from the generals, all of which had to be analysed and discredited, which took time and energy. Meanwhile, the Russians did creep as near to Herat as they could, but no great armies accompanied them to back up these feints. Both Liberal and Conservative governments pressed for talks in an effort to contain the situation but there was no sense of panic. There were, of course, more confrontations to come but Britain's prescience allowed her to keep them in perspective. India's cries of wolf would be ignored. London was not interested in starting a great Asian war. Cameron summed it up for W. H. Smith in April 1885: 'It would scarcely be wise for two great nations to engage in a death struggle and spend hundreds of millions for this tract of country, of so little value as regards revenues, that the Afghans have never taken any adequate steps to secure their hold on it in times past.'

Britain was increasingly able to conduct a confident diplomacy knowing that the Intelligence Department was watching the rear door. As alluded to in the introduction, in October 1885 Cameron sent Salisbury one of the strangest documents he probably ever read, viz the tender document from the Russian Intendance Department for a year's supply of flour for the Russian Army. And, it will be recalled, from this paper alone the ID was able to see there was no planned expansion of the Russian Army (in fact it was downwards as it happened to 14,000 in Transcaspia and 33,000 in Turkestan, a precise 3,416 man shift and a 2,848 addition, but 'the proposed increase is too small to be looked upon as a menace'). But more importantly, there was no mention of contracts for new bakeries anywhere along the probable routes from Russia into Afghanistan. Low-level aggrandisement, yes. An invasion in 1886? No.[205]

‡

Since its formation, the Intelligence Branch, Simla had been a propaganda machine for the Forward School. There were several peculiarly Indian reasons why they behaved in this way. The ten or so officers assigned to the IBS at any one time between 1883 and 1893 were a breed apart. They were the fabled officers who carried out most of the extra-territorial forays of the last two decades of the nineteenth century, the men of whom Kipling and many others wrote and romanticised. Indeed, from the activities of the three directors of the IBS, it is clear that in exploration and adventure they had few equals. Colonel Mark Sever Bell, VC joined the IBS in 1880 after service in Ashanti with Robert Home (where he was awarded his VC). He had numerous adventures, went to northern China, then to several commands in the Bengal Presidency and the Army headquarters of the Madras and Bombay presidencies. In 1884 he was seen in southwest Persia, in 1885–86 Mesopotamia and Armenia and in 1887 back in China and Kashgar after leading the field intelligence effort in the Burma War of 1886–87. The other two directors of that era, Colonel William Lockhart and Colonel R. Woodthorpe, also had 'exciting histories'. They had both carried out extensive examinations of the passes of the Hindu Kush. Woodthorpe then surveyed upper Burma until he received the call to replace Lockhart as head of the IBS in 1889.

Like their predecessors, they spent a great deal of time collecting information about Russia's moves but, as London was proving, such low-level news about Russia's intentions was not half as valuable as information gathered from inside Russia. Some years before, Home had originally intended the IBS to work with the tribes, but as Winston Churchill noted some years later, the IBS was not even doing that. Rather the IBS was playing the Great Game and spoiling for a fight. Grierson, who had passed first into the Staff College in 1882 and after service in Egypt joined the IBS, was the ghost author of *The Defence of India*. He wrote to his father in May 1884: 'I am afraid our chance of a war with Russia is fading daily, but one never knows what hitch may by good luck get into the negotiations.' And the IBS's contribution to the United Services Institution of India's Gold Medal essay competition at that time by Major (later Lieutenant Colonel A. H.) Mason was entitled *The Strategical Measures best adopted for enabling troops to meet an army provided with artillery and all the modern arms of precision beyond our NW Frontier.*

The ID was not impressed. It tried to provide guidance by liaison, letters and even the planned infusion of officers offering advice from the ID (Ardagh and East were asked to go, but declined). It all fell on deaf ears. In mid-March 1885, for example, the ID wired the IBS asking for its much-delayed portion of a planned joint report on the situation in Transcaspia. In due course the IBS answered that the officer assigned that task had retired to Scotland and whilst they had been sending him highly classified documents through the regular post to aid him in writing the piece, they had gone missing.[206] The reaction of the ID can be imagined.

In addition, fresh ideas did not find favour. Those few Indian officers lucky enough to obtain a posting into the staff of the Indian Army regarded it as a long-term assignment and seven or eight years in the IBS was not uncommon. The IBS and the rest of the staff were known to less fortunate officers throughout India as 'the Mutual

Laudation Society' and there is considerable evidence to support this accusation. Mason, who wrote the essay mentioned above, was, like Woodthorpe, a protégé of Lockhart and accompanied him on all punitive expeditions. Younghusband, the fabled explorer, owed his chance for reconnaissance in Siam to Bell, who was trying to find a way around the Siamese mountains when that campaign turned east. Bell thereupon sent a secret messenger *all the way across India* to obtain Younghusband's services. Younghusband came onto the strength as an 'unpaid attaché', a corruption of the ID's Attached Officer scheme. 'Our place in the Military budget helped it to balance nicely both ways, for we were "unpaid attachés" in the Intelligence Branch. Probably we did not do very much work, salving our consciences with the solatum that our mild labours were given, free to a rich Empire.'

When Grierson secured his appointment to the IBS in 1882, with help from the editor of the *Allahabad Pioneer*, he excitedly wrote to his father:

> I need not point out to you that it is usually a stepping stone to a permanent appointment, that I am getting out of the hot weather in the plains, that I am in the midst of the Headquarters of the Army, and that is a billet very much sought after, and that I have been very lucky in getting it.[207]

Physically, the IBS was split into two offices, one at either end of the principal headquarters building at Simla. Like London, time and confidentiality were lost as classified messages, reports and letters were opened by clerks in a central registry outside IBS control. The result was that the IBS could not operate as a secret department even if it had wanted to. When, in 1891, Brackenbury took up his duties as Military Member on the Viceroy's Council, he found that the Indian government's more professional agencies, such as the Foreign and Political and Secret departments, were reluctant to deal with the IBS. Not surprisingly officials from these departments complained that the young, swaggering IBS officers did not conduct themselves with the decorum of those entrusted with great affairs of state.[208]

Yet the Commander-in-Chief in India, General Sir Frederick (later Field Marshal Earl) Roberts, was as pleased with the IBS as he had been when Quartermaster General. He defended it against the slings and arrows, which he put down to jealousy, and made it very clear that under his and MacGregor's aegis, the IBS had made 'great strides'.

Back in London the ID was weaving its web of influence and did not wish to be tainted by the IBS's bellicosity and unreliability. Fortunately, who should arrive in London as the London link of the ill-fated boundary commission but Grierson, slightly under a cloud as previously mentioned, Captain A. F. Barrow, the IBS's only Russian scholar, and George Napier.

Brackenbury had no intention of letting this opportunity pass. He formally asked the War and Indian offices for a separate Indian Section under Napier's command, the fulfilment of a departmental dream stretching back to Cardwell's day. Napier arrived, took one look around and declared that the proposed assignment was not to his liking. The section was stillborn. Brackenbury then had to explain it all to Roberts:

> Neither the India Office nor War Office would pay a clerk. Meanwhile my opinion of Napier was oozing away... His ignorance of Russian was, too, a fatal drawback. The one point in which this office can be useful to the India Office, is in our study of information from Russian sources. And if we could have here a really good Indian Officer with knowledge of Russian, who would take the Indian Frontier Countries, under the DAQMG [Deputy Assistant Quartermaster General] of the Russian Section, he could find ample work to do. At the present moment such an officer is here, Capt. Grierson, RA. But his heart is set on serving with troops...

Thwarted momentarily, Brackenbury set about wooing the India Office in the same way he was winning over the Foreign and Colonial offices. Whilst not perfect, he was still able to comment in September 1886 that the India Office was 'behaving very kindly now about sending us printed papers weekly; but there is still no such cordial and reciprocal interchange of information between my office and the India Office, as exists between us and the Foreign and Colonial offices – I trust to time to improve matters, and if we get a link in the shape of a hard-working pleasant fellow like Barrow, it will, I trust, bring us together. Napier soon snapped and the two ends of the broken chain fell apart.'[209]

Meanwhile the world was turning faster and faster. Whilst the Penjdeh affair was not yet settled in the east, the Russians continued to be active in the west. In September 1885, Prince Alexander of Bulgaria staged a *coup d'état* in Philoppolis and there was unrest in Eastern Roumelia. The Russians sniffed the wind and Ambassador White in Constantinople feared that they had just enough clout to reoccupy Bulgaria as a prelude to a *coup de main* upon Constantinople. Brackenbury agreed and forecast that if the Russians intended to move on the Turks, they would do so through Asia Minor, a whole different scenario than Afghanistan. Indeed, there were indications that this was already happening. Russia was building a Black Sea fleet, renounced Batum's free port status, fortified Sevastopol and made every sign of pressing ahead with the trans-Caucasian railway.

Salisbury, again Foreign Secretary, was concerned. This was not Merv nor Herat. If the military and Pan-Slav parties chose to move in Bulgaria or Turkey in a 'great effort' neither de Giers nor the Czar would be able to stop them. Only Turkey and Britain would stand in the way.

Brackenbury called for advice and Major W. A. H. Hare of the ID's Asia Section produced his October 1885 analysis of the Ottoman armed forces. They were as corrupt and weak as ever. Turkey's attempt at modernisation was bankrupting the Porte and Brackenbury concluded that Turkey neither could nor would stand against Russia alone.[210] Again, that left Britain to face the bear. Brackenbury now produced a Wolfe Murray-style *Sketch* for the Cabinet. After pages of fact and analysis, he concluded:

> If this view be correct, or even plausible the question of our position in regard to the Porte assumes a vital importance ... It is evident that we are practically powerless to defend the Ottoman Empire in any part of its dominions, and the conditions on which we hold Cyprus demand the most careful consideration. Can we longer believe in Turkish promises of reform? In other words can we expect the Turk to cease being a Turk? Shall we not soon have Russia pointing at us as breakers of our Treaty? And should we not, by the acquisition of Cyprus, which becomes daily of greater importance, at any pecuniary sacrifice, get rid once for all of any Treaty obligations with regard to Asia Minor?[211]

If Turkey was a broken reed, reliable intelligence about the Russians in the field was all the more important not least because of the excitable news from Constantinople of Russians here, there, everywhere, even an army corps in Bessarabia. After a meeting between the ID, the NID and the Foreign Office, a number of travellers from the ID were sent out all though Asia Minor. Wolfe Murray and Barrow attended the Russian summer manoeuvres as HMG representatives and then contrived to quietly return via Odessa. Captains Beaufort and Surtees, two temporary officers, were sent travelling in Transcaspia (but as so often happened at that time, were actually contracted to write for the *Daily News* and *The Globe* about their journeys). The Russians lost no time in arresting Beaufort, and the Ambassador, Morier, had to grovel to de Giers to get him released. As Brackenbury told Wolseley: 'We had better be easily appeased by his arrest.' Upon their return the Duke, none other, reprimanded them and forbade them to do any more travelling.[212] Other consuls reported movements according to their several lights and Colonel Henry Hozier, late of the Topographical & Statistical Office, now the influential secretary of Lloyd's of London, regularly monitored and reported on maritime traffic.

Meanwhile the British and Indian press were panicking and the Department was again swamped with a welter of alarmist reports and unwieldy contingency plans. Yet, as in Afghanistan so in the west and Wolfe Murray reported steadily to the Foreign Office that it was 'tolerably certain that no orders for the mobilisation of troops at Sevastopol and Odessa have been given, and so far as I could see nothing of the kind appeared to be contemplated'.

As it was, the Bulgarian affair settled down to 'an uneasy stalemate' and the unfortunate Earl of Iddesleigh, then briefly Foreign Secretary in Salisbury's Cabinet, began to re-examine Britain's relationship with Turkey so pointedly called into question by Brackenbury in September and October 1886. He and Iddesleigh found themselves thinking on the same lines. Britain might yet fight to save Constantinople but 'whether she would do so to obviate the danger of an attack is very questionable' even if it meant the Russians taking the Black Sea and closing the Dardanelles to the British. The Porte must be left in no doubt that if Turkey did not defend itself or Bulgaria adequately, Britain would have to consider its position afresh. If Turkey did not stand up to Russia, added Iddesleigh in sending on the ID's latest threat assessment to Ambassador White in Constantinople, 'England will probably change her tactics, and try to safeguard her Eastern Empire by measures of her own, which would not be framed upon the old model. Our position in Egypt for instance might have to be reconsidered.'[213]

And it was more than that. As Wolfe Murray had indicated the previous year, it would take an impossibly close alliance with the Turks in the west to hold down the Russians, absorb their reinforcements and weaken their thrust into Afghanistan. An Anglo-Persian alliance would be 'indispensable' and even Chinese assistance would help. Brackenbury and Captain William Hall, the Director of National Intelligence (DNI), again looked at hitting Vladivostok, but try as they could, as Brackenbury had suggested in his August *Sketch*, it was better disentangling oneself altogether from Turkish defence before the Russians parlayed it into an excuse for an Asian war.[214]

Britain was better out of it. She had not the troops. Even in those heady days when Buller, Brack and Wolseley were hand in glove, Brackenbury could not imagine interesting the government of any stripe to mobilise an army she did not have in the defence of a crumbling empire spread over thousands of miles. Meanwhile, India had also set up a mobilisation committee under Roberts which planned for two army corps and one reserve department, the formation of which anticipated that, if asked, Britain would send it 30,000 troops, almost the entire total of Britain's reserve.

In ironic timing, the Indian mobilisation report of September 1886 reached Edward Stanhope, the new War Minister, in 1887 just after he feigned ignorance of the ID's recent home mobilisation report. Matters came to a head on April Fool's Day 1887 when Brackenbury attended a War Office Council meeting, significant in itself as he was rarely invited. At that meeting the Council concluded that 'India must not depend upon more Bns. [battalions] from England as part of a plan for mobilisation but that she will always be ready to give what assistance she can in times of emergency'. Stanhope passed this on to the Indians on 5 April and the news no doubt came as a sobering blow.[215]

So how did the Empire fare in 1887 in the golden spring of its imperial era? In Britain, the report of Hartington's Royal Commission on the administration of the Army and Navy was a year away as was the planned dramatic increase of the Royal Navy. Also, Home's mobilisation plans were going ahead slowly. Overseas, there was no question of willingly supporting India and the Turks and Persians were hardly to be counted upon to face up to Russia alone. Plans needed to be brought forward to remove any possible ground of contention between Britain and Russia and so contain an enemy who could not be fought.

The best idea, thought Brackenbury, would be to finally delimit the Russo-Persian boundary. 'For, should the Russians at some future time succeed in annexing the north-west of Persia as far south, say, as Kauf, and find the frontier south of Zulficar in what is believed to be its present indefinite state, they might be tempted to make dangerous encroachments, which a little foresight might have obviated.'[216]

He was much heartened when, at long last in January 1887, West Ridgeway and Barrow wrangled an agreement with the Russians over Penjdeh which was not unfavourable to the Afghans and suggested to Salisbury that it would be well to define a military frontier in Afghanistan 'beyond which we must never allow Russia to pass'.

Salisbury read Brackenbury's 'able paper' and commented on it at length, which was unusual for him. He mused that such a tripwire was possible only if successive administrations were likely to show a 'continuity of policy' towards India, which he doubted:

> If Afghanistan is to be the only or the principal theatre of war the point where Russian aggression is to be checked must depend largely on the circumstances of the moment. The contents of Major General Brackenbury's memorandum tend to show that the alternative course of 'making war with Russia all over the world' is an empty phrase unless Great Britain has command of the Turkish Army, and it is as certain as any diplomatic forecast can be that Gt. Britain will never have that command.

Brackenbury's memorandum and Salisbury's considered reply were sent to Stanhope, Lord Cross at the India Office and the Viceroy as the last word.[217] But the numerous members of the Forward School were not by any means ready to accept Brackenbury's logic. Thus many of the ID's eastern activities from 1886–96 were involved in exposing scaremongering by the IBS and Indian officers, by investigating rumours, criticising the realism of India's grandiose mobilisation plans, posting ID officers to the IBS and scoffing at a new threat: Anglo-Asian railway projects.

‡

Railways were, naturally, all the rage. For some time, prospectors had been lobbying in Constantinople and Tehran for rail concessions, such as their counterparts were doing in South America, the western

United States and Australia, lured on by dreams of profitable haulage. Railways also brought with them informal influence. In July 1887, Ambassador White asked Salisbury to allow the ID to evaluate the competing projects and advise which was most practical. In reply, Brackenbury told White: 'I fail to see what strategical importance there can be to this nation in railways in Asia Minor.' Britain could only defend Asiatic Turkey with Turkish assistance, which was in no way to be relied upon. Any rail line from the Mediterranean to the Persian Gulf would be of use to the Indian or British military only if Turkey allowed Britain to use it. And Brackenbury reckoned that this condition would not be fulfilled unless Britain had command of both the Mediterranean and the Persian Gulf:

> without which it is useless. If we were in a position to command the alliance of Turkey and Persia in a war against Russia, I should attach the utmost importance to a railway from the Mediterranean to the Persian Gulf; but Persia has slipped out of our hands; and Lord Salisbury's despatch implies, if I read it aright, that the game is up in regard to Turkey. As long as we have command of the Mediterranean, we can use the Suez Canal, and if that is blocked, the railways through Egypt, and I think the small gain of time between the Mediterranean and Karachi, which is the sole remaining advantage to be gained for us by such a railway is not of sufficient value to make this line of primary importance to Great Britain under existing political conditions.[218]

The IBS on the other hand enthusiastically backed just those railway projects which the Department in London believed unsound. In 1887 the IBS director, Colonel M. S. Bell, VC, wrote a memorandum urging British merchants to seek trade in Persia and proposed a railway to tie Persia to India commercially and strategically. In November, Bell visited Tehran and suggested to the new envoy, Sir Henry Drummond Wolff, that Britain should press the Shah for a railway concession to Baron Reuters for a line from Quetta to the Seistan border. Bell wanted to use the terminus as a railhead in case the Russians invaded Khorrassan.

Drummond Wolff heartily supported this scheme. When news of this reached Salisbury, he said it was out of the question whereupon Bell proposed metalled cart roads instead![219]

Not long after, Drummond Wolff reported that Prince Dolgorouki, his counterpart in Tehran, was pressing the Shah to grant Russian contractors a concession from the Caspian to Boognord near the headwaters of the Kārun allowing the Russians access to the Persian Gulf. There were also rumours of another line from the Sarakhs along the Afghanistan frontier. He wired for instructions on 26 January 1889. The Foreign Office consulted Brackenbury, who again warned against the railway on strategic grounds and because of the resulting financial and military burden on India.

That did not stop Drummond Wolff, who telegraphed again on 9 February to report that Dolgorouki's proposals were about to put Persia into Russian hands and proposed yet another counter-route. Sir Thomas (later Baron) Sanderson, then the new Assistant Under-Secretary at the FO, consulted Brackenbury and wired back that any concessions awarded to the Russians would have to be matched by concessions awarded to the British. Sanderson was sure, however, that none of the promoters had enough capital in any event. Again, Drummond Wolff returned to his project of building a railway from Quetta to the edge of Siestan through Baluchistan, a project which was warmly greeted, if not inspired, by Bell. To seal his case, the envoy referred to the IBS diary for December 1888, which catalogued Russia's extensive (and in reality largely notional) building programme.[220]

This very same diary had already reached the FO via the ID in February with a note from Brackenbury condemning 'the tone of exaggeration throughout the whole summary which is much to be regretted'. The FO agreed and sent the ID's corrections to the diary directly to Drummond Wolff. The FO and the ID were getting fed up. A few weeks later, Wolfe Murray poured yet more water on the 'most stupendous scheme' and Brackenbury sent to Sanderson a private note from the sound commercial attaché in Tehran, Sir E. Law, which agreed with Wolfe Murray's criticism. Brackenbury then wrote a memorandum demolishing first the commercial and, as importantly, the military arguments advanced by Bell and Drummond Wolff. He recalled Napoleon's campaigns of 1812 and 1815, in which he had 'assumed a bold offensive. In the first he was beaten by climate and distance; in the second by superior numbers... And these are precisely the enemies which we should have to encounter in assuming the offensive against Russia in Central Asia.'[221]

Brackenbury went on. He failed to understand how 'the advance of a single line of railway to a remote corner of Persia would make our influence in that country equal to that of Russia', which virtually controlled most of Persia already. Bell, he agreed, was 'an intrepid explorer in oriental countries and a keen observer' but he was also 'an enthusiast and a dangerous enthusiast'. Citing the moderate Major General Edward Chapman (later General Sir Edward Chapman, Quartermaster General in India and Brackenbury's successor at the ID) Brackenbury concluded that a more important task would be to bring the frontier tribes under British influence. Salisbury sent Brackenbury his 'best thanks' and Sanderson minuted: 'Inform Sir H. Wolff that the scheme, whatever its eventual advantages may be, is premature for the present.'[222]

Tenacious, thick skinned or simply living in a capital where it seemed that rail concessions were the sole topic of conversation, Drummond Wolff returned to the fray again and again in the ensuing three years. The ID's line, and therefore the FO's line, was clear. No railway concessions to the Russians without an equal concession to the British and if so to 'delay by every possible means their construction'. To quote Brackenbury again:

The safety of our Indian Empire from any attack by Russia lies in the distance which separated the Russian base on the Trans Caspian Railway from the Indian frontier, combined with the difficulties of supply and transport throughout that distance which render it impossible for larger forces to be employed against India. Every mile of railway which Russia makes southward into Khorrassan or along the Perso-Afghan frontier diminishes pro tanto those difficulties. Convinced that all idea of an invasion of India by Russia from her present base may be safely dismissed, I am equally convinced that at some future day, when Khorrassan and Northern Afghanistan have been pierced by Russian railways and turned into granaries for Russian armies, unless an unforeseen convolution has broken up the Russian Empire, Great Britain will be confronted with this fearfully difficult problem – how to defend her Indian frontiers against the masses which Russia will then be able to employ. Commercially, every rood of eastern ground that comes under Russian influence is so much lost to British trade; and I hold, therefore, that it is little short of treason to every interest of our Empire to connive at or assent in any way to promotion of Russian railways in the north of Persia.[223]

Salisbury needed no convincing. No railways was the message sent firmly to St Petersburg and Tehran. M. de Giers agreed and on 12 November 1890, the new Russian envoy in Tehran, M. Butzow, signed an agreement with the Shah prohibiting all railway construction for ten years. Everyone except Drummond Wolff and the IBS were relieved. Morier in St Petersburg wrote to Salisbury of de Giers: 'I do not know that I ever saw his Excellency display such unalloyed pleasure. He said "We are quit of the question..."'[224]

There is very little doubt that Drummond Wolff had fallen prey to bad advice from the IBS and from Colonel C. S. MacLean, the Indian consul at Meshed. MacLean was only there because the Indian government had, without recourse to London, given him leave to advise the rulers of Herat. Salisbury naturally objected to this way of proceeding as it implied 'a half-promise of assistance' as MacLean knew it would. Unlike his predecessor in Tehran, Drummond Wolff was inordinately influenced by MacLean's incautious reports. Sanderson called them *canards* and to quote a typical one:

(Private and Confidential) (From MacLean through Wolff to India for the IO and the FO). Please forward to Lord Salisbury. Meshed telegraphs: ... it is reported that Afghans have advanced towards Kerki and Penjdeh, and have killed two or three hundred Russians; that General Komaroff was to start with two battalions, and that he has started; that he had orders to go to Herat. Trains still passing full of soldiers, and all traffic stopped. Reported collision from two distinct sources.

Each time one of these arrived, the ID was called upon to answer, counter and explain away these melodramatic messages. Finally the FO formally warned the Indian government about MacLean's 'very bad habit of telegraphing any rumor [sic] that reaches him without waiting to verify it'. Strong language, indeed, but it did nothing to stop MacLean or dampen the excitement he caused. By the late 1880s MacLean's reports and most of the IBS monthly summaries were receiving the fatal 'X' which by then was also being applied to more and more of Drummond Wolff's despatches, especially after he sent in a note claiming that the Russians were on the verge of attacking Tehran.[225]

As the Department pointed out time and again throughout the late 1880s, the Russians had problems of their own. In the first place the Russian Army was inefficient and corrupt. Its only advantage was its size, but to move it anywhere, with the huge logistical trail which would be involved, was a disadvantage. Senior officers had 'no special merit or capacity'. It was doubtful, even to the Russians themselves, whether they could 'maintain as yet any very large force on active service there (i.e. Afghanistan or neighbouring countries) for any length of time, inasmuch as the resources of those countries for the maintenance of troops are so scanty'. The Russians on the Bulgarian border was one thing, quite another near the Indian border. Throughout Asia, Russian settlements were failing, the trans-Caspian railway was operating at a minimal level and by 1890 it was clear to the ID, as the Russian Intendance Department tender document showed, that Russian troop centres were in the west, towards southern Europe and in the Far East near China.

In 1891, just after he left the Division, Wolfe Murray made his only public pronouncement on his work and the damage done by the Forward School. Writing in the *United Services Magazine* he commented that:

> those whose business it is to follow the progress of the Russian Empire are thoroughly and keenly aware that her path is beset by the same or similar pitfalls as that of her neighbours... By ascribing to her this almost supernatural freedom from restraint, by failing to apply to her the same rules which obtain in dealing with other sublunary powers, we simply place the trump card in her hand.[226]

‡

The remaining obstacle to quiet in the east was the Indian military itself. To set the stage it was not known outside of the highest echelons of government, but Brackenbury and the DNI had come to the conclusion that French naval strength had grown in just a decade to such an extent that the Mediterranean was very much a French lake. The Royal Navy would not be facing just one power, but a combination of powers given the increasingly close understanding between Paris and St Petersburg. In short, British reinforcements (assuming there were any) would be hard pressed to sail eastwards through the Mediterranean without French or Russian acquiescence, as problematic as that might prove.

In addition, Britain's policy towards the Russians in the east was settled in the Salisbury–Brackenbury correspondence of August 1887. In that exchange, Brackenbury had specifically called into question the Indian request for British reinforcements 'without showing what it is they propose to undertake, and what forces that proposed action will demand'. The Indians had more or less ignored this and it was only by accident that the ID and FO learned that it was Indian policy to consider any infringement of Afghanistan's 'borders' a *casus belli*. They had it all planned. They would mobilise, request British reinforcements which would sail through the Mediterranean, assemble hundreds of miles from their point of disembarkation, march on Herat and thence drive a wedge all the way to the Caspian Sea.

Brackenbury wearily commented:

> There is nothing to show that such gain to our prestige as success-ful action at Herat would bring, would compensate for the enormous additional strain, military, political and financial, which it would involve. But what would be the result of failure there, with 500 miles of desert between the beaten army and its base, with the Afghans, and the Persians, too, hanging on the track of the retreating troops? What would be the effect in India? Most careful study of this report has satisfied me that even if we grant all its assumptions as to our ability to move a force of 50,000 men to Herat, the advantages of success there have been greatly overstated, and the consequences of failure have not been considered.[227]

Now that the Indian plan was known at Horse Guards and Whitehall, and anxious to keep what reserve forces there were uncommitted and under imperial control, all factions at the War Office agreed with Brackenbury. Sir Guy Fleetwood Wilson at the War Office wrote to Ardagh: 'We have come to a deadlock as regards India. As far as I can make out, India mildly request, in the event of having to mobilise, rather more men than this country possesses *in toto*.' On 30 July, the Duke, Wolseley, other senior officers including Major General O. R. Newmarch, the military adviser to the India Office, and Brackenbury met to consider what to do. Brackenbury and Newmarch were selected to represent the War Office's view in a memorandum for the Cabinet.

It was ready by 19 August. In it the two generals did 'not hesitate to condemn' Roberts's scheme 'as in the very highest degree dangerous and unsound'. Why, they asked, should the Indians (reinforced by unacclimatised troops fresh from England) march out with 59,350 men and 36,644 animals over hard terrain to Herat where they would still be 275 miles from the trans-Caspian railhead? No. If any trouble came, far better to watch the Russians waste themselves on the long and hazardous march through Afghanistan only to come up on the Indians, fresh and well supplied at the right debouche points.

Eight copies of the Brackenbury–Newmarch report were printed. Brackenbury, in one of his rare letters to Wolseley in this period, wrote: 'I view the Indian scheme with much apprehension & would strongly recommend that it be snuffed out by the Home Government in very decided terms.' Wolseley and the Duke agreed, as did Stanhope, who urged his Cabinet colleague, Cross, to instruct the Indian government 'to accept this report as the basis of their arrangements for mobilisation'. As far as the imperial government was concerned that spelled an end to the matter. India had to work within her means. The Forward School reacted angrily to this instruction and mounted a fresh press campaign, but it was ineffectual.

There was just one more thing to be done: send a senior British general to sit as Military Member on the Viceroy's Council, a position at least equal to and certainly separate from that held by the C-in-C, Roberts. By late 1890 when all this was going on, Brackenbury's five years as Director of Military Intelligence were almost over. Salisbury was as generous in his appreciation of the DMI's advice as he had been of Home's in earlier years. He would be the man for the job. Thus Salisbury wrote to Cross on 6 November 1890:

I have been strongly pressed by several authoritative persons to write to you about Brackenbury that I venture to do so – though I very much dislike the position of seeming to offer advice to one who is much better placed for forming a judgement than I am.

But at the Foreign Office I have had a great deal of intercourse with Brackenbury some personal – most of it written - & I have formed a very high opinion of his ability and clearness of judgement. He is one of the very ablest soldiers we have got – I mean for the council room. Of course I know nothing of his capacity for the field. I am bound to say this for him – he has an independent judgement and may not receive from his superiors the full commendation he deserves.

On 7 November Cross telegraphed the Viceroy, Lord Lansdowne, that Stanhope 'strongly supported' Brackenbury's nomination, repeating on 14 November: 'I have a great fancy for Brackenbury as Military Member. He is without a doubt a very able man.' Roberts quite naturally objected, but he was resoundingly overruled and on 29 December 1890 the Queen approved Brackenbury's appointment to the Council. Cross wrote to Lansdowne: 'She says I am to warn you that he is a good deal of an army reformer.'[228]

‡

As Brackenbury went to India, his place at the Division was taken by Major General Edward Chapman, QMG India, who had dissented from the 1885 report on Indian defences. Chapman and Brackenbury with some help from Ardagh, still the Viceroy's secretary, were soon communicating regularly to control the worst excesses of the IBS. Like his predecessors, Chapman campaigned for extra consuls:

> Our means of communications, through newspapers reporting to our agents in Persia, and in Peshawar and Quetta, is an old and worn-out arrangement. Brackenbury agreed and told Lansdowne that 'the reports of our news-writers are the cause of much unnecessary alarm in this country ...When I was at the War Office, I had repeatedly to call attention to the reckless way in which they accepted the new-writers' reports as Gospel...'

It was time to sort out the IBS. Now in post, Brackenbury wrote to Roberts on 21 September 1891 with the observation that:

> the work proper of the Intelligence Branch in India seems to me to be strictly confined to the recording, collating, compiling, and distributing the information received from political and military officers in the countries bordering upon India, and the preparation of maps and gazetteers of those countries. It should also, I think, in consultation

with the Surveyor-General, prepare confidential maps of all countries in which the army of India might be required to conduct military operations. It should on no account whatever undertake any political work or express any political opinions, which are the distinct function of the Foreign Department under the Government of India.

Brackenbury thereupon set about reorganising the IBS lock, stock and barrel. He proposed that work should be divided between four sections, consisting of one DAQMG and one paid attaché apiece. IBS officers thus assigned were 'on no account [to] be allowed to leave their offices for the purpose of conducting explorations'. The London five-year rule for staff appointments was to be strictly enforced. The head of the IBS was to be responsible for every piece of paper which left his unit and nothing, absolutely nothing, was to be printed without the Foreign Department's approval. Lastly, added Brackenbury:

> I cannot refrain from expressing my opinion that the confidence of Government being a preliminary element of success in any Intelligence Department all its officers should be serious men and should devote their whole time to their duties. Nothing tends more to shake faith in such a department than the idea that its officers, or any of them are idle men, who can find time to take a prominent part in amusements which must of necessity take them away from their special duties.

Brackenbury sought an additional Rs 10,000 for 'the services of the ablest young officers in the army' making it clear that it was 'essential that appointment to it [i.e. the IBS] should be recognised as carrying a good claim for future employment'. The India Office agreed and on 30 May the reorganisation was sanctioned. Immediately a weekly postal liaison was established between Chapman and Colonel (later Major General Sir E. R.) Elles, the new head of the IBS.[229]

It was not going to be easy to bring the IBS up to the standard set by Brackenbury and Chapman. It has been argued that Brackenbury 'did not want rival analyses to interfere with an overall army intelligence assessment' and when Elles drew up a scheme casting the Indian Army in an invading role, Brackenbury abruptly sent him back to his map making. Even there Chapman had to caution Elles not to print boundaries in colour for fear it might be used against India in any future boundary negotiations. Then an officer's name appeared on a secret report. Brackenbury quickly responded: 'It should never appear in these secret reports that the observer was sent by authority... These reports do get into French and/or Russian hands...' The lessons and rebukes came with such frequency that after the DNI had joined the DMI in a withering critique of an IBS report, Chapman felt it necessary to add a soothing note to Elles that their comments were not activated by any motive other than that of the good of the public service.[230]

The immediate gain, of course, was that Brackenbury and Chapman now gained control of Indian strategic planning. Brackenbury began quiet moves to replace Roberts with General Sir George White, as someone less obsessed with every Russian move, and this came to pass in 1893. And young Captain Grierson, who had in all his IBS analyses 'regarded a Russian invasion of India not only as possible but as inevitable', was sent home to Chapman. At 16–18 Queen Anne's Gate, his views changed. Reviewing Grierson's 1892 paper on Russian preparations, Brackenbury sent him his congratulations:

I was immensely interested in your memorandum on the Russian movements in 1892, and in the conclusion which you draw that all these movements point to concentration on their Western Frontier, and that the troops in Central Asia will be left to take care of themselves. I was quite certain that this was the case; but your memorandum strengthened my hands greatly against those in this country, and there are many, who live in constant state of apprehension of Russian aggression against India, an apprehension which they never disguise, which they communicate to a timorous press, and thus play the very game of Russia, which is, and you and I have always agreed, to paralyse the whole Army of India by threats of aggression along its northern frontier.

The Viceroy and India Office agreed.[231]

Whilst on the whole the IBS was no longer the agent for provoking Russian scares, it did not mean, however, that it shrank into a tin can. Whilst Brackenbury was set against any activities, covert or clandestine, which would stir up a diplomatic or murderous hornet's nest, the central Asian consulates remained active and officers from India 'occasionally roamed the mountains and deserts engaged on undercover missions, most of which were not recognised as "official"'.[232] But overall the Forward School, robbed of credence at the highest levels, slid henceforth into a prolonged decline being replaced as appropriate over time by a much more realistic attitude to a 'scientific frontier', a frontier with Afghanistan which was 'closely garrisoned and monitored for any signs of disturbance or sedition' in a way everyone understood.[233]

As for the home Intelligence Division the Russian spectre was now a military problem of manageable proportions. Brackenbury's achievements at home and in Asia liberated Salisbury both from his Asia yoke and from any idea of a rival centre of strategic concern. This allowed him to concentrate on the area where the Empire's security was more at risk: Africa.

CHAPTER SEVEN

WE HAD THE FRENCH 'ON TOAST'

By the last decade of Queen Victoria's reign, Africa was almost as open to Europeans as the Wild West. Traders, explorers, government agents and get-rich-quick boys leapfrogged each other to stake out great tropical tracts, bringing with them European loyalties, European problems and European hegemony. Europe itself was finely balanced and the various powers looked on newly acquired African lands to give themselves added strength and prestige vis-à-vis *their continental neighbours.*

Britain still remained aloof from European entanglements and was reluctant to become involved in the scramble for Africa. It was a futile hope, for Britain's two power centres in India and Britain were divided by Africa, the lifelines between the two lying through the Suez Canal in the north or around the Cape in the south.

Because historically the handling of African issues by the British government was divided between the Foreign, Colonial, War and Indian offices, there was a want of overall direction and policy which disturbed and exercised the ID greatly. It was left to the ID to stand at their doors and point out the threats whilst at the same time resolutely moving to insinuate that want of direction and policy which they believed necessary if Britain was to retain a freedom of action upon which the whole emerging Empire would grow to depend.

That direction and policy sprang from the efforts of Home and Wilson before Constantinople. For convenience and accuracy of attribution, it may be called Wilson's doctrine, a given in the minds of three generations of intelligencers which held that imperial well-being, prosperity in Egypt and the safety of the Nile depended upon a peaceable Sudan in one direction and control over the headwaters of the Nile in the other.

In February 1886, Ardagh angrily summed the ID's frustration in a private letter:

> Tranquillity in Egypt means an active military policy in the Soudan. Egypt can no more ignore and cut herself free from the Soudan, than England can sever her connection with Ireland. The policy of abandoning the Soudan was, in my opinion, a blunder, and the late announcement that British troops were not going to Dongola [26 February] is another piece of stupid frankness of the same sort.[234]

And, true to their word, the Liberals, still reeling from Gordon and its messy aftermath, flatly ordered the final wholesale evacuation of the Sudan on 13 June 1885. The Conservatives on assuming office ten days later did nothing to reverse the decision. They tidied up Egypt's southern border and agreed to hold what had been built of the Wadi Halfa railway. Egypt thereupon receded from the minds of the politicians and the public, too. Whatever dangerous and uncertain future lay ahead, it was far off.

Yet when Henry Brackenbury, the new head of the ID, looked around the coastline of Africa in April 1886 he could point to an increasing amount of activity. There was the secret construction of a splendidly huge French naval base at Bizerta on the Mediterranean and a power vacuum in Morocco which either Spain or France seemed destined to fill. In West Africa, the Department pointed out 'the potential element of great danger' from French-backed Mohammedan armies to Sierra Leone, the only British coaling station between Gibraltar and the Cape. In South Africa, there was the security and the upgrading of the inadequate defences of the Cape. On the coast of East Africa the French were taking control of Madagascar, the Comoro Islands and the building of another large naval station which, 'standing as it does almost directly in the line between the Cape and our Indian possessions, will form in time of war a port of refuge and shelter from cruisers preying upon our commerce east of the Cape'. British Mauritius was too ill defended to respond to this threat. Then the French established yet another port at Zeyla in the Gulf of Aden and even the Italians began scouting the Red Sea, much too near the Suez Canal for sanguinity.

Thus the ID set itself the task of monitoring continental explorations and incursions all across, up and down the continent. It also worked up schemes to keep the Europeans at bay. Yet it was neither the Mahdists nor the French but the Italian advance from the Red Sea which gave Brackenbury the opportunity to take the next step in bringing into existence the ID's long-matured Nilotic strategy.

‡

Italy was, in effect, a new country, recently unified and very keen to have its place in the sun. It spent considerable capital it did not have on colonial ventures. Having established themselves in the coastal port of Massawa a considerable Italian expeditionary force struck westward. This was initially viewed in Cairo and London as ridiculous posturing, but if they were prepared to shoulder some of the responsibility of patrolling the southern Red Sea coast against any other continental incursion and slavers then they might be looked upon as proxy Brits without any claim on the public purse, thus Baring in Cairo suggested to Sir John (later Baron Savile) Lumley, the British envoy in Rome. The Foreign Office, which had not initially been consulted, asked Brackenbury for his opinion. He knew that 'our object is to remain on the most friendly terms possible' with Italy, yet he could not help but point out that the Italians were already extending their influence over tribes within what the British considered was their sphere of influence along the Red Sea.[235]

Brackenbury recommended, and the FO agreed, to send Watson's successor as Governor of Suakin, Horatio Herbert Kitchener (later Earl Kitchener of Khartoum), to Massawa to demarcate spheres of influence on the ground in order to prevent friction between the Italians, the tribes and the British on behalf of the Egyptians. Recognising that dealing with friends can be more difficult than treating with rivals, Brackenbury's idea went to the Cabinet in February 1887. It warily expressed willingness to form, as Salisbury told the Queen, 'as close an alliance as the Parliamentary character of our institutions will permit', and some local agreements were made. This allowed Baring to authorise Kitchener to begin consolidating Anglo-Egyptian influence in the eastern Sudan and Salisbury authorised £10,000 from the imperial Exchequer for that purpose. In a minute which could have been written by Brackenbury, Salisbury noted: 'It will not do – on this ground alone – to allow these Red Sea ports to fall into German or French hands.'[236]

Yet the Italians had no intention of simply patrolling the coast. They lost no time in pressing the British to acknowledge their 'jurisdiction' as far as Ras Kasar, basing their claim upon Massawa's previous suzerainty over that area. Back at the ID, Captain G. A. K. Wisely pointed out that Ras Kasar and Ras Harb lay within territory commonly held to be controlled by the Habab or Beni Amir tribes, the very tribes with which Kitchener was forming links. And again, Brackenbury urged a sounder Anglo-Italian demarcation agreement to bottle up the Italians. Back and forth went the correspondence and Major W. R. R. Fox, chief of the ID's mapping section, produced sophisticated cartographic and demographic support to back the British case.[237]

By 1887, the Intelligence Department recognised that the Italians could only be contained if there was a firm boundary between Egyptian and Italian interests, best settled locally in friendship between Kitchener and General Gene, the Italian commander. It got off to a ragged start when the Italians took an inch and turned it into a mile by ordering surveillance from Massawa to Ras Kasar. This meant that the intelligencers' ideal of a British-controlled Eastern Sudan was being rent daily by Italian shears.

Wilson, vilified by Wolseley for failing to save Gordon, was residing in cold exile with the Irish Ordnance Survey when in December 1888 he sent unbidden to Montagu Corry, Salisbury's private secretary whom he knew well, a reiteration of his doctrine extended with the caveat that Britain must keep the *entire* Nile valley inviolate against any other power.

Corry responded immediately by asking Wilson to write it up into a memorandum for the Prime Minister. Like his influential papers of 1882, 1884 and 1885, this new memorandum of January 1889 carefully argued that Britain must drive away any and all foreign interlopers from the Sudan and the Nile. He cautioned Salisbury that a European power which re-established trade through Suakin:

> will almost certainly drift into an occupation or protectorate of the Sudan. A civilised power controlling in a scientific manner the courses of the Atbara, and the two Niles, would have Egypt completely at its mercy. Sawakin is therefore of importance to Egypt as the Key to the Sudan; and it is of no less importance to England as in a measure the Key of Egypt and the Sudan. What for instance would be the position of this country if France controlled the Sudan and consequently Egypt, from Sawakin?[238]

France? In 1889 it was Italy rather than France which threatened Atbara. On 2 May the Italians extended their influence over the Abyssinians through the sham Treaty of Uccialli and by 2 June Italian forces advanced to Karen. From there they could see Kassala and the Nile itself. This feint was conducted with no little secrecy, but the ID monitored it from listening posts in Rome, Vienna, Cairo and Suakin. Thus on 16 July 1889 it was able to inform Salisbury that in all likelihood the Italians were about to pounce on Kassala and, indeed, the Nile. Salisbury noted that if the ID's prediction was true, then it was 'not very friendly of the Italians' to say the least.[239]

Throughout the summer the ID kept the Foreign Office informed of Italy's push towards the Nile via lengthy extracts from *Suakin Intelligence Reports* which Salisbury almost invariably read. When in August the Italians did as the ID had predicted, Wilson's private memorandum of 1889 was entered into the Foreign Office's official files. The Italian push had focused Salisbury's mind and on 15 November 1889, Salisbury finally decided that the Nile and affluents must be inviolate and he put out signals to the Powers that this was Britain's stand.[240] It is reasonable to posit that if it had not been for the stream of intelligence reports and intelligence advice it is questionable whether he would have attached such importance to the Nile or made his forceful proclamation.

So where did these influential *Suakin Intelligence Reports* come from? Although, as we know, there had been a field intelligence capability operating in Egypt just prior to the invasion and during the subsequent hoo-hahs, it had evolved into consuls on one hand and reconstruction officers on the other. What intelligence capability that was left was divided between the commanders on the frontier and the governors of the Red Sea Littoral and Suakim. There were no funds from the Egyptian Army budget for scouting out into the Sudan.

To the informal network of intelligencers this was unsatisfactory. And whilst the long Egyptian afternoon slumbered on, one of the young Royal Engineers serving with the Egyptian Army, F. R. Wingate, rose from his couch and, of his own accord, set up the Intelligence Division, Egyptian Army: the EID. He had done his homework, the concept was sympathetically received locally, as might be expected with Baring holding the purse strings, and soon the EID was up and running with an office staffed with employees fluent in Arabic, English and often Turkish. Its advent was left unheralded for 'budgetary reasons'.[241]

Wingate was as remarkable as each of the persons involved in this obscure yet critical work. 'Owing to the fortunate accident of his parents' poverty', he grew up in Guernsey and was bilingual. After entering the Army, he developed this into a facility for languages. He mastered Ottoman Turkish and court Arabic much above the street Arabic the English advisers in the Khedive's service spoke.

In setting up the EID, he carefully recruited staff from local British,

Coptic and Syrian officers whose ambiguous position in Egyptian and Ottoman society put their loyalty at the disposal of the British. Top of his list was linguistic ability and so many came from the then Syrian Protestant College, Beirut. Amongst them was the famous soldier and historian Na'ûm Bey (then Effendi) Shuqayyir who was trilingual in English, Arabic and Turkish. His intelligence work took him beyond a mere contemporary knowledge of the Sudan into its tribal history and theology. It was he who authored the seminal history *Ta'rikh al-Sūdān* in 1903. His new staff set about teaching their master the ins and outs of the Sudan and soon Wingate was reckoned by one of the Khedive's most trusted aides to be 'more wily and diplomatic than Lord Cromer himself'. The EID came together remarkably quickly and by the time Baron Rudolph von Slatin Pasha (or Salatin) joined the EID in 1895, it was arguably one of, if not the, foremost field military intelligence team of the age.[242]

Under the cover designation of Assistant Adjutant General-Recruiting, Wingate took over civil as well as military relations on the frontier and Red Sea. He established firm links with the police in Cairo and also formally linked the intelligence officers at Suakin and along the frontier into a collection screen. Indeed, by the beginning of 1892 he had field offices manned by officers, agents and scouts at Aswan, Wadi Halfa, Sarras, Korosko, Shebb, Sudud, Suakin and Tokar. And lest it be thought that their English handlers simply sat back waiting for their agents to ride in from the desert with news, that was not the case. Kitchener, for one, knew what would happen if captured by the Mahdists and always carried a phial of poison with him. It is reasonable to suppose he was not alone in this.

In building his new intelligence division, Wingate took for his model the scouts and operatives of Ardagh's Eastern Sudan Expedition of 1885, who brought in:

> very precise information, knowing the sort of question they have to
> answer. They can recount the names of the chiefs, the districts they

come from, their personal peculiarities, and the number of their followers with as much system as the 'catalogue of the ships' in Homer.

Wingate had some £60 annually to spend on scouts and agents and soon realised that more would be needed if his operatives were to overcome fear of capture by the Mahdists. At first the scouts forged or cooked information for their pay, but after Wingate increased his operational budget ten times in 1893, he could not only undertake low-level penetration of Mahdist outposts, but also actually go into Omdurman itself. This was so successful that Wingate's operatives were able to arrange for the escape of some of the European captives held in the Mahdi's jails there.[243]

The extra money, wisely employed, paid off in better intelligence and a growing esprit. In 1895, for example, eight EID scouts on a long-range reconnaissance patrol from Shebb Station suddenly met 300 Mahdists. In shouted exchanges across the dunes, the patrol convinced the enemy that they had great amounts of ammunition (they had but two boxes) and that hot on their trail was the main body of the Egyptian Army Camel Corps (when they were a hundred miles away). The Mahdists disappeared to the south and Wingate told the home ID: 'It is rather like an Arabian Night's tale; but I am thoroughly satisfied with the intelligence information and with the way the scouts did their duty.'[244]

As in England, the Regular British Army in Egypt was not at ease with the fledgling EID. The feeling was mutual. Wingate railed at British commanders who threw potentially useful sheikhs willy-nilly into their regimental jails and he riled at the quality of British forces field intelligence:

Anyone who has followed Soudan events can see at a glance that the writers know practically nothing of the situation… If I am to be in any way responsible for Frontier and Suakin Intelligence, I would strongly recommend that none of the reports recently received should be sent on; many of the statements are inaccurate and reflect discredit on the Intelligence Department…

Possibly with Baring's backing, but it is not clear, by 1892 Wingate removed the EID from the control of the Egyptian Adjutant General. He now reported directly to the English head of the Egyptian Army, the Sirdar, and began a regular correspondence with the ID in London. Even though he had no control over the General Officer Commanding-Egypt, Wingate somehow achieved the Herculean goal of ensuring that no intelligence reports left Cairo for London and Simla without his personal say-so. And as time went on, the quality of these reports, penned by a new generation of British and Egyptian intelligence officers in miserable and understaffed offices on the frontier, began to provide results.[245]

The EID may have been homespun, but Brackenbury welcomed it and its potential as a vital collection and processing agency, an intelligence operation untainted by the past and the crippling legacy of received wisdom. Within months of its establishment material from a myriad of sources such as no external agency could ever hope to raise up or tap into was being processed. Soon the ID and the EID formed a close bond. Wingate wrote to Brackenbury:

> I feel sure that we have means in our power of assisting you considerably – not only as regards Egypt itself – but many of the adjacent Musselman countries. We have got a greater hold over our native officials than is realised at home and there is lots of information to be had if one only knows how to set about getting it. Now that we have started an Intelligence Department in the Egyptian Army I hope it will develop...

Brackenbury's successor, General Chapman, too, believed in an evolving partnership: 'It is difficult to make this Department as useful, as I hope it may be, unless we maintain at all times the most cordial and intimate relations with our friends in every place.'

To that end, Colonel (later Major General J. C.) Dalton, a mainstay of the Division, who it will be remembered was the pioneer of British document security, entered into a 'quite unofficial' correspondence with Wingate. Both men proceeded cautiously as the GOC-Egypt was very unhappy about Brackenbury writing directly to the Sirdar. As Dalton wrote early on to Wingate: 'If we write officially, we must write through GOC, but for small matters such as we transact together, I see no need to trouble the GOC.' Nevertheless the GOC did hear of this liaison and attempted to prevent Wingate from sending information directly to London. Dalton was non-plussed. 'I daresay you will be able to arrange it so that there shall not be any serious delay.'

Less than a month after this exchange, Egyptian information was arriving regularly at Queen Anne's Gate. Wingate wrote asking for 'any reports, &.c., on the mode of working an Intelligence Department, I mean something elaborate giving the detail of routine...'[246] Captain (later Major General Sir Charles) Callwell took up challenge. And no wonder, for establishing intelligence operations was his *métier*. After Haileybury and Woolwich, Callwell saw active service in Afghanistan and Africa. At Staff College, he won the RUSI Gold Medal like his colleagues at the ID J. F. Maurice and Ross of Bladensburg before him. *Small Wars*, his essay on the conduct of limited operations, rapidly became the standard text. Like other bright officers, he emerged from Staff College with anything but an easy mind until swept up by Brackenbury, who secured his appointment to the Department in 1887. There he brought tradescraft to a new level with his influential *Hints on Reconnaissances in Little Known Countries* and *Instructions for Intelligence Officers Abroad.* Having Godfathered field intelligence offices in the garrisons at Gibraltar and Malta, he was now ready to add Cairo to his list.

In a flurry of letters, Wingate picked up the ID's methodology with Callwell and Dalton as his gentle tutor: 'the old "Diaries" are not going quite right yet,' he would write. But soon enough Wingate was able to provide London with reports which meshed exactly into the home Department's filing system and Wingate was able to tell one of his frontier officers: 'English Intell. Office are quite satisfied with the Frontier Intelligence Reports now, though they were down on us sometime ago.' Within a couple of years Wingate told the DMI: 'I fully appreciate the benefits which have accrued to the Egyptian Intelligence Office by the kind assistance which has been so generously accorded to it by the London Intelligence Department and believe me, my dear General, it is my endeavour to keep you au courant with such Egyptian and Soudan information, as may be of use to you.'[247]

‡

It was the Italians who first felt the results of this new resource. By the autumn of 1889 their every move in Africa was being closely watched. Corroborated by reports gathered in Europe, information gleaned by the EID was analysed by the ID and fed directly to the FO. This gave the British government a whole new prescient power. So, for example, when the Italians airily told Salisbury that they were on the point of taking Kassala, the Prime Minister knew for a fact that they were crying wolf and gave them short shrift.

In pointing out these various advances, each agency reinforced the other; Wingate wrote to Dalton in December 1889 that the EID was contacting Baring about the Italians and hoped that Brackenbury would do the same with the government. Kitchener, as Governor of the Red Sea Littoral, agreed and they both urged the DMI to lobby the Foreign Office, not least because there was no clear indication that Baring subscribed wholeheartedly to Wilson's doctrine. 'I am not sure whether his views on the matter are quite the same as ours,' Wingate told Dalton, '...and, of course, in the official Reports we have only hinted at the possibilities which might occur, but speaking privately one might say more...' If the British sat back and allowed the Italians to take Kassala or push their protectorate westward, Egypt would lose what influence and trade it had left in the region causing 'incalculable harm to British prestige in Egypt and would shake the confidence of all those wavering tribes who look to the Egyptian Government to replace Dervish rule in the Soudan'.[248]

By late 1889 the temperature was hotting up. Kitchener hammered away at Brackenbury to tell the Prime Minister that if the Italians did gain Kassala, first Suakin, then Berber and finally Khartoum would fall under the sway of Rome and 'you can easily realise that irrigating Italy, in possession of the Nile from Berber south, would soon make herself felt in the most unpleasant way in Egypt'. In reply to these concerns, the Division assured Wingate and Kitchener that Brackenbury would 'take up the subject energetically and point out plainly to the Foreign Office the great ultimate loss … if the Italians are allowed to extend too far west'. [249]

The EID and ID kept their ears open and by April 1890 were able to tell the FO that it looked as though the Italians were, indeed, finally poised to advance on Kassala and Tokar. This news moved the FO to formally ask the War Office for advice on the effects of an Italian occupation of Kassala. Stanhope, the War Minister, thereupon replied in terms identical to those used by Wilson, Wingate and Brackenbury, referring to a Brackenbury paper of 28 December the year previous. For Stanhope, not only was prestige at stake but 'any European Power that obtains possession of Kassala is likely eventually to obtain possession of Khartum and Berber'.

Salisbury understood all this. In March he had already warned the Italians not to advance any further west towards the Nile and that would have been the end of it, but Crispi, the Garibaldian republican turned fervent monarchist who, like Salisbury, was Italy's Prime Minister and minister for foreign affairs, still wanted Kassala as an operational base. Salisbury refused and a period of arm wrestling took place. Crispi sent his most able Africanist, dal Verme, to call on Brackenbury. Dal Verme laid his case before Brackenbury but to no avail. Brack advised the FO to stick to its guns (literally) and Salisbury told Tornielli, the Italian envoy, so. Kassala and the Nile were off limits and if compensation were needed that could be arranged in Abyssinia. [250]

Having failed with Brackenbury, dal Verme went to Cairo where Baring gave him the same reception, yet diplomacy was behind Italian boots on the ground and as the intelligencers tracked their progress, the Foreign Office pushed for talks on an ambassadorial level in July, which dragged on into October, every day Crispi hoping for a *fait accompli* by his troops. Kassala did eventually fall and faced with this new reality, Salisbury granted them the use of the place as a temporary operational base. But in licensing the Italians, the British failed to quench their thirst. They repaid Salisbury by renouncing all Egyptian claims over the area and taking Tokar, which exasperated HMG greatly. The Foreign Office and Ambassador Lumley thereupon frogmarched the Italians into new negotiations in March 1891, resulting in a boundary which ran from Ras Kasar to the Blue Nile enclosing all of Abyssinia. Its worth was questionable to say the least.

Meanwhile, the Mediterranean was rapidly becoming a closed lake. Brackenbury and the NID had warned of this in 1886 and by the late 1880s the expanding French fleet had matched its bases in the south of France and Corsica with budding ports in Algeria, Oran and Tunis. In 1888, newly built battleships were stationed at Toulon. Bizerta was next and the ID pointed out to their naval counterparts that the port would soon be the base from which France would undoubtedly control the neck of the Med. The NID could only reply that money spent on naval engineering was money kept away from developing even more technologically advanced warships.

By 1890 the threat of a Russian Black Sea fleet steaming into the Eastern Mediterranean and linking with a French fleet forced the Royal Navy to keep a squadron of its Mediterranean fleet constantly present in the east. In a joint NID–ID contingency plan of 1892, prompted by yet another threat of a Russian *coup de main* on Constantinople, the two divisions warned the government that together the French and Russian navies were far superior to the Royal Navy. This led Chapman to remark that unless Britain was acting with the French fleet, the only road to Constantinople for a British expeditionary force lay across the ruins of that same fleet and that, at any rate, would be a very big task indeed.

Following hard on the heels of the Hartington enquiry into the administration of the Army and Navy, the realisation that the Royal

Navy no longer controlled the Mediterranean burst on an unsuspecting public. Fuelled by politicians like Dilke and Chamberlain, the Naval Defence Act of 1893 was the result. Gladstone would have nothing to do with it and on 2 March 1894 he resigned, his heart and head still in Ireland.

What bothered the ID most, however, was not the incapacity of Britain or India to defend herself, much less make war, it was the slowness of political decision making which, it averred, consistently led to trouble or disadvantage later on. It had been slow to react to French and Italian advances in Africa and it was slow to react to the naval imbalance. The reality was that within a few years, even months, imperial defence had grown to be a problem so portentous, so enormous, so nebulous, that politicians, their civil servants, admirals and generals were unable to grasp it. It was therefore shrugged off as too hard or relegated to the Colonial Defence Committee, which was constantly bogged down in technical discussions over landing rights and such like. The 'animosity' towards it from Horse Guards and Little-Englander Liberals finally killed it off.

Everywhere the officers at Queen Anne's Gate looked, Britain's belated reaction to changing events was frustrating. The private Leopold–MacKinnon Agreement of 1891, which looked as if it would allow Belgian explorers access to the Nile, the success of Italy's move towards the Nile from the east, the unhindered French incursions in Somaliland and along the north and west coasts, and the 'retrograde movement' of disbanding the Colonial Defence Committee, all dismayed the Division, which saw Africa, the rock between Britain's eastern and western fortresses, rapidly becoming a liability of immense proportions which would inhibit, then hobble imperial Britain's freedom of action. It bothered the Division that it alone sensed the enormity of the danger. Officers at Queen Anne's Gate felt, as Ardagh commented later, like a *vox clamantis in deserto*.

The IDs in Cairo and London reckoned that the pressure on the headwaters of the Nile from the east and south-west would soon be matched from Uganda. French, German and British nationals were already there and the French in particular had much to do with stirring up the disastrous native wars between Catholic, Protestant and Muslim tribes. The British presence in Uganda was MacKinnon's British East Africa Company, whose principal agent, Captain (later Sir Frederick) Lugard, had propitiously placed his machine guns with the Protestant faction. Once it was supreme, Lugard negotiated a series of treaties on behalf of the company, trying to drum up exclusive trading rights, excluding other foreigners.

The ID was delighted with Lugard's activities. At least and at last something was happening and the ID came to look upon the British East Africa Company as its unacknowledged instrument for keeping the Nile safe from western or southern encroachment. The ID told the FO that Lugard could now be considered the 'Master of Uganda' and Callwell, the ID's expert in establishing intelligence operations abroad and who 'had a great deal to do with getting him [Lugard] the leave to be in Nyasaland originally', described him to Wingate as 'a cool carful [*sic*] plucky sort of fellow who would do the right thing under almost any circumstances and will turn out alright if left alone.'[251]

But by June 1892 the swashbuckling British East Africa Company had so mismanaged its political and trading affairs that it simultaneously ran out of actual and political currency. Lugard was recalled without explanation and Callwell was left to assume that he had been 'driven' to evacuate for some unspecified 'higher reasons'. The resulting vacuum in Uganda distressed the ID and EID and was, to them, yet further proof that the British government was impervious to its own best interests. When Gladstone returned to power in the summer of that year, Callwell feared for the future of Britain in Africa: 'No one can tell what such a nightmare of a man will do when he gets the chance.'[252]

As it was, Gladstone sent Lord Rosebery to the Foreign Office. Like his fellow Liberal peers Hartington and Northbrook, Rosebery's reputation for hard work and levelheaded thinking went before him and Callwell's letters took on a less pessimistic note. Once in office, Rosebery promptly turned to the question of the British East Africa Company and the evacuation of Uganda. He asked Sir Percy Anderson, now the FO's chief Africanist, for advice. In response, Anderson urged the government to stay put, supporting his argument with a considerable amount of intelligence from the two IDs. On 23 August 1891, the day before Rosebery asked Anderson for his thoughts on Uganda, the ID had sent to the FO a new Wingate memorandum entitled *The Effect on Egypt of the Withdrawal from Uganda* which argued that the French might well invest Equatoria through Uganda if the British left.

Chapman and Currie underlined its possibility and the same day Chapman suggested that Wingate, who was on leave at Tunbridge Wells, should prepare a paper 'outlining the advantages to be derived from the occupation of the Soudan by us, and its value in the future, as a recruiting ground...' Wingate had already met the famous African explorer Sir Samuel Baker, and they both agreed that the French were behind the missionary wars. Baker acknowledged Wingate's premise that 'the Nile basin – in its entirety – must be preserved for Egypt...' This was the key point, which Chapman interpreted to mean: 'Having gone [to Uganda], hang on to it, if you mean to remain in Egypt. The Soudan and Upper Nile mean the command of Egypt to a European power, we must not lose the opportunity of acquiring them.' Wingate concurred and wrote to Baker: 'One is right in supposing that a European power holding Uganda would in time acquire an influence in the Equatorial Provinces... We shall do what we can to prevent France becoming that power.'[253]

Whilst Wingate and Baker were preparing their paper on the British occupation of the Sudan for Chapman, the British Colonies Section of the ID published a succinct history of Uganda for the FO which concluded with the observation that: 'It can hardly be doubted that the object of any power holding Uganda must be to dominate Unyoro and Ankole, and thus acquire a footing on all the lakes, and the command of the sources of the Nile.'

It is not surprising, therefore, that when Anderson's memorandum and Rosebery's amendments were put before the Cabinet on 16 September, Anderson cited Wingate as his authority for concluding:

> It is almost certain that if England withdraws her claim to the Upper Nile watershed one or other of the two powers will at once replace her, and that we must face the contingency of the Nile Basin, in its upper waters, and the Equatorial Provinces, being brought under French rule.

Rosebery told the Cabinet that Britain had to take the Southern Sudan: 'I do not say that it is possible permanently to preserve the Nile for Great Britain and for Egypt, but I do say that if we abandon Uganda, we lose at once and by that fact the control of the Nile.'[254]

Faced with Rosebery's conviction, the Cabinet gave the East Africa Company leave to remain in Uganda until March 1893, ostensibly to satisfy creditors. Gladstone, Harcourt and Campbell-Bannerman had wanted to pull out immediately. Campbell-Bannerman grumbled to Gladstone and Harcourt that Lugard was 'looked on as a lunatic: sort of Gordon on a smaller scale; who thinks his mission is to go all across Africa with a flag' and Harcourt laid much of the blame for the Cabinet's new policy on Wingate. Writing to his Cabinet colleagues on 24 September 1892, he claimed to be 'very much struck' by Wingate's August memorandum, the object of which, he saw, was to:

> lay claim in the name of England and of Egypt to the Nile from its source to Alexandria, and to occupy Equatoria, in order to exclude France and Italy and Belgium. To my mind, this is to carry the Egyptian policy to an extravagance. We have deliberately abandoned the policy of occupying the Soudan from the north, and now the case is put forward for advancing upon it from the South, and making Uganda the base of such an operation. The mere fact that such a policy should be propounded, and the anticipation of collision with other Powers on which it is founded is, to my mind, sufficient to condemn it.

Rosebery defended himself by sending his unconvinced colleagues the ID's *History of Uganda* and after 'running hastily over the valuable memorandum from the War Office' Harcourt and Campbell-Bannerman resigned themselves to Britain's continued presence through the legalistic fiction in their minds' eye that Uganda was attached to Zanzibar!'[255]

With the ID's help Rosebery soon sent Sir G. H. Portal to Uganda to shore up British claims and of the three officers who accompanied him, two, Colvile and Major Julian (later Colonel) Leverson, one of Home's consuls and a highly experienced boundary commissioner, were from the Division.

Like Brackenbury before him, Chapman fostered a sound working relationship with Rosebery, who at that time was reading Father Ohrwaleder's *Ten Year Captivity in the Mahdi's Camp*, which Wingate had ghosted as part of his campaign to keep Sudanese affairs before the British public. It was a bestseller and Chapman was able to tell Wingate that Rosebery had been 'delighted with the careful way in which it is prepared as well as the literary style, & as to the map he said it gave the position of Uganda with reference to the Nile and he is particularly fascinated with your account of Equatoria'. But he cautioned Wingate, who was summoned to meet the Foreign Secretary, 'not to be led into too enthusiastic a view. I mean that you have rightly all along been judicious and it is the duty of an officer of the Intelligence Department to retain that attitude.'[256]

By late September 1892, officers of the ID were less pessimistic. Chapman wrote to Brackenbury in India: 'We have a good deal doing lately – Kitchener, Chermside and Wingate have all been here and E Section [Egypt and Africa] has had a busy time, just as Callwell went [at the end of his five-year tour]. That has given me a bit to do particularly as Lord Rosebery seems inclined to get through his work. We now have Lugard coming and there is altogether a great deal of work in connection with Africa.' The head-waters of the Nile were again, if temporarily, safe and Chapman concluded: 'We had a specially interesting time lately in connection with Uganda and Egypt &c. I think the Dept. has been really useful to the FO.'[257]

‡

An anxious winter followed. Not only was it the government's 'inclination to give way to the French in small matters' in West Africa which so irritated Chapman, but Horse Guards' 'animosity' to the Colonial Defence Committee allowed it to die just as Chapman moved to strengthen it with representatives from the colonies. Then in early December, Wingate received word that the Belgian explorer van Kerkhoven had probably reached the Nile in the region of Lado. He did not know exactly where he was (how could he?) but whenever he was once on the Nile he would no doubt head down it as fast as possible to steal a march on the French. Wingate warned the ID 'that while various powers are wriggling as to who is to get possession of the Sudan the Belgians may quietly take a considerable portion of it'. The home ID corroborated this suspicion with an analysis of the 1893 Congo Free State budget, which revealed substantial allocations for 'greatly increased activity' towards the north and east.

More anxiety from France as well. The ID's Captain Charles à Court (later the brilliant, erratic Colonel Repington of *The Times*) examined the French budget debates, which confirmed, as he told Rosebery, a growing group of colonial activists in the Chamber of Deputies dedicated to *assurer la force et la grandeur de la France Coloniale et exterieure* and 'strong enough to exercise a powerful influence upon the decisions of the Chambers of the Government in Colonial questions, nor is it possible to regard this group as animated by any other than a strong anti-English feeling'. This prompted Chapman, of his own accord, to instruct Colonel Reginald Talbot, the military attaché in Paris, to keep an eye on the French Minister of War and sometime Prime Minister, Charles de Freycinet, who smarted very much over having acquiesced in the withdrawal of the French fleet from Alexandria in 1882. Chapman suspected him of 'keeping very dark'.[258]

That was not to be wondered at. In early 1894 Chapman told Lord Ripon, then Colonial Secretary, that 'the policy of France in north-west Africa is to isolate our possessions from the trade of the interior and then to starve them out of the field of commercial rivalry by prohibitive tariffs'. More intelligence was needed and à Court was sent to Brussels to cultivate the friendship of the French military attaché, Captain Haillot.

Son of a former chief of staff, Haillot proved loose tongued and soon à Court's reports on French military power in Africa and Europe confirmed the ID's growing compendia on French power gathered from more prosaic sources. In a report to the Cabinet Chapman argued that 'it is not too much to say that France has never been so strong, nor, one may add, so confident'. It predicted that Britain would feel this energy in due course and even before the Cabinet saw the report, the ID received confirmation of its prediction. The French were indeed pushing on. From Brussels, à Court reported that Major Monteil's expedition was expected to take Gando, thereby placing France on the Niger for the first time, considerably south of the Say–Bawarra line, supposedly the northern limit of French expansion. The plan was to cut off the British Niger possessions and the Cameroons from Lake Chad and the interior:

> Further, that in course of time, it was hoped to extend the French sphere of influence from the upper regions of the Moomi in French Congo to the Nile and thence to the frontiers of Abyssinia. These are claims for futurity with a vengeance! But after all, as the French have shown us in North West Africa, the dreams of today become the realities of tomorrow.[259]

It was an accurate analysis and the FO sent it to Rosebery eight days before Major Monteil, another important French explorer, reputedly told the French President, Carnot, then shepherding the Franco-Russian Alliance into reality, that 'we must *occupy* Fashoda.'

Convinced of the value of their intelligence and unhappy with the lethargy of the politicians and civil servants, the ID and EID cast about for an extra-diplomatic solution to French aggrandizement on the something-for-nothing principle. The answer was to recruit their own African army and one was to hand. They had long known of a wandering sultanate on the fringe of the Nile Valley led by Rabih Fadl Allah (Rabeh Zubehr), a 'slave-trader and free-booter'. There was no love lost between Rabeh and either the Mahdi or his successor the Khalifa. The two IDs meant for Rabeh to secure Egypt's flank and keep the French away from the west bank of the Nile. They were content, as Wingate told Rosebery, to give him a chance to do just that. Months of time and gallons of ink were expended on finding and recruiting Rabeh, but by October 1893 he had still not been heard from and Wingate became more and more agitated at the increasing possibility that the French would not be stopped.[260]

Chapman and Lieutenant Colonel (later Colonel Sir William) Everett, another one of Wilson's Ottoman consuls who would become the ID's second-in-command in 1895, were by this time fairly certain that Rosebery had been converted into taking offensive action to secure the headwaters. If it were true, it would be welcome news indeed. Fortunately, they did not have long to wait for confirmation. Portal came back with the plea that Britain must annex Uganda and secure it by a treaty with Germany. Wingate, who was home on leave, was asked to call on Rosebery and new letters were drafted for Rabeh which the Germans were told about. They reached Yola in the autumn of 1894. The original letters never arrived.[261] Rosebery may have been on side, but matters were still very much in the hands of the people on the spot.

‡

And that, as ever, was the problem. A decade after the scramble had begun, the Colonial Office still found it difficult to cope with the sudden expansion both of its own Empire and that of the French.

It continued to give way to French demands in West Africa and radiated its confusion by sending to the Foreign Office stream upon stream of undigested reports of explorers and the like, trudging here, trudging there mentioning place locations, rivers, mountains, deserts and savannahs, all of which Rosebery noted with disgust needed a lexicon to read. In June 1893, at the Colonial Office's urging, Rosebery made strong representations to the French about encroachment into British Gambia, yet the villages in question had been in French territory all along. 'This makes matters worse than ever,' Rosebery's private secretary noted. 'I suppose there is no more infernal hole than the Gambia to wh. this Gov[ernor] cd. be sent I think he wd. do better in a small island where boundary questions are quite simple.' Rosebery agreed and archly wrote: 'I shall make no more representations on behalf of the Colonial Office without some scientific basis. Please point out to them privately or publicly the discreditable position in which they place this office.'[262]

The government pressed the French to negotiate over their West African claims but as E. C. H. Phipps, 'the African expert at the Paris Embassy', complained in a letter to Rosebery in August 1893, it was all hellishly complicated and he had no real idea of what Britain was claiming or what it should be claiming. He concluded: 'In view of any discussion taking place, and I would remark that the observation made in the Intelligence Department's letter of the 16 June 1892, relative to the fuller and more accurate geographical information possessed by the French, is now even more valid in regard to the districts to the east of the Middle Niger.'

The ID was in no doubt that this state of affairs had to stop. As long ago as June 1892, and again in January 1893, Chapman had warned Ripon that Britain would continually be bested by the French 'until we are at least as well informed upon the regions in dispute as those with whom we are negotiating'. It was just in time. Negotiations in Paris were going badly. Sir A. Harrington of the Colonial Office admitted that the French were displaying 'an extraordinary amount of chicanery and double dealing'. For example, in 1890 the French claimed that they had neither the men nor the money to delimit the Sierra Leone boundary. They then hurriedly and secretly sent out an officer (who carried, no doubt with pride, the surname Brosselard-Faideerbe), to advance their claim. When Harrington learned of this, he was dismayed. 'It is therefore clear as was pointed out by the Intelligence Division in a memorandum of 15 July 1892, "that the motive of the French for declining to delimit the boundary in 1890–91 was that they might ascertain by a previous survey how far it would be necessary for them to strain the reading of the 1889 Agreement in order to secure a practicable route for a railway" which at that time they were desirous of making.'

Harrington contrasted this method of proceeding with 'that singleminded regard for an honest and fair interpretation which, I venture to think, has characterised our proceedings'. It was clear that incidents like this were far from unusual. Phipps was continually being cheated and from July 1893, Harrington insisted that only ID maps be used.

Now that the ID had gained an entrée of sorts to the negotiations, it worked to resist French claims where it could through superior knowledge of the ground and demography. In October 1893, the ID published a new handbook, *France in West Africa*, which for the first time made the extent of encroachment and local reaction intelligible to the government. When in late 1893 Phipps and the Colonial Office were again in trouble over the Sierra Leone boundary, the Foreign Office suggested that it formally involve Queen Anne's Gate in the negotiations themselves. Thus in January 1894 Colonel Everett and more maps were en route to Paris to assist Phipps.[263] Had the Colonial Office been able to cope itself, Everett probably would never have gone.[264]

Yet just as Everett was taking his place at the table, the techno-logical base from which the ID gained its place was on its last legs. Section (F) (Mapping and Library) had taken the brunt of a growing empire and its diplomatic and military needs. In 1891 it issued more than 34,000 copies of maps, five times that produced in 1887. With only seventeen men, the ID was responsible for almost every ordinary or special map used by the Army and the great offices of state. The FO's map-making capability was reduced to a side-show.

It would not be accurate to say the ID did everything alone. It did receive assistance from the presses of Standfords, the School of Military Engineering in Chatham and the Ordnance Survey in Southampton. But the bulk of the drawing and transferring to stone for the maps was done in the 'unwholesome and inadequate' basements of 16–18 Queen Anne's Gate. Because of the restrictions imposed on the ID by Horse Guards in the early 1870s, there were only two double- and two single-handed hand presses, yet the ID produced full colour maps, requiring numerous pulls, often for a run of only five or ten copies. The eight draughtsmen and three printers worked in cramped, dark and dank pantries and cellars 'choked up with lithographic stones (some 1,154 weighing about 120 tons, besides 572 zinc, and 92 copper plates), and because of this the cubic space is greatly reduced, another is impeded, and the place generally is unsuitable, from sanitary reasons for men to work in'. The dust and variable temperatures played havoc with zinc and the more precise copper lithographic processes. The War Office had twice refused to install electric light. Constantly aware of the risk of fire, the ID spent some £5 every year for 'the inspection of Fire appliances and instruction of staff in their use'.

As the volume of work grew, temporary printers were hired, presenting security problems to the two officers in charge. Increasingly the section worked around the clock and by the early 1890s the War Office forbade anyone to work in the ID for more than three hours overtime without its permission. Neither would the War Office include any of the printers or draughtsmen in a pension scheme. Chapman knew the whole section was collapsing.

Finding little sympathy from his fellow soldiers at Horse Guards, Chapman turned to the Committee on a Military Map of the United Kingdom. Under its chairman, the Quartermaster General, sat Chapman and Wilson, now Director General of the whole Ordnance

Survey, plus the head of Section (F), Colonel Dalton. Chapman gathered support for his case. He wrote to Currie at the FO:

> I feel it very important that Section F should be enlarged, to enable it to deal with the work it now undertakes, and in order that it may be ready to do more. If you feel able to say that Sec. F is useful to the Foreign Office and has at times turned out work that is of value, it would greatly strengthen my hands.

In appealing to the mapping committee, Chapman had come to the right place. Soon plans to expand Section (F) followed, including manning changes and a 'properly qualified civilian geographer' to run it. But it was to no avail. The War Minister was Henry Campbell-Bannerman, the implacable and short-sighted foe of British defence or imperial advancement. He greatly reduced the committee's recommendations and refused to rehouse Section (F). He had obviously been posturing when he called for a strong ID in place of a general staff in his influential minority report to the 1890 Hartington Commission on War Office reform. He had no intention of supporting the ID and with him stood Harcourt, the committed Little Englander and Rosebery's greatest opponent over African questions. As Chancellor of the Exchequer, he forbade any departmental 'increases of this kind'. But such was the ID's behind-the-scenes influence it finally secured the necessary increase on 17 April 1893. To have won this victory in the face of the united opposition of the War Minister and Chancellor of the Exchequer must be regarded as notable.[265]

Once he had the budget, Chapman wasted no time. To preserve secrecy, the Civil Service Commissioners agreed to a closed competition and Mr A. Knox, a Cambridge mathematician from the British Museum, was selected to head (F). His salary was fixed at £300. His appointment brought extra fire power to the Division's armoury of practical, scientific officers who had a deep understanding of nineteenth-century geography and map making. There was Wilson, of course, and Major the Hon. Milo George Talbot, who had surveyed the approaches to the Sudan with a Royal Geographical Society half chronometer and an Admiralty deck watch. There was also the redoubtable Colonel Dalton, who had encouraged Mr Ferguson, the black West African explorer, and secured for him the 1894 Royal Geographical Society Medal, and, of course, the legions of long-suffering stonemen, engravers and printers.

The FO now 'invariably sent the growing number of observations to the Intelligence Division to be worked out or checked before any use could be made of them' because, the Division had blandly told the Treasury, one of their main tasks was the monitoring of the great activity:

> The great activity – more especially in certain parts of Africa – of explor-
> ing parties equipped and sent on missions of a semi-political character
> by Foreign Governments has necessitated the most careful watch on
> their movements, for the Intelligence Division is liable to be called upon,
> at any moment, to give an opinion as to the advantages derived from the
> discoveries made, the political value of the treaties concluded, &c.[266]

With Colonel Everett's appointment to Paris in January 1894, the ID became the linch pin between the Foreign and Colonial offices on West African affairs, both departments feeding the Division with information and observations on an almost daily basis. Everett knew, of course, that Phipps was being outgunned. When he discovered HMG was unwittingly on the verge of yielding to France the entire upper Niger basin he intervened directly and with some relief Anderson told Rosebery that at last the negotiations were about to be rescued. Rosebery wryly commented: 'I presume we rather concur with the I. Dept.'[267]

They did. Everett, Britain's cartographic shaman, began producing arguments for the retention of every acre of ground. 'We might instruct Phipps to try for its [Kalieri's] retention, using the Intelligence Department's arguments,' Anderson told Rosebery, 'but not to insist if the other points are satisfactorily arranged.' The Division had no intention of giving up Kalieri. Colonel (later Major General J. K.)

Trotter, Colonel Sir Henry Trotter's brother and Everett's predecessor as DAAG produced 'the right sort of paper' to show that Kalieri was well within the British sphere as it was shaping up and 'if KALIERI is given up to the French, we concede more than even their extreme claims give them. We have already yielded to them much which we [at the ID] believe they cannot justly demand; to give up that which is beyond their utmost pretensions seems an unnecessary step.'[268]

The ID now proposed, and Rosebery agreed, that it was better to give France the whole of the western watershed of the Niger than Kalieri. The only problem the ID faced was that it was not sure where the watershed lay.[269] In order to redress the cartographical imbalance, which was anything but amusing at the time, the Division pressed its surveyors in Africa such as Trotter and Lieutenant (later Major General Sir Charles) Gwynn to map all the more rapidly. It was no easy feat. Gwynn, for example, did what he could whilst carrying no less than three gunshot wounds in his person. Back in Paris, Everett urged Phipps to accidentally walk off with the maps the French were using. What Phipps thought of this sharp practice is not known, but by February 1894 the ID finally had enough material to urge Anderson to quickly secure a specific line to the rear of Sierra Leone, a line that was, for once, advantageous to Britain. As for the urgency, Anderson told Rosebery that the ID would be pleased 'if we could clinch the delimitation before the French find this out'. Indeed they were. At every step, from Kalieri, the Talla portion and the even more or less notional road between Wulia to Wossu via Lusenia, the ID fought for what-British-interests-should-be in the face of some bewilderment, indifference and dilatoriness by the Foreign and Colonial offices.

A succinct example of this worth quoting at length, coming from a slightly later date, conveys Everett's worry about relations between the French and the King of Nikki, south of the Niger in the Dahomey hinterland. He wrote:

It has seemed to me not impossible that Sire Toro is not a name but merely a title. If that could be proved, Ballot's two declarations would lose value; especially as the Jr: Commrs. make a great deal of the name, even going so far as to assert that Sire Toro Bouay is the brother of Sire Toro, King of Nikki. I can prove that in the Fulbe language Sire = priest and that in Soninke (another West African language) Serekhore, Seredhoru or Serakora-e-u = sheike or religious chief. Thus I am not far off, for 'kh' is only one letter in Arabic; if written 'k' we have a letter greatly resembling T and often mistaken for it. For o and u the same character is used. Will not say more as you will be as anxious as I am to get hold of some document with the King's name on it ... We had the French 'on toast'... two or three times last Friday and we hope to make it warm for them tomorrow...[270]

But in the month of February 1894, all the hard work, all the fiddly negotiations of the previous year were jeopardised when London learned that the Germans had initialled a new, expansive treaty with France effectively scrapping the Anglo-German Treaty of 1893. The intelligence agencies in London and Cairo immediately sent Lugard to Paris as an unemployed explorer, a 'down-and-outer', to sound out the French as to what practical direction the new treaty would take. Lugard fell in with the French explorer Monteil and, when Lugard returned on 10 March, he was convinced that Monteil meant to go to Lado or Fashoda as soon as practicable.

For all its latter successes in detailed negotiations, Britain was being seriously outclassed strategically. The French finally made it to the shore of the Nile, protected by their treaty with Germany, and van Kerkhoven was probably not far behind. Affairs looked increasingly bleak. Then Gladstone resigned the premiership and Rosebery was in the driving seat.

He immediately opened negotiations with the Belgians to hold the western bank of the Nile and the Bahr el Ghazal by the headwaters in trust for the British or Egyptians (they were probably closest) whilst acting as a buffer to keep out the French. This evolved into the Anglo-Congolese Treaty, which the ID drew in such a way as to specifically protect Fashoda. Meanwhile, Wingate echoed Lugard's suspicions about the French and worried that Monteil might ally himself with the coy Rabeh and approach the headwaters of the Nile through Bagirmi and Wadelai or the northern Bahr el Ghazal. In this prediction, the EID correctly presaged Monteil's intention.

Judging from the letters flying between Wingate in Cairo and the officers at Queen Anne's Gate in the run-up to the declaration of a protectorate over Uganda in April 1894, the atmosphere was tense and active. In this sudden flurry of activity, the ID's expertise was heavily relied upon. At the FO 'Qy, ask ID what next'; 'Done' was a routine minute.

At this point, more was to come in the shape of a secret compendium *Handbook on British East Africa* (which contained Captain J. W. Pringle's survey for a railway from Mombassa on the coast to Lake Victoria Nyanza near the headwaters of the Nile). Captain (later Brigadier General William) Fairholme told Wingate that 'our only chance of preventing the Upper Nile Regions from falling into the wrong hands would be an advance from Uganda, and I think there is reason to suppose that Colvile, their only man on the spot, has some special instructions on the subject'. 'Fairy' complained to Wingate that Chapman and Everett were holding back his fresh warnings to the FO and were 'so bally secretive now, that they won't tell me anything. I'm rather afraid that mystery is a weak point of Everett's.' Six days later Britain formally declared Uganda a protectorate and Chapman was appointed to be the unofficial member for 'Administration' on its ruling committee.

Chapman lost no time in joining with Lugard in recommending that Colvile be allowed to recruit and train a substantial African army, numbering some 1,200 and composed of Sudanese and Swahilis. He also requested the immediate assignment of four 'specially trained' officers to support Colvile and obtained specific approval from the FO to keep Colvile up to date with the latest intelligence from home and Cairo. He also backed his request for more weapons and ammunition in case of 'Dervish attack'. The ID knew that there were no Dervishes, but there was the Kabarega of Bunyoro who might get in the way. This thought had also occurred to the French.

By the summer of 1894, Britain's new Ugandan protectorate seemed on a steady course and the Anglo-Congolese Treaty was a fact. Belgian expeditions were to be Britain's buffer against French expeditions. As Everett wrote to Wingate from Paris: 'This idea of leasing territory which does not belong to one is a new departure in "Hinterland Politics" which will probably prove popular in the future.' Writing on the day after the protectorate was declared, he told Wingate that Britain's sudden galvanising came about because 'the attitude of the French, who have intimated to us that they do not recognise that the Say–Bawara line prevents them from stepping into Bornu should they desire to do so'. He added that Britain's 'more vigorous measures than heretofore' might be 'a subject for congratulations but at the same time makes the situation more critical'.

Indeed it was. A few days later, Chapman and Admiral Cyprian Bridge, the DNI, met at the Foreign Office to discuss British reaction in case of war with France or France and Russia together. Meanwhile, negotiations over West Africa continued apace and in September Phipps was able to reach agreement with the French over Sierra Leone. Lord Dufferin, the Ambassador in Paris, who had known Everett since the consular days in Constantinople, bestowed lavish thanks on him for his 'material assistance'. As with the ID's practice of containment hatched in central Asia, Everett immediately pressed for a joint boundary commission and when the French reluctantly agreed, the ID sent out Colonel Trotter. The FO noted: 'I think we may leave the matter in Col. Trotter's hand he knows the views of the Intell Dept. Say that we do not suggest special instructions.' Salisbury, by then again Prime Minister, agreed.[271]

‡

Matters were coming to a head. On one hand there was continued concern about collusion between the Belgians and the French and on the other the fate of the Sudan and the headwaters of the Nile. As for the first, the warm aftermath of the Anglo-Congolese Treaty was proving to be but a lull. Colvile returned from the International Geographical Congress of 1895 to find that he could not get north. Rabeh was reported to be dead (not so), another of Kitchener's planned offensives was vetoed and the French and Germans exerted such pressure on King Leopold of the Belgians that his treaty with the British crumbled. The future no longer looked so rosy.

One of the brightest stars of the last decade now makes his first appearance on the diplomatic stage. Captain Albert Edward Count Gleichen, a Coldstream Guardsman, used his ceremonial duties as a mask for his intelligence work as he knew what he was doing was deeply unpopular with the Duke who told him so to his face. Gleichen called the collapse of the treaty a 'slap in the face' and Wingate thought 'our humiliation could not be greater', predicting that a Franco-Belgian treaty would not share the same fate. He apparently did not know of the ID's part in drafting the Anglo-Congolese Treaty and lamented to Fairholme:

> Why would not the FO have consulted the DMI before they wrote that treaty … I used to urge the folly of Belgium being our caretakers on the Nile – such a plan was both infra dig and unnecessary & now we have been subjected to an even worse blow than when Germany handed over to France the Sharo basin which was thought to be such a concession on our part to the Kaiser – although we seem to have come out of the business very badly … Now therefore is the time for Colvile to make a move if we want to preserve for ourselves (or for Egypt) the headwaters of the Nile.

Diplomatic activity was intense throughout the summer and autumn of 1894 and on the ground the French had some three expeditions on the march. One, Decazes, inherited enough troops from the earlier Monteil expedition to take over those parts near the Nile previously thought to belong to the Belgians as British proxies. Wingate mused: 'Now do you imagine that France is quietly going to give up the advantages Belgium has already gained in these districts? On the contrary I am inclined to think that she will make the most of it…'[272]

In September Wingate's suspicions were reinforced by disturbances in western Darfur which the EID opined were caused by an 'interesting combination in those districts' ostensibly between Rabeh and the French. If it was true, then together they would have the strength to dash straight for the Nile. The French Foreign Minister, M. Delcasse, had long thought that Britain's yielding in West Africa, which the ID deplored and did so much to prevent, was not born out of the weakness of internal Cabinet relations and bureaucratic ineptitude, but was a very deep plot to lull the French in the west and north whilst Colvile came up from the south. Delcasse thereupon authorised the Liotard mission and from 17 November 1894 it became official French policy to sanction the long-held desire by the Colonialists to reach the Nile first.

During the winter rumours and reports of activity reached a fever pitch. The ID watched with growing anxiety the progress of the Decazes expedition and concluded that he was nearer to the Bahr el Ghazal than any other European. Every British ear around the world was as near to the ground as possible for news. And it came soon enough in a map published in the German *Colonial Blatt* from which Everett, through Anderson, warned the Prime Minister:

> It may be observed that according to the Franco-Belgian Treaty of 14 August, 1894, the northern frontier of the Congo Free State was defined as following the M'bomu to its source and then, by a straight line (direction undetermined) joining the watershed between the Congo and Nile basins. The source of the M'bomu is not clearly indicated on the map, but it is known to be somewhere in the neighbourhood of the meridian passing through N'doruma; and as the watershed may be presumed to be at no great distance from the source, it appears that the colour representing the French side of this boundary has been carried about 180 miles too far to the eastward. At the same time, although in Article I of this agreement it is merely stated that the Nile watershed constitutes the frontier of the Free state up to its intersection with longitude 30E of Greenwich, there is strong presumption for suppos-

ing that France intended the clause to represent an assertion of some sort of jurisdiction over the territory to the north of this portion of the frontier as far as that degree. If not, the clause as it stands could hardly be legitimately introduced into an agreement between France and the Congo Free State. Moreover, by Article 4, the latter binds itself to renounce all occupation and to exercise no political influence west of the 30 meridian. It follows therefore that a map maker, if partial to the Franco-Belgian arrangement, or unwilling to wound French susceptibilities, would hardly hesitate to carry the French boundary up to this point and would have no great difficulty in justifying his action. Apart then from the question which has been raised by Sir E. Malet, the map has a certain value in indicating the bias of German public feeling. With respect to the boundaries of the Congo Free State, it is distinctly pro-French and anti-British...[273]

More intelligence was needed and quickly. Thus Lieutenant B. S. Sclater, RE of the Division (who laid out the Kibwezi to Busia portion of the 600-mile-long Mackinnon-Sclater Road from Mombassa to Uganda) paid a casual courtesy call on M. Dhanis, the Interior Minister of the Congo Free State. He, apparently without guile, showed Sclater the secret posts north of the M'bomu in order to convince Sclater that the French were too weak to advance on the Nile. He did not consider the Franco-Belgian Treaty as prejudicing British claims to the Nile basin and implied that Belgium would be happy to see Britain there. If Sclater had taken all this at face value, which he did not, his suspicions were confirmed by the minister's profession that the Decazes mission was a failure, whilst Sclater knew perfectly well he was still on the march.

Back at Queen Anne's Gate and in Cairo, the behaviour of the Belgians gave rise to growing concern that protestations aside, the Belgians and the French were in deep cahoots. This is certainly the mood in the Wingate–Fairholme correspondence where it grew *omni ignotum pro magnifico*. And there was probably some evidence that it was true. One of the Division's sources, probably the same Dr

L. J. Hinde of the Free State who had 'just returned from the Eastern part of the Congo State and who has had exceptional means of judging', told the ID that Leopold had raised a large force of Zanzibaris to go northwards with the explorer Dhanis. The source said that this had taken place in November and December 1894 after the Franco-Congolese Treaty had been agreed.

Wingate told Fairholme:

> The more I see of affairs here, the more convinced I am that the entente between France and Belgium at Bahr el Ghazal exists and your corroboration is very valuable information to me. I have just talked over the matter with Slatin [Baron Rudolph von Slatin, who, it will be recalled, had escaped from a decade of captivity by the Mahdi and who probably knew the Sudan better than any European then living] and when the European situation was explained to him he fully concurred in our view that it would be a matter of no great difficulty for the French or Belgians to install themselves on the Upper Nile...[274]

It was Egyptian Intelligence Division operatives who had secured Slatin's escape and he came out of the desert on 16 March 1895 when he 'brought to Cairo all the experience of an "inside" man'. Wingate had two questions for him. Could the flow of the Nile be affected in the Bahr el Ghazal and could the French occupy the Bahr el Ghazal and the Nile? Slatin did not think the flow of the Nile could be affected in the Bahr el Ghazal (an answer which disturbed Wingate and puzzled Anderson at the FO), but he was certain that the French could get onto the Nile. Another concern was Slatin's understanding that the Mahdists were very weak in the Bahr el Ghazal. In a note to Chapman, Kimberley and Rosebery Wingate warned that the reduced Mahdist activity in the Bahr el Ghazal meant that 'any determined effort on the part of France and Belgium to reach the Nile would in all probability be successful'.[275]

This memorandum did not reach London before 28 March when Sir Edward (later Viscount) Grey told the House of Commons that

Britain would consider any encroachment on the Nile basin as an 'unfriendly act'. But the evidence was overwhelming anyway. And Grey's statement, so unusual for the British, electrified the whole world not least because it was misreported to mean all of Africa and not just the Nile. But bold it was and it immediately became known as the Grey Declaration. He said it and sat down. The first parliamentarian who stood to support him was Major Leonard Darwin MP, late of the Intelligence Division.

CHAPTER EIGHT

PLEASE LAY IN SOME CHAMPAGNE

Looking back, the world's plates were starting to shift perceptibly, nowhere more so than in Africa. Off the shores of the Mediterranean, Turkey was, as usual, a busted flush. Russia and France were in the early days of a mutual defence pact which uncorked the Black Sea and the Sublime Porte was probably at the bottom of the increasing number of massacres against the Armenians, rather than the so-called ungovernable Muslims of Anatolia. The Turks had also strengthened their defences so much along the Dardanelles that by 1892 the Intelligence Division and Naval Intelligence told Salisbury that the Royal Navy was no longer capable of either defending or threatening Constantinople, new keels or no. Salisbury was furious as the fleet could have been critical in preventing more massacres, but they were useless, especially if, as he told the Queen, 'our ships are always to be kept wrapped in silver paper for fear of their paint getting scratched'.

On the other end of Africa, the whites in South Africa were tripping over each other into war and further north the scramble for Africa was on with a vengeance. The Italians were bottled up in Kassala and the French were making it uncomfortable for them through the agency of the Abyssinians. For the Egyptians to the north and west, they were preparing to go back into the Sudan, trusting that the Khalifa and Menelik would continue to be blind to the advantages of their joining their two forces. As for the French, West African interests held sway. They unashamedly pursued a policy of 'effective occupation', i.e. you can claim what you will and even enshrine it in a treaty, but unless you are there on the ground in Africa to occupy it, it is not worth the paper it is written on. This flustered the FO. It wanted an overall understanding with the French but this was not in France's interest. Until the Intelligence Division became involved with the Anglo-French negotiations in Paris in January 1894, British negotiators were simply led a merry dance.

British compromise, indeed capitulation, was always a possibility as matters evolved. The CO, FO and ID all played their parts and Salisbury was generous in acknowledging the contribution of Queen Anne's Gate, but it was Salisbury who at the end called the shots. Thus dealing with the French in the West was always a second-order issue with him until its potential as a route to central Africa became a very real possibility and then his interest grew and his heart hardened against the French.

The hole in the centre of the whirlpool was the headwaters of the Nile. Under the Anglo-Congolese agreement of April 1894, Belgium was free to occupy both the Bahr el Ghazal and the upper Nile ostensibly to keep the French out. Then, sometime in the not too distant future, the British and Egyptians would come to take permanent possession. The Belgians, however, were hardly trustworthy. Leopold was very short of cash and was likely to back any horse at the moment which was backing him.

When they learned of this treaty, the French were furious, especially as they had just offered King Leopold roughly the same bargain. On 17 November 1894, the French Council of Ministers authorised the Colonial Minister to occupy as much territory as possible to forestall any British advance from Uganda. This led directly to the Grey Declaration of 28 March 1895, when, as mentioned above, Sir Edward Grey announced in the House of Commons that a French advance 'into a territory over which our claims have been known for so long ... would be an unfriendly act, and would be so viewed by England'.

It made little difference. In late 1895 Major Jean-Baptiste Marchand set out to reach the Nile and occupy the Lado Enclave, assisted by the Belgians. Marchand set out from Brazzaville in March 1897. There is some evidence that some influential voices in the French Cabinet did not want the headwaters of the Nile other than to have it as a bargaining counter for a general rapprochement over other African territorial issues At the time, however, it was a straight out race.

Keeping track of all this activity was a prime consideration of the ID. As Salisbury told the House of Lords, 'four – if not five – other Powers were now steadily advancing to the upper reaches of the Nile'.[276] The Division's expertise was increasingly valued, both over complex technical issues like the lie of a boundary on a virtually blank map, and in terms of policy. The ID also continued to enjoy its access at the highest level. Lords Cromer and Salisbury were adamant that it would be politics and finances, and not the urging of their military advisers, that would govern the timing of the retaking of the Sudan, and by extension, the headwaters. But as the French and Belgians drew ever nearer the headwaters the intelligence offices in London and in Cairo threw off caution and as this chapter will show paved the way for both the Sudan and the headwaters to turn pink in 1898.

In Egypt and in Tunbridge Wells, Wingate put Slatin through a detailed debrief and printed the result in the Egyptian Intelligence Division's *General Report of the Egyptian Soudan*. Wingate's pre-publication copy still exists and shows very clearly how some of Slatin's answers had to be shaped or reshaped to conform to the intelligencers' notion of what they believed imperial policy should be. Wingate wrote a large 'NO' in the margin next to Slatin's assertion that the possessor of the Bahr el Ghazal could not deflect the Nile. The Egyptian DMI was in no mood for any comments that might give comfort to those in government who could not see the value of pressing on to the headwaters as fast as possible. He thereupon added that deflection could occur 'by extensive irrigation systems north and south of that province', continuing that such a course 'is considered by Slatin Pasha to be by no means unfeasible'.

Then Slatin wrote: 'The possession by Egypt of the Bahr el Ghazal from an Egyptian point of view is not of such paramount impor-tance…' with Wingate writing another large 'NO' and the *General Report* went to the Foreign Office finishing with:

Nevertheless, Slatin Pasha points out that the geographical and strategical position of that province with reference to the rest of Egyptian
Soudan, renders its possession absolutely essential. The presence of
foreigners unconcerned in the preservation of Egyptian interests,
having at their command the vast resources of this great province,
which are estimated at a much higher value in both men and material
than those of any portion of the Nile Valley, would place them in such
a predominating position as to render in large measure valueless the
occupation by Egypt of the remainder of the Egyptian Soudan.[277]

The course was now set. The challenge was to run it.

The *Report* was eagerly read at the Foreign and Colonial offices and
Anderson cautioned Wingate to keep Slatin away from the French.
But he need not have worried. As it happened, Wingate and Slatin
became fast friends and collaborated on Slatin's romanticised life
and escape: *Fire and Sword in the Soudan*. It, too, was an immediate
bestseller. Few, if any, reviewers realised the extent of the editor's
contribution, not least when he inserted as a statement that the
Mahdists were in large numbers in the Bahr el Ghazal when they
were not. That was for the French and Belgians to read.

Despite his years of imprisonment, Slatin had not lost his urbanity
and was a great social success. With Wingate's prompting, he kept
the Sudan question before society and the general British public
without actually saying anything in the press of the remotest use to
French or Belgians about the land from which he had so recently fled.

Lord Cromer, too, was pleased with Slatin, who 'scrubbed up well'.
His rank as pasha was reconfirmed and on 29 April 1895 he joined
Wingate as his assistant in the expanding EID. There Slatin took
responsibility for much of the day-to-day business concerning the
Sudan. It was a very useful addition as much of the EID's work at
that stage was providing the Egyptian and British armies with reliable field intelligence.

The diaries and reports of this period are fulsome and complex,
full of route reconnaissances into the Sudan and topographical and

anthropological information in considerable detail. What had started out as an advance beyond Egypt's border into the Sudan, at some undetermined time in the future, was daily hardening into a fact. When, soon after Slatin's rescue, Wingate was awarded the Companion of the Bath, he wrote to thank Rosebery, assuming it was for his part in facilitating the escape. Rosebery corrected him: 'That was only the last of a long series of services, among which I reckon as chief the information collected, always fresh and available, about the Soudan.'[278]

Armed with the firm tone of the Grey Declaration, Wingate returned to Egypt determined to advance that very matter. Again, he came out with the time-honoured chestnut that the elusive Rabeh might still be Britain's proxy gendarmerie. And Rosebery was enthusiastic. After all, as Anderson and Wingate noted, if left alone the French might secure Rabeh's aid in reaching the Nile. Thus in May 1895 more letters left Cairo with Wingate's hopes riding on them.

Meanwhile, Colvile was having difficulty in proceeding north. The terrain was against him, his bearers unreliable. And there was the failing East Africa Company's territory to deal with. The Division thereupon sent out B. S. Sclater to survey a passable route from Kikuyu to Victoria Nyanza and predicted that if Cabinet approval were gained, a railway would soon be able to start from Mombassa forthwith. As for the company's territory, it was clear that Britain must declare the entire grant and then some into a protectorate. A month later, on 28 May, Rosebery induced the Cabinet to authorise construction to begin on the line of track and by July 1895 the ID was given the agreeable task of creating the first East African Protectorate flag on a theme by Anderson.

The Division welcomed this activity and more was to come. On 25 June 1896 the Conservatives returned to power with Salisbury as both Prime and Foreign Minister. Fairholme intimated to Wingate that he 'should not be surprised' if the pace were quickened. Wingate rushed back to London immediately to brief Anderson. He held to the view hammered out between him and Fairholme in March of that year that the French and the Belgians probably had a 'secret agreement' which, as Hinde had intimated, might take the form of French control over existing Belgian forces in the Upper Congo.

Anderson was sceptical, but Wingate had intelligence, through Slatin, that the French were trying to reach the Nile by Abyssinia in the east in an operation where they 'would be in striking distance of Fashoda, and could join hands with a force advancing down the Bahr el Ghazal'. Through Anderson, Wingate told Salisbury that he still held out hope that Rabeh, 'the redoubtable freelance', would cut off the French if the British were to give him enough rifles and encouragement. It would also complicate matters for the Mahdists. After 'one strong stand at Omdurman', Slatin predicted that the Khalifa would fall.

If at this stage it was clear what the French intended, from the west and from the east, what about the Belgians? Would they continue to assist the French as the ID believed or, for a price, obstruct them? For more than a year the ID had been cultivating Dhanis, who 'indirectly' advised the Division through a friendship with Captain (later Field Marshal Sir Henry) Wilson. He claimed that the Belgians were establishing a strong advance depot just forty miles from the Nile itself. The next day, Wilson sought out Hinde:

> I asked him if he thought that the Belgians were already being paid by the French with a view to a Belgian occupation of the Upper Nile, in French interests (because this is apparently Major Wingate's opinion). He thought it very possible, although he had no information that made him certain of it. He said that practically speaking the King of the Belgians was nearly a bankrupt, and even small sums of money would be very tempting to him.[279]

It was then decided that the Intelligence Division needed to actually see the horse's mouth and the Prince of Wales was asked to arrange a dinner at the Marlborough Club so that Count Gleichen (whose father and sister were the foremost civic sculptors of the era and great favourites of the Queen) could meet Leopold.

Gleichen found the King not overly agreeable and reported that he had 'shifty eyes'. Upon learning that Gleichen knew something of African affairs, the King tried to milk him for information. In return the young Count misled Leopold with 'some small effect' but seems to have come away without having his questions answered.

Henry Wilson thereupon went to Brussels and Antwerp to see Dhanis, the Free State Interior Minister, and came back with the impression that the Belgians were *not* in league with the French. He even concluded that the Belgians 'would rather see England at Fashoda and Khartoum than France'.

Wingate, who was at Tunbridge Wells writing up Slatin's book with him, hurried up to town to see Anderson. As the Egyptian DMI put it, Leopold was too weak to take an independent position:

> It must suit his interests – though not his inclinations – to do nothing calculated to make a row between France and Belgium. If we showed a bold front at present and said we were prepared to fight France rather than let her come into the Nile Valley the King might be prepared to throw in his lot with us – but until we make some such decision we can hardly expect the King to risk self-sacrifice on our account, if we admit that he cannot forever sit on top of the gate; then I think the theory which I ventured to suggest is tenable.

Wingate's debrief of Slatin gave him one grain of comfort: time in which to make the French and Belgian advances 'either practically or politically impossible'. He was convinced that Dhanis was 'trifling with Captain Wilson, or endeavouring for a purpose, to magnify the risk of a French advance' with the hope of convincing the British that only the Belgians could prevent it. But news was not long in coming from Father Neufeld, another captive in Omdurman, that not only were the French on the move but the Belgians as well. It turns out, of course, that this was exactly what Leopold was hoping. At this stage he was backing the French.[280]

‡

The ascendant African stars of France and Belgium were not matched by Italy. It was all going terribly wrong. By late 1895 the Italian garrisons in Abyssinia were beset by Menelik's forces and morale was crumbling. Then on 7 December, General Toselli was routed at Amba Alazi and the Italian Ambassador in London called on the British for help.

This state of affairs presented the two intelligence divisions with a dilemma. On one hand it was encouraging that their East African rival was suffering reverses and Britain's refusal to allow the Italians to open an operational base at Zeila was looked upon in that light. On the other hand, Italy's perilous position might encourage the French to give Menelik the armaments and advice to finish the ouster. Two years previously à Court had warned that France was already alive to the opportunities which such an alliance would bring. Suddenly France would be in possession of Red Sea ports and able to reach the headwaters of the Nile from the east as well as the west with comparative ease.

The analysis from the intelligencers in Cairo and London spelled out the evidence of a Franco-Belgian collusion which would materially assist the fortunes of Marchand when his expedition started. Wingate suspected, correctly as it turned out, that the French and even the Russians were already making overtures to the Abyssinians. With very real pressures from west and east, the time was coming when the British government could make only one possible decision concerning the Sudan, finally, once and for all, to retake it in its entirety.

Since 1875 the Division had been concerned with keeping Egypt stable and since 1882 intelligence officers had argued that the unbridled loyalty of the Sudan was inimitable to Egypt's safety and prosperity. Slowly and surely, calmly and expertly, the Division provided governments of both stripes with reliable intelligence about Africa, usually weekly, often several times a day, in a measured, unexcited

way. Salisbury, Rosebery and their officials understood and appreciated it. Because they were not irrational enthusiasts for ill-considered,
expensive campaigns, the ID was afforded facilities and privileges to
maintain that link. Certainly other soldiers wrote back and forth, but
none, not even the Commander-in-Chief, now Wolseley, would have
the ears of Salisbury or Rosebery like the ID. The ID's sympathy with
Egypt and the non-Mahdist tribes of the Sudan and its understanding of their wish to simply trade and live peacefully combined to make
the intelligence voice heard above others.

As noted above, by December 1895 the government was more
amenable to suggestions of an advance than anytime since 1884–85.
Ostensibly to relieve pressure on the Italians, Cromer suggested a
two-pronged feint from the border and from Suakin. Fairholme
set sail for Egypt and with his help the ID–EID correspondence
swelled with tactical plans drafted and redrafted to meet the changing intelligence picture. Privately, both divisions were still sceptical of
the civilians' efforts to keep up with the fast-changing events in the
Sudan. It was 'possible the FO had not received the Notes through
Ld. Cromer,' Gleichen wrote, 'and their arrangements are always in
such a state of tangle that neither they nor anybody else know what
they have received and they haven't.'

When in February 1896 the Italians threatened to evacuate Kassala
if the British did not help, Cromer for the first time suggested a show
of force. Sanderson and Salisbury formally consulted Chapman but
not the War Office proper. On 29 February Salisbury told Cromer
that 'authorities here' (meaning no doubt the ID as indicated by
the restricted distribution) were rather cautious lest they send the
Egyptian rescue party into a trap. Thereupon Salisbury told Cromer:

> I doubt if we are justified in risking these contingencies for a nominal
> advantage. We have no great interest in the occupation of Kassala by
> Italy who went there without consulting us and rather against our
> wish. We have nothing to gain at present by occupying it ourselves.
> The power of the Khalifa tends steadily to diminish, and a waiting

game is the obvious policy. Whenever we are masters of the Valley of the Nile Kassala will be easily dealt with. Till then it has little value.

Wingate thereupon suggested that a simple diversion from Suakin, such as Cromer was proposing, might take some weight off the Italians and, more importantly, would be '*a first step toward the Soudan*' even though 'the Government will rather shy at any such project as they will fear Dervish retaliation'.[281]

The same day, 1 March 1896, the Italian Army was heavily defeated by Menelik II and his Abyssinians at Adowa, stranding the remaining Italian forces at Agordat and Kassala. Fearing loss of prestige, especially if the Abyssinians were hand in glove with the French and Russians, Wingate pressed Gleichen to urge the government to ride to the rescue and take Kassala. But before anything could happen, the Italian Prime Minister, Sr Crispi, resigned on 5 March 1896 and the fate of the whole Italian colonial effort became an open question.

On 12 March, the Cabinet in London invited Wolseley, as C-in-C to give his views. Gleichen briefed him and after Wolseley gave his evidence worried that he might relapse into his old ways by overplaying the ease of advancing to Dongola. Apparently, Gleichen despaired, Wolseley had told the Cabinet that Dongola was unoccupied, even though he had briefed to the contrary. In the end, to Gleichen's relief, the Cabinet decided on 'an odd blend of timid advance and unprovocative demonstration', which was to say the authorisation of an expedition to Dongola which would, in the Prime Minister's words, 'plant the foot of Egypt rather further up the Nile'.[282]

‡

On 1 April 1896, Sir John Charles Ardagh, late private secretary to the Viceroy of India, Lord Lansdowne, became the new Director of Military Intelligence in place of General Chapman who went on to command the Scottish District. Lansdowne was now Secretary of State for War and together with his old secretary found Egyptian affairs much to the fore. Simply put, Salisbury, Rosebery and Cromer may have said little but undoubtedly the reconquest of the Sudan would go ahead. But how rapidly? What would the French, as obsessed with pushing on to the headwaters of the Nile as the British, think of this new concerted push towards Dongola? What about the Mahdists? What route would work best? Would a railway be necessary? What about the Italians and the Mahdists circling Kassala? Was there a need for large reinforcements from home or from India? Then there was the state of the Egyptian Army to consider and there were the jealousies: Cromer and Kitchener vs Wolseley and Horse Guards.

Haunted by the spectres of Gordon, Hicks and Baker, the Salisbury Government vacillated over the pace of reconquest and how much it was willing to be involved. The memory of 1884–85 was very much alive in the minds of Conservative ministers and they found no comfort in the advice they were receiving from their soldiers at home or in Egypt. Once the order to step back into the Sudan was given, who would be in charge? There were as many firebrands in the Egyptian Army as at Horse Guards, not least Kitchener. The issues of responsibility and meddling complicated the entire push up the Nile.

Throughout the spring of 1896, Wolseley pressed Lansdowne to secure Cabinet approval to plan an expedition involving British troops. Lansdowne put Wolseley's request forward, as he felt he should, but it was so unbalanced Lansdowne disassociated himself from it. In his paper, Wolseley claimed that Kitchener's plans to advance were ill conceived, so much so that the 'only explanation I can formulate in my mind… [is that Kitchener] has been fired by a very natural soldier's wish. To lead a big force and to bring matters to a conclusion speedily, and that his enthusiasm has communicated itself to our Minister [Cromer].' He bemoaned the fact that Kitchener was relying on Egyptian troops, relegating the resident British garrison to a reinforcing role. As they were white men, Wolseley fumed, 'no commander would be so foolish as not to make these the head of his spear'. Again and again Wolseley called for the appointment of a general from home: a man of 'ability and position', perhaps himself?[283]

The FO turned to Ardagh for an appraisal. There was no rush. The retaking of the Sudan could come when it would and as the siege of Kassala had been raised, the Italians were safe enough. The Italians boasted that they had done it themselves, but Ardagh knew that 'the relief of Kassala is due to the advance on the Nile'.

Whether the goal was Dongola or Akasha, the ID and EID were pleased that, at least, an advance was to be made. One key element would be to keep the Italians in place. If the Italians did evacuate, 10,000 Mahdist troops would be free to attack the Egyptian Army anywhere from Suakin to the west. It was beyond thinking. It would be difficult to go to Dongola with such a threat on Kitchener's flank. In the second place any move towards Dongola would be, as Gleichen put it, 'a real big biz' for south of Wadi Halfa lay a vast desert which in 1889 had taken a vast toll on a moving Mahdist Army.

By March the enormity of Wolseley's misleading of the Cabinet had sunk in and Salisbury cautioned Cromer not to rush to Dongola but to advance in pace with the railway relaid on the bed Ardagh had so despaired of losing in 1885. 'It is enough', Salisbury told Cromer, 'to say we are advancing to Akasheh with Dongola as our objective.' But by this time everyone was out of step with everyone else. The Prime Minister urged caution and Ardagh agreed. As he noted on 15 March 1897, Ardagh wrote: 'There may be strong motives for pressing on to Omdurman this year, to anticipate the occupation of the Upper Nile by France, Belgium, or Abyssinia; but, in view of the extremely slow rate at which railway construction proceeds, the final advance should, if possible be deferred until 1898...'[284]

Wolseley on the other hand was planning on an expeditionary force of, depending which memorandum you read, 6,000 British troops costing £600,000 exclusive of the costs to the Egyptian Exchequer or 8,000 British infantry and a whole brigade of cavalry. He continued to disparage the new Egyptian Army as well. 'You may teach a French poodle to do tricks, but you can never teach him to draw a badger.' When Salisbury read this he minuted to Sanderson: 'The WO minute is, like many documents from the same source, defective in taking little or no account of money.'[285]

The Secretary of State for War, Lord Lansdowne, was caught between his Prime Minister, supported by Ardagh, and his C-in-C, Wolseley. He summoned Gleichen to his office on 20 March. Gleichen saw the Secretary of State produce an old map 'shockingly out of date – another proof that the ID was not sufficiently appreciated by the Secretary of State's entourage'. The young officer thereupon had a long interview in which he was questioned about the best time to begin operations and so forth. 'I told him my plain opinion, that we ought to, if we want to save Kassala (though that looks a little healthier this morning), to make little demonstrations on Kokreb, Sangeb, and from Murrat Well, Wady Halfa, and, if you want to go the whole hog think about it before hand well, and have a proper expedition once for all, not earlier than June or July.'

After his interview, Gleichen confided to Wingate:

> My private opinion is that the Government has taken a plunge without looking where they're going, and may find it difficult to extract themselves: unless they have some very deep laid political plot that no one knows anything about. It seems curious, considering what a powerful lot of men our Ministers are. Otherwise I cannot conceive why they took this step without consulting a soul as to the feasibility thereof...[286]

When Lansdowne learned from the ID that the rainy season would probably allow Kassala to hold out until July and furthermore Dongola was occupied and could only be taken by 'severe fighting', he joined Salisbury in advocating a waiting policy no matter what the Italians wanted. Thus on 25 March, the Cabinet rejected Wolseley's proposal for an expedition. It was particularly embarrassing for Lansdowne, who had to apologise to his colleagues for Wolseley's inaccurate estimates.[287]

But London reckoned without Kitchener and Cromer. Having been pushed into this particular form of advance, they decided to execute it in their own time and in their own way 'whatever may be the difficulties and objections'. They went to extraordinary lengths to prevent Wolseley sending out a senior general (perhaps even himself) and curtly rejected the idea of a senior military adviser. They also had to step up their defence of the rejuvenated Egyptian Army against Wolseley's prejudices.

Finally in a letter arriving from Cairo at the end of March from Fairholme the government learned of Kitchener's plans. Kitchener had taken Kasha almost immediately and he would now press on to Dongola with his Egyptian troops in the van and British garrison troops in the wake. He also approved of Wingate's plan to use Indian troops to make a simultaneous move on Berber from Suakin. Never mind what London wanted, Egypt was going back into the Sudan.

But having made their move, there was no need to go further without adequate preparation. Days into his new posting, Ardagh contributed his seminal *Egypt and the Advance up the Nile*, the gist of which was hasten slowly.

In great detail he showed Lansdowne and the Defence Committee of the Cabinet that a slow advance was consistent with the laws of economy, logistics and security. Even if the railway was pushed forward at a mile a day, it could not reach Abu Fatmeh before October at the earliest and in any event 'the necessity for reinforcements from Britain does not at present exist, and may not arise'. In conclusion, Ardagh warned, it was well to remember the past: 'the unfortunate expedition of Hicks Pasha – the troubles which followed the announcement that the Soudan was to be evacuated – the frequent expeditions ending in withdrawal – all of which were, not unnaturally, regarded by the Mahdists as victories over the unbelievers. The motto now would be: *Vestigia nulla retrorsum*. The advance may be slow, but let it be absolutely sure.' And as for the Egyptian Army, it would do very well if seasoned slowly, not exposed to a sudden bloodbath on the doorstep of the frontier.[288]

This steady, calm assessment for the Cabinet was directly opposite to the big push being propounded by the new Commander-in-Chief. Wingate was steadfast. The advance would be made, but carefully, not in some grand rush: 'The soldiers in England appear to me to have rushed the Government into all this business without any adequate knowledge of the facts, and without giving proper warning of the difficulties that lay ahead...' Then there was Kitchener to contend with. For his part, Cromer had no intention of letting him off the lead either, until, as Salisbury and Ardagh urged, the railway was much advanced.[289]

Salisbury began to be worried about Cromer's health and urged him to take a rest at Carlsbad. But Cromer snapped back that if he left Kitchener and his staff alone they would fall into the hands of the authorities at Horse Guards, who 'rightly or wrongly ... are animated by no friendly feelings for them ... this is at times rather tiresome'. When in early June Wolseley wanted to send reinforcements to increase the chance of success, Cromer grumbled to Salisbury that their point was obvious and Wolseley was a disappointment: 'I wish the season for shooting dervishes and grouse did not coincide. It saddens me somewhat.'[290]

For its part, the Foreign Office received Horse Guards' interference with a world-weary air. When Wolseley petitioned Salisbury to be 'given every facility for watching events, in order that it may be able, if necessary, to advise HM Government on any important question that may arise', Salisbury simply minuted: 'Yes, there is no harm in them.' In any event, Salisbury and the Foreign Office did not rely on Horse Guards for their information or advice. There had been a home ID liaison officer co-located with the EID since February. Fairholme had been the first link but was recalled in late March when General Chapman, then within days of finishing his five-year posting to the ID, decided that the government needed a solid Egyptian expert back at Queen Anne's Gate.

His replacement was Count Gleichen, who wrote to Wingate: 'Poor old Fairy; it is rough on him.' But the veteran and chronicler of the Gordon Relief Expedition was absolutely thrilled to be going out. He dashed off a line to Wingate: 'These are stirring times!' and sailed with sixty pounds of maps. When he arrived he was greeted by his old friend Kitchener, 'who thought I was going to be a spy of the War Office – which surmise, as a matter of fact, was a fairly correct one – and would report all his doings home. This was a hateful idea to him, as with his masterful character he intended that this should be a "one-man show" and he would brook no War Office interference. I had therefore to be extremely tactful and not push my nose into too many matters…' Gleichen was honour bound to refuse Kitchener's hospitality at the Headquarters' mess and he stayed in the background working with Wingate, who 'knowing both sides, told me as much as it was good for me to know…'[291]

More tact was needed. Cromer refused to send his telegrams on and complained to the Foreign Office. Ardagh explained to the puzzled officials that 'Count Gleichen has been sent out to keep Intell. D. informed of movements in Egypt, and to collect information which may be useful in event of further developments. We have been, since Capt. Fairholme's return, dependent upon newspaper reports for information as to the location of the Egyptian Army, and Count Gleichen was told to obtain complete and reliable information as to the positions of various units, and to ask that it might be telegraphed home.' Gleichen, he added, was instructed to wire 'should any point of urgent interest arise' and he was careful to keep going through Cromer 'to avoid any semblance of disrespect, and keep Lord Cromer aware of what he was doing'. The Foreign Office leapt to the ID's defence and Cromer was instructed to forward any of Gleichen's telegrams 'which seem to you of sufficient importance'.[292]

Gleichen kept up his charm offensive and soon Cromer was telling Salisbury what a 'clever young fellow' he was. Gleichen certainly earned his keep. Cromer began commending his despatches to Salisbury not least because they varied so from the dark picture being painted by Horse Guards about the combat readiness of the Egyptian Army:

Mind you, the half-drilled rabble which came to such grief under V. Baker and Hicks no longer exists. I really don't think the authorities at home, who haven't been out here since 1885, know what the army is now, or place it at its proper value.

In his letters to 'Fairy', 'Glick' painted a picture of his life in the desert:

I play about chiefly with Wingate, Slatin and Ned Cecil [Salisbury's son] but there's plenty to do all day, somehow: what with helping Slatin, the ciphers and interviewing secret agents and being civil to swarms of correspondents (this I find the hardest work of all, as they use the ID room as a sort of club. If I were Wingate not one should come inside, but he seems to like being pestered in his busiest moments) and making maps and collecting stuff … there's heaps to do.

Gleichen and Wingate worked well together and his letters to the ID which were sent on to the Prime Minister paint a dramatic picture of field intelligence which must have reminded Salisbury of Home and Ardagh in Constantinople twenty years before. As any father would, Gleichen's letters and wires containing news of his son were eagerly awaited by the Prime Minister, who enjoyed the accurate and 'very interesting' picture of the well-directed energy and competence displayed by the Egyptian Army and the two intelligence functions.[293]
Describing the mapping of Firket, Gleichen wrote:

I thought [Section] F was making one, and that it would be ready by now, but my wire to Talbot (in Wingate's name) elicited the fact that things were not so advanced as I hoped, so I have been mugging away at it: been most careful about the names, getting them from the resident natives the districts as far as I could, but its rather difficult; my interpreter, Abu es Salaam, the draughtsman of the ID here, is a colossal old ass, only talks bad French, can't read anything but capitals, and succeeds in tangling up completely any of the confused and already sufficiently entangled statements of the resident gentry.

He painted descriptions of the scouts, 'No. 4 is a ripper', and did not hesitate to criticise Kitchener for allowing the infiltration of Dongola before Wingate and Slatin could make arrangements so as not to compromise their agents there.

Meanwhile, the presses at 16–18 Queen Anne's Gate never stopped. Maps and almanacs were advanced at a great rate. Talbot and Section (F) continually pressed Gleichen for orthographic and topographic information and in July 1896 Talbot came out to assist. He was as thrilled as Gleichen. A loner, he was so sick of civilisation that when the Treasury got into a stew over whether his extra pay should come from the War or Foreign Office, he astounded them by eschewing it altogether. He was a Malahide, but had little money of his own, making up for it by a great sense of adventure. He just wanted to go to Egypt and map the routes to be used for the advance into the Sudan. Soon Kitchener had detailed maps all the way up to Firket and overland from Korti to Metemme, and a massive guide on the country between Dongola and Omdurman.

Ready at last, the advance went as Cromer, Kitchener and Wingate had hoped and in the manner Ardagh had described in April to Lansdowne. It was, in essence, a realistic large-unit training exercise. As the operation progressed, leaders were tried and tested, procedures were proven and revised and when on 7 June they engaged the Mahdists at Firket, the resulting victory convinced Salisbury to let them off the lead. As Fairholme wrote to Wingate two days before the battle:

> The whole move appears to be have been carried out exactly as my recent experiences with the EA led me to suspect that it would be namely – without a hitch and I congratulate you all upon the achievement, and hope, as I confidently believe, that the further progress of the undertaking will be as successful.[294]

On 23 September the Egyptians took Dongola, long before Horse Guards thought possible.

‡

Meanwhile, what about central Africa? What about the Belgians and the French? During the summer of 1896, the ID anxiously looked for signs of French reaction to the advance on Dongola. Then on 1 July Fairholme noted:

> There are signs of renewed French activity in the Ubangi region. A military officer, Capt. Marchand has been sent out... It appears to me that the withdrawal of the Mahdist forces from the Shakka district will open the way for French explorers who will be able to make treaties which they will ultimately produce against us.

Indeed, Marchand had been pressing to go to the Nile since 1893 and, as noted below, his mission had been agreed in principle before the push to Dongola began, but there is some evidence to indicate that its timing was largely as an antidote to the British advance hundreds of miles north. If so, much of the theory behind it hinged on the myth that *Intelligence britannique* somehow controlled the Mahdi and was using them to block the French advance to the Nile. There was also the encouraging news of Colvile's difficulties in Uganda.

Two sources, at least one of whom was in Brussels, conveyed the news that Hanolet, in the Belgian service, had been present when Marchand received his final briefing from M. Gabriel Hanotaux, the French Foreign Minister. From this the Division surmised that Hanolet was to push up from the M'Bomu toward Meshra-er-Rek whilst the ID's old friend, Baron Dhanis, consolidated the advance by establishing strong outposts at Wadelai and Lado. Marchand, with a force from Bangasso would march on the upper Nile whilst Liotard in Bahr el Shagel, in league with the Sultan of Semio and the Chief of Tambura, was already making treaties in the Nile Valley. What was very worrying was that an auxiliary French expedition was reputed to be starting from Djibouti or Obok in the east and, aided by the Abyssinians, would occupy Fashoda *en permanence*.

Colonel Everett told Wingate that 'it would be unfortunate if we should, later on, find the French flag flying in any part of the Bahr el Ghazal. Certainly you are not to blame, nor indeed, I think are we. We have repeatedly warned the FO of danger from the Ubangi side and in your memo of October 1895 you pointed out the possibility of a movement from the eastward. Unfortunately it did not receive the attention it deserved.' Everett reminded Wingate that from what they knew Marchand was 'a most determined fellow who is not likely to be deterred by a few difficulties'.[295]

The Sudan back in play, throughout the summer of 1896 the ID put its many ears to the ground listening for news from as many sources as were thought even vaguely reliable, viz surveyors, consuls, traders, scuttlebutt from the docks in Tunis and Port St Louis. Thus by 21 August, Everett had enough information to plot Marchand's probable route through the Bahr el Ghazal towards Fashoda, some 600–700 miles before him. As he then told Francis (later Viscount) Bertie at the Foreign Office that:

France has always hoped some day or other to connect her eastern possessions in Africa with her western Colonies is ancient history. We have sometimes thought that, now they are no longer troubled by the Italians, the Abyssinians might be a means to this end. We know that there are French officers in Abyssinia, and it is reported that they were not altogether inactive during the recent campaign... The Dervish troops which were at Fashoda have, I believe, been withdrawn northward. The situation wants very careful watching – more, in fact, than we can give it with so few Agents – and if all that is now reported is true, it would seem to point to the necessity our losing no time in disposing of the Khalifa.[296]

Everett accurately forecast France's intention and the means by which it intended to take the Nile. Thus by August 1896, the Division was able to hand to the government the French blueprint for Africa for the next two years.

Three days after Dongola fell on 23 September 1896, Salisbury approved a proposal by Everett to occupy Bona in the rear of the Gold Coast and to make overtures towards Wa and Mossi, which were also equally accessible to the French. Sanderson noted: 'The French and Germans will not like it, but they have no valid grounds for protesting.' Meanwhile the ID carried on its exacting battle against sharp practice in Paris by preventing British negotiators from making even more concessions whilst the French were consolidating their substantial gains. When the Gold Coast boundary was under discussion, Villiers at the Foreign Office asked his Colonial Office counterpart: 'I presume that your Department is in communication on the subject with the DMI?' and when Britain's position (i.e. the ID's position) on Anglo-French delimitation of Sierra Leone and French Guinea was sent to the Foreign Office for approval, the senior official involved could only comment: 'A glance at the Proces Verbaux will show the extremely minute and technical nature of the work, which it is impossible for me to criticise even if, which is unlikely, there were anything to criticise.' The only way to prevent sharp prac-tice, the Foreign and Colonial offices finally admitted in March 1897, was to ensure that no paper concerning Africa went forward without an ID map. They were, as Talbot wrote, thrilling times.[297]

‡

It will be remembered that Brackenbury's 1886 *Sketch* of intelligence predictions was especially valued because it was balanced, well timed and directed at the Queen and incoming Cabinet. It pointed to those areas in which the Division would concentrate its efforts. Ardagh wrote a similar paper in 1896. Looking over the world, Ardagh noted that Britain's 'bungling' of Turkish affairs was so marked that the Porte had no choice but to throw himself 'entirely under the guid-ance of Russia'. This had major maritime implications. Egypt was therefore critical and Britain had to retain control over it. As a senior member of the Cable Landing Rights Committee, Ardagh was well aware that of the four telegraphic cables from Britain to India, three could be easily cut and the fourth went through the Suez Canal.

Unlike in 1882, Ardagh concluded that despite the Suez Canal Convention, any hostilities with the Boers (this was as early as 1896) would find the other major signatories, not least France, Russia and Germany, 'antagonistic to our interests' and the British would have to consider closing the canal 'accidentally on purpose'. Ardagh looked to Alexandria becoming a fortified harbour, which would give the Royal Navy a secure eastern port and would also keep the French in the Mediterranean and Russians in the Black Sea on their guard:

> Africa has been partitioned, and the new spheres of influence in that continent, closely affect Egypt. France is pushing towards the Egyptian Soudan and the Nile, the Congo State has leased from this country a strip of territory on the Nile from Albert Nyanza to Lado. Abyssinia, armed by France and encouraged by Russia, has emancipated herself from the feeble supremacy of Italy, and may undertake or facilitate enterprises directed towards the Eastern bank of the Nile. Germany in her new positions in Africa, has shown a marked unfriendliness.[298]

In order to forestall French designs in Abyssinia which looked like filling the Italian vacuum with weapons and railways, Ardagh proposed taking under British protection a vast track running in a straight line from the neighbourhood of Milmil to the intersection of the River Juba with the sixth parallel of north latitude. The Galla tribes there still considered themselves British subjects, traded through British Somali ports and had suffered from Abyssinian raids. Much of the land involved in his scheme was either vaguely Zanzibari or Egyptian. He also reckoned that the Anglo-Italian Agreement of 1894 was an ethnological disaster cutting through two territories of British tribes and completely excluding the Ogaden. Ardagh was worried that French and Russian influence with the Abyssinians was growing, was, in fact, already predominant and would be used to establish a foothold on the Nile near Fashoda. His objective was to cut off the French, whose Somaliland borders had never been delimited.

As for the Abyssinians, they changed their borders to suit their case, so Ardagh proposed that Abyssinia be recognised internationally as a sovereign state and have its borders regularised, contiguous with Anglo-Egyptian borders. He also thought it prudent to obtain a guarantee from the Negus, Emperor Menelik, that if the Italians left he would honour the new lines. All this, reasoned Ardagh in a minute to Salisbury, could be accomplished by sending a mission to Menelik whilst, at the same time, sending 'properly qualified' officers to reinstate relations with the Galla chiefs south of Abyssinia.

In making this proposal, Ardagh was backing a call originally made by the Division's Captain Henry Wilson in September 1895. The FO, which still considered anything to do with the east coast of Africa as the concern of the India Office, did not see the proposed mission and the expansion of the Somaliland Protectorate as their concern. Nevertheless, the idea caught on. The Queen, Wingate and even Hicks Beach, the cautious Chancellor of the Exchequer, were enthusiastic. Gleichen told Wingate on 31 December 1896:

> The FO has been stirred up with long poles to make up its mind as to a policy and to send a mission to Menelik; it looks rather as if it was coming off. I do hope it will, as we have dawdled and wasted precious time on it already, and if we don't make pals soon, we shall be cut out altogether by the French and Russians. Menelik seems a sensible man and a gentleman. Why not get him to London for the Jubilee? but we'd bar Queen Taiton, as no Royal carriage would be equal to supporting her weight and bulk.[299]

Wingate was delighted. He had long wanted the opportunity to convince Menelik that the Egyptians had no designs on Abyssinian territory. There was no time to lose. He warned Everett that should the French 'make Abyssinia hostile to the Anglo-Egyptian advance up the Nile and utilise her to get on the Nile themselves, they would, if successful, considerably increase our difficulties in Egypt'. If then, as a next step, the French were able to exploit the military and commercial possibilities between the Abyssinians and the Mahdists, the British occupation above Khartoum would be nigh impossible.

Wingate therefore wanted to open up trade with Menelik as soon as possible and assure him that if he did not interfere with Egypt's push up the Nile, he should receive a British guarantee respecting Abyssinia's notion of pre-Mahdist boundaries. Moreover, if the Abyssinians could be induced to actively assist in the reconquest, 'Britain would be prepared to use her good offices to secure some suitable territorial compensation for Abyssinia' on the eastern bank of the Nile.[300]

The idea incubated during the winter of 1896–97 when report after report reached London that the French were on the move, east and west. Salisbury thereupon authorised a mission in January 1897 under Rennell Rodd, Cromer's deputy at the Cairo Agency. Seven officers were to accompany him including his son, Lord Edward Cecil, the famous Captain Speedy, a larger than life Arabist, Wingate and Gleichen. Glick knew that he was to go on 6 February; the War Office was not informed until the nineteenth.

Alas, the Rodd mission was not a resounding success. The consternation of the mission must be wondered when at their first audience with the Negus, they pushed aside the tent flaps to find Menelik flanked by French and Russian officers: Prince Henri d'Orleans, Bonvalot and Leontiev. The French were indeed in play, encouraging Menelik with dizzying promises of vast territories on the Nile and 100,000 repeating rifles in exchange for aiding French expeditions heading towards the Nile. Rodd could not match that and the only real outcome of the British mission was that contact had been made.[301]

Then after months of mixed news following the measured advance into the Sudan, on 16 January the EID reported that the Khalifa was moving his troops out of the Bahr el Ghazal, leaving a vacuum which either the French or Belgians were sure to fill. Meanwhile in

West Africa, the FO learned that the French were taking territory around Bussa and Say, 'entirely ignoring our treaties solely on the ground that we are not in occupation and to admit their rights to do so is to give up all the advantages of priority'. Again, the FO put their trust in paper and were at a loss to deal with this unless 'some sort of understanding with France was reached' which was not what France wanted in the least. It created a gloomier mood, summed up by Ardagh's passing on to the FO a *Temps* article of a mission travelling backwards from the so-called French Sudan to the Gold Coast hinterland. He wearily penned on it: 'Yet another expedition.'

‡

All this added up. From the selection of the Rodd mission in 1897 to Marchand's arrival in Fashoda the next year, both the home and Egyptian intelligence divisions became obsessed with beating the French – no hold barred. And in this goal they had a very firm ally in Salisbury's Colonial Secretary (since July 1895), the Liberal Unionist Joseph Chamberlain. He was more than willing to work with the ID to form a viable African policy and put teeth into it. Wasting no time he told the Governor of the Gold Coast that he was proposing to create a 2,000-man army to trump the French at 'effective occupation'.

The ID thereupon took over the responsibility of creating Chamberlain's new force. Ardagh proposed two forces: one for the Gold Coast and one for the Niger for 'the prevention of encroachments on the British sphere of influence'. In case the French or Germans made an alliance with the Sultan of Sokoto, these forces could be swung south into Dahomey and Togoland from the interior. Ardagh proposed a flying squad of 500 men with two machine guns and two field pieces to stop claim jumpers. Chamberlain told Salisbury: 'Sir J. Ardagh is in cordial agreement with the determination ... to enforce our claims to territories on the west coast of Africa by a display of strength superior to that possessed locally by the French.'

The Colonial Office told the Foreign Office that:

Sir J. Ardagh would observe that the carrying out of this plan, or of the more restricted one proposed by Mr Chamberlain, would sound a note of alarm to the French, and that we must be prepared for a large access of energy on their part throughout West Africa. We should, therefore, be prepared to follow up this first step by further immediate action, and no time should be lost in organising means for the active assertion of our legitimate claims, not only in the territory adjacent to the River Niger, but also in the Hinterland of the Gold Coast and Lagos colonies.[302]

Chamberlain had little trouble in persuading Salisbury to adopt Ardagh's plan for organising a West Africa force especially as the Niger Company would be asked to pay much of the bill. If Sir George Goldie, father of the Niger Company, cavilled at helping himself, Ardagh proposed taking over the company and its affairs, lock, stock and barrel. In any event, Everett knew that the Niger Company's claims were all too often weak. In a memorandum to Salisbury he agreed with Everett that 'in spite of all the tall talk of Sir George Goldie the resources of the Niger Company cannot supply as much local aid as the CO have been counting upon; and that at the same time the resources at the disposal of the French Government have been somewhat underestimated'.[303]

This new energy from the Colonial Office alarmed the officials at the Foreign Office somewhat. A caution was minuted: 'The ID scheme is a very large one and ... can hardly be carried out without bringing us into contact with French forces. It seems to me to go beyond the chess-board policy.' But Salisbury, who was not drawn to Goldie in any event, was no longer prepared to take encroachment lying down either and replied 'there is no doubt that we think the position towards Foreign Powers produced by present arrangements is thoroughly unsatisfactory'. He told Hill to work up a good Blue Book case and Chamberlain thereupon was given a 'free hand to prepare a thorough-going counter-offensive'.

A few days later, Hill was received at Queen Anne's Gate and plans were laid for the new force to get up and running to make the French position at Bussa untenable. The ID did all the detailed operational and intelligence staff work. One of its own Africanists who came to the Division in 1893, Major H. P. Northcott, was picked to be the commanding officer. Northcott lost no time and by October was leading a force from Kumasi into the bush north of Ashanti. As to working up the Blue Book as Salisbury instructed, the ID took over much of that, too, and produced what the Prime Minister called 'a most admirable compilation' including a map which Hill thought 'almost does away with the necessity of a written case'.[304]

It was a time of feverish staff work in the Division. In time for the 23 February Cabinet, the ID produced five detailed contributions to halt foreign encroachments in central Africa and to combat 'the arrival on the Nile of expeditions designed to supplant British and Egyptian interests'. Printed on the ID's own presses they included *Somaliland Protectorate* by Ardagh, in which he outlined his concept of a larger Somaliland for pro-British tribes to offset Menelik, *French Aims in the Nile Valley* by Captain Henry Wilson, *Uganda and the Nile Valley* by Major H. P. Northcott and *The Dhanis Expedition* and *Resistance to be encountered by a European Expedition into the Bahr-el-Ghazal* by Captain William Fairholme. In his overall conclusion Ardagh argued that no time should be lost despatching a small force from Uganda down the Nile to make treaties and assert sovereignty. 'If nothing is done, we may soon hear of a belt of French Treaties from Ubangi across the Nile Valley to Abyssinia.'

As ever, the tipping point was collusion between the Belgians and the French. As Martin Gosselin, the British envoy to Belgium, wrote:

> There is serious ground for fearing that the French are endeavouring to engage the Congolese authorities in some combined action hostile to us, such as Sir J. Ardagh anticipated, and I venture to think that no time is to be lost in taking such steps as HM Government may think desirable and feasible for securing our own interests in the Upper Nile Valley.[305]

Then on April Fool's Day 1897, Gosselin in Brussels forwarded the startling rumour that Liotard had come from the west, joined Marchand and that together they were at or even beyond the Nile. In his memorandum he recalled Henry Wilson's note of 25 September 1895 warning of Abyssinian support from the east if a French mission could reach Fashoda from the west, and by 20 March the French had secured such a treaty. Of course the Foreign Office knew nothing of that and sent the rumour on to Everett, who responded on 2 April by reminding the FO of the Division's warning of 4 February about the advanced state of French intrigue in the east. Nevertheless, he thought it improbable that Liotard could have crossed the Nile with Marchand, who was last reported in Brazzaville. (Marchand set out in late March.) But the country they would have to transverse was held by a French ally, the Sultan of Semio:

> All this points to a steady advance of French forces and French influence towards the Nile Valley, and it is not difficult to imagine that an enterprising and ambitious officer, such as M. Liotard undoubtedly is … being assured of a friendly reception should he be tempted to march across the Nile Valley … It may be found that M. Legarde's visit to Abyssinia is not unconnected with M. Liotard's movements in to the Nile Valley.[306]

Rumours and reports of this kind increased dramatically and by the spring of 1897 Salisbury finally decided on a secret mission under a Royal Engineer, Major J. R. L. Macdonald, who would come through Uganda at speed and take the headwaters. The genesis for this was in Northcott's memorandum of 4 February and blossomed in the Prime Minister's mind to become a highly mobile flying column without the encumbrance of the substantial number of troops Northcott thought necessary to accomplish the task.

Macdonald was to carry out this mission in the strictest secrecy. His cover story was that he was to explore the Juba River, investigating the feasibility of using it, as Ardagh had suggested, as a boundary line between British and Italian Somaliland. As soon as he got far enough north, however, he was to cut across to the east bank of the Nile and establish himself there.

A week before Macdonald got his instructions, the ID suggested that if, as seemed likely, effective occupation was the be-all and end-all, then the fastest way into the Bahr el Ghazal would be to build a 140-mile branch of the Uganda Railway to the southern end of Lake Rudolph. Piggy-back steamers in sections up the railway, reassemble them at water's edge and soon they would be patrolling the 200 miles of lake.[307]

Wingate and Gleichen told Macdonald that if he was not careful he would run afoul of the Abyssinians 'in considerable force' and would 'excite suspicion and distrust amongst the Abyssinians with whom it was in the highest degree important we should avoid any possible cause of friction at the present moment'. They were right. Tentative contact was already being made between the Khalifa and Menelik and an alliance would be exceptionally inconvenient for the Anglo-Egyptian force carefully crawling up the Nile.

Wingate, not yet knowing the real mission, thought the whole plan as he understood it from the cover story was ill conceived. Macdonald was decidedly undermanned. He depreciated the £35,000 it would cost and, given the need not to irritate the Abyssinians, felt certain that if the FO would listen they would modify Macdonald's instructions to do exactly what Macdonald was being secretly instructed to do. He told Gleichen: 'Major Macdonald appeared to fully appreciate the necessity of some such steps being taken instead of carrying out the exploration of the Juba…'

Cromer agreed and instructed Rodd to report Wingate and Gleichen's views directly to Salisbury. The Mahdists, although weak south of Fashoda, had, as the two IDs feared, co-operated with the Abyssinians to the extent of a non-aggression pact which secured the Khalifa's eastern flank. If the Italians withdrew from Kassala as they threatened to, then the Mahdists would have become considerably stronger. This news caused both IDs 'some anxiety' and they successfully pressed Salisbury to urge the Italians to stay at least until Christmas.

For his part, Ardagh sent in another operations plan urging Macdonald's diversion towards the Nile with the object of meeting the Anglo-Egyptian force. This was now feasible. Kitchener's rail-head was by July 1897 far enough advanced to allow him to launch an attack on Abu Hamed and Ardagh reckoned the railway would reach it by October. Ardagh told the Foreign Office that if Macdonald's instructions were modified to fit in with his plan to bring up steamers along with a sizeable force from Uganda, then the result would be a 5,000-man Anglo-Egyptian force under a senior British general which could be mechanically transported by ship, train and boat from England and Egypt directly to a battlefield of choice outside Omdurman! At the same time, Ardagh proposed a 5,000-man contingent from India heading from Suakin to Berber. The whole operation could be taken care of by the end of the year, for the 210 miles from Berber to Omdurman was passable even at low Nile.

The DMI was well aware that delay worked to Egypt's advantage, nevertheless:

> it has been represented by the ID in other papers, that the Middle Nile from Fashoda to Uganda is the aim and goal of expeditions by France, by the Congo State and by the Abyssinians. Even though these expeditions are on foot and their strength is not known, it is manifestly desirable that we should not be forestalled in the effective occupation of this region, and that no part of the course of the Nile between Uganda and Egypt should be allowed to pass out of the British sphere of influence. In order to attain and assure this important object, there is not time to be lost in obtaining the command of the navigation of the Nile over and above Khartoum. When that is granted, our armed steamers, or those of the Egyptian Government can penetrate as far as Rejaf; leaving the portion between that place and the Albert Nyanza to be dealt with from Uganda.

As for Kassala, if such measures as Ardagh suggested for the Nile were carried out, the Italian problem would disappear.

Although he might not have known that Ardagh was recommending Kitchener's supercession, Wingate agreed that it was advisable to finish the work that winter. 'We can only dictate to Menelik when we are in possession of Khartoum and our gun boats are patrolling the river to Fashoda and I therefore urged the present season as a favourable one for giving the Khalifa his quietus...'

With his memorandum and the culmination of mounting anxiety over many months, Ardagh mentally moved away from the Foreign Office and into the soldiers' camp. It did not go unnoticed. Sanderson was taken aback. He dutifully sent it on to Salisbury but wrote: 'Here is a fresh mem. from Ardagh advising expeditions up and down the Nile. I think we might keep it for our private consumption. If it is printed and sent to any our missions abroad it may cause misconceptions.'[308]

On leave in England following his journey to Menelik, Wingate promoted the combined force concept, which he believed Kitchener also now supported, and found complete agreement amongst the senior officers he consulted. When calling on Salisbury he transferred his enthusiasm to the Prime Minister. To Wingate, Salisbury seemed 'keen to go to Khartoum but dreads the effect on the French populace of the despatch of a British Expedition, though he did not seem to mind so much the Quai d'Orsay'. In this, Salisbury was right as the French press and much public sentiment was behind every French mission in Africa, burning with the thrill of the chase and motivated not a little by the shame of being pushed out of Egyptian affairs in 1882.

As it was, Hicks Beach at the Treasury and senior officials at the FO combined to influence Salisbury not to deviate from his steady but sure plans. Ardagh and Wingate did not know this until Wingate was summoned to see Cromer, also in London. Wingate wrote to Kitchener:

The night before I left London I had a long talk to Lord Cromer, and presuming that I should see you, he gave me the benefit of his views in his usually forcible manner; he seemed much amazed with the attitude of the Horse Guards authorities in pushing for a British expedition; I told him about my various interviews and he then gave me to understand that that Gov had not the slightest intention of sending out British Troops this winter, that he himself was most strongly opposed to any such action and that the plan of a gradual and slow advance by the Egyptian Army was not in any degree altered by the Abyssinian situation ... he impressed upon me the necessity of not giving the WO authentic intelligence to aggravate the situation but rather to 'feed them with back history and tribal statistics.' My impression is that WO and FO are by no means agreed [and] that he does not intend WO to interfere in his preserve; as usual it is all a question of money and the government does not wish to ask the English taxpayer to subscribe for the reconquest of the Sudan – about which her interest seems rather to have waned – though from conversations I had with certain other people of some influence, I gathered that there is considerable interest in the retaking of Khartoum and a strong desire to see it accomplished at any early date; but, be that as it may, I think there is practically no chance of British aid this winter ... I do not gather that the FO are at all perturbed about the Abyssinian and Sudan situations, their hands are apparently rather full of other matters, Greece and Turkey, India and America.

After years of close co-operation and influencing, this rebuff must have been heavily felt and Wingate lamented: 'I cannot help thinking that it may prove a matter for regret that circumstances so fell out as to make the delivery of the final blow impossible this season.' Wingate deeply resented being set up, as he suspected, by Kitchener when in London. The Egyptian DMI had made his rounds amongst the men of power speaking about the need for the winter advance, believing that he enjoyed 'the entire concurrence of the Sirdar'. Yet after Cromer's rebuke it was clear to Wingate that Kitchener had 'kept his views in the background waiting to see how the cat would jump'.[309]

But matters were not standing still. The day after Wingate's reprimand, the Egyptians took Abu Hamed and on 31 August Berber fell. Wracked by internecine wrangling and shortage of food and weapons, the Mahdist forces of 1897 were a far cry from the great movement of the 1880s.

On top of this good fortune came the disturbing but inevitable news that the French were nearer Fashoda than ever. Wingate again recommended an Anglo-Egyptian push that winter. Sanderson told him that the government 'preferred to let things take their course'. Ardagh then asked Sanderson outright if the government planned to secure the Nile in 1898. Sanderson said he would ask Salisbury if Ardagh's new information would incline him towards 'a speedy advance' to Khartoum with British troops. In his note to the Prime Minister, Sanderson went to pains 'in fairness' to explain the DMI's points even though he dissented from them. 'His reasoning is', he wrote to Salisbury, 'that the French are not at present in any force on the Upper Nile, and that if we advance to Khartoum, they will have the opportunity of establishing a hold upon the country between Uganda and the southernmost Egyptian possessions, and that when [they] are so established we shall not be able to dislodge them without risking a war.'

For his part Salisbury agreed with Sanderson. He did not believe the French could have arrived on the Nile in any substantial numbers. 'I suspect the whole thing of being a bogie. The judgement of the War Office in this matter is slightly biased by a desire for something brilliant.' Sanderson answered Ardagh fully but concluded that whatever happened 'we must in fact take our chance'.[310]

‡

Kitchener, too, was under severe strain owing to the 'hasten slowly' policy. Although much of the entire strategy of reconquest was based on strong lines of communications and supply, they were becoming stretched and he might possibly have the Abyssinians to contend with as well as the Khalifa. Although reluctant in the extreme, in the early autumn of 1897 the Sirdar finally called for British troops. Cromer refused to sanction the request and the impetuous Sirdar resigned. Cromer talked him out of it, giving him permission to take Kassala, but the cracks were beginning to show. The ID's man on the spot, Captain à Court, found the Sirdar 'showing the effects of the hard work and worry of the past campaign'. He described the gloom from the front of those facing another year of 'grilling' inactivity and even after Kassala was taken in late December there was little to relieve the pessimism and despair. The EID then learned that the Khalifa was massing his troops near Berber and everyone finally agreed that British reinforcements would be needed. À Court wrote: 'I have not seen a single suggestion in any letter that the E.A. can finish the show by itself.' Wingate recorded in his diary that 'the decision to ask for British reinforcements quite lightened the atmosphere'.

Reinforcements were authorised and as they moved up to the line during the spring of 1898, Ardagh wrote another of his *tour d'horizons* for the Cabinet. In West Africa, negotiations with the French over access to the Niger were plodding to a conclusion with the ID deeply involved. The mission of 'that ass Macdonald' as Wingate called him was stalled and there was no knowing when it would get on, if at all. But on a brighter note the combined Anglo-Egyptian force was on the point of investing Atbara whereupon Khartoum would be in view. The Abyssinians were, as predicted, filling the vacuum left by the Mahdists and the Italians and as for the ultimate prize:

Two French expeditions are advancing towards the White Nile from the East and West respectively, hoping to join hands about Fashoda. It is possible that they may have done so already (though the Dervish force at Bor may prove an awkward customer); but is unlikely, for it is almost certain that the Eastern expedition has been obliged to retire. An Abyssinian expedition is moving westwards – object unknown. Though the king of the Belgians has now a footing on the Nile at Regaf, it is a very precarious one. The British forces from Uganda will not be able for some time to advance North without reinforcements. The Dervish supremacy in the Bahr-el-Ghazal and regions bordering on the Upper Nile has been greatly diminished owing to their severe defeat at Regaf, and also owing to the necessity of reinforcing their threatened centre about Omdurman and Mettemmeh. Altogether, if the star of any of the contending Powers in these regions may be considered as being in the ascendant, it is that of France and not of Great Britain, the Dervishes, or the Congo Free State.[311]

Fortunately for Britain, reports coming in during the spring of 1898 spoke of the difficulties Marchand was facing, which was true, and one source even reported that it 'had completely failed', which, of course, it had not. The Bonchamp mission had to return to Addis Ababa. The ID commented 'that it would appear that the whole scheme of establishing a French belt from east to west across Africa has broken down for the moment'.

By the end of May, Gleichen could tell Wingate that Macdonald was starting again and as for Marchand, Gleichen was altogether more cheery:

> I have taken the opinion of an eminent QC as to what to do with Marchand & Co. when we get them. He agrees with me that we ought to invite them to a champagne dinner and then cast loose and steam down stream with them at once, so will you please lay in some champagne.[312]

The end came quickly. In August, Cromer obtained the Cabinet's permission to send gunboats up the Nile as high as was practicable to occupy both banks of the Nile and on 2 September Kitchener crushed the Mahdists at Omdurman. The next step was to oust Marchand at Fashoda, which Kitchener wasted but little time in doing, yet doing it with courtesy, despite Marchand's deputy's ill-disguised fury. As for the Khalifa, he escaped the battlefield at Omdurman and, after a year, Wingate tracked him down and he, too, was defeated in November

1899. The Mahdia was finished and so were the French. There was still some wrangling over boundaries in West Africa which lasted into the 1920s, but in diplomatic terms the way was being paved for the two powers to work together sufficiently to result in the Entente Cordiale of 1904 and the Intelligence Division, in new clothes, would be there as well.

CHAPTER NINE

A *VOX CLAMANTIS IN DESERTO*

During the last quarter of the nineteenth century, Britain was involved in thirty or so 'minor' armed interventions around the world (such as the Uganda Mutiny, the Sierra Leone Rebellion and other operations in West Africa), besides a regular series of potentially more major scares involving the main western powers. They all reflected the growing rivalry of continental powers which slowly but surely were kicking Britain's 'splendid isolation' into touch. Grave were the concerns, but at least Africa was no longer Britain's Achilles heel, an outcome in which the home and Egyptian intelligence divisions played a key part.

But that was now the past. With the retirement of the Duke of Cambridge and the fiasco of the Second South African (or Boer) War, Britain was forced finally to face the future and to get to grips with its higher military organisation. It was a changing world in which intelligence would play a larger part than ever before.

A small knot of officers watched in the gathering dark of All Hallows Eve 1895 as the aged Duke of Cambridge was driven out of Horse Guards for the last time. He returned his personal sentry's final salute and when the guard relief came a few minutes later, that sentry fell in, leaving no replacement. The Duke's sentry box was empty for the first time in almost four decades and it was soon removed as well. An era really had closed.

The Duke had finally been persuaded to retire after thirty-nine years as Commander-in-Chief by none other than the Queen, who at the end was blunt with him on the verge of being rude.

He never forgot it and even after the passage of eleven years wrote angrily 'I was pushed!' His ouster came on the heels of the abortive attempt by the Hartington Commission to create a modern general staff. This and the longevity of the Duke's time in office made the choice of his successor particularly difficult. Campbell-Bannerman, whose dissenting report had sabotaged the commission, intended to appoint General Redvers Buller, whose stand against Irish landlords and management of the Duke whilst filling the post of Adjutant General made him a favourite with many Liberals. The Duke of Connaught, as a member of the Royal Family, was favoured by the Queen and a number of senior officers. Brackenbury had been packed off to India and that left Wolseley, then commanding in Ireland.

In 1895, John Charles Ardagh arrived back in London from India where he had been Lord Lansdowne's secretary and the universal choice to replace Brackenbury when his tour ended. Lansdowne now moved from the Viceroyalty to become the new Secretary of State for War. With the C-in-C's post coming up, Wolseley, knowing how close professionally Lansdowne and Ardagh were to each other, eagerly pounced on him:

> Very Private Midnight 5-8-95 My dear Ardagh What I really want to know is this: am I still fairly in the betting for employment in the new organisation of the War Office, or not? ... I have no wish to push myself forward to beg of Lord L[ansdowne] to employ me if he thinks someone else would do the work better, for I do not believe in 'claims' in such a matter. But at the same time I should esteem it a real kindness to me – no matter how indirectly – such as that I had better sell my horses for example – as he can do so in the public's interest, that another man will be placed at the head of the Army.

Wolseley arranged to meet Ardagh a few days later and it cannot have been easy for either man. He wrote to Ardagh on the same day that 'the blow nearly stunned me.' He took the government's silence as evidence of intrigue and asked Ardagh to nominate him as attaché to Berlin if he did not resign altogether to make his living by writing. 'When my disgrace is made public and the shock of it has somewhat passed away, I shall be better able to make plans for the future.'

A few days later he told Ardagh that he had gone to console his wife and anxiously added:

If you at any time ascertain anything upon the matter in question, do please tell me. I don't mind so much being executed but being kept on the scaffold with the glint of the axe constantly blinding my power of seeing clearly around me, is a torture worse than that which Damocles underwent. Again thanking you for the friendly part you have already taken for me…

Wolseley knew, of course, that Ardagh was Lansdowne's trusted adviser. The new Secretary asked Ardagh for his perspective on each of the potential candidates. On 6 August Ardagh replied that he felt that the Duke of Connaught would not abuse patronage, but he was not especially popular with the Army as a whole. Buller was certainly *persona grata* with the Liberals but 'if however the history of Army administration in the last five years is examined into, it would be found that Sir Redvers policy was *quieta non movere*. Progress has been exceedingly slow under his regime.'

A plebiscite would elect Major General Roberts, but his long service in India had put him out of touch with Britain, the Army and Parliament. They both knew that 'English staff officers had not a very high opinion of the Indian Army'.

As for the British Army, much remained to be done and:

the two men with the most brains to do it are Wolseley and Brackenbury. The great talent of the latter is marred to some extent by an underlying self-seeking and selfishness, which has made him distrusted in the past; but whatever he takes in hand he is sure to do thoroughly well – e.g. as head of the Intelligence Dept. and as Military Member of Council. He would no doubt have made an admirable Chief of the Staff, in the system devised by the 'Hartington Commission' – if it could have worked at all, but it could only have worked by his being virtually Cr. in Chf.

Ardagh concluded that whilst many might be called, the British Army 'would prefer Lord Wolseley'.[313]

To what extent Ardagh's influence with Lansdowne made him a king maker is debatable, but Wolseley certainly thought him so: 'Let me thank you from the bottom of my heart for your efficient service in my cause and for your friendship and kindness to me at a time when I did indeed feel so low that I felt ashamed to look my old comrades in the face.' On 14 September he told Ardagh: 'I feel that I owe you much more than I care to put on a sheet of paper – for the fact that I am to have a term of office of any sort again.'

But Wolseley was hardly to repay the favour. He fought hard against any implementation of the Brackenbury–Hartington system, the legacy of the ill-fated commission, which would, he believed, diminish his powers as Commander-in-Chief, and in doing so became as much an obstacle to progress as the Duke. Brackenbury told Grierson: 'I do not see how anything else could be expected when Ld Lansdowne has sought his advice from Lord Wolseley and Sir Redvers Buller, the two men who are responsible for the existing War Office organization, which was so condemned by the Hartington Commission.' Indeed, Wolseley admitted to Ardagh that 'my endeavour is consequently to keep things very much as they are'. Almost immediately, Wolseley's limitations became more and more obvious. He was often ill, was out of favour with politicians of every stripe and as far as reformation of the Army was concerned, 'had no ideas about the value he might get from the assistance of a Chief of Staff'.[314]

Faced with the failure of the Hartington Commission and the bubbling pot of South Africa, Lord Salisbury created a Defence Committee of the Cabinet under Hartington, now the Duke of Devonshire from 1891, at the beginning of his third and final administration. Burdened with petty inter-departmental squabbles and inadequate energy, it did not settle broad principles of national and imperial defence, even though many thought that was why it had been established.

None of this spelled any good for the ID, which did not receive the enhanced role which Devonshire had planned for it. Lansdowne himself was a problem, too. Like so many others he had not worked out the potential value of a C-in-C working with a Chief of Staff. He, again like so many others, was confused as to roles, and looked in vain for an English von Moltke. He and Wolseley were increasingly at each other's throats over authority, accountability and responsibility. He worried that a Chief of Staff might overrule the proposed board of senior generals and be in fact a 'political officer who advocated some military policy in favour of the Government'. He looked to give the Commander-in-Chief all the functions which the Hartington Commission recommended for its Chief of Staff. Lansdowne envisaged the ID and the Military Secretary helping the Commander-in-Chief to perform his duties but he, too, shied away from a separate 'department of thought'. Here was Campbell-Bannerman speaking with his distrust of 'Continental ways and his suspicions of soldiers who "sit apart and cogitate"'.

At the War Office, Lansdowne preferred to make the DMI responsible to the Commander-in-Chief. It was logical. If he were accountable to the Secretary of State alone, 'he would acquire, in virtue of his membership of the Board an influence equal to that of his colleagues, without the responsibility from which they ought not to be able to escape. Such an arrangement might also be objected to as giving the Commander-in-Chief, whose subordinate would sit beside him on the Board, an undue share of influence over its proceedings.'[315] Therefore the ID, formally a *division* from 1888, was projected to become a *department* under the Commander-in-Chief, but without any special responsibility for planning for war. It is from this mistake that later generations blamed for the disaster which was the Second South African War.

The irony was that Wolseley, the reformer from outside, eschewed reform when in power and spent his term as a reactionary, adrift in liberally dispensing spite and wallowing in what Lansdowne called 'the graver problems of military administration'. The actual result of it all was that the ID more or less continued on its own path as a virtually separate department of state.[316]

Whilst the succession issue was keeping Horse Guards and the politicians busy, the DMI, General Chapman, it will be recalled, went to the Scottish District when his five years were up. He was replaced by Ardagh, who assumed the mantle on 1 April 1896, the thirty-seventh anniversary of his commission. He had been in line for the post for some time and Wolseley had alluded to it as a *fait accompli* as early as 1892. Gleichen, who himself would become in effect a DMI in the new century, wrote of his then new boss:

Ardagh, silent, monocled, skinny-necked (he always reminded me of a marabou stork, I fear), the writer of beautifully expressed far-seeing memoranda on the most abstruse questions, was always something of a mystery to us. He never spoke, and when he sent for us to give him information on certain subjects there was dead silence on his part whilst we talked. I once gave him a full account of Morocco matters during the space of something like half an hour. He leant back in his chair, never interrupted once nor took a note, and at the end he slowly screwed his eyeglass in and said in a hollow, faded voice, 'Thank you.' Yet he had absorbed painlessly all that I had told him, and the issue was a masterpiece of writing.'[317]

Promoted to major general upon appointment, Ardagh was an honorary aide-de-camp to the Commander-in-Chief, a Knight Commander of the Indian Empire and a Companion of the Bath in both military and civil divisions. The latter honour, it will be recalled, dated from his work with Salisbury on the Eastern Question in 1878. Although a discreet, shadowy figure, he was not without substance or regard. In 1897 he received an LLD from his alma mater, Trinity

College, Dublin, and like other ID officers he was a prolific writer, sat on the council of the Royal Geographical Society, and was an associate of the Institute of Civil Engineers and a member of the Club, founded in 1764 by Dr Samuel Johnson. There were only forty members, all key figures, including Lord Rosebery and Wolseley.

Brackenbury was delighted with Ardagh's appointment and wrote to him from India:

> I would rather see you there than anyone else, not only for your own sake, but for the sake of the Department, in which I take so deep an interest. My experience is that Everything in the ID depends upon your having the complete friendship and hearty cooperation of the Foreign Office. So long as you have that, as I had, you can command the use of all their staff at home and abroad, and they will never let you want for money – With the India Office and Colonial Office, if you continue to show them how useful you can be to them, they will help you all they can. Keep close touch with the NDI [Naval Director of Intelligence]. I hope the Intelligence Department will never cease to be not only the eyes & ears of the Army, but a most valuable Department to the State generally. It was my object to make it so; and I am quite certain that your power of obtaining military information depends directly upon your friendly relations with Departments of State – Foreign, Colonial, and India Offices – and these friendly relations depend upon the help you give them … I shall pay you an early visit at Queen Anne's Gate…

For his part, Ardagh knew exactly what he was about. 'The most important duty of an Intelligence Division is foresight.'[318]

‡

The Division's intense effort to ensure Britain was paramount in East, West and Central Africa and the Sudan began to take its toll on the Division. With the rise to power of the Japanese, the Division's work there was growing and Grierson, then military attaché in Berlin, was sending ever more worrying reports back to the Division about German intentions as well.

Gleichen and Talbot, both of whom would rise to prominence before the Great War, were still in the Sudan helping Wingate set up the new administration. There were also an increasing number of boundary commissions to run, and experienced junior ID officers were called from Queen Anne's Gate to do so. Colvile was still in Uganda, Northcote was commanding the new West African force, Everett's work with the Anglo-French Niger Commission was disrupted as overwork and ailments from his consular days laid him low. Then he was at work delimiting in Togoland and even Ardagh, who was far from being well, was called away in March 1899 to a lengthy and futile disarmament conference in The Hague.

But the demands on the Division did not cease. Quite the opposite. The map-making abilities of Section (F) were again stretched to breaking and the ID's large secret library was in trouble, too. This library was extraordinary. It was indeed the wellspring of the Division's ability to provide accurate intelligence. Within a year of the invention of the Dewey Decimal System in 1877, the Department was classifying not just titles, but material within sources *to five and nine divisions*. Between 1879 and 1883, £1,600 was spent paying ID officers some ten shillings a day to compose, in their spare time, a 537-page quarto catalogue of seven columns with numerous cross-entries. Although mind-numbing in construction, this database, for so it was, allowed the ID to provide its unique expertise far more accurately and rapidly than other departments of state could even hope to do.[319]

In 1886 the post of librarian went to W. H. Cromie, who had come to the ID as a private soldier. Cromie advanced through the ranks as fast as the ID could push him, to sergeant, then quartermaster, lieutenant to late entry captain. Obviously ambitious, he was publishing articles in the *United Service Magazine* whilst still a quartermaster. By 1890 he had completed reading law at Gray's Inn and took his LLB. He also taught himself – and became an expert in the process – how to make secret inks, at which the English had excelled in Elizabethan times.[320]

When Cromie took over the library, it contained close upon 38,000 volumes and a further 1,500 works were coming in annually. The Foreign Office had four librarians with only twice the volume of works and most were historical. The Colonial Office had but 12,000 volumes. The officers in each section of the ID (A to F) indexed the periodicals of interest to their section. Cromie and two clerk sergeants did everything else including all the classified documents. By 1891 the Division needed to update its system again and the DMI applied to the Treasury for £500 to accomplish the task. The Treasury acknowledged that the ID possessed what was 'believed to be the best Military Library in the world' but was unable to comment on the proposal. Sir E. Maunde Thompson, principal librarian and secretary to the British Museum, was asked to evaluate it. He greeted the whole project with scathing amusement. He had never heard of the Division or its library. Cromie was despatched to see Thompson. This was no little occasion as only the year before the DMI had complained that the low-ranking officer was:

unable to meet other librarians on equal terms. In fact they have hitherto refused to grant him an audience. This is a serious drawback for occasions sometimes arise when their assistance would be invaluable to us. The varied nature of our work necessitates, if high efficiency be aimed at, our securing for ourselves the entrée into every depot of information.

The interview was a success and the expenditure authorised.[321]

During the Brackenbury and Chapman years the work grew steadily and when the West African negotiations and the jobbing for the reconquest of the Sudan was rising to a boil in 1894, Chapman urgently requested the War Office to give Cromie a rise and at least three more assistants. In exchange, the ID offered to house the estimated 7,000–8,000 books scattered around the rest of the War Office, probably many more.

Possibly because the Liberals were in power and the War Office was under tight budgetary restrictions, nothing more was heard of that proposal. But Chapman kept at it until the War Office and Treasury gave in, and in 1895 F. J. Hudleston was transferred from the British Museum as Cromie's assistant. Quiet and effective, he was much more acceptable in 'the great age of Victorian snobbery' and would eventually rise to be the librarian for the whole War Office.[322]

Ardagh, too, did what he could to improve Cromie's lot, but it was too little, too late. In 1898 Cromie resigned from the Army but stayed on as librarian. By August 1898 – whether it was the years of non-recognition or the low pay is not clear – Cromie had fallen under suspicion of selling secrets to the French.

The overworked officers of the Division, heavily taxed over India (again), the Sudan, and West, Central and South Africa, did not discover the leak themselves. It was probably uncovered in France. When Ardagh heard of it, he cooked up 'a bogus scheme open for betrayal to the French' of a planned attack on Brest. Copies of the scheme were, pro forma, lodged with the Division's library. It worked. The French learned of it and sent over two agents to meet their informer. But Cromie, if it were he, eluded Ardagh's trap by sending rather than taking a copy of the plan to his handlers. The DMI tried again, hoping to secure evidence by means of Cromie's handwriting, but nothing conclusive was gained.

Nevertheless, from that moment Ardagh kept Cromie away from classified documents and eventually had him transferred out for 'irregular conduct' leaving Hudleston in charge. Strangely, Cromie was transferred to the Inspector General of Fortifications' Office and as late as the 1930s rumour was alive in the War Office library that Cromie had been sacked for participating in a gun-running scheme. This, too, is plausible as the Division and the Foreign Office were involved in working up just such a scheme in Abyssinia, but the real reason in all its complexity has quietly slipped away.[323]

This incident was, however, indicative of the limit which the ID had reached. Whilst Ardagh was at The Hague, he was not avail-able to throw his political weight behind the increasing number of worried memoranda which the Division was sending to the Foreign and War offices about the Boers and their growing military preparations. Upon reading one by Ardagh in the aftermath of the Jameson Raid, Salisbury told Lord Lansdowne: 'I am astounded at reading the recommendations of Sir J. Ardagh. I suppose he reflects the dominant view of the Horse Guards.'[324]

That was hardly likely. As there were no accurate maps of the probable area of operations and other information from the Transvaal and Orange Free State was deficient, Ardagh urged the War Office time and again to allow him to set up a proper field intelligence office for the collection of information which would be useful to an expedition, especially as the Boers were said to be spending some £170,000 during 1898 alone on secret service. Gleichen recorded with disgust that Ardagh was given 'as a *great* concession, £100'. As it was, the entire fund for extra-channel information and travel expenses, worldwide, was only £600. Ardagh's requests for more money were, as he told the post-conflict Royal Commission investigating the want of pre-war arrangements, 'scoffed at by the Financial authorities of the WO and had never been referred to the Treasury'.[325]

The Colonial Section (B) under Captain (later Lieutenant General Sir E. A.) Altham and Captain (later Field Marshal Sir William) Robertson had long since given up arguing the toss about the likelihood of war (which they first predicted on 11 June 1896) and were deep in planning route reconnaissances, updating handbooks and preparing summaries of useful information. As the commission established to investigate the war was told, between June 1896 and the beginning of large-scale conflict, the ID sent some seven detailed warnings to Wolseley. All were ignored.

Matters deteriorated and the politicians realised that decisions had to be taken about a possible expedition. Lansdowne was firmly under the impression that General Sir Redvers Buller, who had been selected to head an expeditionary force if there was to be one, was consulting Ardagh. But that was not so, Buller airily saying that he had been told to keep his appointment secret. When his appointment was known, the ID sent him a written briefing which was returned unopened with Buller saying that he knew as much about South Africa as there was to know! This was only equalled by the actions of General Sir George White, who also admitted that 'there was no interview of mine with the [DMI] of sufficient importance to impress itself deeply on my memory'. In fact, he later admitted, he had not spoken with Ardagh or his officers at all.[326] Robertson sourly commented on the result. 'Britain', he said, 'would be penalised with the greatest of all handicaps in war – a bad start.' By 22 June 1899 the Bloemfontein Conference had broken down and the ID, for lack of anyone else in the War Office to see the need, took in hand the arrangements for transportation and supply of an expeditionary force.

In July 1899 Ardagh returned from The Hague to take up his normal ten-hour day and soon collapsed. His doctors ordered him to take three months' complete rest. Everett and Altham redoubled their efforts although Everett's illness was taking its toll, too. More chaos. Ardagh despaired. He wrote to his new wife, Susan, the Countess of Malmesbury: 'I wish Gladstone were alive to realise what he has done and be made to suffer for it. A pillory in Johannesburg would be a nice warm place for him. It is a sore subject to those who have foreseen and warned in vain.'[327]

When war came in mid-October, Altham was sent immediately to Africa and Robertson was left to carry on a bewildering number of operational and intelligence functions by himself with only the help of an ever-changing assistant. From dealing with crank inventors to preparing the daily situation report for the Queen and Cabinet, Robertson worked day and night. As the ID did not enjoy that easy access to information from the War Office which it had with the other great departments of state, Robertson was short of hard news from the various fronts and to his disgust had to cobble most of his reports from the newspapers.

Matters became worse and the 1879 cry of 'Ichabod!' by young Captain Grover was heard once again. The officers chafed to see active service and Ardagh did not stand in their way, but the toll was considerable. By February 1900 the head of Section (A) (France, Belgium, Italy, etc.) was senior aide-de-camp to Sir Francis Clery in Natal. Altham of Section (B) (British Colonies) stayed on to become Sir George White's Chief of Intelligence at Ladysmith. The head of Section (C) (Germany, etc.) was serving in a similar capacity with General French. Lieutenant Colonel W. H. Waters, the Oriental scholar who headed (D) (Russia and all Asia), was in north-western Cape Colony with Sir William Gatacre and Gleichen of (E) (Austro-Hungary, the Ottoman Empire and much of Africa) was on the Modder River with Lord Methuen, as was his handpicked replacement, Captain Forestier-Walker. Save Mr Knox, the map maker, and Mr Hudleston in the library, the entire personnel of the monitoring sections changed at least twice during the war and 'a newcomer in this pursuit is of little value until he has made himself thoroughly acquainted with the previous history of the cases he deals with'. Even Robertson was given permission to go to Africa.

At the seat of war, the British forces found themselves up against a sophisticated and well-armed enemy. Reverse followed reverse. Public incredulity at Britain's lack of preparation mirrored that of the Crimean War. In their defence, the government and the War Office in particular denied that they had known anything of the Boer's militarism or their strength before hostilities broke out. In January 1900, Balfour told the House of Commons that 'the man in the street knew as much as the man in the Cabinet'. Even the faithful Salisbury perjured himself on 30 January when he replied to a question from Lord Kimberley: 'When the noble earl says that we must have known about the artillery and munitions of war that the Republics were introducing, I ask how on earth were we to know of it?' Their ignorance was, of course, feigned and came back to haunt them when the truth finally became public.

Wolseley was, true to form, no help either and only when confronted by Ardagh, who was again now very ill, did he promise to give the ID its due in a forthcoming Mansion House speech. This he failed to do.

But had the ID itself failed? Faced with accusations from both politicians and soldiers, Ardagh sent a memorandum to Lansdowne's successor, St John Brodrick (later Earl Midleton), on 30 January 1901:

> In reference to South Africa … The ignorant attacks made on the ID at the time of the early reverses have been entirely disproved by the capture and publication of our secret documents which show that we furnished full information upon the numbers, armament and plan of campaign of our enemies and for many years had formed plans of campaign of our own. The latter, which were not followed at the outset of the war, we still believe to have been perfectly sound and it may be remarked that they met with considerable opposition among high military authorities when first propounded. Only a fortnight ago, Mr Fischer a South African statesman when told that the announcement that the Orange Free State was going to throw in its lot with the Transvaal, came upon all the British public as a surprise for which they were not at all prepared, he replied 'Surely not to all – I myself found among documents captured from the British at Dundee, a military plan for invading our Free State in which all the routes were described and characterised; and there must have been more than one such plan of campaign, because the editor of this one expresses here and there his dissent from the views of another military man who had done the work before'.[328]

Ardagh was referring to the ID handbook *Military Notes on the Dutch South African Republics*. In November 1899, the victorious Boers took a copy from General Sir Penn Symons's luggage at Glencoe and, reading it, learned to their astonishment that Altham's Colonial Section had overestimated the total fighting force of the Transvaal (53,000) and Orange Free State (32,000) by only two hundred men. The count of weapons and dispositions was so accurate that the Boers reprinted the handbook, unchanged, for their own use.

Even before the loss of *Military Notes* was known in London, Ardagh had pressed the War Office to expand the official circulation of this key work. This the War Office flatly refused to do and would not even let it be seen by Members of Parliament on the grounds that it was a classified document. This was preposterous but such were the times. It was only when parts of it appeared in the press in New York and then in *The Standard* that Ardagh was able to demand its reprinting and tabling before both houses of Parliament. Grudgingly, the War Office permitted the printing of just fifty more and Lady Malmesbury later remarked: 'From that time on members of the Government, when they were driven to it, defended the Intelligence Division in a half-hearted, apologetic sort of way, which made things look blacker than if they had said nothing at all.'

At the end of the debacle, the government was forced to constitute a Royal Commission under the Earl of Elgin. The commission's report condemned every aspect of Britain's war machinery, except the conduct of the Intelligence Division. Some weeks before the Royal Commission was convened Brodrick commented publicly that when the report of the Royal Commission was made known 'it would be found that Sir John Ardagh had not been so much to blame'. His discomfort can be imagined when just a few days later he found himself taking Lady Malmesbury in to dinner. She remembered him saying:

'I suppose you read the report of the Intelligence Division?' I replied: 'Yes, Mr Brodrick, I have. It is public property now.' – 'I suppose you are very angry with me?' 'I must say I am. I cannot understand how you could allow him to be so wrongfully accused.' – 'Oh, well, Lady Malmesbury, you must remember that if I had admitted that Sir John Ardagh told us the truth, people would naturally say: If you were told the truth, why did you not act upon it, and they would think it was my fault.'

‡

Everything changed in the aftermath of the Second South African War. The War Office, Horse Guards, its civil servants and soldiers alike, had existed in mutual chaos for years. The prosecution of the small colonial wars, indeed the taking of the Sudan and the headwaters, happened despite the want of system and lack of co-operation. Whilst that had not made much difference before, the blood of thousands of British troops killed or wounded and the public outcry for efficiency meant that the loud calls for a great and proper planning staff could no longer be ignored.

Lord Roberts, successful in the field, was called to supervise the much-needed reform of the War Office. This coincided with the end of Ardagh's term and an Indian Army officer, Sir William Nicholson, took over the ID. It was now to be physically integrated into the new War Office at Winchester House. The denizens all along Queen Anne's Gate, who had unwittingly benefited for years from the constant patrolling of a constable on their street all night, every night, stood in amazement as huge presses, stones and safe after safe were removed from the two knocked-together houses and trundled down the street.

It was a new century in other ways, too. The Victorian giants Salisbury, Devonshire, Rosebery and the Queen herself had left or were leaving the stage. The Queen died in 1901. Salisbury left office in 1903. Visiting Edinburgh that year with the new King, Lord Esher remarked that he was struck at seeing Rosebery looking old and frail and the same was said of his peers. Salisbury, seventy years old in 1900, was now visibly slower and tired. After the general election in October of that year, he removed the mantle of the Foreign Office from his shoulders and put it around Lansdowne, even though his conduct during the South African War had been found wanting by the Elgin Commission on the conduct of the war.

Lansdowne's successor as Secretary of State for War was St John Brodrick, who was equally mired down by the constant tiffs racking the War Office. Able, yet he too 'inspired little confidence' amongst the soldiers. In 1903, he was replaced by H. O. Arnold-Forster, who also tried to take reform further and, indeed, a General Staff was created in 1904, just before Viscount Haldane became Secretary of State for War in the following year. Behind all these men were significant unofficial personalities as well who also played significant roles in the shaping of reform from time to time, such as Clinton Dawkins, Reginald Viscount Esher, Colonel Repington of *The Times* (aka Charles à Court, late of the ID) and Spenser Wilkinson, a prolific writer who would become the first Chichele Professor of War at All Souls, Oxford.

Each played his part, but based on actual achievement, issues of imperial defence, military reform and security seemed to overwhelm politicians, officials and military reformers alike. Military politics reached new heights and it was intelligence and mobilisation issues which concerned and connected them all. As the investigation into the Boer War brought to light, there was insufficient appreciation of the value of strategic intelligence. There was also a dawning awareness that intelligence was potentially 'a big biz', a split between support for the Foreign and Colonial offices, the increasing need for intelligence to serve the Army and Navy within an imperial context, and, playing across all these issues, espionage and counter-espionage. As the enquiry to the Boer War found, the Intelligence Division, the government's uncomplaining Sally Ann who behind the scenes had been doing all the washing up providing the Crown with expertise in all these areas, was found to be too small to continue doing it all.

As one of his first acts upon appointment to the War Office, Brodrick appointed Clinton Dawkins from the Administrative Reform Association to look into War Office organisation in January 1901. Ardagh, nearing the end of his time, provided a characteristically concise memorandum:

> The name of the 'Intelligence Department' was originally applied to a small branch for the collection of information about foreign countries. As necessities arose, it has gradually been extended over a much larger field, and the original designation is now somewhat of a misnomer, as the expansion has included many of the subjects dealt with by the 'general staff' of other armies; and it is, in my opinion very advisable

that further development should take place in the same direction, and that it should eventually take that position, and become the authoritative advisory and consultative branch of the War Office, and the general remembrance on all questions of offence and defence, military surveys, and all abstract military questions throughout the Empire. It should not be an executive Department, but many advisory matters now referred to executive branches should be transferred to it. The work required by the Foreign, Colonial, and other offices should continue as at present.

The Mobilisation and Defence Section, which, for convenience was transferred from Queen Anne's Gate to Pall Mall in 1887 has drifted from the Intell Div of which formed a part, towards the Adjutant General's Department. It appertains more to the former than the latter, and should be closely connected with it.

The Secret Section should, as now, be practically under the direction of the Foreign Office.

The Topographic Section has now no means of executing new surveys, which are much needed in many British possessions. I have applied for a small survey party to be permanently allotted to remedy the deficiencies gradually; and have submitted to the Colonial Office a project for surveying South Africa which now under their consideration. [This happened: a Colonial Survey Section was formed in 1902 and in the forthcoming reorganisation of 1904 became the Topographical Section (Geographical Service) of the General Staff.]

A general and historical section for publishing comiliations, disseminating military information to the Army, and studying questions not dealt with by the special sections is much required. The superior staff of the Intelligence Division is inadequate to perform the many special duties which constantly devolve upon it.

Both Sir William Everett and myself have had almost always important questions in hand outside our ordinary duties which necessitated continual attention, and one or the other of us has been employed for long periods exclusively on such work as Boundaries Conferences in Paris, Berlin, Constantinople, the Peace Conference in the Hague, etc. Committees also take up a considerable portion of our time. It is to the interest of the public service that these duties should be performed by those considered most suitable, but a provision should be made for a state of affairs which is the rule and not the exception, by an addition to the staff.

In order to give proper weight to the Intell Div I think that it should be placed in the same category as the AG, QMG, IGF, and DGO and that there should be an intelligence officer in every command at home and abroad. At present we are dependent upon voluntary and unpaid efforts, which we cannot expect to be adequate in all cases.

It would be also desirable to arrange for more frequent visits of officers to foreign countries, to familiarise themselves with personalities and institutions. The funds at our disposal are not sufficient for this purpose and the minor states have to be neglected. Foreign States largely practise the employment of officers other than Military Attaches, where information is wanted.

With the modifications proposed I have no doubt that the SofS and the CinC would find their labours lightened, and the conduct of military affairs facilitated, by giving due weight to the recommendations made after deliberate study by an advisory and consultative branch, whose information and warnings in the past, have not, I venture to think, received the attention they deserve.

It is manifestly quite impossible for any of the heads of the great departments of the War Office to devote the necessary time to the details upon which the Intell Division opinions are based, yet I have often felt that those opinions certainly would have carried conviction had they been studied, and what I am anxious to attain, is, the acceptance on the part of the SofS and the CinC of a presumption that these opinions should hold the field until they have been successfully impugned and that they should not be summarily overruled or departed from without sufficient cause shown. I abstain purposefully from entering into any particular instances in which this has occurred in the past, as my object is not to justify what I conceive the SofS is satisfied requires no exculpation, but rather to assure that in the future my successor as DMI shall not be – as I have often been – a *vox clamantis in deserto*.[329]

The Dawkins recommendations were ready by July. It was a bit of a *tour de force* and led to an Order in Council in November 1901. The Army Board became a council upon which both key civilians and soldiers sat, but the C-in-C, now Lord Roberts, was to be, indisputably, the Secretary of State's principal adviser and therefore the government's. He was to 'control' key functions, viz the Adjutant General's Office, the Military Secretary and Intelligence, now remerged with Mobilisation. Other functions, such as Fortifications, Quartermaster and Ordnance, were to be 'supervised' by the C-in-C but responsible to the Secretary of State. [330]

Almost all of these recommendations were accepted, at least notionally, but the blockbuster was about Intelligence and Mobilisation. Ardagh's advice had not fallen on deaf ears. The ID, as a thinking and operational department, was to be doubled in size. This, too, had Cabinet approval, even before the sitting of the exonerating Elgin Commission, which when it came in 1903 also looked on the ID 'with friendly eyes, and are disposed to help us all they can as to the future'. But, as ever, the Treasury and the civilians at the War Office were the problem and it took all of the energy and wit of Ardagh's successor, Major General Sir William (later Field Marshal Lord) Nicholson, an Indian officer who had never been to Staff College nor commanded troops in action, to bring it about in the face of stiff opposition. He eventually won and became 'an immense success, grasping the potential of his new department and willing to fight for it against all comers'.[331] Nicholson would become the first Chief of the Imperial General Staff and in the new set-up Gleichen, Altham and Lieutenant Colonel W. R. 'Wully' (later Field Marshal) Robertson were amongst those on his strength, Grierson later taking on the Mobilisation role.

Dawkins's work was followed by the Elgin Commission into the South African War. Despite the efforts of Lord Esher for it to focus on the organisation needed for the future, it kept its eye resolutely on the past. It made no real recommendations for further staff reforms, apparently hoping the November 1901 Order in Council would suffice. Esher told the King that in his evidence Ardagh had given the commission a clear steer that a general staff, somewhat on the German model, should be formed 'involving a very proper increase of expenditure upon the Intelligence Branch, if that Branch is to be made really efficient'. He added: 'Sir John Ardagh struck the Commissioners as a man of great ability, who might have done far more valuable work had he not been hampered by an organisation altogether out of date. By raising the military status of his successor to that of a Lt.-General, an excellent advance has been made, and Sir William Nicholson should succeed where Sir John Ardagh failed.'[332] This was hard lines especially as the Elgin Commission roundly condemned Wolseley and the other generals over their failure to heed the ID's warnings.

In response to the commission, Brodrick announced a number of reforms in March 1903 including an increase in Intelligence but he, too, was hampered by the endless bickering by 'high military officials, all pulling in different directions, each man anxious to absorb the authority of his neighbour...' As Esher told the King: 'The task is hopeless.'[333]

When the new Prime Minister, A. J. Balfour, sought to replace Brodrick at the War Office, the obvious candidate was Viscount Esher, the Edwardian 'incarnate paradox', to quote the crusading journalist W. T. Stead, 'who carved out for himself a unique place in the world of affairs'. He had been a Liberal MP, Hartington's private secretary between 1878 and 1885, and then became absolutely indispensable to the Queen as chief of works and master of ceremonies. Above all, he was very clever, loyal and a wholly reliable confidant of the King and successive ministers. He was a knowledgeable observer of military affairs who preferred to exercise his considerable influence behind the scenes. This unusual man was summed up to a T in a Beerbohm cartoon which showed him lecturing an attentive but apprehensive Britannia, saying to her: 'Never mind who I am. Just go do what I tell you.'[334]

To Balfour and the King's exasperation, Esher refused to take up the post of Secretary for War and it went to H. O. Arnold-Forster,

Arnold of Rugby's son. A single-minded man, he began concentrating on Army reform from the bottom up and became deeply involved in recruitment issues. This suited Esher, who wanted to form and lead a committee which would tackle reform from the top down, i.e. advance general staff reform through the agency of a committee consisting of himself, Admiral 'Jacky' Fisher and Brackenbury. Unfortunately for Brack, Fisher said he had found him a difficult person to work with. To this Arnold-Forster sagely commented: 'Perhaps Sir Henry would make a similar remark; perhaps he would make it justly.' With Brackenbury ruled out, Esher selected the Governor of Victoria, Sir George (later Lord Sydenham) Clarke.

Brought into existence as the War Office Reconstitution Committee, it was a power house of purpose, recommending the creation of a general staff, to be known as the Army Council, with a brief to concentrate on the complicated issue of imperial defence. Intelligence was not forgotten. Largely as a result of the Esher Committee the Foreign Section, already enlarged, was raised to eight subsections in 1904 under Robertson to cover all the first- and second-class military powers, and all of it under Grierson as Director of Military Operations (including intelligence), who had had a meteoric rise from captain to major general in just eight years and three months.

Yet the political infighting, moves and counter-moves went on and on. Nicholson was eventually forced out. Clarke thought Grierson idle and conceited. Gleichen was not universally well regarded and few, it was averred, could understand how James Wolfe Murray kept advancing. Like Wilson or Ardagh he 'could hardly fill the eye'. Little wonder his nickname was 'Sheep'.

‡

The next few months were no more edifying than the three previous years, yet behind the scenes Esher breathed new life into the Committee of Imperial Defence (CID), which was, at long last, to be 'the machinery necessary to

compile a comprehensive strategic scheme for action within the Empire'.
It was also meant to undertake intelligence work, as Arnold-Forster put
it, 'different from and additional to' work done by the naval and military
intelligence divisions.

It was at this point that R. B. (later Viscount) Haldane became the new
Secretary for War. Justly credited with the founding of the Territorial
Army, he could also be credited with banging heads together and
forging the first General Staff. Haldane noted that the Esher Report
was 'far from being Holy Writ. But for the present it does to work
under' and it has been said that his reforms were as much Esher's
and Balfour's as his own. Again, commenting publicly and privately,
Haldane was much assisted by Repington and Wilkinson, although
both managed to infuriate. But at least in 1904 a General Staff was
approved and another new day and age had dawned. [335]

In any event, almost every issue concerning the nascent General
Staff or imperial defence centred around intelligence. After the
Algeciras Conference the military and naval intelligencers refo-
cused on Germany as Britain's main threat and the ID's subsections
were reorganised so that Europe (Gleichen) and Asia (Col. Aylmer
Haldane) now received much more attention. The intelligencers and
politicians also agreed with 'Jacky' Fisher that the primary purpose
of the Army was offensive, leaving the defence of Britain and Ireland
to the Royal Navy. 'England', the almost universal phrase for Great
Britain during the whole of the Victorian era, was now, more and
more, supplanted by the phrase 'United Kingdom'.

The other side of the strategic intelligence coin was espionage and
counter-espionage. Like the various rides into Afghanistan which so
alarmed Salisbury thirty years before, officers on official and unofficial missions now took to cycling the Franco-German borders and
sketching emplacements and harbours. And so, too, German tourists
were to be watched. As Michael Smith recalls in *Six* it went to absurd
lengths. The *Daily Mail* 'instructed its readers to "refuse to be served
by a German waiter", adding as an afterthought: "If your waiter says

he is Swiss, ask to see his passport.'" When Erskine Childers's *Riddle of the Sands* appeared, it appeared so plausible that steps were taken to ascertain whether or not the launch of the whole of Germany's navy as set out was feasible. The conclusion was that it was not.[336]

Spies and spy stories excited not only the public but the ID as well. As Ardagh reported to Brodrick in 1901: 'It may not be generally known that the Intell Div has another section known by the letter H, which deals with Secret Service, Censorship, and various other matters of a confidential nature with which the War Office has less concern than the Foreign Office ... This section, originally created in connection mainly with the war in South Africa, is likely to outlast it.'[337] And so it proved. It was this section, under Major (later Brigadier General Sir James) Edmonds, which evolved into MI5. Edmonds was wholly in the ID mould. Passing out first from his Staff College class, he was appointed to the ID in 1899 where he assiduously promoted the need for an expanded secret service. (And assiduous is the right word. He later edited the twenty-eight volumes of the *Official History of the Great War* and personally authored some seventeen of them.) He was the right man at the right time and place. A subcommittee of the CID on foreign espionage urged the DMO to set up a proper secret service bureau and Edmonds to create a proper counter-espionage section. The enhanced ID produced a plan for a secret service 'In the Event of a War in Europe' in 1905 and Edmonds, who already ran a small band, appointed his Far Eastern expert, the able linguist Colonel Sir Vernon Kell, to head this counter-espionage work in 1909. Kell retained this appointment until 1940 rubbing along with or bumping against the Admiralty's nomination to lead the active espionage arm, Commander (later Captain Sir Mansfield) Cumming. The espionage arm became MI6 and in accordance with Ardagh's advice of 1901, this arm of the secret service was, despite several attempts by the War Office and Admiralty to have it otherwise, at least notionally the operational responsibility of the Foreign Office.[338]

‡

It was a whole new world and one in which intelligence issues blossomed. It was a very far cry from the days when intelligence and its collection were considered beyond the pale, as when Gladstone told Lord Granville in 1880:

> It may seem ridiculous, but it is a positive fact that in this my 12th Parl. and after 20 years of office, I have never had any such knowledge of S.S. as to enable me to form any original judgement whatever on the question of its necessity...[339]

Those who carried the intelligence lamp in the last half of the preceding century quietly faded away, scarcely recognised. Ardagh, denied the customary leaving rank of lieutenant general, went on to serve as the Crown's representative on various international commissions and as a director of the Suez Canal Company, but his health declined steadily and he died in 1907, without issue. Everett briefly took up the post of military attaché in Berlin but had by this time formed a revulsion for active collection. 'I so dread the thought of being compelled to continue in communication and contact with the class of man who must be employed in this sort of work, while the measures to which we are obliged to resort are repulsive to me.'[340] What prompted this late change of direction is not known as he likewise laid down his pen, retired in silence to France and died without an heir in 1911. Brackenbury, who like Ardagh married late in life, went to his grave in the summer of 1914, again without issue.

For the younger intelligencers now in senior positions like Altham, Edmonds, Gleichen, Grierson, Robertson, Trotter, Tulloch, Wilson and Wolfe Murray, they had all served in what had been Britain's only real general staff, the Victorian-era Intelligence Division. And it proved as good an experience as any British officer was bound to get, a good stable to be from. Indeed, from Queen Anne's Gate came three chiefs of the Imperial General Staff (Wolfe Murray, Wilson and Robertson), two field marshals (Wilson and Robertson) and over a score of general officers.

They and their able colleagues from those earlier years were officers, each of whom Ardagh joked 'could be relied upon [to]... hold his
tongue ... instigating and committing the most atrocious crimes, and
yet be an honest, hardworking, intelligent gentleman' and all of whom
'had the qualities disowned by the bishop who "thanked God that
Providence had not endowed him with the low cunning necessary for
the solution of a quadratic equation"'.

As these officers reaped the rewards of backing the long shot,
finishing their careers building a large, formal general staff for Great
Britain and her Empire, it would be interesting to know if they ever
thought back to the exciting days of their youth, when under the dark
cloud of career-limiting opprobrium, they answered with accuracy,
speed and care the Foreign Office's urgent 'Query: Ask ID what next'
and in so doing played their part in gaining and retaining the foremost empire the world has ever seen.

NOTES

1   A. Roberts, *Salisbury: Victorian Titan* (London, 1999).

2   Sir Michael Howard, *War in Euorpean History* (Oxford, 1976, 2009).

3   *Vide* especially H. Strachan, *From Waterloo to Balaclava: Tactics, Technology and the British Army* (Cambridge, 1985); *The Pre-Cimean Origins of Reform in the British Army* (Cambridge PhD, 1977) and 'Soldiers, Strategy and Sevastopol', *Historical Journal* (Cambridge, 1978).

4   Clarendon and Russell correspondence, E. L. Woodward, *The Age of Reform* (Oxford, 1938).

5   A. Shepperd, quoted in C. Pugsley and A. Holdsworth, *Sandhurst* (London, 2005). There were 178 cadets and two 'professors'; J. Luvass, *Education of an Army, 1815–1940* (London, 1965).

6   W. P. Jervis, T. B. Jervis, *Christian Soldier, Geographer, and Friend of India*, (London, 1898).

7   TNA War Office [hereafter WO] 32/ 7290, T. B. Jervis to Frederick Peel, Institution of a Topographical & Statistical Office, 31 December 1855 and B. A. H. Parritt, 'Intelligence Corps to INTELLIGENCE CORPS', *Rose & Laurel*, viii, no. 29 (Ashford, 1966).

8   S. A. Wilks, *An Independent in Politics, JA Roebuck*, DPhil (Oxford, 1979). This led to the Roebuck Committee which almost immediately became bogged down in detail, its witnesses 'not necessarily the best qualified to take a comprehensive view of the weakness of the British military system'.

9   St Aubyn, *The Royal George* (London, 1966). The Duke did not become Gazetted as Commander-in-Chief until 1887, the fiftieth year of his military service.

10 D. Galton, *Memorandum on War Office Organisation*, November 1868; O. Wheeler, *The War Office* (London, 1914) and B. Parritt, *The Intelligencers* (Ashford, 1972).

11 TNA WO 32/7290, Jervis to Peel, 12 June 1855.

12 TNA WO 33/1, *System of Organisation and Administration of the French Army*, 5 March 1855. The concluding sentence of the report was entirely capitalised. *Vide* also *Military Expenditure of France*, 8 June 1855.

13 TNA WO 32/7290, Jervis to Peel, 31 December 1855; A. C. Cooke, *Catalogue of Maps, Plans and Views in the Topographical & Statistical Depot of the War Office*, (London, 1859) ii vols.; B. Bond, *The Victorian Army and the Staff College, 1854–1914* (London, 1972).

14 Capt E. E. H. Collen, *Report on the Intelligence Branch* (hereafter Collen, *Report*), 1878.

15 TNA GD (HO) 45/8/445 (Panmure Papers), J. R. Godley, *Report on the Topographical and Statistical Department*, 18 July 1857; TNA/WO 32/6053, Lord Northbrook, *Report of a Committee on the Topographical and Statistical Department*, 24 January 1871; Col. C. M. Watson, *Life of Major General Sir Charles Wilson* (London, 1909).

16 TNA Treasury/1/7035A/1869; TNA WO 139/1, WO to James, 3 March 1864; TNA WO 139/6, 28 January 1867; TNA 30/48/5/22 (Cardwell Papers) James to Lowe, 22 November 1869; *Parliamentary Papers*, xliii 1870; C. W. Wilson, *Royal Engineer Journal*, Chatham, 1 November 1874.

17 TNA GD 45/8/502 (Panmure Papers), undated (hereafter u.d.) memorandum, probably 1858, 'The changes introduced since 1857 have entirely changed the original organisation laid down by Lord Panmure'; TNA WO 30/125, H. R. Dreury to James, 12 February 1859, James to Peel, 17 February 1859.

18 Ripon held an office in every Liberal administration from 1861–1908. He had been the Under-Secretary of State for War between 1861–63 and Secretary of State for War from 1863–66.

19 *Vide* especially C. Woodham Smith, *Florence Nightingale* (London, 1950); Bond, *The Victorian Army and the Staff College* (London, 1972); Galton, *Memorandum on War Office Organisation*; anon., 'General Lord Airey' *Colburn's United Service Magazine*, October 1881; and Collen, *Report*.

20 C. B. Otley, *The Origins and Recruitment of the British Army Elite, 1770–1959* (Hull 1965); Bond, *Staff College*, C. M. Watson, *History of the Corps of Royal Engineers*, (Chatham 1913); TNA 30/48/22 (Cardwell Papers), ltr 72, 26 March 1870; WO 30/125, James to War Office.

21 TNA/GD 45/8/522 (Panmure Papers), J. T. Delane to Panmure, 3 September 1867, *Parliamentary Papers* 1867–68, xli (3834) and TNA WO 139/11, *Annual Register of Correspondence*, 6 November 1867. *Vide* also Capt. H. M. Hozier, *The Seven Weeks' War* (London, 1867).

22 Col. Sir C. M. Watson, *Life of Major General Sir Charles Wilson*, (London, 1909) and TNA OS/1/17 Palestine Exploration Fund.

23 India Office [hereafter IO] C/144/20 (Northbrook Papers), Sir R. Biddulph, *Lord Cardwell at the War Office*, (London, 1904); TNA WO32/6050, James to Lugard, 1 April 1870, James to Cardwell, 9 May 1870; TNA T/1/7021B/1870, James to Treasury, 14 January 1870, Lowe to Treasury, 5 February 1870; TNA T/1/4065/1870, James to Treasury, 10 March 1870; TNA 30/48/5/22 (Cardwell Papers), Lowe to Cardwell, 5 February 1870.

24 R. Owen, *Cromer*, (London, 2004) and Professor Richard Hill, interview, Oxford, 1977; Lord T. H. Sanderson, 'Memoir of Evelyn Earl of Cromer', *Proceedings of the British Academy*, viii (1919); Bond, *Staff College*; Marchlow, J. March, *Cromer in Egypt*, (London 1970).

25 Firepower, the Royal Artillery Museum, unaddressed letter from Baring, 7 June

1870, found in the Museum's copy of *Staff College Essays*, 1870.

26 J. Haswell, *British Military Intelligence*, (London, 1973); TNA 30/29/53 (Granville Papers), Cardwell to Granville, 5 November 1870; 30/48/1/2: Ponsonby to Cardwell, 20 July 1870; M Howard, *The Franco-Prussian War* (Oxford, 1962).

27 TNA WO/32/6053, Lord Northbrook, *Report of a Committee on the Topographical & Statistical Office*, January 1871; Watson, *Life of Major-General Sir Charles Wilson*.

28 TNA 30/48/5/29, Cardwell to Granville, n.d., Cardwell to Granville, 14 September 1870 and March 1871; TNA 30/48/3/14, Cardwell to Duke of Cambridge, 23 September 1870, TNA 30/29/53, Cardwell to Granville, 5 November 1870; Granville to Cardwell, 1 January 1871. *Vide* also BL/Add MS 44119 (Gladstone Papers) Cardwell to Gladstone, 22 September 1870, Duke to Cardwell, 24 September; TNA 30/48/1/2, Queen to Cardwell, 9 November 1870, Cardwell to Queen, 10 November 1870, Cardwell to Queen enclosing Baring's paper on the fortress of Paris, 31 August 1870 and 12 October 1870 enclosing another map of Paris. For examples of distain in which attachés were held: TNA 30/48/5/22 Lowe to Cardwell, 21 January 1869 and TNA FO 366/398 n.d.

29 Sir B. Mallet, *The Earl of Northbrook*, (London, 1908); TNA WO 30/48/4/19, Northbrook to Cardwell, 26 October 1870; 30/29/53, Cardwell to Granville and TNA WO A Series 0436; C. W. Wilson, *Notes on a visit to Metz and Strasbourg*, November 1870.

30 TNA WO 32/6053, Lord Northbrook, *Report of a Committee on the Topographic & Statistical Department*, January 1871.

31 Watson, *Life of Major-General Sir Charles Wilson*; H. M. Hozier, *Seven Weeks' War*; M. Kitchen, *The German Officer Corps* (Oxford, 1968); D. Johnson, *France and the Dreyfus Affair*, (New York, 1966).

32 Charles Brackenbury, *Report on Departments of Foreign States Corresponding to the Intelligence Branch*, 1874.

33 W. S. Hamer, *The British Army, Civil-Military Relations, 1885–1905* (Oxford, 1970); BL Add Ms 44119 (Gladstone Papers) Cardwell to Gladstone, 20, 22 September 1870; H. Strachen, *Wellington's Legacy* (London, 1984); Wheeler, *War Office*; Earl of Kimberley, E. Drus, ed., 'A Journal of Events during the First Gladstone Ministry, *Camden Miscellany* (London, 1958); St Aubyn, *Royal George;* TNA 30/48/1/2, Northbrook Report, Queen to Cardwell, 26 February 1870; Duke to Cardwell, 4 March 1870.

34 C. Brackenbury, *Report*.

35 J. Luvaas, *Education of an Army, 1815–1940* (London, 1965); A. Tucker, 'Army and Society in England, 1870–1900', *Journal of British Studies*, May 1963; Northbrook, *Conduct of Business in the Army*, 3rd Report, 16, Command Paper 54 of 1870; National Army Museum (hereafter NAM) 6804-3-38 (MacDougall Papers): MacDougall to Lord March Kerr, 27 November 1873.

36 Hansard, Series 1873; Collen, *Report*, Sir Robert Biddulph, *Cardwell at the War Office* (London, 1904)

37 Comment on C. Brackenbury's 'French Army Reforms', *United Service Magazine*, October 1874; *vide* BL Add MS 44119 (Gladstone Papers), Cardwell to Gladstone, 22 September 1870, TNA 30/48/4/19, ltr 6: Delane to Cardwell, 6 January 1870; C. Brackenbury, 'Military Systems of France and Russia, RUSI lecture, 12 May 1871.

38 Porter, *History Royal Engineers*; 'WHJ' 'Colonel R. Home' *Royal Engineer Journal*, 1879 and H. Vetch, *Dictionary of National Biography*, ix, 1921. Home even received a gratuity from the Treasury for *Precis* of £500 as it 'gave great satisfaction; was most favourably reviewed and was translated into several foreign languages as a standard work...', TNA T1/7728/21378/1878; Collen, *Report* and Bond, *Staff College*.

39 TNA WO33/6, 'Popular Fallacies with regard to our Security against Invasion', June 1858, TNA WO139/7, T&S to Home Office, 30 November 1866, TNA WO 30/125, Lord Longford to James, 5 January 1867.

40 This is an immense subject. For its beginnings *vide* for example: TNA T/1/7374B/9756/1874, MacDougall, *Defensive Organisation*, 6 November 1873; Colburn's *United Service Magazine*; F. J. Maurice, *Hostilities without a Declaration of War*, January 1884; T. B. Collinson, 'Mobilisations and its aftermath', *Royal Engineer Journal*, February 1877; WHJ, Obituary of Col. Home, *Royal Engineer Journal*, March 1879; Maj. Gen. Sir George Aston, *Secret Service*, (London, 1930); Collen, *Report*; Maj. Gen. Sir A. B. Tulloch, *Recollections of Forty Years' Service*, (London, 1903); Sir G. Aston, *Memories of a Marine*, London 1919; TNA 30/40/13, J. C. Ardagh, 'Defence of England, Mobilisation of the Regular and Auxilliary Forces for Home Defence', April 1888; Hugh Cunningham, *The Volunteer Force*, (London, 1975); 'A Prussian Critic', 'Invasion and Mobilisation' in Coburn's *United Service Magazine*, March 1876.

41 TNA T/1/7657/1877, Home to F. Stanley, 27 July 1877.

42 TNA 30/48/5/24, Cardwell to Lowe, 12 May, 7 June 1873; TNA T/1/7374B/2708, Campbell-Bannerman to Treasury, 12 February 1874. *Vide* also TNA T/1/7374B/3339 and 3340/1874.

43 A. Preston, *The South African Journal of Sit Garnet Wolseley*, (Cape Town, 1973).

44 Johnson, *Diaries of the Earl of Cranbrook*, T501/296, 1874.

45 TNA WO 193/8, *Annual Register of Correspondence*, November 1874.

46 A. L. Kennedy, *Salisbury*, (London, 1953), Salisbury to Lytton, 1877.

47 Salisbury to Lord August, 24 December 1878; L. P. Morris, *Anglo-Russian Relations in Central Asia* (London PhD, 1968) and TNA FO 519/284 (Wellesley Papers) and Wellesley to Loftus, 7 October 1873; Kazemzadeh, Firuz, *Russia and Britain in Persia, 1864–1914* (Yale, 1968).

48 E. C. Mouton, *Lord Northbrook's Indian Administration* (London, 1968).

49 *Parliamentary Papers*, 1878, C-2190, 'Correspondence respecting the Relations between the British Government and that of Afghanistan since the accession of the Ameer Shere Ali Khan' quoting the Indian Commander-in-Chief, 1868.

50 Collen, *Report*

51 TNA FO 96/174, Memorandum (Morier) on cover of Kabul Diraires; *vide* also notes on Pollock's despatches, 117–733, 18 May 1870.

52 C. W. Wilson, *Russian Advances*, March 1873 and D. Gillard, *Salisbury and the Indian Defence Problem* (London, 1968).

53 TNA 30/48/6/35:Cardwell-Argyll correspondence, ltrs 126, 129, 131, 25–26 November 1873.

54 A. C. Cooke (1869) and C. S. Wilson (1873), *Russian Advances*.

55 Capt. G. L. Ervin, *Time and Space Analysis*, (Murnau, 1971); Owen, *Cromer*, 'Rules for the Conduct of the War Game', T&S 1872.

56 Lady MacGregor, *Life of Sir Charles Metcalf MacGregor*, (London, 1888).

57 Morris, *Anglo-Russian Relations*, TNA FO 519/278 (Wellesley Papers): Wellesley to Loftus, 7 January 1875; TNA T/1/7615A/15533/1877, Thomson to Derby, 8 December 1875 and Derby to Treasury and IO, 23 November 1875.

58 C/2/69 (Salisbury Papers), Salisbury to Northbrook, ltrs 18,27,33,86, 1873–74.

59 *Parliamentary Papers*: C-2190, January 1875.

60 S. Gopal, *British Policy in India, 1858–1905* (Cambridge, 1965).

61 *Vide* E. C. Mouton, *Lord Northbrook's Indian Administration* (London, 1968).

62 R. Blake, *Disraeli* (London. 1966).

63 TNA FO 65/1102, Butler to Roberts in enclave (encl.) to Currie and Granville and Gov of India, 25 May 1880.

64 Morris, *Anglo-Russian Relations*, quoting Salisbury to Northbrook, 10 June 1874.

65 Collen, *Report*, quoting Roberts to Haines, 17 June 1876 and 1 September 1876.

66 This did not come out of the blue. The Indians had been working on establishing a permanent IBS for some time. A committee to bring this into effect was convened under the able leadership of Sir George Pomeroy Colley (1835–81), a reformer in the Ashanti Ring, who was killed at Majuba in 1881. Edwin Collen, the author of the seminal report on the ID, was Colley's assistant secretary.

67 TNA FO 633/16, *Memorandum on the Central Asian Question*, ID, 8 January 1877.

68 *Vide* TNA FO 458/5, et al, A. Alison, *Memorandum on the Northwest Frontier of India*, 26 November 1878; *Memorandum on the Choice of a Military Frontier for India on the Northwest*, 9 December 1878 and *Memorandum on Herat*, 9 December 1878, and Colley to Alison, 18 February 1879.

69 TNA FO 65/1065, Salisbury minute to Currie, 15 June 1879. *Vide* also F. H. W. Milner and L. Marshall, *Notes on the Russian Expedition to the Tekke-Turcomans in 1879*, 28 November 1879.

70 TNA FO 65/1063; TNA FO to WO, 30 April 1879.

71 TNA FO 65/1100, Alison memorandum, 16 April 1880; minutes by Sanderson and Tenterden, seen by Salisbury, to IO and Tehran; Thomson to FO, No 145, 19 June 1880.

72 B. Holland, *The Life of Spencer Compton, VIIIth Duke of Devonshire*, (London, 1911); Morris, *Anglo-Russian Relations* and Hartington Papers C-2776. Further

correspondence relating to the affairs of Afghanistan, Hartington to Viceroy, 21 May 1880.

73 BL Add Ms 44545: Gladstone to the Queen, 18 September 1880; *vide* also BL Add Ms 44145: Hartington to Gladstone, 21 September 1880 and BL Add Ms 44117: Campbell-Bannerman to Gladstone, 13 July 1882; also Hartington Papers 340 1015A, Hartington to Ponsonby, 18 September 1880.

74 Military *Parliamentary Papers*, C-2811: C. J. East, *Memorandum on our Future Policy in Afghanistan, No.7*, August 1880.

75 Kandahar was, in the minds of the Forward School, key to defending the Northwest Frontier and plans were laid for making it an independent region when suddenly Sher Ali's second son, Ayub, ruler of Herat, decided to try for Abdur's throne by taking Kandahar. A British force was defeated at Maiwand and, again, Roberts marched from Kabul at the amazing speed of three hundred miles in three weeks to reassert Indian authority.

76 As the ID was in the midst of establishing relations with the new government, it may have been somewhat hesitant of corresponding directly and secretly with the India and Foreign offices as it had during Disraeli's government. In any event, copies of East's paper went to Wolseley and finally the Duke. Wolseley warmly approved of it. The Duke did not.

77 340.1018 (Hartington Papers): Queen to Hartington, 8 October 1880; 340.1026A: Hartington to Ponsonby, 6 November 1880 and Hartington to Ripon, Sect No 45, 11 November 1880, PSD to India, vol. 6, 1880.

78 Anon, *Honour or Shame*, 1878, quoting Grant Duff, 'The Situation', *Nineteenth Century*, u.d.

79 TNA FO 78/2532, TNA WO to FO, 3 July 1876 and TNA T/1/7592/7958/1877, TNA WO to Treasury, 10 July and HWP to W. H. Smith, 11 November 1876.

80 They were W. S. Cooke, *Ottoman Empire and its Tributary States*, R. A. Vincent, *Offensive and Defensive Condition of the Ottoman Empire*, and F. C. H. Clarke and H. B. Moffatt, *Report on Russia in the Balkans*, all 1875.

81 R. H. Vetch, *Dictionary of National Biography* (hereafter *DNB*), 1901–11; TNA 30/40/1, S. Malmesbury, *The Life of Major General Sir John Ardagh* (London, 1909).

82 A. Gathorne-Hardy, ed., *The Life of Gathorne Gathorne-Hardy* (London, 1910).

83 E. Baring, *Memorandum on the Probable Course of Action which would be adopted by the Russians in the Event of their Attempting to Occupy Bulgaria and March on Constantinople*, 16 October 1876.

84 Johnson, ed., Hardy, diary entry for 24 October 1876.

85 *Ibid.*, i, 376–380, November, December 1876.

86 T. Fraser, *Recollections with Reflections* (Edinburgh 1914). The other officers were Lieutenants Chermside and Cockburn.

87 H43: T50V296 (Cranbrook Papers): 27 October 1876 and TNA FO 358/1 (Simmons Papers): Simmons to Lord Cadogan, 10 February 1877.

88 Fraser, p. 289, 310. *Vide* also Malmesbury for detailed accounts.

89 Collen, *Report*.

90 TNA FO 78/2663, Home to Simmons, 18 November 1876.

91 TNA WO 147/6, (Wolseley's Diary), 5 November 1878, FO 363/4 Tenterden Papers, 27 December 1876.

92 TNA FO 78/2663: Home to Simmons, 11 December 1876, minutes by Tenterden and Derby on same, 12 December 1876; Blake, *Disraeli*, Hardy vol. 1.

93 Blake, *Disraeli*.

94 TNA FO 78/2687, Home Memorandum: 'Under Certain Contingencies England Might have to seek some Compensation or Equivalent in the Eastern Mediterranean', 23 December 1876.

95 TNA FO 78/2688, Home to Simmons, 12 January 1877; FO 358/1, Home to Simmons, 15 January 1877 and D. E. Lee, *Great Britain and the Cyprus Convention Policy of 1878*, Harvard Historical Studies, 1934.

96 FO 358/1 (Simmons Papers), Lennox to Simmons, 26 December 1876 and 13 February 1877. FO 358/2, Deedes to Simmons, 6 February and 13 February 1877. *Vide also* FO 78/2534; T/1/7592/1877, 11 November 1876.

97 FO 358/2, (Simmons Papers): Simmons 'On certain instructions given to Colonel Home by Lord Salisbury', 2 February 1877.

98 *Ibid.*, also HA 43:T501/297 (Cranbrook Diaries), 2 February 1877; *vide*, for example, FO 78/2893, 26 July 1878 and 340.1115 (Hartington Papers): Childers and Hartington, 1877.

99 340.742 (Hartington Papers), Granville to Hartington, 28 December 1877.

100 TNA FO 358/1 (Simmons Papers): Home to Simmons, 7, 15, 16 January 1877.

101 TNA HA 43: T501/297 (Cranbrook Diaries), 17 April 1877

102 TNA CAB 41/8/12: Beaconsfield to the Queen, 23 April 1877.

103 Fraser, *Recollections* and TNA FO 358/3: Hardy to Simmons, 31 July and 28 August 1877.

104 TNA FO 579/2789 (Wellesley's Attaché Journal) 14 April 1877 (qy).

105 TNA FO 519/280 (Wellesley Papers): Wellesley to Loftus, 9 February 1877; TNA FO 519/276, Wellesley to the Duke of Cambridge, 20 March 1877 and TNA FO 519/281: Wellesley to Secretary British Embassy, Vienna, 18 August 1879.

106 FO 358/1 (Simmons Papers): Simmons to Lennox, 24 October 1877; FO 78/2673, December 1877 and HA 43: T501/297 (Cranbrook Diaries), 10 January 1878.

107 Fraser, p. 406–7, FO 78/2672, WO (Home) to FO 22 November 1877, FO 78/2665: FO to WO, 7 May 1877.

108 TNA 30/40/7 (Ardagh Papers): Deedes quoting Hardy to Ardagh, 6, 22 September 1877.

109 Hardy, ii.

110 *Chronology of Events connected with Army Administration, 1858–1907* (WO, 1908) p. 31. More than 35,000 men were called: 13,000 from the Army Reserve and 22,000 from the Militia Reserve. The order went out on 2 April and they were disbanded on 31 July 1878.

111   Capt. F. C. H. Clarke, *Memorandum on Recent Russian Military Preparations in Central Asia*, 26 July 1878.

112   BL Addit MSS 39137 (Layard Papers), Home to Tenterden, 10 April 1878.

113   *Ibid.*, TNA FO 78/2886-2891, FO 366/456, E/Home/5 (Salisbury Papers): Salisbury to Home.

114   FO 358/1 (Simmons Papers): Home's Cyprus Memorandum, Hardy, ii; BL Add MSS (Iddesleigh Papers): Derby to Northcote and Northcote to Derby, 19 July 1878.

115   TNA 30/40/7 undated note, TNA 30/40/1, Ardagh to T. Gowan, 26 July 1878.

116   Collen, *Report*, quoting from Turkey no. 37, *Correspondence relating to the Congress of Berlin* 1878, FO to WO, 17 July 1878.

117   E/Home/9 (Salisbury Papers): Home to Salisbury, 2 August 1878 and E/Home/10, Salisbury to Home, 5 August 1878.

118   BL Add MSS 50019 (Iddesleigh Papers): Salisbury to Northcote, 10 October 1878.

119   TNA 30/40/1 (Ardagh Papers): Grover to Ardagh, 17 June 1879 and 24 June 1879.

120   TNA 30/40/7, 4 December 1878, BL Add MS 39023 (Layard Papers): 27 November 1878 and TNA FO 364/7 (White Papers): Layard to White, 19 August 1879.

121   WHJ/Walter James/Colonel R. Home, CB, RE, *Royal Engineer Journal*, ix, (1 March 1879); W. Porter, *History of the Corps of Royal Engineers*, p. 533; Vetch, *Dictionary of National Biography*, *The Times*, 31 January 1879; and a number of professional papers.

122   A/21/11 (Salisbury Papers): Salisbury to Temple, 20 September 1878.

123   A/13/45 (Salisbury Papers): Salisbury to Trotter, 16 September 1879, A/33/46: Salisbury to Wilson 4 December 1879, Wilson to Salisbury, 9 January 1880, TNA FO 195/1363L Wilson to FO, seen by Dufferin, A/13/64: Trotter to Salisbury, 8 October 1879, TNA FO 195/1363: Wilson to Dufferin, Bennett to Dufferin, 23 October 1881.

124   C. J. Lowe, *Reluctant Imperialists*, (London, 1967) quoting Salisbury to Layard, 6 November 1879.

125   TNA FO 195/1363, Memorandum by Tenterden, 15 December 1881.

126   TNA T/1/7444B/13830/1873, Hammond (FO) to Treasury, 13 September 1873; TNA T/1/7444B/15702/1874, Lister for Derby to Treasury, 10 October 1874; Chancellor of the Exchequer to W. H. Smith, 16 October 1874; Smith to Disraeli, 27 October 1874 and Sutherland (P&O) to Smith, 26 November 1874 enclosed in Smith to Disraeli, 5 December 1874.

127   TNA WO 33/335: *Parliamentary Report of the Committee appointed to consider the movement of Organised Bodies of Troops by sea*, 30 November 1875.

128   P. MacDougall, *Report on Egypt*, 16 June 1876 and TNA T/1/7444B/13830/1873, Lister to Treasury, 10 October 1874 and Chancellor of the Exchequer to W. H. Smith, 16 October 1874.

129 TNA FO 358/2, *On certain Instructions given to Colonel Home by Lord Salisbury*, 2 February 1877.

130 TNA FO 78/2670 WO to FO, 11 August, 22 August 1877.

131 *Vide* for example, A. A. H. Knightsbridge, *Gladstone and the Invasion of Egypt 1882* (BLitt Thesis, Oxon) 1960.

132 340.656 (Hartington Papers): Cavendish to Hartington, 30 January 1876 and Gladstone to Hartington; 340.657 Gladstone minute, 14 February 1876; D. A. Farnie, *East and West of Suez* (London, 1969); Add MS 44766: 5 July 1882.

133 TNA 30/29/118, Granville minute, 12 November 1881; TNA 30/29/137, Granville to Northbrook, 15 December 1881; Northbrook to Granville, 20 December 1881 and TNA FO 78/3337 FO to WO, 9 December 1881; TNA FO 195/1363, Memorandum by Tenterden, 15 December 1881.

134 Maj. General Sir A. B. Tulloch, *Recollections of Forty Years' Service* (Edinburgh, 1903).

135 WO 2A54, Tulloch 'Report on Egypt', 1882 and *Recollections*.

136 BL Add MS 44545 Gladstone to Childers, 6 January 1992; Gladstone to Granville, 6 April 1882 and *Hansard* 267.831, 13 March 1882; TNA FO 195/1363 'Memorandum by Tenterden on Wilson's proposals to use British consuls to counteract French intrigue', 15 December 1881; Capt H. Jekyll (ID) 'Royal Commission on the Defence of British possessions and Commerce Abroad', 23 March 1882.

137 TNA FO 78/3470, 16 June 1882, Tulloch, *Recollections*. Only two copies are known to exist, Mons Archives Comm and Old WO Library, now untraceable. TNA FO 78/3481, Granville to English Suez Canal Company, 27 June 1882.

138 BL Add MS 44545, Gladstone to Granville, 24 June 1882, 1 July 1882.

139 R. E. Robinson and J. Gallagher with Alice Denny, *Africa and the Victorians*, 1967; TNA 30/40/9 Ardagh's diary, July 1882; Add MS 44766 5 July 1882.

140 Tulloch, *Recollections*; BL MS 45/246 *Handbook on Egypt*, 13 July 1882; *Royal Engineer Journal*, 2 October 1882; TNA FO 78/3471 Seymour to Admiralty, 9 August 1882; TNA FO 78/3430, Granville minute, n.d. (probably July 1882).

141 TNA FO 78/3470, Alison to Childers, 14 July 1882; Alison to Childers, 15 July 1882 and throughout TNA FO 78/3471; Royal Commonwealth Society MS 5/144 (Childers Papers), Childers to Gladstone 16 July 1882; Lord Charles Beresford, *Memoirs of Lord Charles Beresford* (London, 1914); TNA FO 78/3471, Alison to WO, 19, 24, 26, 29 July 1882.

142 TNA FO 78/3471, Granville to Admiralty, 14 August 1882, seen by Gladstone; BL Add MS 44545 Gladstone to Ripon, 6 September 1882; Porter, *History of the Royal Engineers*; Maurice, *Military History of the Campaign of 1882 in Egypt* (IBWO 1887); BL Add MS 50020 Salisbury to Northcote, 29 September 1882 and Gardiner, *Harcourt*.

143 Roberts, *Salisbury*.

144 BL 5/149 Gladstone to Granville, 16 September 1882; TNA FO 222/8/1, Wilson to Dufferin, 8 November 1881 and TNA FO 195/1363, Tenterden memorandum,

15 December 1881; Ramm, *Political Correspondence*; TNA FO 78/3440 WO to FO, 29 July 1882, Tenterden to Granville, 1 August 1882, Childers to Granville, 2 August 1882 and 340.1081 (Hartington Papers) Northbrook to Hartington, 12 February 1881. Northbrook told Hartington: 'Wilson might have his division.'

145 TNA FO 78/3431 Hayter (WO) to FO, 5 December 1882 and FO 78/78/3590-1; P. Magnus, *Kitchener* (London ,1958); TNA T/1/14189/821883 FO to Treasury, 11 January 1883; FOCP 4724 Granville to Malet, 26 October 1882; TNA CAB 41/16/56, Gladstone to the Queen, 16 November 1882; TNA FO 78/3591, Wilson to Lord Edmund Fitzmaurice, 12 May 1883; E. W. C. Sandes, *Royal Engineers in Egypt and the Sudan* (Chatham, 1937); various obituaries.

146 TNA CAB 37/9/92 Malet to Granville, 1 October 1882 encl. 'Project by Lt Col. Sir C. Wilson for the Re-organisation of the Egyptian Army, 29 September 1882, copy to Baker Pasha; FOCP 4725, Malet to Granville 4 November 1882; TNA CAB 37/9/92 Northbrook's criticism of Baker's report; FOCP 4724 Granville to Malet, 31 October 1882 and TNA FO 78/3589 WO to FO, 22 February 1883.

147 R. L. Hill, *Egypt and the Sudan* (London, 1967); TNA FO 78/3703 Malet to Granville, 2 October 1882 encl. Wilson memorandum of 29 September 1882; FOCP 4724 Granville to Malet, 28 October 1882, Malet to Granville 4 November 1882; FOCP 4725 Granville to Dufferin, 3 November 1882; TNA FO 78/3707 Bertie memorandum, 14 January 1884 quoting Malet to Granville, 4 November 1882; Barrington memorandum, 22 January 1884, re: Granville to Malet, 30 October 1882, Malet to Granville, 28 October 1882, 11 November 1882; TNA FO 78/3431, Chief Clerk's minute, 15 November 1882; Ramm, *Political Correspondence*, quoting TNA 30/29/126, Granville to Gladstone, 17 November 1882.

148 TNA T/1/14819/82/1882 FO to Treasury, 11 January 1883; BL Add MS 44175 Granville to Gladstone, 6 April 1883; Gladstone to Granville, 22 March 1883, Granville to Gladstone, 10 April 1883 and TNA 30/29/170, 21 July 1883.

149 TNA 30/40/2, Dufferin to Ardagh, 10 January 1884.

150 TNA FO 78/3707, Wilson memorandum, n.d. c.early January 1884.

151 BL Add MS 44547, Gladstone to Granville, 7 January 1884 and FO 141/241, Ardagh 'Note on the Obligation of Her Majesty's Government to defray the cost of defending the Frontiers of Egypt', 1886.

152 *Vide*, for example, BS 10097.aa.30, 'Report on the Egyptian Provinces of the Soudan, Red Sea and Equatoria (ID June 1883); TNA FO 78/5392, Dufferin to FO, 12 September 1883; FOCP 4940 Baring to Granville, 9 October 1882; Add MS 44175 of 86 Granville to Gladstone, 17 February 1883; 340.1308 Ponsonby to Hartington, 8 January 1883 and 340.1309, same date, Alison to Hartington.

153 TNA CAB 37/12/7 'EF' (FO), memorandum for Egyptian debate, 1 February 1884; 340.1396 Granville to Hartington 11 June 1884.

154 FOCP Egypt, Granville to Baring, 25 March 1884.

155 H. Russell, *Ruin of the Soudan* (London, 1892).

156 340.1434 Wolseley to Hartington, 23 March 184; TNA WO 33/43 WAH Hare (ID), 'Despatch of Troops to Upper Egypt and the Soudan', 11 March 1884.

157 BL Add MS 44547, Gladstone to Northbrook, 24 April 1884, Gladstone to Hartington, 13 May 1884.

158 BL Add MS 44130, Hartington to Gladstone, 11 April 1884.

159 BLAdd MS 44547, Gladstone to Childers, 30 May 1884.

160 Russell, *Ruin of the Soudan*.

161 BL Add MS 44547, Gladstone to Hartington, 10 February 1884 and A. B. Cook and J. Vincent, *The Governing Passion* (London, 1974); WO 147/8 Wolseley Diary, 5 December 1884.

162 TNA WO 33/44, Sawyer (ID) 'Diary of the Suakin Expedition' quoting Wolseley to Hartington, 11 February 1885, Hartington to Wolseley, 4 March 1885; BL Add MS 44547, Gladstone to Hartington, 12 February 1885; TNA WO 32/6351, Hartington to Wolseley, 12 March 1885; TNA WO 147/8, Wolseley Diary, 24 February 1885.

163 340.1703 Hartington to Gladstone, 31 March 1885.

164 TNA WO 147/8 Diary, 24 February, 29 March, 14, 26 April 1885.

165 340.1664 Wolseley to Hartington, 23 February 1885; 340.1704 Gladstone to Hartington, 1 April 1885.

166 TNA WO 33/44 Sawyer, 'Diary' quoting Wolseley to Hartington, 2 May 1885; 340.1686 Wolseley to Hartington, 23 March 1885.

167 FOCP Egypt, Baring to Granville 3 May 1885.

168 R. Deacon, *History of the British Secret Service*, (London, 1969); Gleichen, *Guardsman's Memories* (London 1932); Sir George Aston, *Secret Service* (London, 1930); TNA WO 139/11, 4 January 1878, December 1886.

169 A. Cochrane, *Dictionary of National Biography*, 1912–21; *Morning Post*, 21 April 1914; BL Add Ms 454: Gladstone to Welby, 22 June 1882; BL Add Ms 44766, Gladstone memorandum, 9 June 1882; Gladstone to Lord Spenser, 21 July 1882; and A. G. Gardiner, *The Life of Sir William Harcourt*, (London, 1923).

170 TNA T/1/8211B/18845/1885, Smith to Welby, 5 December 1885; Maj. Gen. Lord Edward Gleichen, *Guardsman's Memories*; St Aubyn, *Royal George*; BL Add Ms 41230, R. Gipps to Thomson, 11 May 1894.

171 Gardiner, *Harcourt*; Add Ms 41658: Colvile to Mrs K. R. Colvile, quoting Brackenbury, 16 September 1885.

172 In 1881, Gen. Steele, GOC Dublin attributed an unsigned *Times* article calling for the Duke's resignation as 'evidently the production of Brackenbury dictated by Wolseley'.

173 TNA WO 147/6 and WO 147/8, 30 November 1884; Hamer, *British Army*; Royal Commonwealth Society 5/37 (Childers Papers) ,Wolseley to Childers, 23 August 1881; TNA 30/40/13, Fleetwood Wilson to Ardagh, 15 August 1889.

174 Bond, *Staff College*; Gleichen, *Guardsman's Memories*; TNA WO 147/8, 31 December 1884; TNA WO 147/6, 102/10 (Wingate Private Diaries), 6 April 1885; F. Maurice and Sir George Arthur, *The Life of Wolseley* (London, 1924).

175 TNA WO 132/2 (Buller Papers), Wolseley to Buller, 15 September 1886 and Lt Col. W. R. V. Isaac, *History of the Development of the Directorate of Military*

Intelligence, 1855–1939 (Ashford, 1957).

176 TNA CAB 37/20/33, Stanhope to Cabinet, 18 June 1887; MS 113: Brackenbury to Lansdowne, 17 October 1892; Maj. General Sir Charles Callwell, *Stray Recollections* (London, 1923); TNA FO 65/1288, shows examples of the yellow slips; TNA 30/40/2, Brackenbury to Ardagh, 7 April 1896; TNA FO 78/4068, Leverson to Hervey, 2 November 1887; Dallas to Pauncefote minute, Brackenbury to FO, 13 December 1887; Salisbury minute, n.d.; BL MS 113, Brackenbury to Lansdowne, 17 October 1892.

177 TNA T/1/8106A/1884, A. D. Hayter (WO) to Treasury, 8 February 1884; TNA T/1/8624C/16232/1891, Ryder (Treasury) to Thomson, 23 November 1891, F. J. Hudleston, *Warriors in Undress*, (London. 1925); Collen, *Report*; Callwell, *Stray Recollections*.

178 TNA T/1/8211B/18845/1885, Smith to Welby. 5 December 1885, Ridley, Rider, 11 December 1885; Luvaas, *Education of an Army*; TNA WO139/9 *ARC* 'Request of the PM that officers should be prohibited from publishing Confidential opinions', January 1889; 'Circular from the Premier as to divulgence of opinions of officers who have been consulted on particular matters', January 1887 and CAB 37/23/1, Baring to Salisbury, 21 December 1888 and TNA CAB 37/23/2, Salisbury to Stanhope, 2 January 1889; WO 139/6 *ARC*, 'Question whether officers of the Intelligence Branch may without permission enter into discussion as to papers officially prepared', June 1888.

179 TNA WO 139/11 *ARC*, August 1886 (7606/9242); TNA WO 32/6174, *Classification and Custody of Documents*, C-in-C approval, 5 October 1889, Chapman to Robinson, 2 June 1891; TNA WO 32/6173, *Custody of Secret and Confidential Documents*, Brackenbury minute, 26 September 1890 and *vide* notice to executors label found on WO 32/6349, Brackenbury-NewMarch memorandum, 19 August 1889.

180 IO MSS Eur D 735, Brackenbury to Lansdowne, 14 October 1891.

181 TNA FO 65/1280, Brackenbury to Villiers, 1 February 1886; Villiers: 'Done'; TNA FO 106/12 Brackenbury to Sir R. Herbert, 26 January 1886; Meade: 27 January 1886, Fairfield: 10 March 1886; ID and DQMG minutes, February 1886, and *vide* for example: TNA WO 106/11, Morier to FO 4 May, 14, 28 August 1886.

182 TNA WO 106/12, Thomson to Brackenbury, 8 February 1886; TNA 30/40/12 Ardagh to Lansdowne, paper 27 n.d.; Villiers to ID, 25 June 1886; TNA FO 64/1152, Pounsfort to Malet, 8 April 1886; TNA WO 139/11 *ARC*, August 1887; Order in Council, 21 February 1888 (also in this order the IGF was removed from all overseas work) *vide* also *REJ*, 2 April 1888.

183 TNA T/1/8302B/5728/1887, TNA ADM 116/3106, TNA 30/40/10, Beresford to Ardagh, 10 November 1888 and C. Beresford, *Memoirs of Admiral Lord Charles Beresford* (London, 1914); WO 106/12, Cameron to Lord Walter Kerr, 4 September 1885; Hall to ID, 3 March 1886 and TNA FO 78/3174, Admiralty to ID, 8 December 1880; TNA FO 78/3357, Admiralty to ID, 30 November

1880. Also *vide* TNA WO 106/1122, September 1886 and *Parliamentary Papers* 1890/91, The Hartington Commission 'Intelligence Department testimony by Brackenbury and Col .Charles à Court Repington, *Vestigia*; TNA T/1/8626C/19032/1891, Capt. L. A. Beaumont, RN, DNI memorandum to FO, IO, CO 24 June 1896.

184 TNA T/1/8302B/1887, Brackenbury, 'Extract for a memorandum addressed to the Secretary of State for War by the DQMG, 11 June 187; Jackson minute on Treasury suggestion, 2 July, 8 August 1887; TNA WO 106/12, H. Campbell-Bannerman minute, 19 January n.d.; BL Add MS 41232, Brackenbury to Dalyell, 20 April 1886; M. Wright, 'Treasury Control 1854-1914 in G. Sutherland, *Studies in the growth of Nineteenth Century Government*, London 1972; Isaac, *Intelligence Directorate* and TNA WO 139/9, May 1888.

185 A. G. Marder, *The Anatomy of British Sea Power*, 1972; TNA CAB 37/18/31, Brackenbury memorandum, 22 March 1886; TNA CAB 37/19/8, Brackenbury memorandum, 25 January 1887; TNA WO 132/4A, Brackenbury to Buller, 9 November 1886; TNA WO 110/8, Smith memorandum, 18 November 1886; TNA 30/40/13, *Mobilization of one Army Corps for Foreign Service*, 14 April 1886; H. Cunningham, *The Volunteer Force* (London, 1975).

186 TNA 30/40/13, Thomson-Brackenbury memorandum to SS War, 7 December 1886; TNA CAB 37/19/8, Brackenbury memorandum, 25 January 1887; TNA 30/40/2, Brackenbury to Ardagh, 15 August 1887 and TNA T/1/8302B/1887 WO to Treasury, 15 September 1887. *Vide* also TNA 30/40/13 ID to Lansdowne, n.d. and Brackenbury to Ardagh, 13 October 1887.

187 TNA 30/40/13, Mobilisation Subcommittee, Brackenbury to Wolseley, 17 November 1886, Ardagh, 17 April 1888; TNA WO 163/4 WO Council Meeting, 11 January 1887; TNA CAB 37/19/8 25 January 1887; C-5979 quoting from Hartington Commission second report of the Select Committee on Army and Navy Estimates, 1887; Hamer, *The British Army*, Hansard, III series, 53-54 *Victoriae*, 1890, vol. cccxlii.

188 MS 113, Brackenbury to Maj. Gen. Sir O. R. NewMarch, 16 August 1892; WI 139/11 *ARC* November 1887; Isaac, *Intelligence Directorate*, IO MSS Eur D 735 (Northbrook Papers), Brackenbury to Northbrook, 14 October 1894; TNA WO 33/50, 'Memorandum on the Relations between the Intelligence Department of the War Office, Admiralty and India' quoting WO memorandum 171, 8 February 1888; TNA CAB 37/21/14, Salisbury memorandum on the defence of London, 6 June 1888.

189 340 (Devonshire Papers) Campbell-Bannerman to Hartington, 12 January 1890; *Report of the Commission*, Campbell-Bannerman, 10 February 1890; TNA 30/40/2 Wolseley to Ardagh, 4 October 1895; J. Wilson, *C-B*, (London, 1973); Luvaas, *Education of an Army*; St Aubyn, *Royal George*; Hamer, *British Army*; Robertson, *From Private to Field* Marshal (London, 1921).

190 L. Penson, *Foreign Affairs under the Third Marquis of Salisbury* (London, 1962).

191 *Vide* for example TNA FO 65/1149 ID to FO, 30 August 1882, tasking D. R.

Peacock; TNA FO 65/11531 ID to FO, 13 November 1882, tasking the Consul General at Odessa; TNA FO 65/1170 ID to FO, 31 March 1883, 17 November 1883; TNA FO 181/663/4, Consul at Tagarrog to Thornton, 14 January 1884; TNA FO 593/24, Chenevix-Trench on the Mertvi-Kultuk Railway, 2 December 1884; TNA FO 65/1205 FO to Thornton, 16 April 1884; TNA FO 65/1209 ID to FO 8 August 1884.

192 TNA FO 65/1203, Granville to Hartington, 1 February 1884; TNA FO 65/1250, C. W. Bowdler Bell (ID) to FO, 10 September 1885; Fox (ID) to A. Oakes, n.d. 1883, re: Turco-Persian boundary, TNA FO 65/1151 FO to WO, 1 April 1882 and FO 65/1250, Bowdler Bell to FO, 10 September 1885.

193 NA FO 65/1205, Hertslet memorandum, 19 April 1884.

194 A. Ramm, *Political Correspondence*, quoting TNA 30/29/129, Gladstone to Granville, 10 April 1885; TNA FO 65/1235, Kimberley to Granville, 28 January 1885 and TNA FO 65/1238 FO to Lumsden, 27 March 1885.

195 TNA FO 65/1235, Condie Stephen to Currie, seen by Kimberley and Granville, 1 January 1885; Kimberley to Granville, 28 January 1885; TNA FO 539/26, Currie to Godley, 9 June 1885.

196 *Vide* for example TNA FO 65/1235, 1236, 1207 and FO 65/1239, Rumours of Military Movements: Government of Kandahar.

197 C. M. MacGregor, *Defence of India: a Strategical Study* (Simla 1884); W. H. H. Waters, *Secret and Confidential* (London, 1926); N41 (Royal Archives), Ponsonby to the Queen, 7 September 1884; TNA FO 539/26, 11 March 1885; L. A. Gregson and A. C. Cameron (ID) critique on MacGregor's *Defence of India*, March 1885.

198 F. Beaufort (ID), 'Memorandum on Herat', 17 March 1885 and Cameron, ditto, 28 March 1885.

199 TNA FO 539/25, Thompson to Granville, 10, 12, 13 March 1885.

200 TNA 30/40/12, Ardagh to Lansdowne, n.d., re: Horse Guards jealousy '…it is now admitted that these special secret studies are necessary, and official sanction has been extended to [this] practice, with very satisfactory results.'

201 J. Wolfe Murray, 'Russian Communication with the East', 13 March 1885, signed off by Cameron and TNA WO110/9, Cameron: 'Some observations as to the military value of a suggested frontier line between Afghanistan and the Russian Empire', 19 April 1885.

202 TNA FO 65/1237 and 12388 ID to FO March 1885; TNA FO 539/25, Thompson to Currie, 18 March 1885; Granville to Thompson, 18 March 1885.

203 BL Add MS 44631, J. S. Rothwell, 'England's means of Offence against Russia', 7 July 1884, updated by Cameron on 27 January 1885 and sent on to Alison, briefly A. G., on 10 April 1885. Rothwell had taken over Section (D) from Clarke in 1880, travelled in Africa, Russia, returned to Staff College in 1884 as professor of staff duties and administration.

204 J. Wolfe Murray, 'Military Operations in the Event of War with Russia', 17 April 1885; Cameron to Wolfe Murray, 10 April 1885; Cameron memorandum, 13 October 1885, seen by Salisbury.

205 TNA WO 110/9, Cameron: 'Some Observations as to the Military Value of a suggested Frontier Line between Afghanistan and the Russian Empire', 19 April 1885 and TNA FO 65/125.

206 TNA FO 65/1238, Cameron to Pauncefote, 21 March 1885.

207 *Vide* MacDiarmid, Grierson and F. Younghusband, *Forty Years a Soldier* (London, 1923).

208 IO MS Eur D 735, (Northbrook Papers), Brackenbury memorandum to the Viceroy, 14 October 1891.

209 TNA WO 106/12, ID to PUS, 15 February 1886; NAM 7101-23/11/1,2.3 (Roberts Papers) Brackenbury to Roberts, 22 July 1886, 16 December 1886.

210 Major W. A. H. Hare, 'The Ottoman Empire', 31 October 1885.

211 Brackenbury, 'Sketch', August 1886.

212 TNA WO 106/11, Brackenbury to Thomson, 15 July, 4 August 1886.

213 TNA WO 106/11, Wolfe Murray memorandum, 8 September 1886; Sanderson to ID, 11 August 1886, TNA FO 65/1281, Grierson, 'State of the Russian Army and Preparation for War', 12 August 1886, seen by Salisbury; Brackenbury to FO, 4 October 1886, enclosing Wolfe Murray memorandum seen by Iddesleigh; C. Smith, *The Embassy of Sir William White at Constantinople, 1886-1891* (London, 1957).

214 TNA FO 364/1, Iddesleigh to White, 12 October 1886 encl. ID memorandum; Brackenbury 'Report on the Russian Pacific Provinces', 1 May 1886; WO 106/11, 31 May, 2 June 1886.

215 TNA WO 163/4 WO, Council Meeting, 1 April 1886; Add MS 44548 Gladstone to Harcourt, 28 May 1886, Gladstone to Campbell-Bannerman, 15 July 1886; Add MS 44549 Gladstone to Rosebery, 18 August 1882; WO 32/6349 NewMarch memorandum, November 1891.

216 TNA FO 539/31, Thompson to Pauncefote, November 1891, enclosing Wolfe Murray memorandum, 19 July 1886, to Cross, 29 July 1886.

217 TNA FO 65/1321, Brackenbury to Barrington, 17 August 1887, Salisbury reply, 19 August 1887. *Vide* also FO 65/1291 ID to FO, 29 October 1886, enclosing Wolfe Murray's 28 October 1886.

218 A/75/42, White to Salisbury, 25 July 1887 and TNA FO 364/4, 'Remarks applying to different British schemes for the Construction of Turkish Railways in Asia', 25 July 1887; TNA FO 195/1564, Brackenbury memorandum, 7 September 1887.

219 TNA FO 65/1327, M. S. Bell, 'British Commercial Enterprise in Persia and Communications required to Develop it', 20 November 1887; FO 539/40, Wolff to Salisbury, 14 November 1888, Salisbury to Wolff, 23 November 1888; TNA FO 65/1347, Bell Memorandum, 30 November 1888.

220 TNA FO 65/1377, Wolff to FO 26 January 1889, FO minute, seen by Salisbury; Brackenbury to FO 9 February 1889, enclosing Wolfe Murray's 'Reported Russian Projects for the Construction of Railways in Persia in Russian Interests' and FO 539/41, Salisbury to Wolff, 4 February 1889, Wolff to Salisbury and FO to Wolff, 9 February 1889; Sanderson to Salisbury n.d. (mid-February 1889).

221 *Ibid.*, Wolff to Salisbury, 19 February 1889; Brackenbury to FO enclosing 'Alarmist Indian Views' (Sanderson), 4 February 1888; TNA FO 78/1378, Wolff to FO, 9 March 1889.

222 TNA FO 65/1392, Currie to Brackenbury, n.d.; FO 65/1378, Sanderson minute, 28 March 1889.

223 TNA FO 539/44, Brackenbury to FO, enclosing memorandum, 8 October 1889.

224 Kazemzadeh, *Persia* quoting Salisbury to Wolff, 19 May 1890; TNA FO 539/50 Morier to Salisbury, 12 November 1890.

225 TNA FO 65/1322, Sanderson to Salisbury, n.d. 1887, ID (encl. IBS report) to FO, 5 September 1887; TNA FO 65/1310, Sanderson minute, 19 March 1887; TNA FO 65/1353 Sanderson minute, Currie and Salisbury, 27 September 1888.

226 *Vide* Wolfe Murray, 'Russia's power to concentrate troops in Central Asia', 4 May 1888, seen by Salisbury and relevant ambassadors; Wolfe Murray, *United Service Magazine*, August 1891.

227 TNA WO 33/49, C. H. Brownlow and Brackenbury, 'Secret Memorandum on the Report of the Indian Mobilisation Committee regarding the Strategical Situation in Central Asia', 1 February 1899.

228 IO Add MS 51264, Salisbury to Cross, 6 November 1890, Lansdowne to Cross, 27 November 1890 and MSS Eur D 668, Cross to Lansdowne, 31 December 1890.

229 TNA WO 106/16, Chapman to Brackenbury, September 1892; IO MS 113, Brackenbury memorandum ,14 March 1892, Brackenbury to Lansdowne, 19 October 1892; Mss Eur D 735, Brackenbury memorandum, 14 October 1891, 27 February 1892; TNA WO 106/16, Chapman's letter books 1892–93.

230 TNA WO 106/16 Brackenbury to Elles, 25 August 1892, September 1892, Brackenbury to Elles 17 December 1892, 9 December 1892.

231 *Vide* for example, TNA FO 65/1416, Chapman memoranda, 30 October, 24 November 1891 and IO response, FO 65/1417 IO to FO, 10 November and Chapman's, 22 December; re: White *vide* IO MSS 113, Brackenbury to Col. Brackenbury, 3 June 1892 and MSS 114 Brackenbury to Buller, 20 May 1893. D. S. MacDiarmid, *Life of Sir James Moncrieff Grierson* (London, 1923); J. Wolfe Murray, *United Service Magazine*, August 1891.

232 Robert Johnson, *Spying for Empire* (London, 2006).

233 *Ibid.*; MS 114 Brackenbury to Thompson, 10 February 1893 and M. Howard, *The Continental Commitment* (London, 1972).

234 TNA 30/40/9, unaddressed confidential letter, 28 February 1886.

235 TNA FO 78/3975, Brackenbury ,'Italy and Egypt in the Red Sea', 21 December 1886.

236 *Ibid.*, Pauncefote minute, Brackenbury memorandum, 21 December 1886, seen by Iddesleigh; TNA CAB 41/20/31, Salisbury to the Queen, 10 February 1887; FOCP Egypt, Baring to Kitchener, 15 January 1887;TNA FO 78/4066, Peel to FO, 18 March 1887, Salisbury minute, 21 March 1887 and TNA CAB 41/21/19, Salisbury to the Queen, 7 December 1888.

237 TNA FO 78/4080, Wisely memorandum, 9 May 1887, with Brackenbury,

Pauncefote and Salisbury minutes; Fox to FO, 30 May 1887.

238 TNA FO 78/4251, Wilson memorandum, 5 January 1889 with Barrington minute, seen by Salisbury.

239 *Ibid.*, ID to FO enclosing Suakin report, 16 July 1889 and FO 78/4253, seen by Salisbury.

240 Robinson and Gallagher, *Africa and the Victorians.*

241 155/9 (Wingate Papers): Wingate to Dalton, 23 December 1888; 179/3/1 'Organisation of Military Intelligence', n.d.

242 R. Hill, *Notes on the importance of language in Egyptian Army Intelligence*, 1973; *Biographical Dictionary of the Sudan*, 1967; *Egypt and the Sudan*, 1967. Shuqayyir was educated at the Syrian Protestant College in Beiruit. The other Christian college (French, Roman Catholic) provided no intelligence officers. Shuqayyir was commissioned in 1884 and joined the EID in 1890. His *Tārikh al Sūdān* is the Sudan's revered history. He died in 1922.

243 TNA 30/40/9, Ardagh, unaddressed, n.d., 1885. He added *Cantabit vacuus coram latrine victor*!; 253 Wingate to GOC, 24 February 1892; Wingate to Callwell, 16 May, 2 June 1892; NAT FO 78/4513, ID to FO.

244 258 Palmer to Wingate, 24 December 1894, tradescraft was taught and rewards issued commensurate with results, viz 'A watch for No 1 Agent'; Wingate to Fairholme, 2 January 1895.

245 233/2 Chapman to Wingate, n.d. 1892; 248/39 Comment on C6561, *Reoccupation of Tokar*, 1892; 258 Palmer to Wingate n.d. and Wingate to Lloyd, 27 January 1895 re: Palmer's death from overwork and pneumonia.

246 155/4 Dalton to Wingate, 25 January 1889, 155/3Dalton to Wingate 7, 20 December 1888, 25 January, 6 February 1889; Wingate to Dalton, 16 March 1889.

247 155/5 Wingate to Bimbashi H. G. Dunning, DAAG Int, Frontier Field Force, Halfa, 3 April 1889; 256/1 Chapman to Wingate, 38 November 1894; Wingate to Chapman, 7 December 1894.

248 179/2 Wingate to Dalton, 8 December 1889; FO 78/4253 Wingate to Leverson, 15 December 1889.

249 *Ibid.*, Leverson to Wingate, 24 December 1889.

250 FOCP Egypt, FO to WO, 13 February 1890, WO to FO 4 March 1890; TNA FO 78/4318 Brackenbury to Bertie, 27 March 1890; Sanderson, *England, Europe and the Upper Nile,* (Edinburgh, 1965).

251 253 Foster 'Uganda', September 1892; M. Perham, *Lugard, the Years of Adventure* (London, 1956); 233/2 Callwell to Wingate, 24 June 1892

252 233/2 Callwell to Wingate, 16, 24 June, 19 July 1892; Wingate to Callwell, 11 June 1892.

253 TNA WO 106/16 ID to FO 23 August 1892; 253 Chapman to Wingate 23, 24 August 1892, Wingate to Baker 24 August 1892; Foster 'Uganda'.

254 TNA CAB 37/31/22, Anderson memorandum, 10 September 1892; TNA CAB 27/31/23, Rosebery to Cabinet, 16 September 1892.

255 TNA CAB 37/31/24, Harcourt to Cabinet, 24 September 1892; BL Add

MS 44549, Gladstone to Rosebery, 21 October and Gladstone to Harcourt, 22 October 1892; BL MS 4417 Campbell-Bannerman to Gladstone, 6 October 1892.

256 233/2 Chapman to Wingate, 14 October 1892.

257 TNA WO 106/16, Chapman to Brackenbury, 29 September 1892, Chapman to Brackenbury, 21 October 1892.

258 253 Wingate to Everett, 5 December 1892; TNA WO 106/16 Chapman to Talbot, 20 December 1892; FO 27/3149 à Court to FO. Seen by Rosebery.

259 TNA FO 27/3159 à Court to Hill, 25 April 1893; FO 27/3149 ID to FO, 19 May 1893.

260 There is so much on Rabeh that even the scantiest of footnotes would endanger a forest. *Vide*, to begin with, Hill, *Biographical Dictionary of the Sudan* and TNA FO 7219, Gleichen, *A Short History of Rabeh Zubeir*, December 1898.

261 Sanderson, *England, Europe and the Upper Nile*; TNA FO 2/118, Anderson to Rosebery, 31 October 1893, 26 November 1893; Gleichen, *Rabeh Zubeir*.

262 TNA FO 27/3159, CO to FO, 2 June; FO to CO 18 July 1893.

263 TNA FO 27/3374, Phipps to Rosebery, 8 August 1893; TNA FO 27/3162, Chapman to FO, 10 October 1893; TNA FO 27/3133, Everett to Hill, 8 January 1894, Sir A. Harrington, 12 December 1893, quoting ID memorandum 15 July 1893.

264 TNA FO 27/3184, min of Phipps to FO 3 January 1894.

265 TNA T/1/8748D/11946/1893, Baker et al., *Supplementary Report of the Committee on a Military Map of the United Kingdom –as to the present condition and requirements of the Topographical Section (Section F), Intelligence Division, War Office*, 1 July 1892; TNA WO 139/11, June 1886; WO 106/16, Chapman to Currie, 9 June 1893, Chapman to Thompson, 31 July 1893; TNA T/1/8748D/11948/1893, Cane to Treasury, 21 March 1893, Ryder-Welby, Sir J. Hibbert, 17 April, 26 June 1893.

266 TNA T/1/8980B/1895, de la Bere to Treasury, 11 June 1895, 30 November 1895; WO to Treasury and Mowatt to WO, 9 December 1895.

267 TNA FO 27/3206 CO to FO, 17 January 1894.

268 *Ibid.*, Anderson to Rosebery, 17 January 1894.

269 TNA FO 27/3206, Everett to FO, 23 February 1894, ID to FO 24 July 1894.

270 TNA FO 27/3300, Everett to Hill, 3 March 1896

271 TNA FO 78/3256, Kimberley to Everett, 4 February 1895; Everett to FO, 25 January 1895, Meade to FO, 1 February 1895, Kimberley to Dufferin, 6 February 1895; TNA CO 267/362 ID to CO, 2 February 1886; TNA FO 27/3258 CO to FO, 5 November 1895.

272 257 Wingate to Fairholme, 9 September 1894, Gleichen to Wingate, 17 September 1894; 258 Wingate to Everett, 12 November 1894, Fairholme to Wingate, 7 December 1894.

273 TNA FO 27/3256 ID to FO, 6 March 1895, minute by Anderson for Rosebery.

274 FOCP 6758, Chapman enclosing Sclater, 2 March 1895; 258 Fairholme to Wingate, 14 March 1895.

275 258 Fairholme to Wingate, 14 March, 25 March 1895; TNA FO 78/4676 n.d., seen by Kimberley and Rosebery; Hill, *Slatin Pasha.*

276 Roberts, *Salisbury*

277 TNA FO 78/4668, Cromer to Wingate, Wingate to Cromer, 12 April 1895; 261 *General Report* Wingate's copy, FO Copy.

278 TNA FO 78/4676, Anderson memorandum, 15 April 1895; Hill *Slatin Pasha,* 440/1 (Slatin Papers), 'Duties of the ADMI and Reorganisation of the Bureau', 16 November 1895; 262/2 Rosebery to Wingate, 14 June 1895 and FOCP 6694 Cromer to FO 24 March 1895.

279 FOCP 6758, 'Congo State', Anderson to Salisbury, 11 July 1895, Anderson memorandum, 22 July 1895, H. Wilson to FO, 23 July 1895.

280 Gleichen, *Memories,* FOCP 6758 ID to FO, 14 August 1895, 261 H. Wilson to Wingate, 17 August 1895, Wingate to Wilson, 18 August 1895.

281 261 Gleichen to Wingate, 13 February 1896, 1 March 1896; TNA FO 78/4986 Cromer to FO, Sanderson minute, 26 February 1896, Salisbury to Cromer, 29 February 1896.

282 Robinson and Gallagher, *Africa and the Victorians.*

283 TNA CAB 37/41/24.

284 TNA 30/40/14/I, Ardagh memorandum, 'The Advance up the Nile from Dongola', 15 March 1897, TNA CAB 37/41/24, Lansdowne memorandum, 29 April 1896, quoting Salisbury to Cromer, 16 March 1896.

285 TNA FO 78/4874 WO to FO, Wolseley memorandum, 26 March 1897; TNA FO 800/2, Salisbury to Sanderson, 27 March 1897 and A/110/21, Cromer to Salisbury. Cromer related an incident in 1884 when Wolseley had lied to him.

286 Gleichen, *Memories,* 261 Gleichen to Wingate, 20 March 1896.

287 TNA CAB 37/41/21, Lansdowne memorandum, 24 March 1896.

288 TNA 30/40/14, Ardagh to Sanderson, 14 April 1896.

289 A/109/48, Cromer to Salisbury, 7 May 1896.

290 A/109/53, Cromer to Salisbury, 17 May 1896; A/109/59, Cromer to Salisbury, 5 June 1896.

291 261 Gleichen to Wingate, 4 March 1896, Chapman to Cromer, 20 March 1896 and Gleichen to Wingate, n.d., March 1896; 262/1 Fairholme to Wingate, 5 June 1896; A/93/72 Gleichen to Ardagh, 6 May 1896; Gleichen *Memories.*

292 TNA FO 78/4771 Ardagh to Sanderson, 20 April 1896; FO 78/4893, Sanderson to Cromer, 22 April 1896 and A/93/73, Gleichen to Fairholme, 2 May 1896.

293 A/109/52, Cromer to Salisbury, (probably early May) 1896; A/93/73, Gleichen to Fairholme, 2 May 1896; FOCP 6928, Cromer to Salisbury, 15 April 1896; FO 789/4893, February and March 1896; A/93/71, Fairholme to Barrington, 28 May 1896, Salisbury minute; A/93/72, Gleichen to Ardagh, 6 May 1896.

294 262/1, Fairholme to Wingate, 5 June 1896.

295 FOCP 7042, Gleichen 'Précis of Events on the Upper Nile', 15 March 1898; Everett to Wingate, 9 October 1896. The first mention of French approaches to the Abyssinians was between Wingate and Anderson, 11 July 1895.

296 TNA FO 27/3301, Everett to Bertie and Balfour, 31 August 1896; CO to FO, 14 September 1896.

297 TNA FO 27/3369, *Proces Verbal*, 1897, Hill minute; TNA FO 78/4874, Everett to FO, 16 March 1897.

298 TNA 30/40/2, Lansdowne to Ardagh, 24 September 1896, 261 Everett to Wingate, 9 October 1896; TNA 30/40/14, Ardagh to Lansdowne, 13 October 1896; TNA T/1/8626C/18416/1896, E. A. Altham (ID) memorandum, 14 June 1896, Ardagh to Sanderson, 2 July 1896.

299 TNA 30/40/14, Ardagh to Sanderson, 23 December 1896, TNA FO 27/3368, H. Wilson to FO, 25 September 1896; TNA FO 78/4785, 17 December 1896, ID to FO, 24 December 1896; A/83/44, Queen to Salisbury, 17 December 1896; 263 Gleichen to Wingate, 31 December 1896.

300 263 and FO 78/4885, Cromer to Salisbury, 17 January 1897.

301 Gleichen, *Memories*; Robinson and Gallagher, *Africa and the Victorians*; Wingate and Gleichen, 'Précis of Information obtained by the British Mission to Abyssinia'.

302 TNA FO 27/3371 CO to FO, 20 August 1897, 25 August 1897 enclosing ID to CO, 17 August 1897; Ardagh to CO, 16 August 1897.

303 A/115/87, Monson to Salisbury, 14 November 1897.

304 *Ibid.*, CO to FO, 2 September 1897, Ardagh minutes, 4 September, 11 September 1897; COCP442 CO to Gov. Gold Coast, 24 September 1897; TNA FO 27/3372 ID to FO, 11 October 1897, minutes by Hill and Salisbury.

305 TNA FO 3368 ID to FO, 4 February 1897 with enclosures and Hill minute. Seen by Salisbury, 9 February 1897, 24 February 1897; FOCU 7019, 7 March 1897; Robinson and Gallagher, *Africa and the Victorians*; TNA 30/40/14/I, Ardagh memorandum, 'The Advance up the Nile from Dongola', 15 March 1897.

306 TNA FO 27/3368 ID to FO, 2 April 1897; 263 Fairholme to Wingate, 29 April 1897.

307 TNA 30/40/14i, Ardagh to Sanderson, 3 June 1897

308 *Ibid.*, Ardagh to Sanderson, Wolseley, 'Kassala and the Advance up the Nile, 6 July 1897, TNA FO 78/4875 Ardagh, 'Report on Rodd's Mission', Sanderson and Salisbury, 10 July, 23 July, 24 July 1897.

309 263 Wingate to Kitchener, 6 August 1897; TNA 30/40/14/i Ardagh 'The Situation in Uganda' 16 August 1897; TNA FO 800/2 Sanderson to Salisbury, 16, 18 September 1897; 262/2 Wingate to Wood, poss. 9 September 1897, 5 November 1897; 262/1 Wingate to Grenfell, poss. 9 September 1897.

310 233/2 Wingate to Bigge, poss. September 1897, TNA 30/40/14/i Ardagh 'The Situation in Uganda'; 262/2 Fairholme to Talbot, 11 June 1897; FO 800/2, Sanderson to Salisbury 16, 18 September 1897 and replies.

311 TNA 30/40/2, Ardagh to Goldney, 19 February 1898, à Court to Fairholme, 12 November 1897, 102/1 Wingate Diary, 31 December 1897, 14 January 1898, 31 January 1898.

312 FOCP 7092, Pickersgill to Salisbury, 26 April 1898; TNA FO 78/4978 ID to

FO, 2 May 1898 and 266'4, Gleichen to Wingate, 27 May 1898.

313 Wheeler, *The War Office* (London, 1914); TNA 30/40/13, Ardagh memorandum, 6 August 1895; TNA 30/40/12, Wolseley to Ardagh, 5 July 1895; TNA 30/40/2, Wolseley to Ardagh, 12 July 1895, 16 July 1895; Gooch, *Plans of War*, p. 21.

314 TNA 30/40/2, Wolseley to Ardagh, 24 August 1895, 14 September 1895, BL MS 114 Brackenbury to Grierson, 26 August 1895, Brackenbury to Lake, 30 September 1895; TNA 30/402 Wolseley to Ardagh, 10 November 1895.

315 TNA CAB 37/40/41, Lansdowne to Cabinet, 12 August 1895, 'Changes Consequent upon the Retirement of HRH The Duke of Cambridge'; CAB 37/40/58, Lansdowne to Cabinet, 9 November 1895.

316 Malmesbury, *Ardagh* and MS 114 Brackenbury to Colvile, 30 April 1895, Brackenbury: 'There is not as far as I can see to be any thinking department, responsible for organisation, Intelligence'; TNA CAB 37/40/41, Lansdowne to Cabinet, 12 August 1895, 'Changes Consequent upon the retirement of HRH The Duke of Cambridge; CAB 37/40/58, 9 November 1895.

317 Gleichen, *Guardsman's Memories.*

318 TNA 30/40/2, Wolseley to Ardagh, 19 July 1892, February 1893, 7 April 1896; Watson 'Ardagh' *RE History* iii, Maitland to Ardagh, 19 February 1895 and Buller to Ardagh, 23 February 1895; Gleichen, *Memories,* Vetch, *Dictionary of National Biography 1901–1911*; Malmesbury, *Ardagh.*

319 Collen, *Report*; TNA T/1/8624C//1891, Ryder (Treasury) to Thompson (British Museum), 23 November 1891. In his light work, *Warriors in Undress*, Hudleston considered the 1878 system 'a lamentable instance of misplaced energy'.

320 TNA WO 32/654, Brackenbury minute, 1 September 1890; Wingate Papers 266/8: Gleichen to Wingate, 4 August 1898.

321 TNA T/1/8624C/16232/1891, Ryder to Thompson, 23 November 1891; Treasury to ID, 30 November 1891, ID to Treasury, 1 December 1891; Thompson to Ryder, 15 December 1891. The original letter by the financial authorities in the WO is a typical example of the inadequatee support given by the WO. The Treasury granted the increase on 15 December 1891.

322 D. W. King OBE, letter from the late MoD Librarian, 23 January 1976.

323 BL Add MS 49717 (Balfour Papers): Broderick to Balfour, 27 August 1898; TNA 30/40/2 (Ardagh Papers), 17 September 1898; WO 332/3640, Nicholson memorandum, 6 August 1902, King interview January 1976.

324 Newton, *Lord Lansdowne*, Salisbury to Lansdowne, 21 April 1897.

325 Gleichen, *Guardsman's Memories*. When the War Office finally involved itself, the want of direction led to disastrous errors. The ID, for example, had for some years concerned itself with the location of suitable large herds of serviceable horses throughout the world. In this it had been much encouraged by horse-racing Lord Rosebery. It had even secured an arrangement with the Austro-Hungarian Remount Department, through which the best military horses in Europe could be had. When the Quartermaster General's department became involved its officers went to the wrong brokers. The

substandard animals it purchased at premium prices either perished en route or succumbed during their first month on active service in Africa. This same type of sad occurrence would happen again on a much more tragic scale when, in 1914, General Sir Ian Hamilton was told by one of his staff officers returning from a desultory search for information on the Dardanelles or Gallipoli, that none was to be had, whereas the ID had been amassing intelligence, creating maps and up-dating maps on just these places since the 1870s.

326 Roberts, *Salisbury*; Parritt, *Intelligencers.*
327 Malmesbury, *Ardagh*
328 TNA 30/40/16, Ardagh to St John Broderick, 30 January 1901.
329 TNA 30/40/16, JCA to St John Broderick, 8 March 1901; TNA WO 32/7134 file 80/248/1907, Watson, *History of the Royal Engineers.*
330 Hamer, *Education of an Army*; Gooch, *Plans of War*, p. 107.
331 Gooch, *Plans of War*, p. 23; TNA 30/40/3, Altham to Ardagh, 28 October 1902.
332 M. V. Brett, *Journals and Letters of Reginald Viscount Esher*, vol. 1, p. 361, (London, 1934).
333 *Ibid.*, vol. i, p. 401.
334 Lees-Milne, *Enigmatic Edwardian* (London, 1986).
335 Gooch, *Plans of War*, 99, 158; Haldane, *Haldane.*
336 Gleichen, *Guardsman's Memories*, p. 344.
337 TNA 30/40/16, Ardagh to Brodrick, 30 January 1901.
338 M. Smith, *Six*, (London, 2010); K. Jeffery, *MI6: The History of the Secret Intelligence Service*, (London, 2010); C. Andrews, *Defence of the Realm* (London, 2009); Gooch, *Plans of War*, J. Bullock, *MI5*, Hennessey and Thomas, *Spooks* (London, 2009).
339 B M Add Mss 44544, Gladstone to Granville, 18 September 1880.
340 M Smith, *Six.*

BIBLIOGRAPHY

(Manuscript and Printed Primary Sources include by title only those Intelligence Division reports and memoranda the location of which is not clear in the citation.)

A. Manuscript Sources

The British Library
Arnold-Foster Papers
Balfour Papers
Campbell-Bannerman Papers
Dilke Papers
Gladstone Papers
Hutton Papers
Iddesleigh Papers
Kilbracken Papers
Layard Papers
Moffatt (Gordon) Papers
Sydenham Papers

Ministry of Defence Library (Central & Army)
Catalogue of Foreign Reports, 1757–1870, containing Dec. 1875 note by Wilson
Isaac, Lt Col. W. R. V., _A History of the Development of the Directorate of Military Intelligence_ (1957)
Wall, Maj. E. L., _The Development of the Intelligence Department_ (n.d.)

National Archives
Admiralty Papers, ADM 116
Ardagh Papers, TNA 30/40
Balfour Papers
Brodrick Papers, TNA 30/67
Buller Papers, WO 132
Cabinet Papers, CAB 37; CAB 41; CAB 7
Cardwell Papers, TNA 30/48

Carnarvon Papers, TNA 30/6
Colonial Office Papers, CO 267; CO 879
Cross Papers
Foreign Office Papers 27, 30, 60, 65, 78, 83, 96, 97, 141, 181, 195, 222, 363, 366,
   519, 537, 538, 539, 633, 800
Granville Papers, TNA 30/29
Grey Papers, TNA 800/35
Kitchener Papers, TNA 30/57
Lansdowne Papers
Lascelles Papers, FO 800/17
Ordnance Survey Papers, OS 1
Northbrook Papers
Panmure Papers, GD (HO) 45/8
Ponsonby Papers, FO 800/3
Royal West African Frontier Force, CO 879
Sanderson Papers, FO 800/1
Simmons Papers, FO 358
Smith, W. H. Papers, WO 110
Tenterden Papers, Po 363/1
Treasury Papers, T/1 (1854–1905)
War Office Papers, 1, 25, 28, 30, 32, 33, 43, 106, 139 (A.R.C.), 163
Wellesley Papers, Po 519; Po 579
White Papers, FO 364
Wolseley Diaries, Po 147

National Army Museum
MacDougall Papers
Roberts Papers

Miscellaneous
All Souls College, Oxford
Wilkinson Papers (Ogilby Trust copy)

Birmingham University
Ukpabi, S. C., *The West African Frontier Force, 1897–1914* (unpublished MA
   thesis, 1964)

Chatsworth House
Hartington Papers

Christ Church, Oxford and Hatfield House
Salisbury Papers

Durham University
Slatin Pasha Papers
Wingate Papers

Hull University
Otley, C. B., *The Origins and Recruitment of the British Army Elite, 1870–1959* (unpublished PhD thesis, 1965)

University of London
Morris, L. P., 'Anglo-Russian Relations in Central Asia, 1873–1887' (unpublished PhD thesis, 1968)
Simpkin, A. P., 'Anglo-Russian Relations in the Far East, 1879–1904' (unpublished PhD thesis, 1967)

Maggs Bros.
East Diaries

Oxford University
d'Ombrain, N. J., 'The Military Departments and the Committee of Imperial Defence, 1902–1914' (unpublished DPhil thesis, 1968)
Knightsbridge, A. A., 'Gladstone and the Invasion of Egypt in 1882' (unpublished BLitt thesis, 1960)

Reading University
Johnson, Nancy A., ed., Gathorne-Hardy, *The Cranbrook Diaries*

Firepower: The Royal Artillery Museum
Brackenbury Papers

Royal Commonwealth Society
Childers Papers

Scottish Record Office
Dalhousie Muniments

B. Printed Sources
(1) Printed Primary Sources and location

Alison, Sir A., 'On Army Organization' 1869 (BL)
Alison, Sir A., 'Memorandum on the Northwest Frontier of India' 26 Nov. 1878 (MoD)
Baring, Evelyn, 'Memo. on the Probable Course of Action which would be adopted by the Russians in the Event of their Attempting to Occupy Bulgaria and March on Constantinople' 16 October 1876 (MoD)

Baring, Hozier, Jessop et al., 'Extracts from the Reports of the Military Attaches who accompanied the French and Prussian Armies during the Campaign of 1870–71' 1871 (MoD)

Beaufort, F., 'Memorandum on Herat' 17 March 1885 (MoD)

Beaufort, F., 'Russian Advances in Asia' 1887 (MoD)

Brackenbury, C. B., 'Military Systems of France and Prussia' 1871 (MoD)

Brackenbury, C. B., 'Report on Departments of Foreign States Corresponding with the Intelligence Branch of the Quartermaster General's Department' 1876 (MoD)

Brackenbury, Sir H., 'Report on the Russian Pacific Provinces' 1 May 1886 (MoD)

Callwell, Sir Charles, 'Hints on Reconnaissances in Little Known Countries' n.d. (BL)

Callwell, Sir Charles, 'Instructions for Intelligence Officers Abroad' n.d. 1889 (MoD)

Cameron, Sir A. G., 'Memorandum on Herat', 28 March 1885 (MoD)

Clarke, F. C. H., 'Memorandum on Recent Russian Military Preparations in Central Asia' 26 July 1878 (MoD)

Clarke, F. C. H., 'Papers on Western Turkey and Greece' 1878 (MoD)

Clarke, F. C. H. and Moffatt, H. B., 'Report on Russia in the Balkans' October 1875 (MoD)

Collen, E. H. H., 'Memorandum on the Employment of an Indian Force in Egypt' 18 January 1878 (MoD)

Collen, E. H. H., 'Report on the Intelligence Branch, Quarter-Master-General's Department, Horse Guards' 1878 (Intelligence Corps Library)

Colonial Office Confidential Prints (Oxford)

Cooke, Sir A. C., 'Catalogue of Maps, Plans, and Views in the Topographical and Statistical Depot of the War Office' 1859, ii (BL)

Cooke, Sir A. C., 'Russian Advances in Asia' 1869 (MoD)

Cooke, W. S., 'Ottoman Empire and its Tributary States' October 1875 (MoD)

Cooke, W. S., 'French Operations in Madagascar' 1886 (MoD)

Fairholme, W. E., 'The Dhanis Expedition', 2 February 1897 (MoD)

Foreign Office Confidential Prints (Oxford)

Galton, D., 'Memorandum on War Office Organization' 1868 (MoD)

Gregson, L. A. and Cameron, A. C., 'The Defence of India by Sir C. M. MacGregor, QMG India' March 1885 (MoD)

Hare, W. A. H., 'The Ottoman Empire' 31 October 1885 (MoD)

Home, Robert et al., 'Memoranda relative to the Defence of Constantinople and other Positions in Turkey and also Routes in Roumelia' 1878 (MoD)

Jekyll, Sir H., 'Royal Commission on Defence of British Possessions and Commerce Abroad', 2nd report, 23 March 1882 (MoD)

MacDougall, Sir Patrick, 'Report on Egypt' 16 June 1876 (MoD)

Milner, F. H. W., 'Herat, with Reference to the British Occupation of Kabul and Kandahar' 6 November 1879 (MoD)

Milner, F. H. W., 'Memorandum on Afghanistan with Reference to the probable British Operations consequent on the Murder at Kabul of the Resident and Escort, on 3 September 1879' 15 September 1879 (MoD)

Northbrook, Earl of, 'Conduct of Business in the Army', third report under the Military Department no. 16, Cmd. pp.54 of 1870 (Oxford)

Parliamentary Papers, 1859 viii; 1860; 1861 xxvii; 1862 xxxii; 1863 xxxiii; 1864 xxxv; 1865 xxxii; 1866 xli; 1867–68 xli; 1868–69 xlii; 1870 xliii; 1878 E1290; 1881 E2811 (Oxford)

'Report (Handbook) on Egypt', ID 13 July 1882 (BL)

Report of Hon. R. Churchill's Committee 'Second Report of the Select Committee on Army and Navy Estimates' no date [n.d.] (MoD)

Report of Lord Hartington's 'Royal Commission to Enquire into the Civil and Professional Administration of the Naval and Military Departments and the Relation of those Departments to Each Other and the Treasury' 1890 (MoD)

'Report on the Egyptian Provinces of the Soudan, Red Sea, and Equatoria' ID June 1883, February 1885 (BL)

'Topographical Section of the General Staff' n.d. c.1905 (MoD)

Tulloch, Sir A. B., 'Report on Egypt' May–June 1882 (MoD)

Vincent, R. A., 'Offensive and Defensive Condition of the Ottoman Empire' 1875 (MoD)

Wilson, Sir C. W., 'Russian Advances in Asia' 1873 (MoD)

Wingate, Sir R. and Gleichen, Count E. A., 'Precis of Information Obtained by the British Mission to Abyssinia' 1897 (MoD)

Wolfe Murray, Sir James, 'Russian Communication with the East' 13 March 1885 (MoD)

Wolfe Murray, Sir James, 'Military Operations in the Event of a War with Russia' 17 April 1885 (MoD)

(2) Printed Secondary Sources (all London published except where indicated)

À Court Repington, C., *Vestigia* (1919)

Andrews, C., *Defence of the Realm* (2009)

Anon., 'Colonel the Hon. Milo George Talbot, CB (late R.E.)' (u.d. memoir and appreciation)

Anon., *Honour or Shame* (1878)

Anstey, R., *Britain and the Congo in the Nineteenth Century* (Oxford, 1962)

Arden-Close, Sir C. F., *The Early Years of the Ordnance Survey* (Chatham, 1926)

Army and Navy Illustrated (1890–1905)

Arthur, Sir George, *Life of Lord Kitchener*, iii vols. (1920)

Aston, Sir George, *Memories of a Marine* (1919)

Aston, Sir George, *Secret Service* (1930)

Atkinson, C. T., 'Maurice', *Dictionary of National Biography, 1912–21* (Oxford, 1922)

Baring, E. (Lord Cromer), *Staff College Essays* (1870)

Beckett, I. F. W., 'The Volunteers and the RUSI' *Royal United Services Journal* (1977)

Benians, E. A. et al., eds., *The Cambridge History of the British Empire, vol. iii* (Cambridge, 1967)

Beresford, Lord C., *The Memoirs of Admiral Lord Charles Beresford* (1914)

Biddulph, Sir R., *Lord Cardwell at the War Office* (1904)

Blake, Lord Robert, *Disraeli* (1966)

Blunt, W. S., *Secret History of the English Occupation of Egypt* (1907)

Bond, B., *The Victorian Army and the Staff College, 1854–1914* (1972)

Bonham-Carter, *Soldier True* (1963)

Brackenbury, Sir H., *Ashanti War* (Edinburgh, 1874) vols. ii

Brackenbury, Sir H., *The River Column* (Edinburgh, 1885)

Brackenbury, Sir H. and Huysche, G. L., *Fanti and Ashanti* (Edinburgh, 1873)

Buckland, C. E., *Dictionary of Indian Biography* (1906)

Bulloch, J., *MI5* (1963)

Bury, J. P. T., ed., 'The Zenith of European Power', *New Cambridge Modern History* (Cambridge, 1971)

Busch, B. C., *Britain and the Persian Gulf, 1894–1914* (Berkeley, 1967)

Butler, Sir W., *Sir George Pomeroy-Colley* (1899)

Callwell, Sir C. E., *Field Marshal Sir Henry Wilson*, ii vols. (1927)

Callwell, Sir C. E., *The Memoirs of Major-General Sir Hugh McCalmont* (1924)

Callwell, Sir C. E., *Service Yarns and Memories* (1912)

Callwell, Sir C. E., *Stray Recollections*, vol. i (1923)

Cecil, Lady Gwendolen, *Life of Robert, Marquis of Salisbury* (1932), and unpublished final volume in Salisbury Papers

Chronology of Events Connected with Army Administration, 1858–1907 (1908)

Churchill, W. S., *The River War*, ii vols. (1899)

Clarke, G. S. (Lord Sydenham), *My Working Life* (1927)

Cochrane, A., 'Sir H. Brackenbury', *Dictionary of National Biography, 1912–1921* (Oxford, 1922)

Cook, A., *M: MI5's First Spymaster* (2004)

Colburn's *United Service Magazine* (1854–1890 and successor 1890–1906)

Coldstream, W., ed., Sir W. Muir, *Records of the Intelligence Department, During the Mutiny of 1857*, ii vols. (Edinburgh, 1902)

Cole, D.H., *Imperial Military Geography* (1936)

Collier, Basil, *Brasshat, A Biography of F.M. Sir Henry Wilson* (1961)

Cunningham, H., *The Volunteer Force* (1975)

'Major General J. C. Dalton, Colonel Commandant R.A.', Private Memorial (Wingate Collection, University of Durham)

David, Saul, *Victoria's Wars* (2006)

Dawson, D., *A Soldier Diplomat* (1927)

Deacon, R., *A History of the British Secret Service* (1969)

Douglas, Sir G. and Ramsay, Sir G., *Panmure Papers* (1908) ii

Drus, E., ed.,'A Journal of Events During the Gladstone Ministry, 1868–1874', by John, First Earl of Kimberley', *Camden Miscellany* (1958) xc

Duke, Sir C. W., *Problems of Greater Britain* (1890)

Edinburgh Review (clxxv, 1 January 1892)

Edwards, M., *Playing the Great Game* (1975)

Ellison, G. E., 'Lord Roberts and the General Staff', *Nineteenth-Century and After* (December 1932)

'England', *What are our Legions? or the Truth about the Indian Armies* (1878)

Ensor, Sir R., *England, 1870–1914* (1936)

Ervin, Capt. G. L., Time and Space Analyses (Murnau, 1971)

Fage, J. D., *An Atlas of African History* (1965)

Farnie, D. A., *East and West of Suez* (Oxford, 1969)

Flint, J. E., *Sir George Goldie* (Oxford, 1966)

Foreign Office Lists

Fraser, Sir Thomas, *Recollections with Reflections* (Edinburgh, 1914)

Fyfe, C., *A History of Sierra Leone* (1962)

Fyfe, C., ed., *Sierra Leone Inheritance* (1964)

Gabre-Sellassie, Z., *Yohannes IV of Ethiopia* (Oxford, 1975)

Gallagher, J. and Robinson, R., 'The Imperialism of Free Trade', *Economic History Review*, 2nd series, vi, no. 1 (1953)

Gardiner, A. G., *The Life of Sir William Harcourt,* ii vols. (1923)

Garvin, J. L., *The Life of Joseph Chamberlain*, ii vols. (1932)

Gathorne-Hardy, A., ed., *Gathorne Hardy*, ii vols. (1910)

Gibbs, N. H., *The Origins of Imperial Defence* (Oxford, 1955)

Gifford, P. and Louis, W. R., *Britain and Germany in Africa, Imperial Rivalry and Colonial Rule* (Yale, 1967)

Gilliard, D., *Salisbury and the Indian Defence Problem* (1968)

Gleichen, Lord Edward, *A Guardsman's Memories* (1932)

Gleichen, Lord Edward, *With the Camel Corps up the Nile* (1888)

Gleichen, Lord E. A., *With the Mission to Menelik* (1898)

Gooch, J., *The Plans of War* (1974)

Gopal, S., *British Policy in India 1858–1905* (Cambridge, 1965)

Grenville, J. A. S., *Lord Salisbury and Foreign Policy* (1970)

Haldane, R. B., *Richard Burdon Haldane* (1926)

Hamer, W. S., *The British Army, Civil–Military Relations, 1885–1905* (Oxford, 1970)

Hansard, 1856–1904.

Haswell, J., *British Military Intelligence* (1973)

Haywood, A. and Clark, F. A. S., *History of the Royal West African Frontier Force* (Aldershot, 1964)

Hennessey, T. and Thomas, C., *Spooks* (2009)

Hill, R. L., *Biographical Dictionary of the Sudan*, 2nd edition (1967)

Hill, R. L., *Egypt and the Sudan* (1967)

Hinsley, F. H., ed., 'Material Progress and World-Wide Problems', *New Cambridge Modern History* vol. xi (Cambridge, 1940)

Holdich, T., 'Lt. Col. Sir Henry Trotter, KCMG, CE', obituary *Royal Engineer Journal* (December 1919)

Holland, B., *The Life of Spencer Compton, Eighth Duke of Devonshire*, ii vols. (1911)

Holt, P. M., *The Mahdist State in the Sudan* (Oxford, 1958)

Hopkirk, P., *The Great Game: On Secret Service in High Asia* (2006)

Howard, M., *Continental Commitment* (1972)

Howard, M., *Empires, Nations and Wars* (2007)

Howard, M., *War and the Liberal Conscience* (2008)

Hudleston, F. J., 'The War Office Library', *Army Quarterly*, i (1920)

Hudleston, F. J., *Warriors in Undress* (1925)

James, D., *Lord Roberts* (1954)

James, R. R., *Rosebery* (1963)

James, Sir William, *The Eyes of the Navy* (1955)

Jeffery, K., *MI6, History of the Secret Intelligence Service, 1909–1949* (2010)

Jervis, W. P., *Thomas Best Jervis: Christian Soldier, Geographer and Friend of India* (1898)

Johnson, D., *France and the Dreyfus Affair* (New York, 1966)

Johnson, F. A., *Defense by Committee* (Oxford, 1960)

Johnson, R., *Spying for Empire* (2006)

Kanya-Forstner, A., *Conquest of the Western Sudan* (Cambridge, 1969)

Kazemzadeh, F., *Russia and Britain in Persia, 1864–1914* (Yale, 1968)

Kebbel, T. E., 'Disraeli', *Dictionary of National Biography*, v (1908)

Kennedy, A. L., *Salisbury 1830–1903* (1953)

Kilbracken, Lord, *Reminiscences* (1931)

Kitchen, H., *The German Officer Corps* (Oxford, 1968)

Knapland, P., 'Intra-imperial Aspects of Britain's Defence Question, 1870–1900', *Canadian Historical Review*, iii (June 1922)

Lane-Poole, S., *Watson Pasha* (1918)

Lee, Dwight E., 'Great Britain and the Cyprus Convention Policy of 1878', xxxviii *Harvard Historical Studies* (Cambridge 1934)

Lees-Milne, J., *The Enigmatic Edwardian, the Life of Reginald 2nd Viscount Esher* (1986)

Lewis, Bernard, *The Emergence of Modern Turkey* (1968)

Lloyd, Alan, *The Drums of Kumasi* (1964)

Lowe, C. J., *The Reluctant Imperialists* (1967)

Lowe, C. J. and Marzari, F., *Italian Foreign Policy, 1870–1940* (1975)

Luvaas, J., *Education of an Army, 1815–1940* (1965)

Macdiarmid, D. S., *Life of Sir James Moncrieff Grierson* (1923)

Macdonald, J. R. L., *Soldiering and Surveying in British East Africa* (1897)

MacGregor, Lady, *Life of Sir Charles Metcalf MacGregor*, ii vols. (1887)

Magnus, Sir P., *Gladstone* (1954)

Magnus, Sir P., *Kitchener* (1958)

Mallet, Sir B., *The Earl of Northbrook* (1908)

Malmesbury, Susan, Countess of, *The Life of Major General Sir John Ardagh* (1909)

Marcus, H. G., *The Life and Times of Menelik II* (Oxford 1975)

Marder, A. J., *The Anatomy of British Sea Power* (1940)

Marlowe, John, *Cromer in Egypt* (1970)

Matthew, H. C. G., *The Liberal Imperialist* (Oxford 1973)

Maurice, F. B., *Haldane* (1937)

Maurice, F. B., *Sir Frederick Maurice, A Record of his Work and Opinions* (1913)

Maurice, Sir J. F., *Military History of the Campaign in Egypt* (1887)

Maurice, Sir J. F. and Arthur, Sir G., *The Life of Wolseley* (1924)

Maxse, F. I., *Seymour Vandeleur* (1906)

Maxwell, R. P., *Memorial to the late Earl of Cromer, 12 May 20* (1920)

Melville, C. H., *Life of General Sir R. Buller*, ii vols. (1923)

Milner, F. W. H., *Anglo-Afghan War* (26 October 1881)

Morgan, G., 'Myth and Reality in the Great Game', *Asian Affairs* (February 1973)

Morning Post, 25 July 1892; 21 April 1914

Moulton, E., *Lord Northbrook's Indian Administration* (1968)

Moyse-Bartlett, H., *The King's African Rifles* (Aldershot, 1956)

Moon, P. T., *Imperialism and World Politics* (New York, 1926)

National Review, June 1908

Newbury, C. W., *British Policy towards West Africa* (1971)

Newbury, C. W., 'The Development of French Policy on the Lower and Upper Niger, 1890–98', *The Journal of Modern History* (xxxi, no. 1), March 1959

Newton, Lord, *Lord Lansdowne* (1929)

Oliver, R. and Mathew, G., eds., *History of East Africa*, vol. i (Oxford, 1963)

Owen, R., *Lord Cromer* (2004)

Pall Mall Gazette

Panikkar, K. M., *Asia and Western Dominance* (1953)

Parliamentary Papers, 'Memorandum of the Secretary of State relating to the Army Estimates 1887–8' (Cd. 4985, 1887)

Parliamentary Papers, 'Reports and Other Documents relating to Army Organization', vol. xxi (Cd. 2792, 1881)

Parliamentary Papers, 'Report of a Committee of General and other Officers of the Army on Army Reorganization', vol. xxi (Cd. 2791, 1881)

Parliamentary Papers, 'Report from the Select Committee on Army and Navy Estimates; together with the Proceedings of the Committee, and minutes of evidence', vol. viii (1887)

Parliamentary Papers, 'Proceedings of the Colonial Conference', vols. i–v (Cd. 5091, 1887)

Parliamentary Papers, 'Proceedings of a Conference between the Secretary of State for the Colonies and the Premiers of the Self-governing Colonies, at the Colonial Office, London, June and July 1897', vol. lix (Cd. 8596, 1897)

Parritt, Lt Col. B. A. H., 'Intelligence Corps to INTELLIGENCE CORPS', *Rose and Laurel*, viii (1966)

Parritt, Lt Col. B. A. H., *The Intelligencers* (Ashford, 1972)

Penson, Dame L., *Foreign Affairs under the Third Marquis of Salisbury* (1962)

Penson, Dame L., 'Lord Salisbury's Foreign Policy', *Cambridge Historical Journal*, 29 January 1935

Perham, Dame M., *Lugard, the Years of Adventure* (1956)

Perham, Dame M. F. and Bull, M., *The Diaries of Lord Lugard*, iii vols. (1959)

Petherick, E., *Colonial Book Circular and Bibliographical Record* (1887)

Porter, W., *History of the Corps of Royal Engineers* (Chatham, 1951) ii

Preston, A., ed., *The South African Journal of Sir Garnet Wolseley* (Cape Town, 1973)

Ramm, A., *Political Correspondence of Mr. Gladstone and Lord Granville*, ii vols. (1962)

Ramm, A., *Sir Robert Morier* (1973)

Roberts, A., *Salisbury* (1999)

Roberts, Lord, *Forty-one Years in India*, ii vols. (1897)

Robertson, Sir W., *From Private to Field Marshal* (1921)

Robinson, D. and others, *Army List* (1854–1909)

Robinson, R. and Gallagher, J. with Denny, A., *Africa and the Victorians* (1961)

Royal Commission on the war in South Africa, vols. xl–xlii (Cd. 1789–92, 1904)

Royal Engineer Journal, 1879–1906

Royal Engineer Occasional Papers

Royal Engineer Professional Papers

Royal United Services Journal

Russell, H., *The Ruin of the Soudan* (1892)

St. Aubyn, C., *The Royal George* (1963)

Sandes, E. W. C., *The Military Engineer in India*, vol. i (1933)

Sandes, E. W. C., *The Royal Engineers in Egypt and the Sudan* (1937)

Sanderson, G. N., *England, Europe and the Upper Nile* (Edinburgh, 1965)

Sanderson, Lord T. H., 'Evelyn, Earl of Cromer: Memoir', *Proceedings of the British Academy*, VIII (1919)

Shibeika, Mekki, *British Policy in the Sudan, 1882–1902* (1952)

Slade, R., *King Leopold's Congo* (1962)

Slatin, R., *Fire and Sword in the Soudan* (1895)

Smith, C., *The Embassy of Sir William White at Constantinople, 1886–1891* (1957)

Stanmore, Lord, S. H., *Lord Herbert of Lea*, ii vols. (1906)

Steiner, Z. S., *The Foreign Office and Foreign Policy* (Cambridge, 1969)

Stigand, C. H., *Equatoria: The Lado Enclave* (1923)

Strachan, H., *From Waterloo to Balaclava* (1985)

Strachan, H., *Wellington's Legacy: Reform of the British Army 1830–1854* (1984)

Taylor, R., *Lord Salisbury* (Edinburgh, 1975)

Thornton, A.P., *The Imperial Idea and its Enemies* (New York, 1968)

The Times, January 1879; September 1879; January 1891

Tripodi, C., *Edge of Empire, the British Political Officer and Tribal Administration on the North-West Frontier, 1877–1947* (2011)

Trotter, Sir J. K., *The Niger Sources* (1898)

Tulloch, Sir A. B., *Recollections of Forty Years' Service* (Edinburgh, 1903)

Tucker, A., 'Army and Society in England, 1870–1900: A Reassessment of the Cardwell Reforms', *Journal of British Studies*, vol. ii, no. 2 (May, 1963)

Vetch, R. H., 'Ardagh', *Dictionary of National Biography, 1901–11*

Vetch, R. H., *Life of Sir Andrew Clarke* (1905)

Wade, S., *Spies in the Empire* (2007)

Wade, S., *Victoria's Spymasters* (2009)

Waters, W. H. H., *Secret and Confidential* (1926)

Watson, Sir C. M., *History of the Corps of Royal Engineers*, iii (Chatham, 1913)

Watson, Sir C. M., *Life of Major-General Sir Charles Wilson* (1909)

Watson, Sir C. M., 'Major General Sir Charles Wilson', *Royal Engineer Journal* (1905)

West, R., *Back to Africa* (1970)

Wheeler, O., *The War Office* (1914)

Who-Was-Who

Wilkinson, S., *Brain of an Army* (1890)

Wilkinson, S. and Dilke, Sir C., *Imperial Defense* (1892)

Williams, Sir E. T., 'Queen Victoria', *Encyclopaedia Britannica* (New York, 1974)

Wilson, J., *C-B* (1973)

Wingate, Sir F. R., *Mahdiism and the Egyptian Sudan* (1891)

Wingate, Sir R. E. L., *Wingate of the Sudan* (1955)

Wood, G. S., 'Collen', *Dictionary of National Biography 1901–1911*

Wright, M., 'Treasury Control, 1854–1914', in G. Sutherland, ed., *Studies in the Growth of Nineteenth Century Government* (1972)

Wyatt, C. M., *Afghanistan and the Defence of Empire* (2011)

Younghusband, F., *Forty Years a Soldier* (1923)

INDEX

Abdul Hamid, Sultan 70
Abdur Rahman, Amir 61, 62
Abyssinia 24, 208–9, 239, 253–5, 259–60
à Court, Colonel Charles (Repington)
    215–16, 239, 265
Administrative Reform Association 284
Afghanistan
    Anglo-Indian campaign in 57–8,
        60–61
    boundary commission 166–71
    'disintegration' of 61–2
    feared Russian invasion of 4–5, 45–7,
        162–3
    military intelligence on 48–9, 52–3, 63
    and Russia border maps 166
    strategic importance of 46
Ahmed, Mohammed ('The Mahdi')
    119–20, 124, 126, 131–2
Airey, Sir Richard 22, 29
Alexandria 103, 111, 113
Algeciras Conference 290
Alison, Sir Archibald
    appointed head of ID 42
    and Ashanti campaign 40
    and Consuls network 107–8
    and Egyptian campaign 111–14
    and Egyptian intelligence 108–10
    and Foreign Office sources 58–9
    and Sudanese threat to Egypt 120
Allahabad Pioneer (newspaper) 178
Altham, Lieutenant General Sir E. A.
    278–80

American Civil War 9, 20–21, 27
Anderson, Sir Percy 212–13, 222–3, 228–9,
    236–7
Anglo-Congolese Treaty (1894) 224,
    226–7, 233
Anglo-German Treaty (1893) 224
Anstruther, Captain E. C. 74
Ardagh, Major General Sir John
    and Abyssinia 253–4
    appointed deputy to Brackenbury
        142, 143
    appointed Director of Military
        Intelligence 241, 273–4
    and Berlin Congress 90–91
    and Boer War 278–9, 281–2
    and Boundary Commissions 94–5
    and Cable Landing Rights
        Committee 252–3
    and control of the Nile 258, 261–2, 264
    and Cromie affair 277
    death of 292
    and Egyptian intelligence 105, 113
    and general staff 287–8
    and ID recommendations 284–6
    joins ID 69–70
    and mobilisation plans 153–5
    and proposed Turkish reforms 78
    and recapture of Sudan 243, 244–7,
        261, 265
    records of 6–7
    and replacement head of army
        269–71

Ardagh, Major General Sir John *cont.*
report on Constantinople's defences
71, 74
and Secret Service Section 291
and Sudan campaign 127, 198
and War Office communications 148
and West Africa force 256–7
Argyll, Duke of 49–50
Armed Strength (orders of battle series)
31, 34, 40
Armstrong gun 20
Army and its Reserves, The (book) 35
Army Council 289
Army List (orders of battle) 38, 39
Ashanti Expedition 40, 136–7
'Ashanti Ring' 40–41, 42, 114, 136–7
Association for the Discouragement of
Duelling 12
Asterabad 63
Austria 17, 24, 32, 33, 36, 45–6
Austro-Prussian War 17, 24, 32, 36
Ayub Khan 61

Baghchetsh 75
Bahr el Ghazal 224–5, 230, 233–5, 251, 255,
260, 266
Baker, Sir Samuel 212
Balfour, Arthur 280, 288
Bamian 59
Baring, Captain Evelyn
and African expansionism 199, 207
and Central Asia Question 56
and creation of IBS 50–51
and Franco-Prussian War 28–9
joins T&S Department 27
and reorganisation of T&S 31
and Russian threat to Bulgaria and
Turkey 71–2, 79
and Turkish intelligence 69
and war gaming 50, 56
Batum 84, 174, 180
Beaconsfield, Lord (Benjamin Disraeli)
and Berlin Congress 90–91

and Bulgarian insurrection 67
and Constantinople intelligence
70–71, 72–3, 75, 77
and death of Home 96
and Egyptian intelligence 104
and India 45, 47
and Northbrook's resignation 54
and Russo-Turkish War 81–3, 85
and Suez Canal 102
Beaufort, Captain 181
Belgium 215, 224, 226–30, 233, 237–9
Bell, Colonel Mark Sever 176, 178, 185–7
Bengal 53
Berber 119, 125–6, 128, 131
Beresford, Lord Charles 129, 149
Berlin Congress (1878) 90–91
Bihar 53
Bismarck, Otto von 32, 45, 90
Black Sea 174, 180, 182
Bloemfontein Conference 279
Boer War 2, 268, 278–82, 284
Bokhara 47
Bosnia and Herzegovina 69
Bosphorous 71, 73
Boulac 117
Brackenbury, Major General Charles
36–7, 103
Brackenbury, Lieutenant General Sir
Henry
and African expansionism 198–200,
207–8
and Ardagh's ambition of 139, 141,
158–9
and Ashanti Expedition 136–7
and confidentiality 147–8
death of 292
appointed DMI 136, 137–8, 141, 157,
274
at Dublin Castle 137
and Egypt campaign 137
and EID 205
enthusiasm for intelligence 138, 141–2
and French naval dominance 209

and general staff 141, 156
and Hartington Commission 271
and IBS 178
and ID secondments 150–51
and India Office 179–80
and Indian mobilisation plans
    190–92
and military reform 138–9, 146
and mobilisation plans 151, 153–6, 183
and Persian rail links 185–8
and printed material 141–3
relationship with Wolseley 140–41,
    156, 158–9
and reorganisation of IBS 193–6
and replacement head of army 269,
    270–71
and Royal Commission 157–9
and Russian threat on Turkey 180–83
and threatened conflict with Russia
    183–4
appointed to Viceroy's Council
    (India) 192–3
and West Africa information 40
Brijuk-Tchechmedjie line 83
Britain
    and Afghanistan campaign 57–8,
        60–61
    and African expansionism 197, 200
    management of warfare 9–10
    mobilisation plans 151–6
    reform of 16–17, 24, 26, 43–4, 138–9
    replacement Commander-in-Chief
        of 269–71
    unpreparedness for war 11, 15–16,
        24
    weakness of 81, 95
    belated reactions of 210
    and Boer War 280–82
    coastal defences of 37–9
    and Crimean War 9–11, 14–15
    and defence of Herat 168, 170–71, 173,
        190–91
    diplomatic machinery of 1

and 'Eastern Question' 66–7, 102
and Egyptian campaign 111–15
and Entente Cordiale 267
and evacuation of Sudan 131, 171,
    173, 198
importance of Nile to 197–8, 201–2,
    210–13, 227–31
importance of Suez Canal to 101–2
and Indian Empire 46–7
navy of 134, 148–9, 152, 190, 209–10,
    232
negotiations with France 252, 265
occupation of Egypt 103
occupation of the Nile 266
potential French invasion of 152
proposed Turkish reforms 77–8
and recapture of Sudan 242–9, 261–5
sends fleet to Alexandria 111, 113
sends fleet to Dardanelles 86–7
'splendid isolation' of 268
and Sudan campaign 125–30
support for Egypt 102–3, 115
support for Turkey 66–7, 71, 90
threatened conflict with Russia
    171–6, 181–2, 183–4
and Treaty of Berlin 91–2
and Treaty of San Stefano 87
British East Africa Company 211–13
British National Society for Aid to the
    Sick and Wounded 136
British Red Cross 136
Brodrick, William St John 281, 282, 283,
    284, 288
Brussels 13
Bulgaria 67, 71, 87, 180, 182
Bulgarian Commission 94, 97
Buller, General Sir Redvers 114, 138–9,
    269, 270, 271, 278–9
Burdett-Coutts, Baroness Angela 25
Burgoyne, General J. F. 37
Buyuk-Tchekmedje-Derkos line 73

Cable Landing Rights Committee 252–3

'Cabul Diaries' 49
Callwell, Major General Sir Charles 144,
    206, 211
Cambridge, Duke of
    and creation of ID 35–6
    and general staff 33–4
    and military reform 43–4, 139
    and mobilisation plans 153, 191–2
    opinion of Henry Brackenbury 138
    as reactionary 28
    retirement of 268–9
    uselessness of 157
Cameron, Colonel Aylmer 135, 137–8
    169–70, 175–6
Campbell-Bannerman, Henry 150, 158,
    159–60, 213–14, 221, 269
Canadian Defence Plan (1865-66) 74
Cardwell, Viscount Edward
    and creation of ID 35–6
    and Franco-Prussian War 27, 28
    and general staff 33
    and Indian Intelligence Department
        49–50
    and military reforms 43–4
    moves ID offices 40
    and reorganisation of T&S 29–31,
        34–5
    appointed Secretary for War 25–6
Carnarvon, Lord 82
cartography 12–15, 17–18, 163–4
Cavagnari, Major Louis 57, 60
Cecil, Lady Gwendolen 123
Central Asia Route-book 51–2
Chamberlain, Joseph 256
Chamberlain, Sir Neville 57
Chapman, General Sir Edward
    and EID 205
    and French expansionism 215–17
    appointed head of ID 193
    and Library & Mapping Section
        220–21, 276–7
    and Persian rail links 187
    and reorganisation of IBS 193–5

at Scottish District 241, 273
    and Uganda 212, 214–5, 225
Chermside, Lieutenant General Sir
    Herbert 74, 116, 118, 125–6, 128, 129
Childers, Hugh 80, 108, 110, 112, 116
Churchill, Lord Randolph 133–4, 153, 156,
    157–8
Clarke, Major F. C. H. 163
Clarke, Sir George 6, 7, 289
Collen, Lieutenant General Sir Edwin
    H. H. 3–4, 55, 75
Colonial Defence Committee 6, 210, 215
Colonial Office 148, 217–19, 257, 276
Colvile, Lieutenant General Sir Henry
    138, 225, 227
Colvin, Sir Auckland 121
Committee of Imperial Defence (CID)
    289–90
Confidential Mobilisation Committee
    112
Congo Free State 215, 228–30
Congress of Berlin 56, 59
Connaught, Duke of 269, 270
Constantinople 66, 67–8, 70–77, 86, 180,
    209
Constantinople Conference 77–8, 80
Cooke, Lieutenant General A. C. 20–21,
    23, 24
Coptic Christians 103
Corps of Guides 48–9
Corry, Montagu 102
Crimean War 9–11, 13–14, 15–16, 24
Crispi, Francesco 208–9, 241
Cromer, Lord 235, 240–41, 243, 245–7, 262
Cromie, W. H. 145, 275–7
Cross, Lord 184, 192–3
Crowe, Sir Eyre 162
Currie, Baron Philip 115–16, 165, 167, 169,
    212, 221
Cyprus 78–9, 89–90, 92–3, 96, 105, 114, 115

Daily Mail (newspaper) 290–91
Daily News (newspaper) 181

Dalton, Major General J. C. 146, 205–6, 207
Dardanelles 71, 73, 80, 82–3, 86–7, 232
Dawkins recommendations 284–7
Dawkins, Clinton 284, 287
de Freycinet, Charles Louis 103, 215
de Giers, Nikolas 46, 162, 165–6, 168, 188
Decazes expedition 227–9
Defence Committee 271–2
Defence of England, The (report) 154
Defence of India: a strategical study (report) 169–70, 177
Defence of London, The (report) 154
Delane, J. T. 24
Depôt de la Guerre (French map repository) 14
Derby, Lord 47, 53, 67, 70, 72, 77, 81, 87, 101
Dervishes 119, 225
Dewey Decimal System 145, 275
Disraeli, Benjamin *see* Beaconsfield, Lord
Dolgorouki, Prince 186
Domesday book 21
Dongola 131, 198, 241–2, 243–5, 249
Dreikaiserbund (triumvirate) 45–6
Dreyfus, Captain 33
Drummond Wolff, Sir Henry 185–9
Drummond, Admiral Sir James 76
Duff, Grant 67
Dufferin, Marquis of 27, 116, 121, 123, 266

East African Protectorate flag 236
East India Company 48
East, General Sir Cecil 62–4
Edmonds, Brigadier General Sir James 291
Effect on Egypt of the Withdrawal from Uganda, The (report) 212
Egypt
 and control of the Nile 233–9, 250–51, 258–9, 265–6
 army reinstated 117–18
 army revolt in 106–7

British campaign in 111–15
British occupation of 100, 103
British support for 102–3, 115
French designs on 101, 102–3, 106, 111
instability of 100, 106–7
intelligence collected from 103–5, 108–13
nationalist movement in 102–3, 111, 113–14
prison reforms in 117
threat from Sudan 118–25, 131–2, 197–8
see also EID
Egypt and the Advance up the Nile (report) 245
EID (Egyptian Intelligence Division)
 and African expansionism 207–8, 217, 228
 established 202–3
 and recapture of Sudan 243, 246, 265
 relations with ID 205–7
 and Slatin 230
 and Sudan intelligence collection 203–4, 235–6, 239–40
 and Uganda 211
Elgin Commission 282, 283, 287–8
Elles, Major General Sir E. R. 194–5
Elliot, Sir Henry 67, 71, 76
England and Russia in the East (book) 54
England's Means of Offence against Russia (report) 173–4
Entente Cordiale (1904) 267
Erzeroum 97
Esher Committee 289–90
Esher, Viscount Reginald 283, 287–90
Everest, Colonel Sir George 12
Everett, Colonel Sir William 99, 217, 219, 222–3, 226, 228–9, 251, 279, 292

Fairholme, Brigadier General William 225, 227, 229–30
Fife, Captain 88
Fire and Sword in the Soudan (book) 235

Firket 249
Fisher, Admiral 'Jacky' 152, 289, 290
Fitz-George, Captain G. W. A. 76
Foreign Office
    and African expansionism 199–202,
        207–8
    and Consuls network 107
    and Egyptian intelligence 105, 108
    and Home's Constantinople mission
        76–7
    Indian reports received 168–9
    information collection methods 162
    library section of 276
    and Persian rail links 186–7
    and recapture of Sudan 246–7
    relations with ID 58–9, 85, 88–9,
        142–3, 148, 157
    reliance on ID 165, 169, 222
Fortification Committee (1868) 70
'Forward School' 51, 56, 63, 176, 184,
    189–90, 192, 196
Fox, Major W. R. R. 165, 200
France
    and African expansionism 198–9,
        209–13, 215–19, 222–30, 232
    Anglophobia of 111
    British secrets sold to 277
    and control of the Nile 233–4, 236–7,
        239, 250–51, 258–9, 265–6
    and Crimean War 10
    and designs on Egypt 101, 102–3,
        106, 111
    development of general staff 17
    'effective occupation' policy 232, 256,
        260, 261
    and Entente Cordiale 267
    and Franco-Prussian War 17, 27–9, 32
    and Grey Declaration 233
    growing militarism of 31–2
    influence in Abyssinia 253–5, 259
    influence on Egyptian Khedive 121–2
    Mediterranean naval dominance
        190, 198, 209–10

military intelligence units 33
    negotiations with Britain 252, 265
    potential invasion of Britain 37–9, 152
    sends fleet to Alexandria 111, 113
    treaty with Germany 224
France in West Africa (handbook) 219
Franco-Belgian Treaty (1894) 228–9
Franco-Congolese Treaty (1894) 230
Franco-Prussian War 17, 27–9, 32
Fraser, Captain 83, 85, 86
Fraser, Major General Sir Thomas 73–4
French Suez Canal Company 101

Gallipoli 73, 78, 82, 86
Galton, Captain Douglas 22
Gambetta, Léon 103, 111
Gambia 218
Gathorne-Hardy, Gathorne 41, 70–71,
    72–3, 77, 82, 84–6
Gene, General 200
General Staff 3, 283, 289–90, 293
Germany 31–2, 33, 45–6, 224
Girishk 59
Gladstone, William Ewart
    and Afghan boundary commission
        167–8
    and Berlin Congress 91
    and Egypt 105–7, 110–12, 114–15
    and general staff 33
    and Irish problem 137
    loses power 41
    opinion of ID 292
    re-elected 61–2, 211
    resignation of 210, 224
    and Royal Commission 159
    and Sudan 122, 124, 126–8, 131
    and Uganda 213
    appoints Viscount Cardwell as
        Secretary for War 25–6
    and withdrawal from Kandahar 64
Gleichen, Count Edward 227, 237–8,
    240–41, 244, 246–9, 254, 260, 266,
    273, 278

Globe (newspaper) 181
Godley Committee 19–20, 22
Godley, J. R. 19
Gold Coast 252, 256–7
Goldie, Sir George 257
Goldsmid, Major General Sir Frederick 108, 112
Gordon, Major General Charles 120–21, 125–7, 129–30, 137, 217
Goschen, George 134, 161
Gouko, General 83
Graham, General 125
Granville, Lord 27–8, 60, 108, 110, 115–16, 120, 122, 135, 166, 168–9
'Great Game' 5, 56, 97, 177
Grey Declaration 231, 233, 236
Grey, Admiral Sir Frederick 70
Grey, Viscount 230–31, 233
Grierson, Lieutenant General Sir James 170, 177, 178, 195
Großstab (Prussian general staff) 17
Grover, Captain G. 85–6, 93
Gwynn, Major General Sir Charles 222–3

Hadem Keue 75, 76
Haillot, Captain 216
Haldane, Viscount 290
Hall, Captain W. H. 149
Handbook on British East Africa 225
Handbook on Egypt (book) 112
Harcourt, Sir William 137, 213–14, 221
Hare, Major W. A. H. 180
Harrington, Sir A. 218–19
Hartington, Marquess of
    cautiousness of 134
    and Defence Committee 271–2
    and India Office 61–2
    and Sudan campaign 125, 127–8, 129–30
    opinion of Simmons 80–81
    records of 6
    relationship with Salisbury 133–5
    reliance on ID 162
turns down premiership 133
and withdrawal from Kandahar 64
Hartington Commission 157–9, 183, 209–10, 221, 269–72
Herat 47, 50, 57, 62, 163–4, 168, 170–71, 173, 190–91
Herbert, Sidney 16, 20–21, 22, 25, 43
Hewitt, Admiral Sir William 113–14
Hicks, Pasha William 119, 122, 245
History of the Royal Engineers (corps history) 7
History of Uganda (report) 212, 214
Home, Colonel Robert
    advises Salisbury 75, 78–9, 80, 87, 91–2
    appointed to ID 37
    and Boundary Commissions 95–6
    at Bulgarian Commission 94
    Constantinople mission 73–7
    and Dardanelles intelligence 80
    death of 96–7
    and Egyptian intelligence 105
    and French invasion plans 38–9
    and mobilisation plans 152, 154, 183
    and overseas collection 39–40
    and proposed Turkish reforms 78
    and Russo-Turkish War 82, 85, 88–9
Horse Guards
    and Colonial Defence Committee 215
    conflict with War Office 11, 15
    and Home's Constantinople mission 73
    and military reform 139
    and recapture of Sudan 246–7
    relations with ID 2, 40–41, 58
    and T&S Department 16, 19, 21–2, 28, 30, 33, 34–5
    and threatened conflict with Russia 174
Hoskins, Admiral 113
Hozier, Colonel Sir Henry 24, 27–8, 31, 32, 34, 36, 181
Hume, Joseph 16

IBS (Intelligence Branch Simla)
and Afghan boundary commission
166–7, 170–71
aggressive attitude of 176–8, 184
creation of 50–51
and *Defence of India* (report) 169–70
and Persian rail links 185–6, 188
reorganisation of 193–6
structure of 178–9
unreliability of 58
ID (Intelligence Department 1873–88/
Division 1888–1904)
absorbed into General Staff 3
access to Foreign Office resources 157
and Afghan boundary commission
166–7, 169
and African expansionism 197–202,
207–8, 215–19, 222–6
and Anglo-Congolese Treaty 224,
227
and Anglo-French negotiations 252,
265
and Anglo-Indian campaign in
Afghanistan 57–8
appointments to 3–4
Asia Section 180–81
and Berlin Congress 90
and Boer War 278–82, 284
and Boundary Commissions 94–7
breaks from War Office 160
and British East Africa Company
211–12
and confidentiality 146–9
and Consuls network 98–100, 105–8,
115–17, 145–6
and control of the Nile 236–8
creation of 3, 35–6
and Dawkins recommendations
284–7
as department under Commander-
in-Chief 272
discrimination against 3
displaced to front lines 93–4, 149

as Division of the War Office 157,
283
and East African Protectorate flag
236
and Egyptian intelligence 103–5,
108–14
evidence for 5–7
expansion of 287, 289–90
and Foreign Office sources 58–9
and French designs on Egypt 106
and Indian Intelligence Department
50, 52–3, 58
as 'indispensable' 85–6
influence of 136
as 'key player' 135
legacy of 292–3
Library & Mapping Section 85, 93,
145, 163–5, 219–21, 275–7
and mobilisation plans 151–6
and Naval Intelligence Department
148–9, 150, 152
and 'news' 68, 72
organisation of 143–4
and overseas collection 39–40
and Persian rail links 186–7
as potential general staff 93–4, 141,
156, 158, 287–8
printing presses of 141–3, 220
and recapture of Sudan 243, 246–9
recruitment for 36–7
relations with Colonial Office 148
relations with EID 205–7
relations with Foreign Office 85,
88–9, 142–3, 148
relations with government 44–5
relations with Horse Guards 40–41,
58
relations with IBS 177–8, 179, 184
relations with India Office 179–80
relations with War Office 148
reliability of 4–5, 144
reliance upon 1–2, 162, 165, 169, 222
relocation of 40, 135

report on 55
reputation of 68, 157
resentment of 149–50
resources overstretched 274–7
respect for 85–6
Russian Section 163, 171–6
and Russo-Turkish War 83–5, 88–90
secondments to 150–51
Secret Service Section 291
security classification system 146–7
sophistication of processes 68–9,
    144–5
'special secret studies' of 172
status of 136
subjugated to the Quartermaster
    General's Office 41
success of 4–5
and Sudan campaign 127–30
and Sudan intelligence collection
    201–4, 239–40, 251
and threatened Russian attacks 62–3,
    64–5
and Turkish defence of Dardanelles
    232
and Turkish intelligence 69, 71–6
and Uganda 211–15
and West Africa force 256–8
Iddesleigh, Lord 134, 182
imperial fire brigade 151, 155–6
India
    campaign in Afghanistan 57–8
    famine in 53
    feared Russian invasion 4–5, 45–6,
        54–6, 62–5, 163–4, 168, 171–3,
        195–6
    Intelligence Department of 48–50, 58
    mobilisation plans 183, 190–92
    mutiny in (1857) 47
    reports to Foreign Office 168–9
    and Russian expansionism 163–4
    'scientific frontier' of 46, 57, 196
    as unwilling imperial partner 152–3
    'vulnerability' of 54–6

India Office 165, 179–80, 194
Indian Boundary Commission 171
Invincible (HMS) 112
Ismailia 114
Italy 199–202, 207–9, 239–41, 243,
    260, 261

James, Lieutenant General Sir Henry
    20–26
Jaserin 76
Jena 13
Jerusalem 25
Jervis, Major Thomas Best
    appearance of 12
    appointed head of T&S Department
        16–18
    and cartography 12–15, 42
    and Corps of Guides 48–9
    death of 18–19
    and importance of intelligence 12–14
    reputation of 12, 14

Kabul 54, 57, 60, 61
Kalieri 222–3
Kandahar 54, 57, 61–4
Kars 89
Kassala 201, 207–9, 240–41, 243, 244, 260,
    261, 265
Kauffman, General 88
Kell, Colonel Sir Vernon 291
Key, Sir Cooper 111
Khalifa Abdulla 132
Khartum 119–20, 122–4, 129, 208, 262–5
Kimberley, Earl of 34
Kitchener, Field Marshal Earl
    and African expansionism 199–200,
        207–8
    and Mahdists 203
    and recapture of Sudan 242–3, 245–7,
        249, 261–5
    and Sudan campaign 125–6
    and Wilson 118
Kiva 46

kriegspiel (war games) 50, 175
Kuropatkin, General 166
Kushi 63

Lake, Lieutenant General Sir Percy
153–4
Lansdowne, Lord 242, 244–5, 269–71,
272, 273, 278, 281
Layard, Sir Henry 83, 88–9, 96
Lefroy, Colonel J. H. 18, 22
Lennox, Colonel 79–80, 84
Leopold, King 233, 237–8
Leopold-MacKinnon Agreement (1891)
210
'Liberal Imperialists' 133
'Liberal Unionists' 133
Lockhart, Colonel William 176–7, 178
'Lost Legions' 145
Lowe, Robert 26
Lugard, Sir Frederick 211, 213, 224–5
Lumley, Baron Savile 199, 209
Lumsden, Major General Sir Peter 166–8
Lytton, Lord 44, 54–7, 61

Macdonald, Major J. R. L. 259–61, 265–6
MacDougall, Lieutenant General Sir
Patrick 35–6, 38–9, 41–2, 103–4
MacGregor, General Sir Charles Metcalf
51–2, 169–70
MacLean, Colonel C. S. 188–9
Malet, Sir Edward 110, 116, 120, 122
Malmesbury, Lady 282
Malta 88
Marchand, Capt. 250–51, 256, 259, 266
Mason, Lt Colonel A. H. 177–8
Maule, Fox 15
Mecca 119
Memorandum on our Future Policy in
Afghanistan 63–4
Memorandum on the Central Asia
Question 56
Memorandum on the Probable Course of
Action which would be adopted by the

Russians in the Event of their attempt-
ing to occupy Bulgaria and march on
Constantinople 71–2
Menelik, Emperor 239, 241, 254–5, 258,
260, 262
Merv 47, 50, 54, 56, 57, 163, 165
Meshed 63
Messoweh 120
Metz 30
MI5 291
MI6 291
Military Notes on the Dutch South African
Republics (handbook) 281–2
Ministry of Defence Library 5
Monteil, Major 216, 224–5, 227
Morier, Sir Robert 147

Na'ûm Bey Shuqayyir 203
Napier, Lieutenant Colonel George
51–2, 58, 179–80
Napoleon III 14–15
national map repository 12–13, 14–15
Naval Defence Act (1889) 134
Naval Defence Act (1893) 210
Naval Intelligence Department (NID)
129, 148–9, 150, 152
Newcastle, Duke of 13–15
Newmarch, Major General O. R. 191–2
'news' 68, 72
Nicholson, Field Marshal Lord William
158, 283, 287–8
Niger Company 257
Nightingale, Florence 16, 20, 22
Nile, River
British occupation of 266
race for control of 233–9, 250–51, 258–9,
265–6
strategic importance of 197–8, 201–2,
210–13, 215, 227–31
Nisch 70
North American Boundary Commission
22, 25
Northbrook, Earl of

and creation of IBS 50–51
and Egyptian intelligence 108
and French designs on Egypt 106
and general staff 33
and military reforms 43
relationship with Salisbury 52–4
and reorganisation of T&S 29–30,
     34–5
and Sudan campaign 127–8
and withdrawal from Kandahar 64
Northbrook Committee 29–31, 34
Northcott, Major H. P. 258
Notes on a Visit to Metz and Strasbourg
     (report) 30

Official History of the Great War (series) 291
Ordnance Survey Department 19–20,
     26, 165
*Organisation, Composition and Strength of
     the Army of Great Britain* (book) 24
Osman Pasha 83
Oxus Valley 55

Pacific & Orient Steamship Company 101
Palestine 25
Palmerston, Lord 10, 15, 37
'Palmerston's follies' 10, 37
Panmure, Lord 15–16, 18–20, 22–6
Pauncefort, Sir Julian 125
Peel, Major General Jonathan 20
Peel, Robert 20
Penjdeh region 163–4, 166, 171
Penson, Dame Lillian 161–2
Persia 47, 51–2, 59, 92, 162–3, 183, 185–9
Peshawar Diary (report) 168
Petrie, Captain Martin 23–4
Phipps, E. C. H. 218–19, 223
Phoenix Park Murders 110, 137
photozincography 20–21
Pishin Valley 57, 63–5
Plevna 83
Political & Secret Department (India) 48
Ponsonby, Sir Henry 62, 158

Port Said 104, 113
Précis of Modern Tactics, The (book) 37
Prussia 17, 24, 27–9, 32, 36
Punjab Administrative Report 49

Quetta 57

Rabih Fadl Allah (Rabeh Zubehr) 217,
     227, 228, 236, 237
Raglan, Lord 13–14
Rattigan, Sir Terrance 6
Rawlinson, Sir Henry 53–4
*Report on the Intelligence Branch, Quarter
     Master General's Department* 3–4
*Report on the late Movement of the Russian
     Force in the Trans-Caspian District* 58
*Reports and Memoranda relative to the
     Defence of Constantinople and other
     Positions in Turkey* 74–5
Rhodes 78
Rice, Vice-Admiral Sir Edward 108
Ricketts, Consul 84
Ripon, Marquess 22, 61, 62, 64
Roberts, Field Marshal Earl 51–2, 55, 57,
     60–61, 179, 183, 191
Robertson, Field Marshal Sir William
     156, 278–80
Rodd, Rennell 255–6
Roebuck, John Arthur 15
Romanian Boundary Commission 94–5
Rosebery, Lord 6, 148, 211–14, 217–18,
     223–4, 236
Rothwell, Major J. S. 173–4
Royal Artillery 149
Royal Commission on Military
     Education 27
Royal Engineer Establishment
     (Chatham) 25
Royal Engineer Journal (corps history) 7
Royal Geographical Society 22, 25, 146,
     222
Royal Navy 134, 148–9, 152, 190, 209–10,
     232

Royal United Services Institute (RUSI) 21, 25

Rumours of Military Movements: Government of Kandahar (report) 169

Rundle, General Sir Leslie 125–6

Russell, William Howard 15

Russell, Lord John 11

Russia

and Afghan border maps 166, 170

and Afghan boundary commission 166–7, 170–71

and Berlin Congress 90–91

Black Sea fleet 180, 209

conflict with Turkey 47, 63

and Crimean War 9–11, 13–14, 66

declares war on Ottoman Empire 81–2

growing militarism of 31–2

influence in Abyssinia 253–5

influence over Sher Ali 56–7

and Ottoman states 66–7, 69

and Persian rail links 186

and Russo-Turkish War 67, 81–7

size of army 189

southward expansion of 45–7, 49–50, 55–6, 66, 162–3, 165–6

support for Serbia 70

threatened conflict with Britain 171–6, 181–2, 183–4

threatened invasion of Afghanistan 4–5, 45–7, 162–3

threatened invasion of Bulgaria 71

threatened invasion of India 4–5, 45–6, 54–6, 62–5, 163–4, 168, 171–3, 195–6

threatened invasion of Persia 59, 92, 162–3, 183, 188–9

threatened invasion of Turkey 71, 180–83

and Treaty of Berlin 91–2

and Treaty of San Stefano 87

triumvirate with Austria-Hungary and Germany 45–6

Russian Abstract (report) 168

Russian Advances in Asia ('Blue Book' series) 50

Russian Communications with the East (report) 172–3

Russki Mir (newspaper) 84

Russo-Turkish War 67, 81–7

Salisbury, Marquess of

advised by Home 75, 78–9, 80, 87, 91–2

and African expansionism 200, 201–2, 207–9

and Berlin Congress 90–92

and Boer War 278, 280

and Boundary Commissions 95–6

and Central Asia Question 55–6

and confidentiality 146

and Constantinople intelligence 75, 77

and Consuls network 98–100

and control of the Nile 233–4, 237

and credible intelligence 72

and Defence Committee 271–2

and Egyptian intelligence 104–5

energy of 134

and Foreign Office resources 157

and foreign policy 161

appointed Foreign Secretary 87

and impotence of Royal Navy 232

and India Office 45, 47–8, 50

leaves office 283

and Kassala 240–41

and Khedive of Egypt 115

and military advisers 44

and Napier expeditions 58

and naval cuts 133–4

and Naval Intelligence Department 149

opinion of Brackenbury 192–3

and 'pacific invasion' of England 98

and Persian rail links 187–8

and proposed Turkish reforms 77–8

and recapture of Sudan 242, 243–4,
246, 248–9, 262, 264
records of 6
relationship with Hartington 133–5
relationship with Northbrook 52–4
reliance on ID 162
and Royal Commission 157
and Russo-Turkish War 81–2, 88–90
and threatened conflict with Russia
184
and warfare 9
and West Africa force 257–8
Samarkand 47
Sanderson, Baron 186, 188, 262, 264
Sandhurst (Royal Military College) 11
'scientific frontier' (Indian) 46, 57, 196
Sclater, Lieutenant B. S. 229
Serbia 70
Servian Boundary Commission 94
Sevastopol 14
Sher Ali, Amir 46–7, 54, 56–7, 60
Shipka Pass 83
Sierra Leone 148, 219, 223, 226
Simmons, General Sir John Lintorn
73–4, 75–6, 79–81, 86, 90, 105
Slatin Pasha, Baron Rudolph von 203,
230, 234–6, 238, 249
Smith, W. H. 40, 67, 101–2, 134, 138, 151
Speke, John Hanning 22
spying 32–3, 291
Standard (newspaper) 282
Stanford & Co. (map makers) 165
Stanhope, Edward 155, 183, 192, 208
Stanley, Lord 39–40
Stewart, Major General Sir Herbert 60,
116–17, 125–6, 129–30
Stone, General Charles P. 104
Suakin 119, 122, 124–5, 126, 128–9, 131,
201–3
Suakin Intelligence Reports 201–2
Sudan
British campaign in 125–30
British evacuation of 131, 171, 173, 198

British recapture of 242–9, 261–5
intelligence collection from 201–4,
235–6
and Italian expansionism 200
as threat to Egypt 118–25, 131–2,
197–8
Suez Canal
and Cable Landing Rights
Committee 253
British control of 78–9, 102–3, 106,
113–14
British survey of 103–4
potential sabotage of 109–10, 111–12
strategic importance of 101–2
Suez Canal Company 292
Suez Canal Convention 253
Sydenham, Lord 6, 7, 289

T&S (Topographical & Statistical)
Department
'Blue Book' series 50
creation of 16–17
and Godley Committee 19–20
as embryonic general staff 33, 34
recruitment to 17–18, 23
reorganisation of 26, 29–31, 34–5
restrictions upon 20–23, 28, 30
role of 26–7, 29–31
Ta'rikh al-Sudan (book) 203
Talbot, Colonel 248–9
Tancred (novel) 89
Tashkent 47, 88
Tekke-Turcomans 52, 54, 58, 63
telegraph system 11, 47, 162
Tel-el-Kebir 114, 117
Temple, Sir Richard 49, 98
Ten Year Captivity in the Mahdi's Camp
(book) 214
Tenterden, Lord 77, 84, 107, 116
Territorial Army 290
Tewfiq Pasha, Khedive 102–3, 104, 115,
121–2
Thompson, Sir E. Maunde 145, 276

Thompson, W. Taylour 47
Thomson, Sir Ralph 148, 151, 153
Times, The (newspaper) 15, 24
Tokar 208–9
Tonnage Admeasurement Commission
    101–2
Topographical Depôt 19
Transcaspia 163, 170, 172–3, 176, 181
Treaty of Berlin (1878) 91–2, 98
Treaty of Gandamak (1879) 60, 63
Treaty of San Stefano (1878) 87
Treaty of Uccialli (1889) 201
Trotter, Lieutenant General Sir Henry
    97, 98–9, 100, 107
Trotter, Major General J. K. 222–3, 226
Tulloch, Major A. B. 108–14
Tunis 106, 111
Turkey
    and Armenian massacres 232
    and Berlin Congress 90–91
    and British Consuls network 98–100
    and British reforms 77–8
    and Bulgarian insurrection 67
    conflict with Russia 47, 63
    independence of 9, 10
    military intelligence collected 69
    and rail links 185
    and Russo-Turkish War 67, 81–7
    support from Britain 66–7, 71, 90
    threatened Russian invasion of 71,
        180–83
    and Treaty of Berlin 91–2
    and Treaty of San Stefano 87
    war with Serbia 70

Uganda 210–14, 225–6, 258–60
United Service Magazine 36, 189–90
Urâbî Pasha 103 112, 113–14, 117
Uthman abu Bakr Diqna 123, 125, 128

Victoria, Queen
    and appointment of Brackenbury 138
    death of 283

and Franco-Prussian War 27, 28
    knowledge of foreign affairs 4
    and Northbrook Committee 34
    and retirement of Cambridge 268–9
    and Royal Commission 158
    and Russo-Turkish War 82–3
    and withdrawal from Kandahar 64
Villiers, George 11
Volunteer movement 36, 38, 39, 154–5

Wadi Halfa 118, 127, 131, 243
Walker, Colonel 28
war gaming 50, 56, 175
War Office
    and Boer War 279, 280, 282
    and Confidential Mobilisation
        Committee 112
    and confidentiality 146–8
    and conflict with Horse Guards 11,
        15–16
    and Dawkins recommendations 287
    and Home's Constantinople mission
        74, 76–7
    and ID's Mapping & Library Section
        220, 276–7
    and ID's potential as general staff
        93–4
    and mobilisation plans 151–2, 191–2
    reform of 283–4, 288–9
    relations with ID 2, 148
    and Sudanese threat to Egypt 120,
        122
    and T&S Department 16, 19, 26
War Office Reconstitution Committee
    289
warfare, management of 9–10
Watson, Charles 118, 125–6
Wellesley, Colonel 84
Wellington, Duke of 18
West Africa force 256–8
West-Ridgeway, Colonel Sir Joseph
    166–7, 171
White, General Sir George 195, 279–80

Wilkinson, Spencer 158
Wilson, Lt Gen. Sir Charles William
 appointed Colonial Governor of
  Egypt 121
 and Consuls network 98–9, 100,
  106–7, 115–17
 and Egyptian Army 117–18
 and Franco-Prussian War 28–9
 and French invasion plans 38
 joins T&S Department 24–5
 leaves ID 41–2
 and reorganisation of T&S 29–31,
  34–5
 and role of T&S 26–7, 29
 secrecy of 6
 at Serbian Boundary Commission
  94
 and Sudan campaign 125–7, 128–30
 and Sudanese threat to Egypt
  118–24, 131, 197–8, 199–200
 and Turkish intelligence 69
Wilson, Sir Guy Fleetwood 140, 191
Wilson, Field Marshal Sir Henry 237–8
Wingate, General Sir F. R.
 and Abyssinia 254–5
 and African expansionism 207, 217
 and control of the Nile 236–8
 correspondence of 6
 and EID 202–3, 205–7, 235–6
 and Kassala 241
 and Macdonald Mission 260
 and recapture of Sudan 247–9, 262–4
 and Slatin Pasha 230, 234–5, 238
 and Sudan intelligence collection
  203–4
 and Uganda 212–14, 225–6
Wingate, Sir Ronald 6
Wisely, Captain G. A. K. 200
Wolfe Murray, Lieutenant General Sir
 James 6, 142, 151, 171–5, 181–2, 189–90
Wolseley, Field Marshal Viscount
 ambition of 139
 and Ashanti Expedition 40–41, 136–7

 and Boer War 278, 280, 288
 appointed Commander-in-Chief of
  army 269–71
 and Dongola 241
 and Egypt campaign 114, 118
 and general staff 141
 and Indian mobilisation plans 191–2
 and military reform 138–9, 146
 and mobilisation plans 156
 reactionary administration of 273
 and recapture of Sudan 242–6
 relationship with Brackenbury
  140–41, 156, 158–9
 relationship with Lansdowne 272,
  273
 and Royal Commission 158–9
 and Sudan campaign 127–30, 137
Wood, General Sir Evelyn 118
Woodthorpe, Colonel R. 176–7, 178

Yakub Khan, Amir 60–61
Younghusband, Lieutenant Colonel Sir
 Francis Edward 178

Z cipher 147
Zagazig 109
Zulficar Pass 164

Also available from Biteback

SIX: THE REAL JAMES BONDS 1909–1939
MICHAEL SMITH

The first part of bestselling author Michael Smith's epic
unauthorised history of Britain's secret intelligence service.

"*Engrossing... As a rollicking chronicle of demented derring-do,
Smith's book is hard to beat. His research is prodigious and his eye
for a good story is impeccable, and his book, while perfectly scholarly,
often reads like a real-life James Bond thriller.*"
Dominic Sandbrook, *Sunday Times*

480pp paperback, £12.99

**Available from all good bookshops or order from
www.bitebackpublishing.com**